Program
Evaluation

Program Evaluation

METHODS AND CASE STUDIES

Fourth Edition

Emil J. Posavac
Loyola University of Chicago

Raymond G. Carey
Lutheran General Health Care System

PRENTICE HALL
Englewood Cliffs, New Jersey 07632

Library of Congress Cataloging-in-Publication Data

Posavac, Emil J.
    Program evaluation : methods and case studies / Emil J. Posavac,
Raymond G. Carey.—4th ed.
        p. cm.
    Includes bibliographical references and index.
    ISBN 0–13–678129–2
    1. Evaluation research (Social action programs)—United States.
I. Carey, Raymond G. II. Title.
H62.5.U5P62   1992
361.6′1′072—dc20   91–10726
                                                            CIP

Acquisitions editor: Susan Finnemore
Editorial/production supervision and
    interior design: Mary McDonald
Cover design: Carol Ceraldi
Prepress buyer: Kelly Behr
Manufacturing buyer: Mary Ann Gloriande

Printed in the United States of America
10 9 8 7 6 5 4 3 2 1

ISBN 0-13-678129-2

Prentice-Hall International (UK) Limited, *London*
Prentice-Hall of Australia Pty. Limited, *Sydney*
Prentice-Hall Canada Inc., *Toronto*
Prentice-Hall Hispanoamericana, S.A., *Mexico*
Prentice-Hall of India Private Limited, *New Delhi*
Prentice-Hall of Japan, Inc., *Tokyo*
Simon & Schuster Asia Pte. Ltd., *Singapore*
Editora Prentice-Hall do Brasil, Ltda., *Rio de Janeiro*

To
Wendy and Steve
Rita, Mike, and Mark

Contents

5. Ethical Standards of Conducting Program Evaluations   85

PART III   QUANTITATIVE EVALUATION OF OUTCOME

8.   Nonexperimental Approaches to Outcome Evaluation   140

9.   Quasi-Experimental Approaches to Outcome Evaluation   159

10. Analysis of Causes of Change   178

PART IV   ADDITIONAL APPROACHES TO PROGRAM EVALUATION

11. Analysis of Costs and Outcomes   193

12. Qualitative Evaluation of Need, Process, and Outcome   209

PART VI   CASE STUDIES

Preface

Few people list reading research methods books among their favorite activities. We suspect that people find methods books tedious because the topics are hard to relate to life outside of the classroom or laboratory. We have tried to make *Program Evaluation* an exception.

Program evaluation deals with the planning and the success of activities that are important to society—topics that evaluators deal with include education, rehabilitation, health care, tax reforms, welfare policies, criminal justice, and job training. How do we go about evaluating the success of public policies? How can we compare the validity of assertions made by city officials with those made by their critics? Is the Department of Education spending its money in the most effective manner? Are there any effective approaches to helping drug dependent people? Should welfare policies include compulsory training for employment? These are issues that we read about in newspapers, learn about on "60 Minutes," and hear discussed in bars, at church, and across family dinner tables.

There are no organizations whose activities are not affected by the central concerns of program evaluation. We urge you to watch newspapers and magazines for examples of debates on social issues and policies. If you read carefully you will discover examples of self-serving assertions, confused thinking, and ignorance of valid research methods. We hope that you will find well-reasoned and well-supported positions as well. After reading this book, the differences between empirically supported arguments and unsupported positions should be easier to spot.

A difference between descriptions of program evaluation methods and presentations of basic research methods is the attention paid to the interpersonal skills needed to work effectively with the people who provide services to populations in need or who make decisions about what services are going to be offered. A major part of program evaluation involves listening to people describe their need for information, helping them clarify what they need to know, and then gathering and presenting the information in a manner that encourages its use in practical ways. As you can imagine there are ways of presenting new information that reduce the likelihood that the information will be used; there are also ways to present new information that facilitate understanding and application.

This book is divided into six parts. Part I provides an orientation to the role of the program evaluator in organizations. The core tasks and the types of questions evaluators work with are discussed. In Part II the contributions of evaluators to program planning and monitoring are illustrated. Part III is the part that is the most similar to other social science methods books in that a number of standard research designs useful to program evaluation are presented. Part IV includes some of the most difficult, yet essential, approaches to program evaluation. This part includes the major strategies for cost analyses of the effectiveness of services and the procedures that permit the evaluator to develop a thorough personal understanding of services, policies, and the people involved. Part V contains practical suggestions about communicating the findings of program evaluations and encouraging policy makers and agency staff members to use the information that has been learned through the evaluation. The last part of the book includes five case studies that illustrate several types of program evaluations.

Whether in the role of a professional, a member of a voluntary group, or as an informed citizen, you will be called upon to participate, sometimes only indirectly to be sure, in the planning and offering of effective services to people in need and in the development of constructive government policies. These are the fundamental concerns of program evaluation. We hope that this book instills an interest in this discipline: it is still evolving, but we believe that program evaluation does and will continue to contribute to the well-being of people.

Emil J. Posavac
Raymond G. Carey

Acknowledgments

The following journals and organization are thanked for permission to reprint or adapt material for this text: *General Hospital Psychiatry; Journal of Alcohol & Drug Education; Evaluation Review; Evaluation & The Health Professions;* and American Psychological Association.

The authors are grateful to their respective institutions for encouragement during the writing of this text. The first author's contribution to the first edition was greatly facilitated by a sabbatical leave awarded by Loyola University of Chicago. The second author acknowledges with thanks the explicit support received from Lutheran General Hospital.

The authors also wish to express their appreciation for the helpful comments of the following reviewers: Amado M. Padilla, University of California at Los Angeles; Alan Siman, School of Social Work, San Diego State University; Ross F. Conner, University of California at Irvine; Brian T. Yates, American University; Myron Mast, School of Public Service, Grand Valley State Colleges; Clara Mayo, Boston University; Richard M. Wolf, Teachers College of Columbia University; Robert J. Calsyn, University of Missouri at St. Louis; Francis G. Caro, Institute for Social Welfare Research of the Community Service Society of New York; Fred B. Bryant, Loyola University of Chicago; Melvin M. Mark, Pennsylvania State University; James R. Cook, University of North Carolina at Charlotte; Steven R. Heyman, University of Wyoming at Laramie; and Mark W. Lipsey, Claremont Graduate School.

1

Program Evaluation and Organizations

Program evaluation is a new and exciting applied social science. A productive society recognizes both the importance of human resources and the importance of providing human services in an efficient manner. Program evaluators provide information about human services in the same way accountants and auditors provide information about financial resources. The mission of program evaluation, or simply evaluation, is to assist in improving the quality of human services. Program evaluation is a collection of methods, skills, and sensitivities necessary to determine whether a human service is needed and likely to be used, whether it is sufficiently intense to meet the unmet need identified, whether the service is offered as planned, and whether the human service actually does help people in need at a reasonable cost without undesirable side effects. Through these activities evaluators seek to help improve programs, utilizing concepts from psychology, sociology, administrative and policy sciences, economics, and education. Before discussing specific applications of program evaluation methods, let us describe the field as a whole and illustrate how evaluation and evaluators fit into organizations.

WHY PROGRAM EVALUATION DEVELOPED

Quality of Service Not Assumed

No longer is it assumed that well-meaning individuals or groups who institute health, education, training, rehabilitation, or other services actually help people. Rejecting the assumption that all human services help people receiving the service

1

has made the efforts of many people who teach, counsel, provide medical care, or work with community groups more challenging—but possibly more productive. Today innovative programs as well as extensions of standard services can seldom offiunded without some means of demonstrating that the costs of the service are justified by the improved state of the clientele. Although Congress initiated the requirement that services supported by federal grants be evaluated (see, for example, Neigher et al., 1982), the source of a program's funding has little effect on whether the program must be evaluated: It must.

The increasing use of social science methods to improve the effectiveness of human service programs and institutions made evaluation a "growth industry" during the 1970s (Guttentag, 1977). There were several reasons for this growth. Well-meaning, expensive, and ambitious attempts planned during the middle and late 1960s to overcome the effects of disadvantaged backgrounds were by and large ineffective; the impact of these efforts did not measure up to the optimistic expectations held by program developers, government officials, and the general public (Cook and Shadish, 1986). During the 1970s considerable caution was expressed about beginning national programs whose effectiveness had not already been demonstrated. Boruch et al. (1983) show, however, that such warnings often were not heeded.

Besides the need to show that proposed programs are likely to be effective, there are persistent needs to demonstrate that existing programs are worth having and are managed efficiently. Frequently, government programs are not explicitly terminated. Instead, new approaches to problems are implemented alongside old programs. One suggestion is to authorize programs for a specific length of time—five years, for example. After the period of time expires, the program goes out of existence unless its success has been documented and it has been reauthorized (Chelimsky, 1978). Although federal legislation has never been passed requiring this degree of evaluation, it can be argued that a rigorous use of program evaluation should be part of any legislation authorizing government programs.

Difficulty in Defining and Measuring Results

Another reason why the demand for the evaluation of people-oriented services grew is that it is difficult to describe the intended outcomes of human service organizations as compared to those of product-oriented organizations. Whenever the intended outcome is hard to define, assessments of success are very complicated. Industrial firms make things that can be seen, weighed, and counted. Department stores, supermarkets, and bakeries sell merchandise. To evaluate the success of such organizations is easy—at least in theory. It is necessary to determine whether the products were in fact made and sold, and whether the amount collected for the products exceeded the cost of making and selling them. In practice, these questions are complex, due to the nature of large businesses; however, the approach to judging the ultimate success of such an organization is easy to define and widely accepted.

The use of human resources is just as important as the use of financial resources but the nature of the "products" is as difficult to describe as are the methods of assessing their quality. What are the goals of a remedial education program? How do we know that a child has obtained what a program was designed to offer? When is an injured person rehabilitated? What level of rehabilitation should be hoped for? If the state provides hot lunches to a school, but the children throw out the vegetables, is the program a failure? Should we change the menu or teach nutrition to the parents? If a couple gets a divorce after marriage counseling, was the counseling inadequate?

Regulation of Human Services

If human services were available only on a fee-for-service basis, evaluating them might be left to free-market forces. The services that were purchased would, by definition, be successful; unwanted services would fail because there would be few, if any, buyers. The free-market approach has not been permitted to govern the field of human services. There are two major reasons for this. First, it has been assumed that the public cannot easily differentiate between poor and good human service providers. How many patients, for example can really tell when a physician is competent? For this reason, physicians and many other service providers are required to obtain a state license before providing services to people. Traditionally, qualifications for offering services were based on training; however, a trend is developing that would require a demonstration of skill before licensing.

A second reason why free-market forces do not control human services is that the recipient usually pays for the service indirectly. Private insurance companies, large charitable organizations, local governments, and increasingly, federal and state governments cover the costs of many human services. Once a service program is developed, the intended recipients have little to say about how it is administered or what is provided. However, it is important that insurance and public funds be used wisely and productively. The need to demonstrate the effectiveness of human services is critical.

HOW PROGRAM EVALUATION IS USED IN ORGANIZATIONS

Types of Organizations Requiring Evaluations

The preceding paragraphs have been very general, and the reader may have had some difficulty knowing just what sorts of activities are being discussed. The following is a brief discussion of the types of human services that can and ought to be evaluated.

Health care. Hospitals, clinics, extended care facilities, nursing homes, mental health centers, and similar organizations sponsor many services for their patients and clients. Such facilities expend much money on services whose effectiveness has never been fully documented. Educational services for patients, some forms of psychotherapy, certain novel medical treatments, recreational programs, and innovative ways of treating medical/behavioral problems are among the types of health services that should be evaluated in some fashion. Common sense and good management practices call for the documentation of the effectiveness of such programs in order to justify the continued expenditure of funds.

Criminal justice. Police departments, court systems, and prisons sponsor programs to encourage respect for law enforcement, to develop citizen–law enforcement officer rapport, and to intervene in the lives of potential and convicted criminals. The effectiveness of these and other criminal justice programs is often questioned. Evaluations can aid in the selection of new programs and in the improvement of existing programs when done carefully.

Education. Schools and colleges should evaluate the effectiveness of their teaching staffs as well as specific programs (such as enrichment and remedial programs). The effectiveness of new curricula should be assessed before dissemination to other schools. It is not unknown for special programs to be watered down or to be provided to students other than those identified in the program proposal.

Industry and business. Training programs are widely used in all types of business. Newly designed training programs are especially in need of evaluation. A new company-sponsored safety program, for example, would be an ideal program to evaluate using cost-benefit techniques, because both the cost of the program and the cost of accidents can be calculated.

Public administration. Local communities support a variety of service programs. Preventive medicine (such as blood pressure checks), park district programs, and fire safety inspections are among the service programs sponsored by local communities. Taxpayers should be assured that the services reach the intended population, that the recommendations of safety inspectors are followed, and that people in need of medical care are diagnosed and treated.

Various Kinds of Programs

Human service programs are developed to help individuals with acute but temporary needs; others seek to correct or alleviate longstanding problems; and others help to prevent future problems or to develop the potential of students, workers, and managers.

Acute problems include the need for health care for injuries and illnesses, the need for emotional and financial support after accidents or criminal attack, and the need for housing after a home or apartment fire. Such needs are pressing and must be met without delay if suffering is to be minimized, lives are to be saved, or further emotional harm is to be averted. We are all aware of hospital care and emergency rooms, which alleviate physical needs. Acute emotional needs are sometimes met through community mental health crisis services. Some police departments try to help victims of crimes handle their emotional reactions. The help these programs offer is short term and must be mobilized quickly for maximum effectiveness.

Alcoholism counseling, drug abuse treatment programs, psychotherapy, physical rehabilitation, and training services in correctional facilities seek to help people with longstanding problems. There is a very high failure rate within such programs. Often both the cause and the actual nature of the problem are hard to define. Thus, the programs are difficult to design, to run, and to evaluate. Evaluation of these services has traditionally been minimal. However, because the amount of money and human resources devoted to mental health and criminal justice programs is staggering, evaluation work in these fields is being encouraged, if not required, by funding bodies.

Evaluation should play a part in programs developed to reduce the effects of economic disadvantages. Welfare, job-training, Medicare, Medicaid, and Social Security were planned to help people maintain dignity and health despite limited financial resources.

Some human services are designed to prevent problems. For example, law enforcement agencies suggest ways to make a home or a store less inviting to criminals; health education programs provide nutritional information to enable people to avoid certain health problems; and health screening programs detect illness or weakness that, if unchecked, could lead to serious disorders or even early death.

Educational programs constitute a major part of the human services industry. The products and goals of these programs are difficult to describe fully. Americans sponsor education at many different levels and for a variety of purposes from preschool through postgraduate work—and in settings ranging from formal classrooms, to IBM management seminars, to the U.S. Army. People participate in educational programs to gain accreditation or become licensed to practice various occupations or professions, to learn specific skills, for enjoyment, for self-help, to enhance their social standing, and for intellectual and psychological growth. Accounting for the funds spent on education must take into consideration the specific purposes of the program being studied.

Programs are delivered by a variety of agencies with very different characteristics. Human services can be administered as regional or national projects involving millions or even billions of dollars. At the other extreme, a program can be directed to a small group of people in a given institution over a very short time period.

Local Level Focus

We have concentrated our discussions throughout this text on evaluations of the smaller programs likely to be encountered by evaluators working for school districts, hospitals, personnel departments, social service agencies, city or state governments, and so on. Although some national programs are described, the focus on smaller programs is useful in an introductory text because most readers are more familiar with local government or organization-level programs than they are with national programs. Johnston (1983) envisioned organization-level, internal evaluators carrying the major responsibilities for program evaluation in coming years, with the number of major, national evaluation projects decreasing. Political trends and an appreciation of the difficulties in carrying out and interpreting national-level programs have led to the situation Johnston anticipated (Lincoln, 1990).

Although complex analytical tools are useful, the use of simpler techniques is sufficient for most evaluators and may lead to greater utilization by administrators who find statistics to be an incomprehensible—if not intimidating—topic.

Some writers prefer to reserve the term *program* to refer to major government-funded human services (for example, Cook, Leviton, and Shadish, 1985). However, this text uses the term in a more flexible manner, as do many other writers.

Reasons to Evaluate Programs

There are many reasons for conducting program evaluations, including:

- Fulfillment of accreditation requirements
- Accounting for funds
- Answering requests for information
- Choosing among possible programs
- Assisting staff in program development and improvement
- Learning about unintended effects of programs

These uses of evaluation are described in detail in the chapters on methods. At this point we discuss them only briefly.

First, many facilities are required to evaluate their programs for accreditation purposes. Colleges, hospitals, and mental health centers need accreditation to maintain viable facilities. Although a high level of effectiveness might not be required, the threat of the loss of accreditation helps maintain a certain quality of service.

Second, a majority of grant applications to government and philanthropic agencies require a discussion of the techniques to be used to evaluate the effectiveness of the activities supported by the grant. If a program to teach elderly people about nutrition is supported, the program administrators are required to gather empirical evidence that the elderly are being reached and that the program has increased nutritional knowledge and practices. If programs are to be accountable to government or charitable agencies (and, indirectly, to the public), it should be possible to show some results for the expenditure of funds.

A third reason is to facilitate the completion of the vast number of surveys government bureaus require for the continuation of funds. If an agency does not keep systematic records, each request for information requires a time-consuming manual search through files.

Fourth, many administrative decisions can be enhanced by evaluation data. An agency may be requested to expand its programs. However, budgets cannot be stretched to cover all the services that the community or an enthusiastic staff suggests. Administrators are ultimately responsible for allocating resources. They must face questions such as: If job counseling is begun, what current service is to be eliminated or deemphasized? Is the proposed program suited to the needs of the local community? If evaluation activity has been a routine aspect of the some material should be at hand already to help in the decision and it is m that an empirical approach to making decisions would be followed. An approach to decision making would be an improvement over the typical s......., selecting programs solely on the basis of impressionistic and anecdotal evidence, or political pressures.

A fifth purpose of evaluation is to obtain information to improve practices and program structure. Providers of human services need information on how well they do their work. Also, evaluators can provide feedback on how well human service providers are viewed by those receiving the service. Good interpersonal relations are more important to human service providers than to people who primarily use technical skills in their work.

Sixth, a program's unintended effects should be discovered. Just as effective medicines can have negative side effects, so too can useful and successful social programs. The most useful evaluations include procedures to detect unanticipated and unwanted outcomes. This is a crucial, but an often overlooked, contribution of program evaluation.

What Program Evaluation Is Not

In seeking to define what program evaluation is, it is helpful to describe what it is not. Program evaluation is not to be confused with basic research or individual assessment.

Basic research concerns questions of theoretical interest, without regard to the immediate needs of people or organizations. In contrast, program evaluations include information to help people improve their effectiveness, assist administrators make program-level decisions, and make it possible for programs to be accountable to the public. If evaluators do not provide information that is relevant to decisions, they are not fulfilling their major purpose. Furthermore, evaluation is often done under time pressure and in settings such as hospitals, courts, schools, and training offices, which are designed for the delivery of a service, not for research.

If program evaluation is indeed a new social science with unique methods, it requires basic research on new evaluation methods and new procedures to encourage implementation of findings. Those who create such advances are essential to the practice of program evaluation but they do not fill the role of a program evaluator. Readers who have taken social science courses in which basic research is held up as an ideal may be surprised to find that application holds such a central place in this text.

The second professional activity often confused with program evaluation is individual assessment. Educational psychologists, personnel workers, and counseling psychologists traditionally have provided diagnostic information for human service organizations. They administer intelligence, aptitude, interest, achievement, and personality tests for the purpose of "evaluating" a person's need for a service or qualifications for a job or for advancement. These activities are not part of the program evaluator's role. In program evaluation, information describing people is derived from measures of performance in their jobs or from measures thought to be sensitive to changes caused by a human service program. For example, program evaluators might measure depression to examine the effects of counseling or another service, but not for the purpose of analyzing someone's mental state.

Common Types of Evaluations

This text divides evaluations in two ways: (1) according to the type of question asked about the program; and (2) according to the purpose of the evaluation.

The questions asked by evaluators can be classified into four general types: *need*, *process*, *outcome*, and *efficiency*.

The evaluation of need. An assessment of need seeks to answer questions such as:

- What is the socioeconomic profile of a community?
- What are the particular unmet needs of a target population with respect to the type of program being considered (for example, health, mental health, employment, education, crime prevention)?
- What forms of service are likely to be attractive to a particular group?

The measurement of needs is a prerequisite to effective program planning. Evaluators view planning as closely related to evaluation. Planning is, in fact, a form of evaluation—one that occurs before the program is implemented. The title of the journal *Evaluation and Program Planning* illustrates the close association of planning and evaluation.

To be a good advocate and a good planner, one must have correct information about need. Certain techniques are useful for measuring or estimating social needs. Although some of these techniques are less quantitative than are other aspects of evaluation, the accumulation and synthesis of information is a necessary aspect of need assessment. This text includes a brief discussion of the evaluation of need. Those readers who become involved in this area can find references to some key works on this subject at the end of Chapter 6.

The evaluation of process. Once a program has been developed and begun, evaluators turn to documenting the extent to which the program was implemented as designed, serves the target population, and operates as expected. The kinds of questions a process evaluation seeks to answer are:

- Is the program attracting a sufficient number of clients?
- Are clients representative of the target population?
- How much does the staff actually contact the clients?
- Does the workload of the staff match that planned?
- Are there differences among staff members in effort expended?

While the answers to these questions do not indicate whether the program is successful, they are still important. It is conceivable that a good plan has been inadequately implemented or that a successful program is not serving the population it was commissioned and funded to serve. Early warnings provided by a process evaluation would give the directors an opportunity to redirect the program to give it a chance to be successful.

An extreme illustration of the need to verify program implementation concerns a Russian tractor factory that was reported to be a model of efficiency when, in fact, construction problems had been so severe that it was not even built. To avoid criticism for failure, those responsible for having it built faked confirmation of construction and fabricated the production records ("The Potemkin Factory," 1980).

The information necessary for a process evaluation is often available in the agency; however, it is typically not in a usable form. Material describing the clients is on application or intake forms, but it might not be summarized. Details of services received are part of prose notes made by care givers and added to the files. Retrieving filed information requires a special effort and considerable expense. Process evaluations are best conducted when a system of reporting is designed to facilitate gathering and summarizing useful information. In Chapter 7 we illustrate the use of simple information systems for human service settings. References are provided for descriptions of more ambitious systems.

The evaluation of outcome. If a study of implementation does show that the program was successfully put into place, an assessment of the program's outcome may become a major focus of evaluators. For example:

- Do the people who take a speed-reading course read fast?
- Do they read faster than those not taking the course?
- Can evidence be found that taking the course causes increased reading speeds?
- How much support for the theoretical foundation of the program was found?
- What evidence is there that the program can be implemented effectively elsewhere?

Although it it reasonable to ask these questions, it is difficult to identify the causes of behavioral changes observed in people. For example, many people begin psychotherapy during a life crisis. If several months later they feel better and seem better adjusted, the change may be due to therapy, to the natural resolution of the crisis, to a combination of both, or to something else entirely. If a change in on-the-job requirements is followed by better morale, can we say that the change caused the better morale, or should we conclude that it was simply the attention of management that led to improvement? Perhaps a better national economic outlook was the actual cause.

The presentation of methods ranges from the very simple to the very complex. There are situations in which a research plan with many technical weaknesses is quite appropriate for answering the questions facing administrators and public representatives at certain times. Other more demanding questions require more complicated research plans. In fact, evaluators might work with more complicated research designs than do laboratory research scientists. While laboratory social scientists can control some of the experiences of the people involved in the research, evaluators gather data from people participating in actual, ongoing programs. Although these people are very interested in the benefits they can obtain from the program, their interest in the needs of the evaluators is marginal at best. The evaluators are seen by some as requiring their energy and time without providing any service in return.

When designing and conducting outcome evaluations, evaluators need to select appropriate criteria to indicate program success. The PUSH/Excel program was designed to raise the aspirations of inner city youth through a variety of local initiatives. It was very unfavorably evaluated. House (1988, 1990) argued that evaluators of PUSH/Excel treated it as other programs with standardized services that could be offered at different sites. They concluded that there was no program when in fact the program was to encourage local initiative. Thus, no common criteria of success could be used at all sites because the program differed from site to site.

The definitions of successful outcome may well vary if we compare the opinions of various interested groups, such as the agency funding the program, the program staff, and the participants. A job-training program may be funded to provide job skills so that the long-term unemployed may obtain jobs with private companies. The staff may view the training as a reward for participation in local elections, and the trainees may view the program as a good, albeit temporary, job. Whose definition of outcome is to be used?

At times the outcome sought by one or more of the groups is hidden purposely from evaluators. In politically sensitive settings careful evaluators are in an uncomfortable position if publicly stated goals conflict with privately held goals. Developing methods to measure success is difficult when goals are clear; when they are hidden, evaluators' jobs are all the more difficult. There are ethical concerns that are relevant when evaluators believe a program is using resources for purposes other than those intended. For example, in Dade County, Florida, an investigator charged that some funds for unemployed workers were used to hire relatives of politicians (*Time*, July 24, 1978). If the outcomes of programs are regularly evaluated, such misuse of money should be more readily discovered than it usually is.

Another problem centers on the issue of how long after participation the outcome is supposed to be maintained. People leaving a program typically return to the same environment that was at least partially responsible for their problems. The good intentions of alcoholics may not withstand the social pressures of their peers. Cigarettes are smoked by habit in a number of situations, such as after meals, or from worry or boredom. Breaking longstanding habits is very difficult. Although changes may be observed after participation in a program, the changes may only be superficial and dissolve in a matter of months, weeks, or days. If so, was the program a failure? Such questions about outcomes are treated in Chapters 8 through 11.

The evaluation of efficiency. While a program may help the participants, administrators and legislators must also address the issue of cost. Evaluations of efficiency raise the following questions:

- Are funds spent for the intended purposes?
- Does the program achieve its success at a reasonable cost?
- Can dollar values be assigned to the outcomes achieved?
- Does the program achieve a better level of success than other programs costing the same or less to administer?

There are often competing suggestions for the best ways to help people in need. Do people who are convicted of a crime need psychological counseling for emotional conflicts, moral instruction on values, vocational training for holding a job, or academic instruction to help them complete school? Institutions cannot do everything. Choices must be made among possible services and criteria on which to base the choice must be defined.

Two important criteria used to compare programs are effectiveness and cost. If two programs appear equally effective, then the less expensive program is getting more results per dollar. If the more expensive program is more effective, the problem becomes more difficult. Is the additional improvement worth the additional cost? Another complication is that most programs seek to involve more than one behavior or skill. Weighing the relative effectiveness of two such programs is very difficult if the decision maker wishes to be objective. An introduction to cost-benefit and cost-effectiveness analyses is given in Chapter 11.

Note that there is a logical sequence in these evaluation questions and in the order of this text's chapters. Without measuring need, programs cannot be planned rationally; without effective implementation, successful outcomes cannot result from the program; and without valued outcomes, there is no reason to worry about cost-effectiveness. A premature focus on an inappropriate evaluation question is likely to produce an evaluation with little value (Wholey, 1983).

PURPOSE OF PROGRAM EVALUATION

There really is only one major purpose for program evaluation activities, although this purpose is often broken down into several subpurposes. Human behavior is adaptive only when people obtain feedback from the environment. Our physical existence literally depends on the feedback within our bodies to regulate activities such as breathing and heart rate, levels of hormones and chemicals, and eating and drinking. Organizational behavior also requires feedback. Delayed feedback, not clearly associated with the behavior being examined, is not very informative. Some writers have said that environmental problems are hard to solve because of the long delay between environmentally destructive policies and the feedback indicating a weakening of natural systems (Meadows and Perelman, 1973). Program evaluation seeks to provide timely feedback in social systems.

What effect do social interventions such as jail sentences, nutrition counseling, community hotlines, crime prevention measures, or job-training programs have on the people expected to need these interventions? Figure 1.1 illustrates the place of program evaluation as the feedback loop in human service activities. Program evaluation can be a powerful tool for improving the effectiveness of organizations

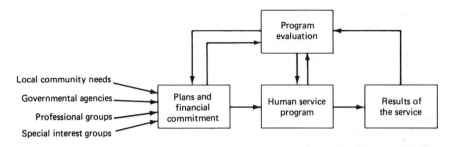

FIGURE 1-1 Schematic diagram of the place of evaluation as a feedback loop for a human service program.

(Davis, 1982; Zammuto, 1982). The rational processes of assessing needs, measuring the implementation of programs to meet those needs, evaluating the achievement of carefully formed goals and objectives, and comparing the degree of achievement and the costs involved with those of similar programs serves to improve the use of human and material resources in organizations. Michael Hendricks' comments on the role of evaluation are included in Evaluator Profile 1.

Feedback can be provided for two different purposes. Evaluations can strengthen the plans for services or their delivery, to raise the outcomes of programs, or to increase the efficiency of services; such evaluations are called *formative evaluations* (Scriven, 1967) because they are designed to help form the programs themselves. Evaluations may also help us decide whether a program should be started, continued, or chosen from two or more alternatives; such evaluations are called *summative evaluations* (Scriven, 1967). There is a finality to summative

EVALUATOR PROFILE 1.

Michael Hendricks: The Role of the Program Evaluator

Michael Hendricks was president of MH Associates, a Washington, D.C., based firm specializing in program evaluation, organizational development, and training before moving to India. Prior to setting up his own consulting firm, he had been Chief of Field Inspections for the Office of Inspector General of the U.S. Department of Health and Human Services. His Ph.D. from Northwestern University is in Social Psychology.

In light of his wide experiences in program evaluation, Dr. Hendricks was asked about changes in evaluation he has seen in the past ten years. He answered: "I'm an incurable optimist, but I really do think that the field has blossomed and is still blossoming. . . . From a fairly narrow technical specialty, which basically wrote 'report cards' on programs, we've grown to fill many different roles during all phases of a program—planning, implementation, operationalization, as well as after [the program is over]. We have a much more sophisticated understanding of the importance of the environment, and . . . we recognize much more the need to be useful."

Adapted from Sporn, D. L. 1989. A conversation with Michael Hendricks. *Evaluation Practice, 10*(3), 18–24.

---

evaluations; once the value of the program is assessed, it is possible that the program might be ended. In actuality, few evaluations really determine whether or not a program will be terminated (Cook et al., 1985). There are many sources of information about programs available to administrators, legislators, and community leaders. Because program evaluation is only one of these sources, evaluators are not surprised when clear evaluation reports are not followed by specific decisions. Thus, nearly all evaluations are formative, ideally serving to improve the program evaluated.

Evaluations are also done for less than noble purposes (Kytle and Millman, 1986), some of which are discussed in the next chapter.

TRENDS MAKING EVALUATION NECESSARY

The growing interest in program evaluation is the result of several trends in American society. *Accountability* has become a word often heard in government and human service settings. Accountability refers to the justification of how resources have been used, and to the responsibility to achieve realistic results from one's efforts (Scriven, 1981). The call for accountability has come from the consumer movement, professionals' own desires to improve services, an awareness of good management practices, a recognition of society's limited ability to support human services, and legislation.

The Consumer Movement

In recent years numerous groups have been organized to make the needs of consumers known to large corporations. This movement has had repercussions in human service fields. The philosophy behind this approach is that "the assumption that *operating* a service is equivalent to *rendering* service, and that both are equivalent to rendering *quality* service are no longer being honored as inherently valid" (Speer and Trapp, 1976, p. 217). The right of professionals to make unchallenged judgments has been curtailed. A form of medical care evaluation—malpractice suits and the threat of malpractice suits—has already altered the practice of medicine. No professional is above being held accountable. Government administrators, teachers, nurses, military officers, and priests are among those whose performance is now being analyzed more closely. Increasingly, respect and acceptance have to be earned by performance, not by certification or status.

Professional Concern

The service providers themselves have often cooperated and provided leadership in the movement toward the evaluation of human services. In the first decades of the twentieth century, American medical care was evaluated by the medical societies themselves. Such cooperation has its limits, however. One early outcome evaluation conducted by the American College of Surgeons revealed such a poor level of outcome that the reports were destroyed (*National Standards for Commu-*

nity Mental Health Centers, 1977). Medical outcome evaluation on a national scale was not attempted again until the 1970s.

Managerial Effectiveness

Good management procedures have become more widely used in human service fields. McConkey (1975), while serving as a statewide United Fund chairperson, was distressed to learn that some organizations requested funds but provided neither a description of their services nor evidence that the services produced positive outcomes. Human service administrators are much more aware of the necessity of effective management than they were in the past. The Crusade of Mercy (United Fund) of Chicago, Illinois, ran full-page ads picturing their "priorities committee." The caption under their picture stated that the "hardest noses of Chicago run the Crusade of Mercy." The caption went on to describe the auditing procedure used and how some agencies are dropped from support.

There are two major reasons for the tardy development of careful management procedures in human services: the difficulty of specifying the outcome of an effective human service and the origins of many human services in small charitable settings. Commercial firms can be clearer about the goals they seek to attain than can human service agencies. In addition, commercial managers have not had the "God-will-provide" attitude of the people who traditionally ran charity services. This is not to say that human service settings do or should act on the same values as business firms (see Sirotnik, 1990), but there is much to be learned from modern management methods.

Program evaluation in human services received impetus from the development of several data-oriented tools for managers. Tools for studying and improving how organizations accomplish their purposes, such as operations research (Lesourne, 1990) and systems analysis (Cornes, 1990), have helped evaluators with their work in human service organizations. Program evaluation can help managers learn which programs are successful and which programs are serving target populations. Such information can permit administrators to make more informed decisions.

Limitations on Resources

The recognition that society cannot fulfill every need that people may have requires that priorities be set. Which is more valuable—treatment of alcoholics in the workforce or park programs for potentially delinquent children? Devoting resources to one program means that these resources cannot be devoted to another program. Each program has its own supporters and beneficiaries. The conflicting wishes of these groups can pull decision makers in two, three, or more directions. Programs, of course, can be ranked on the basis of the power of their backers. Still, it would be better to rank programs on the basis of their potential effectiveness to meet unsatisfied human needs. In this way the resources of society may be expended in a fairer and more useful manner than has been the case traditionally.

Legislative Mandates

Increasingly, the federal government insists on the evaluation of programs. Social programs grew considerably during the 1960s and 1970s. Health, Education, and Welfare (HEW) programs required approximately $2 billion in 1953, which was 3 percent of the federal budget. By 1975 HEW programs made up 14 percent of the federal budget, not counting Social Security costs (*U.S. News & World Report*, 1975). Social programs have a reputation for costing more than initially planned. Medicare and Medicaid, for example, cost $39 billion in 1977 but only $6 billion in 1967 (*Newsweek*, 1977). Important for our purposes was the result of congressional reaction to rapid cost escalation. Congress sought to contain Medicare costs by monitoring the time required for treatment and by examining the quality of treatment given (Gosfield, 1975). More recently, Medicare has paid hospitals a fixed amount on the basis of the illness being treated rather than the actual costs incurred. The "diagnostic-related groups" approach was developed to encourage hospitals to provide care in an efficient manner.

The government's role in evaluation is also evident in the requirement that recipients of grants be directed to evaluate their work. For example, in 1964 Congress mandated some program review in hospitals treating Medicare patients (Egdahl and Gertman, 1976), and the evaluation requirements in the Elementary and Secondary Education Act of 1965 (McLaughlin, 1974) encouraged the development of educational evaluation. Although requirements are often met with less than adequate research methods, we believe that thinking in evaluative terms is a step forward.

THE ROLES OF EVALUATORS

Work Settings

Before actually describing the specifics of program evaluation, it would be worthwhile to describe where evaluators work. There are three major work settings for professional evaluators. Some work as internal evaluators for the organizations that provide the service to be evaluated. It is undesirable for the evaluator to work directly under the manager of the service being evaluated; the explicit or implicit demand for favorable reports would be too severe (Cook, Leviton, and Shadish, 1985). Working for the central administration of a large organization that sponsors the services being evaluated helps to insulate the internal evaluator from some of the pressure.

A second role is employment with governmental or regulatory agencies. The U.S. General Accounting Office, for example, reports to Congress on how legislative programs are working out. The GAO's reports can influence any area of Federal legislation. The Office of Inspector General carries out evaluations for the Secretary of Health and Human Services. Some states have created evaluation units, often in the offices of the state auditor. The act creating the Legislative Auditor in Minnesota states that this official is to

. . . determine the degree to which the activities and programs entered into or funded by the state are accomplishing their goals and objectives, including the evaluation of goals and objectives, measurement of program results and effectiveness, alternative means of achieving the same results, and efficiency in the allocation of resources ("Spotlight," 1982, p. 2).

Since states have responsibilities in the areas of education, health care, welfare, safety, and highways, evaluators in state offices work on a variety of topics. Since government-sponsored programs have supporters who carefully guard their turf, evaluations of government-based programs can be "explosive" (Nienstadt and Halemba, 1986).

The third major work setting for evaluators is private research firms. Such firms submit proposals in response to "Requests for proposals" announcing competitions for evaluations of governmental programs. The proposals are judged on the basis of cost and quality of methods proposed. They are evaluated in much the same way as are competitive bids for construction projects; a contract for the project is given to the firm or evaluator group that has submitted the highest quality proposal within the allotted budget. Some university faculty members conduct evaluations independently; they work in much the same way as evaluators who work with research firms.

In addition to professional evaluators, many individuals in educational, personnel, training, rehabilitation, management, and corrections roles perform evaluations as part of their responsibilities. Readers who currently fill or intend to seek positions in such settings may find that the concepts and skills presented in this text are valuable in their work even if they never have a position labeled evaluator.

Consultants Compared to Internal Evaluators

There are two general ways an evaluator can relate to the organization needing the evaluation: (1) Evaluators can work for the organization and do a variety of evaluations; or (2) they can come to the organization from a research firm or a university to work on a specific program only. For the purposes of discussion, the terms *internal evaluator* and *consultant* are used to summarize these two different roles. The particular role filled has implications for the size of the evaluation project attempted and for some of the characteristics of the research itself.

Factors related to competence. In terms of knowledge about a program, internal evaluators have the advantage, since they have better access to program directors and to the organization's administration. A person who is physically present 40 hours a week is likely to see the program in action, to know the staff, and to learn about its reputation from other people in the organization. The information gained informally by a secretary in the cafeteria would be unavailable to a consultant not based in the organization. The more that is known about the actual workings of the program, the easier it is to ask the relevant questions in an evaluation.

The technical expertise of the evaluator is important. An internal evaluator often works with a small group of two or three. Some evaluators work alone.

However, working alone provides limited opportunities for helpful feedback. In contrast, the consultant can draw from the resources of a larger organization.

A different facet of the question of technical expertise is suggested by the need to perform evaluation work in many different areas of an organization. During one period of two years, the authors of this text performed work on topics that included psychosomatic illness, stroke disability, a dietary supplement, patient satisfaction, medical education programs, and employee satisfaction. It is challenging and stimulating to work in new areas; however, there is also a risk that inexperience in a given area may lead to oversimplification. By selecting a consultant with experience in a specific program area, an organization can avoid the errors that may occur when an internal evaluator faces a problem in a new area of the organization.

Personal qualities.   There are personal qualities unrelated to technical competence that are important to evaluators. Evaluators can do more effective work if they are objective, trusted by administrators, and interested in improving the program being evaluated.

Being well known and, let us hope, having been found worthy of trust, internal evaluators usually find program directors and staff more willing to devote time to the evaluation, to admit problems, and to share confidences than they would be with a consultant not previously known. Being trusted may make it possible for the evaluator to fulfill the organizational educator role suggested by Cronbach (1980).

An internal evaluator can also be expected to have a desire to improve the organization sponsoring the program and paying the evaluator's salary. Although intentions are sometimes misunderstood, it is always in the best interests of evaluators to find ways to improve the organizations in which they work. Consultants might not have the same motivations, being less dependent on the organization sponsoring the program for continuing support.

On the other hand, whether or not one is dependent on the organization for a job may affect one's objectivity, which is important if reports are to be credible. The objectivity of internal evaluators may be questioned because they may know the program designer and the staff delivering the service. It is not easy to criticize the work of a friend. The consultant, on the other hand, is unlikely to have developed personal relationships within the organization and thus may be more objective. An internal evaluator may also hesitate to report critical findings because future work may be jeopardized. Research in an applied setting depends on cooperation. If people believe that negative outcomes will result from the project, the needed cooperation may be hard to obtain.

There is yet another side to the question. Evaluators lose their credibility and, thus, their effectiveness if they ignore sensitive issues. The authors prepared a report that showed positive outcomes for the patients in a medical/psychological program (Carey and Posavac, 1977). If the report had stopped there, it would have been welcomed. However, it went on to show that other patients obtained the same degree of positive benefit at less cost in a different program. This observation was not welcome. It is important to emphasize, though, that this short-term problem should be weighed against the likelihood that willingness to report negative or ambivalent findings will increase one's credibility in the long run.

The purpose of the evaluation required.   Earlier in this chapter two purposes of evaluations were described—formative and summative. Internal and consultant evaluators can and do perform both types of evaluations. However, there are certain situations that are better served by one or the other type of evaluator. An internal evaluator is likely to be more effective than a consultant in implementing procedures to follow for formative evaluations. Such evaluators are available and committed enough to see the project through, and because formative evaluations cannot lead to a traumatic decision to end a program, negative results do not damage the evaluator's role in the organization. If, in contrast, a summative evaluation is wanted because there is a strong suspicion that a program is failing, an outside evaluator probably is more helpful. A school board, knowing that it had to close one of three grade schools because enrollment had dropped, decided to select a consultant with no ties to the school district to recommend which school to close. The consultant performed an evaluation of efficiency for each school and recommended that the least efficient school be closed. Although there were some hard feelings, and a number of verbal attacks were leveled at the consultant and his report, the selection of the school to be closed was made and implemented with fewer difficulties than in neighboring school districts that made similar decisions, but relied on local expertise.

Conflicts Between Evaluators and Organizations

Evaluators fill a position between the role of the research social scientist concerned about theory, the design of experiments, and the analysis of data (but for the most part uninvolved in the delivery of human services) and the role of the practitioner dealing with people in need and seldom interested or trained in the methods of data collection and analysis. Evaluators are able to read the language and to use the tools of the research social scientist. Research design, validation, reliability, and statistical significance are familiar to evaluators. In addition, the effective evaluator is sensitive to the concerns and style of the service delivery staff. Finally, evaluators interact with administrators, who are ultimately responsible for the effectiveness and cost of the program. Because the field is still new and the tasks assigned to the evaluator are so varied, the role of the evaluator is not widely understood.

Participating in such a new field has advantages and disadvantages. The advantages include the intellectual stimulation provided by exposure to people serving various roles in human service programs and the satisfaction of seeing research methods used in ways that can be of potential benefit. The disadvantages include being viewed as intrusive and unnecessary by some service delivery personnel. The most effective evaluators show that they are allies of service providers, while at the same time asking searching questions and requiring documentation of answers. It must be recognized that evaluators might fail to see their own biases since they are affiliated with the organization offering the program (Cook, Leviton, and Shadish, 1985).

It is unfortunately true that shortsighted self-interest has opposed objective evaluation. Spinney testified to Congress that military planners ignored the findings of their own research and those of evaluation analysts when ambitious officers wanted pet projects funded (Isaacson, 1983). It should also be noted that some political orientations are opposed to government participation in many social services, regardless of the effectiveness of these governmental activities (Levin, 1982; Walsh, 1983). Campbell (1983), one of the early leaders in the evaluation field, has become concerned about the possibility of collecting valid information when people are threatened by an evaluation of their work or ideas. Others expect active, but changed, roles for evaluators in future years (Johnston, 1983; Lincoln, 1990; McClintock, 1983). These observers foresee a growth in the use of information prepared by people working in the organizations sponsoring the program or service. A responsible investment of resources by federal, state, and local governments, as well as by business and charitable organizations, requires careful monitoring as well as evaluations of effectiveness (Rossi, 1983).

It is true that requirements to evaluate programs do not necessarily mean that evaluations are uniformly good (they are not), that evaluations are always utilized (sometimes they are ignored), or that ineffective programs no longer exist (they do). However, many social scientists believe that the widespread requirement for evaluation, if coupled with increased sophistication in evaluation methods, contributes to the achievement of the desirable goals of improving the effectiveness of social programs and making new programs more sensitive to the needs of the people to be served.

Getting a Job as an Evaluator

As mentioned above, many organizations conduct evaluations but do not call their evaluation activities program evaluations. Some entry-level jobs go under the names *program analyst* or *planner*. A number of graduate students have gotten such positions in city government during some phase of their studies. To get a job in program evaluation, a person must sometimes be creative in suggesting how organizations can use an evaluator's skills. For example, an analogy could be drawn between an auditor working with financial matters and an evaluator working with people-oriented issues. Just as you would not run a business without adequate monitoring of cash flow, you should not run an organization without knowing how employees react to company policies and benefits, whether customers like the services, or if managers work better after being trained (Perloff, 1983).

In order to understand the problems of organizations that might hire an evaluator, it is helpful to learn something about the ways individuals in those organizations think. There are professional organizations for people in personnel, marketing, training, and so on; and the journals they publish can usually be found in libraries. Capper (1983) has suggested joining the organizations and meeting people in the businesses that might need evaluation skills. The crucial question is: How will evaluation improve the quality of the work done by the organization? To provide a credible answer, the evaluator must understand the needs of the organization.

A number of people have suggested that conducting a project for free is a way of becoming known and demonstrating the value of program evaluation. Several students of the first author have been offered jobs after doing a class project for an organization.

Even after getting a job as an evaluator, it is still important to demonstrate that evaluation can help in running an effective program. Some managers will be threatened by the idea of someone collecting data on the effectiveness of their work groups. Still, becoming known in the organization as competent and trustworthy, and developing a broader knowledge of how feedback about effectiveness can help different aspects of the organization, helps keep a steady flow of work for the evaluation office.

Evaluation and Other Activities of an Organization

Professional interaction among people with similar interests often is beneficial to all concerned. An evaluator working alone finds it hard to grow and develop professionally. If an organization is too small to employ more than one full-time evaluator, it may be wise to attach evaluation to another function of the organization. Four functions that are sometimes joined with evaluation are research, education, planning, and human resources.

Research. Some human service organizations routinely sponsor research directly with operating funds or indirectly with grant funds. Evaluation can become one function of the research team. For example, a police department was awarded a grant to study the effect of providing emotional support to the victims of crime. The social scientists responsible for that research would be excellent colleagues of an evaluator. University-affiliated hospitals carry on research. Individuals conducting research into psychiatric problems or emotional issues related to serious illness have interests similar enough to those of evaluators to serve as colleagues.

Education. Some organizations have joined the functions of education and evaluation. There is a longstanding precedent for this marriage in educational psychology. New study materials and curricula are evaluated before being widely used by schools. Universities are combining faculty development and evaluation into one office. Many organizations besides schools sponsor educational programs that need monitoring. For example, industries have safety education programs, apprenticeship programs, and job-training programs.

Planning. Planning is an activity in which evaluators can assist. It is common for service providers to serve as a planning group. This choice is wise; however, many direct-service providers are not data oriented, feel uncomfortable constructing need surveys, and may be unable to analyze the information obtained. Evaluators can help estimate the probable effectiveness of planned programs and consumer reaction to proposed projects or services. Sometimes evaluators can help planners simply by asking hard-to-answer questions about the assumptions implicit in the plan for the program itself or for the implementation of the program.

Human resources. Large businesses often have a vice-president of human resources. This office oversees all policies concerning hiring, compensation, and the professional development of employees. Compensation plans, training programs, and management effectiveness seminars all require evaluation if an organization is to be as effective as possible.

SUMMARY AND PREVIEW

National trends, such as the consumer movement, professional concern, increased managerial effectiveness, limitations on resources, and specific congressional mandates have converged to create a need for methods to make rational managerial and legislative decisions in human services. The social science methods of program evaluation include planning, program monitoring, outcome assessment, and benefit/cost considerations. Evaluators are quantitative social scientists working to improve the delivery of human services. Their efforts to effect such improvements are on a program level, not on the individual person/client/patient level frequently associated with human service organizations.

To obtain the maximum benefit from an evaluation, evaluators work closely with the groups who have an interest in the program while planning and conducting the evaluation. Although such cooperation can be time-consuming, wide interest and participation are essential for an evaluation to be useful and used. Chapter 2 addresses the steps in planning an evaluation.

STUDY QUESTIONS

1. One of the interesting aspects of program evaluation is its relevance to a variety of activities. From newspaper and magazine articles, gather examples of the use of program evaluations in the formation of public policy. You might find articles dealing with medical care (malpractice, peer review, costs), education (children reading well or not reading well), program planning (need assessment), relative costs of programs with similar goals, or other issues.
2. What aspects of program evaluation might be used in organizational settings with which you are familiar? Illustrate.
3. List the advantages and disadvantages of making program evaluation a part of American human services delivery systems. Save your list, and when you have finished the text, consider how you might change the list.

4. Some people suggest that while society wants to believe that something is being done about social problems, most people really do not care if the programs actually have an impact on the problems. Consider the question of whether people really want to know if educational, welfare, health, and other services actually work.

FURTHER READING

Cook, T. D., and Shadish, W. R. 1986. Program evaluation: The worldly science. *Annual Review of Psychology 37*: 193–232.
Fairweather, G. W., and Davidson, W. S. 1986. *An introduction to community experimentation.* New York: McGraw-Hill.

2

Planning an Evaluation

Most program evaluations begin in one of three ways. Program personnel themselves may initiate the evaluation or seek to have an evaluation team conduct one; the funding agency or central management may require an evaluation of a sponsored or planned program, or an internal evaluation department might suggest that the organization would benefit from an evaluation of a particular phase of its activities.

Whatever the source of the proposal initiative, evaluators need to address a number of issues and make certain decisions before the collection of data begins. They need to learn about the goals and mechanics of the program, about the people who sponsor the program, about the program personnel, and about groups that may resist the evaluation of the program. After obtaining this information, evaluators must decide whether an evaluation can be done. If the program is planned in a way that permits evaluation, then a decision needs to be made as to whether an evaluation should be done immediately, whether it should be done in the way in which it is proposed, or whether it should be done at all.

In the first part of this chapter, we provide an overview of several models of program evaluation. Next we outline the sequence and manner in which the issues can be approached, identifying the steps to be taken between the time of the initial proposal and the beginning of data collection. The time and effort devoted to each step varies, depending on the complexity of the program, the relationship of the evaluator to the program sponsors and personnel, and the urgency of time constraints. Some steps, such as selecting or developing measures, are very complex. Chapter 3 treats the complicated issue of the specification of the criteria that is used to decide whether a program has been implemented as planned or shows the level of success that is desired. Chapter 4 deals with the more technical questions of what makes a good measure of the criteria selected by the evaluator and the stakeholders.

AN OVERVIEW OF EVALUATION MODELS

A number of different approaches to evaluation have been put forward to guide the planning and implementation of program evaluations. At times disagreements over the best way to carry out an evaluation have been based on different assumptions about the best or even the proper way to evaluate a program. This overview highlights these different assumptions and, consequently, clarifies possible ways to go about evaluating programs. Each of the models outlined emphasizes a valuable aspect of evaluation. The specific questions being addressed by an evaluation or the unique aspects of the program setting often make one or another of the models especially useful. It is crucial for evaluators and stakeholders to avoid selecting a model as the "correct" approach before thoroughly analyzing the setting and the questions that are to be answered by the evaluation. Most evaluations, in fact, use multiple approaches. The order in which these approaches are discussed is not random; however, readers should not see the order as indicating increasing objectivity, or increasing validity. Many of these model descriptions have been adapted from Scriven (1981), House (1980), and Madaus, Scriven, and Stufflebeam (1983).

The Traditional Model in Practice

In the past, those who delivered services to students, patients, prisoners, or welfare recipients were free to work as they felt best with little regard for formal evaluation. The evaluations of their work were confined to impressionistic self-evaluations by the teacher, physician, welfare office, warden, social worker, or psychologist offering or supervising the service. It is not surprising that such evaluations tended to be self-serving and to produce very little to challenge the program directors and staff. This is not to say that human service professionals were dishonest or uninterested in providing quality care or education, but without the disciplined analysis encouraged by formal models of evaluation, the informal evaluators were limited by the cognitive biases that have become well-known (see, for example, Kahneman, Slovic, and Tversky, 1982).

Social Science Research Model

In an effort to make evaluation more rigorous and to control self-serving biases, some evaluators came to view program evaluation as a specialized form of social science research. The way to determine a program's level of success was to form two random groups, providing one group with a service and using the second one as a control group. After the program was administered, the members of each group were observed or they described themselves on the appropriate dependent variables. Statistical tests developed for basic research were applied to the results: if the contrast between treatment group and control group means was statistically significant, the program was pronounced a success. If the results were not significant, the program was deemed a failure. Concluding that a program failed because a statistical test was not significant would have been a mistake, of course, because a nonsignificant finding means that we should suspend judgment; it does not mean that the group means are equal. Unfortunately, this fundamental point was overlooked by some users of the social science model and harm was done to effective programs. The failure was on the part of the evaluator rather than the program (Lipsey, 1990a). The social science approach to program evaluation served to introduce a degree of rigor and objectivity into program evaluation, but its inherent limitations in applied settings and the potential for misuse has become evident.

Goal-based Evaluation

In an effort to make an evaluation sensitive to the particular program, some approaches emphasize that evaluators work with the staff to get the goals and objectives stated clearly and then measure the degree to which these goals are achieved. Examining goals and objectives seems to be an essential aspect of evaluation; however, some evaluators were so focused on the stated goals that they neglected to examine why programs succeeded or failed and to consider any additional positive effects or undesired side effects of the program. For the most part, goal-based evaluations, even when done well, primarily served only one stakeholder group since program managers usually provided the statement of the goals, paid the evaluator, and received the evaluation reports.

Goal-free Evaluation

An attempt to avoid a premature focus on goals led to a suggestion that evaluators work better if they do not know the stated goals of the program. Evaluators who know the goals of the program might unintentionally focus on information that supports the goals and not observe how the program is actually administered or assess the total impact on the program's clients. A goal-free evaluator would spend a considerable amount of time studying the program, the staff, the clients, the setting, and the records to identify all the positive and negative impacts of the program. The evaluator would work in the way that an anthropologist studies a culture for the first time. Later the program staff and its financial supporters would decide whether the evaluator's findings were compatible with the purposes of the program and consider how to make adjustments in the program.

Black Box Evaluation

Black box evaluation refers to those evaluations that examine the output of the program without examining the internal operation of the program. In some situations this is precisely what is needed. Before purchasing an automobile, many people examine *Consumer Reports*, a magazine reporting tests of consumer products. Since car buyers are not in a position to correct the faults of completed automobiles, it is irrelevant why a transmission shifts in a rough manner, or why an engine is hard to start. What consumers need to know is which cars perform better than others, not why. Black box evaluations serve well when examining manufactured objects like cars and TVs. Such evaluations do not serve well when examining social programs for which the evaluation is expected to lead to program improvement.

Fiscal Evaluation

Potentially, the most objective evaluations compare the financial investment needed for a program with the return on that investment. When a company introduces labor-saving machines, it expects to save on labor costs or to increase output in order to pay for the equipment and provide a return on the dollars invested. When deciding to make an investment, planners project how the change may affect the amount of money coming into the organization. While such projections cannot be completely accurate, the final evaluation of the purchase is based strictly on financial considerations. When the item being evaluated does not depend on objective standards of quality, it may be that a strictly bottom-line, financial evaluation is needed. For example, popular culture items such as magazines, top-ten music, or films are usually based on consumer reactions as detected by the number of subscribers and buyers.

Accountability Model

The accountability or audit models developed out of fiscal evaluation (Davis, 1990). Publicly funded programs must devote resources to the activities that were mandated when the programs were funded. Large programs, such as all federally funded program, involve many managers, in numerous sites, scattered across many states and government bases. The Office of Inspector General of the Department of Health and Human Services is an evaluation arm of the department's Secretary. Although the office seeks to help individual agencies become more effective, its primary mission is to be sure that the federal government's funds are supporting the defined services for the appropriate groups of people.

Expert Opinion Model

An approach that seeks to remove the self-serving biases in the traditional approach and avoid the limitations of black box and fiscal evaluations involves having experts examine the program. Art and literary criticism are forms of evaluation in which a learned person carefully examines the work and renders a judgment about its quality. Although art criticism is subjective, expert opinion evaluation can make use of objective data. Findings in post-occupancy evaluations of recently completed buildings include how well buildings were designed and constructed, how efficiently the heating and air conditioning systems function, and whether a building is conducive to effective work. Clearly some decisions in such studies are based on objective, quantified information as well as qualitative impressions. Expert opinions are often used when the entity being evaluated is large, complex, and unique. For example, university accreditation decisions are based on the recommendations of a team of experts who examine quantitative records, inspect the buildings, and talk with students, administrators, staff, and faculty. Since it is impossible to produce some set of numbers indicating the quality of a college, an expert opinion is used.

Naturalistic Model

Evaluators who do not wish to restrict their vision by focusing on stated goals but want to improve the chances of remaining sensitive to the richness of the program, sometimes carry out what is called a *naturalistic evaluation* or a *qualitative evaluation*. When using this model, the evaluator is the data gathering instrument, does not enter the setting with preconceived ideas about the crucial variables, and seeks to understand the program and the stakeholders. The lengthy report includes rich descriptions of the program. The most well-known proponents of qualitative evaluation (Guba and Lincoln, 1989) have adopted philosophical views that are quite different from those held by many evaluators. In fact, Guba and Lincoln eschew the terms *naturalistic* and *qualitative* and instead emphasize *constructivist* philosophical ideas that treat truth as socially defined. If reality is a social and political invention, effective evaluation must involve the empowerment and enfranchisement of the program stakeholders, goals that proponents of other models of evaluation would not espouse. Qualitative methods and the philosophical issues related to them are treated in a later chapter.

The Model Used by the Authors

Goal-based evaluation seems to be the most obvious way to begin planning an evaluation and selecting the evaluation criteria. When we use the term *goal* or *objective*, we do not mean outcome goals and objectives alone. Some goals refer to meeting the needs of the community successfully, some focus on getting a service system in place on time, and others concern efficiency. However, successful evaluators adopt and adapt aspects of any approach that is useful. At times, a simple black box evaluation is appropriate for part or all of the evaluation, but, at other times, a thorough analysis of the program's conceptual underpinnings is essential.

Evaluators seek to help stakeholders find discrepancies between program objectives and the needs of the target population, between the program implementation and the program plans, between the expectations of the target group and the actual program delivered, or between the outcomes achieved and the projected outcomes. These discrepancies show where the program needs to be improved. To improve a program, evaluators examine the program inputs, how the organization functions, and the type of people served, not just the results of the program. Objective, quantitative data are important, but quantitative data also need to be interpreted using qualitative observations. We have found that personal observations provide direction in selecting what to measure and in forming an integrated understanding of the program and its effects. The best evaluators do not select methods until learning what specific questions the program's stakeholders need to answer. As this text unfolds the implications of this model become more apparent.

We now turn to practical steps in getting a program evaluation planned. Our comments are particularly aimed at the work of an internal evaluator; however, these steps must be followed by consultants in very similar ways.

SIX STEPS IN PLANNING AN EVALUATION

Before discussing the steps in planning an evaluation, we want to stress that when working in applied settings or with politically charged issues, it is crucial that communication during planning be explicit. Oral agreements made between the evaluation team and administrators should always be followed up with a memo describing the agreement and the obligations each has accepted. Since administrators are busy and must be concerned with many different issues during any day, it is unwise to depend on memory. Evaluators and the administrator may forget precisely what was decided or may never have understood the agreement in exactly the same way. If the evaluator puts the agreement on paper, ideas that were not discussed because they seemed obvious are brought to the attention of stakeholders. It is better to take this time during the planning stage than to try to untangle problems later.

Identify Stakeholders

The first thing effective evaluators do is identify the stakeholders. Stakeholders are those who are personally involved in the program, who derive some or all of their income from the program, whose future status or career might be affected by the quality of the program, or who are the clients or potential recipients of the program services (Bryk, 1983).

Program personnel are usually more personally involved in the program than either the sponsors or the clients. The program director is a key person with whom evaluators relate during the entire project. It helps to learn as much as possible about the background, interest, attitudes, and reputation of the program director. In addition, other people involved in the delivery of program services must not be overlooked. They should be involved in the planning stage so that they will assume ownership of the project and provide maximum support during the data collection stage (Bank, 1987). If possible, evaluators should learn about the relationship between the director and other program personnel, so that they can be dealt with more effectively during the planning meetings. If the director manages in an authoritarian manner, it is more difficult for evaluators to draw out the ideas of other personnel and determine when a consensus exists or when a decision has been made by the director alone.

Program sponsors should be considered next. At times program personnel are the sponsors; in other cases sponsors are funding agencies, governmental bodies, or administrators of the institution sponsoring the program. Often there is a single person with whom the evaluators are to relate. The funding agency may delegate one or two representatives to handle the commissioning and supervising of an evaluation project. In an organization the program sponsor might be the vice-president or administrator to whom the program director reports and who is ultimately responsible for the management of the program. Contact with the program sponsor is especially important during the initial stages of planning and at the end of the evaluation. At the beginning it is important that the sponsor fully supports the proposed evaluation and that all the program personnel are aware of that support. At the end of the evaluation, it is important that a report be presented to sponsors in a way that encourages its use in decision making. The presentation of reports and ways to encourage utilization of findings are discussed more fully in Chapters 13 and 14.

The clients or recipients of the program services also need to be identified. The amount and type of contact with the clients also depends on the nature of the program and of the evaluation. Primary schoolchildren are stakeholders who cannot participate in the same ways as other groups, but parent representatives would be involved.

Arrange Preliminary Meetings

Before a final decision is made to undertake an evaluation and to write a detailed proposal, it is advisable to meet with stakeholders to gather background information on five questions: (1) Who wants the evaluation? (2) What type of evaluation is desired? (3) Why do they want it? (4) When do they want it? and (5) What resources are available?

Who wants the evaluation? Ideally both the program sponsor and the program personnel desire to have the program evaluated. In such situations evaluators usually interact with competent people who are secure in their professional expertise, who are open to suggestions for improvement, and who welcome the opportunity to have documentation for what they feel is a successful program.

If the program sponsors initiate the evaluation proposal—either without the knowledge of or against the desires of the program personnel—the evaluators are faced with making the program personnel comfortable with the goals and methodology of the evaluation before data collection begins. If evaluators do not succeed in doing this, they face the possibility of open opposition or a lack of essential cooperation on the part of the program personnel. On the other hand, when the program personnel see the evaluators as "allies" rather than as "the enemy," they are more likely to give the evaluators much-needed assistance in the difficult job of data collection and valuable insights into the interpretation of the data. Gerald Barkdoll describes the importance of working with stakeholders in Evaluator Profile 2.

If the program personnel initiate the evaluation proposal—either without the knowledge of, or against the desires of, the program sponsors—the evaluators need to convince the sponsors of the usefulness of the evaluation. Sponsors who do not

EVALUATOR PROFILE 2.

Gerald L. Barkdoll, DPA: Working Closely with Stakeholders

Gerald Barkdoll directs strategic planning, program evaluation, and economic analysis for the Food and Drug Administration. After working as an industrial engineer and consultant, he came to the FDA in 1971. His B.S. is in engineering. He has an MBA (Drexel) and a Doctor of Public Administration (University of Southern California). He is also an accomplished volleyball player.

He was with the FDA evaluation staff when its mission was enlarged to carry out evaluations of programs making up the FDA. Dr. Barkdoll was asked how he handled the change in role. He replied: "We did three things to make the evaluations a positive experience for the program managers. First, we used teams including people from the program and selected by the program managers to do the evaluation. Each team was headed by a member of the evaluation staff. Second, we had a 'no surprise' rule. We shared our plans, our schedule, our activities, and our preliminary insights and findings with the program manager on a real time basis. And last, we finished each evaluation in three months. One program manager told us that this was most important since he knew he could tolerate almost anything for three months."

Adapted from Sporn, D. L. 1989. A conversation with Gerald L. Barkdoll. *Evaluation Practice,* 10(1), 27–32.

---

assume ownership of the evaluation project during the planning stage are inclined to ignore the findings.

What type of evaluation is desired? Early in the evaluators' meetings with program sponsors and personnel, it frequently becomes clear that the term *program evaluation* does not have the same meaning for everyone. More often than not, program personnel think in terms of a formative evaluation that would help them modify and improve the program. Program sponsors may desire a summative evaluation; they may be under pressure to divert resources to another program and must decide whether or not to continue the present program. Finally, some program personnel and sponsors have little knowledge of the concept of program evaluation and expect individual performance appraisal. For example, when Bauer and Toms (1989) tried to measure the degree of implementation of a science curriculum, their student tests were assumed to be individual student assessment tools.

The task of evaluators at this point is to clarify the pertinent concepts for those who do not understand them and to help the relevant people decide what type of evaluation best meets their desires, needs, and resources. The choice is seldom between one type of evaluation and another. Often it is possible to incorporate some elements of various types of evaluations into the total scope of the project, depending on the complexity of the program goals and the resources available for the project. For example, in the evaluation of "Sesame Street" conducted by Cook et al. (1975), various types of assessment were included in the overall evaluation. They assessed (1) whether the program reached its target audience; (2) effectiveness by analysis of learning scores; (3) the magnitude of effects relative to the magnitude of the need that gave rise to the program; (4) the ratio of benefits to cost; (5) the aspects of the complex home viewing situations that led to learning, and the conditions of TV viewing that most promote learning; and (6) the value of program objectives—that is, the importance of stimulating the growth of all social groups of preschool children versus that of narrowing the academic achievement gap between economically advantaged and disadvantaged children.

Why is the evaluation desired? Closely tied to the previous question is the issue of why evaluation is desired. The commissioning of an evaluation is rarely the product of an inquiring scientific spirit. More often it meets the needs of political forces. Program sponsors often need to satisfy constituents and want to keep politically advantageous programs alive. Effective evaluators put a high priority on identifying the reasons why the evaluation is desired. Were there some groups in the organization who objected to the evaluation? What were their motives? Is there real commitment among the program personnel and program sponsors to use the results of the evaluation to improve decision making? Ideally, program personnel are seeking answers to pressing questions about the program's future: How can it be improved? Are we serving the right people? Should we expand? Evaluators expect that different stakeholder groups have differing priorities. Some want a smoothly functioning program, others want tips on making their work more effective, and still others want to see improvements in the service (Cook et al., 1985).

One aspect of the evaluators' role is to help both the sponsors and program personnel arrive at a consensus on the precise decision(s) to be made. For example, in the evaluation of a physical medicine and rehabilitation program (Carey and Posavac, 1978), no consideration was being given to discontinuing the program. What concerned program personnel was the condition of patients who were discharged as apparent successes. Staff members wanted to know whether these patients maintained their regained abilities. After extended discussion it became clear that the primary focus of the evaluation was whether a follow-up program was needed for those patients who were discharged as successfully rehabilitated.

Some reasons for program evaluation are undesirable. For example, an administrator may use program evaluation as a ploy to avoid making a decision. Administrators who are pressured about the viability of a given program can buy time by saying that the program is being evaluated; by giving as little support as possible to the evaluators, they ensure that the evaluation will take a long time to be completed. If there is a need to buy still more time when the evaluation is completed, administrators may appoint a committee to study the evaluation report. Evaluation is also inappropriate when administrators know what decisions they will make but commission a program evaluation solely to give their decision legitimacy.

When is the evaluation desired? It is not unusual for stakeholders to want an evaluation to be done overnight. Part of the planning process involves agreeing on a balance between the preferences of the stakeholders and the time needed for carrying out the best evaluation possible. Time to obtain access to records, to arrange meetings, to develop measures of criteria of intermediate and long-term success, to find and observe a reasonable number of program participants and sites, and to draw together the observations and prepare a report must be considered in setting a viable end date. Internal evaluators are often restricted in how many observations they can perform because schools, hospitals, and businesses only include a finite number of students of a certain age, patients of a given diagnosis, or employees in a specific job. Furthermore, the type of evaluation requested leads to different constraints on the time needed to plan and complete an evaluation.

There is no magic formula to determine how long a project should take. Experienced evaluators develop a sense of the relationship between the scope of the project and the time it takes to complete it. A good technique is to estimate how much time each step in the project requires. The steps in the evaluation process are: developing measures of criteria, collecting observations or answers to surveys, compiling and analyzing the data, interpreting the findings, preparing drafts of reports including drawing recommendations, and presenting the reports to stakeholders. The amount of time needed varies depending on the size of the project and the ability to gain access to the information needed.

What resources are available? Besides time, another situational factor that can limit an evaluation is the availability of resources. Grants only include a specified amount for the evaluation. Of course, internal evaluators cannot be reckless with resources either. The assistance of program personnel can hold down the expense of data collection.

Even if no formal contract is signed, it is advisable for evaluators to put into writing an exact list of what is covered and not covered in the cost estimate and to specify when payments should be made. The evaluator's understanding of his/her obligations should be sent to the program director and the manager of the institution sponsoring the program. Ideally, the manager indicates in writing that the statement accurately summarizes the agreement. This approach does not indicate a lack of trust; it recognizes that the memories of busy people can fail. Honest misunderstandings have led to hard feelings between evaluators and program directors.

Assess the Evaluability of the Program

The next step is to decide whether an evaluation should be done. This process, referred to as an *evaluability assessment* (Schmidt, Scanlon, and Bell, 1979; Wholey, 1979), is intended to produce a reasoned basis for proceeding with an evaluation. Meetings with the stakeholders are held to learn about the conceptualization and the objectives of the program. Furthermore, the stakeholders need to agree on the criteria of program success (as discussed in Chapter 3). If they do not agree about what makes a program successful or unsuccessful, some types of evaluations are impossible to carry out. After such discussions, evaluators make a conscious decision to conduct or not to conduct the evaluation.

A program is not ready to be evaluated until its theoretical basis has been developed. Lipsey et al. (1985) reported that less than 30 percent of published evaluations described programs with theoretical formulations linking the program to the hoped for outcomes. A helpful discipline to aid in deciding whether a program has a good theoretical basis is to try to construct an impact model showing how the elements of the program led to the changes in the program participants that the staff expects. Upon questioning, it may turn out that some programs are no more complicated than "we tell them what to do, and they will do it." On the basis of what you know about the health benefits of regular exercise and a balanced diet that is also low in sugar, fat, and salt, would you agree that knowledge is enough to motivate people? Many steps intervene between the provision of knowledge and actions. The steps can include the reinforcement of appropriate behaviors, social support, reminders, skill in applying knowledge, belief in the personal applicability of the information, and so forth. Discussions initiated by evaluators can reveal that planners have not developed a clear rationale on which to base a program or do not have the freedom to make changes in response to an evaluation. Recognizing such situations even before gathering any data is a contribution that evaluators can make (Cook and Shadish, 1986).

Examine the Literature

When evaluators work in an area that is new for them, it is important to make a careful search of the literature before designing or developing new instruments. Evaluators should learn from the successes and failures of others and get a picture of the methodological, political, and practical difficulties that must be overcome.

Depending on the type of evaluation, computerized search services might be a good place to begin. MED-LINE, Psychological Abstracts Search and Retrieval (PASAR), and Educational Resource Information Center (ERIC) are three such systems. A search of professional journals recommended by program personnel is also helpful. After a few useful articles have been identified, the bibliographies of these articles provide additional references.

While reading the articles, evaluators should keep these key questions in mind: Has any evaluation been done on this type of program? What designs were used? Were new measures developed? How reliable and valid were the measures? What type of statistical analysis was used? Was it appropriate? Is there a consensus among the findings of various studies? If there is conflict, is this due to sampling procedures, design, or interpretation of findings? What issues were not addressed or investigated?

Determine the Methodology

After reviewing the literature, the evaluators are ready to make some methodological decisions regarding sampling procedures, research design, relevant criteria, data collection, and statistical analysis. Separate chapters are devoted to some of these issues, but it is helpful to examine the main issues now so that the reader can better understand their interrelationships and how they fit into the planning stage of an evaluation.

Population and sampling. Once the program's target population has been identified, evaluators need to decide whether to use the entire population, a random sample, or a purposive sample. One argument for including the entire population is political—namely, people may be offended if they were not included. If a state auditor's office is evaluating a state-wide program, it would be wise to gather information from every county, or at least from every state legislative district. Evaluations within a large organization possess more face validity if all employees have an opportunity to participate rather than a random sample only.

Sometimes it is best to select certain groups in order to examine particular evaluation questions. There may be concern about types of program participants or people with particular problems. Some writers suggest that evaluators take special care to be sure that participants from a variety of program settings are included. If the program is effective in different settings, considerable confidence in the findings of an evaluation is merited (Campbell, 1986). Thus, for example, an evaluation of a reading program in a large urban school system could be based on schools whose students represent different ethnic and economic backgrounds rather than making a random selection of students from all schools.

There are two main arguments for using a sample of participants rather than the entire population when the populations are large—namely, time and money. Program evaluation must be done within a budget and usually there are time restraints. Selecting a representative sample and devoting resources to obtaining data from as many as possible produces a more representative sample than a halfhearted attempt to include the whole population would yield. In other words, a 75 percent response from a random sample of one hundred is better than a 25 percent response from a population of 1,000. Observers untrained in social science research methods frequently confuse a sample's size with its representativeness.

Regardless of how sampling is done, evaluators know that some people do not cooperate and some cannot. Thus, it is advisable to seek a larger sample than is essential. It is important to identify the characteristics of nonparticipants and those who drop out at various points of time. Both the attrition rate and the reasons for dropping out have a bearing on the conclusions to be made from the data collected.

Research design. Another crucial step in planning a program evaluation is selecting a research design. This decision depends on such constraints as the purpose of the study, the preferences of the stakeholders, the time when the project must be completed, and the funds available. Some evaluations simply require a series of interviews conducted by a knowledgeable evaluator, others involve a creative examination of existing records (see Evaluator Profile 5, in Chapter 7), and still others require a design similar to those used in basic research involving random assignment to program and control groups. Since a large portion of this text is devoted to the various designs that evaluators use, we stress at this time that evaluators should remain flexible, selecting a design that matches the needs of the stakeholders rather than routinely selecting a favorite design. The evaluation projects proceed more smoothly when the stakeholders have participated in the selection of the design and understand the reasons for whatever design is ultimately chosen.

Selection of criteria. Using multiple criteria gathered from different sources yields the best information for an evaluation. The program participants themselves are one of the most important and accessible data sources. They can describe their reactions to the program and their satisfaction with it, and they can report their current behavior. People close to the participants, such as family members, may sometimes provide information, especially when the participants are very young or incapacitated. Program personnel at times provide crucial information; program records are often essential. For some programs community-level variables are the most relevant. Last, evaluators must not overlook their own observations; this point is expanded in Chapter 12 on qualitative methods.

Data collection. Who handles the day-to-day mechanics of data collection? This usually involves an on-site coordinator who keeps abreast of the whereabouts of the program clients, personnel, and other sources of data, so that they can be contacted at appropriate times by the evaluation team. This is ordinarily a tedious task, but a reliable person must handle it.

Data collectors need to be sensitive to the issue of confidentiality. First, confidential information must be kept confidential. If information was obtained with an understanding of confidentiality, it should not be released until explicit approval is obtained. Second, the obligation of others to keep information confidential must be respected. Evaluators do not have an ethical right to all information, even when it might have a bearing on the evaluation. Other values may at times conflict with the needs of evaluators. Care must be taken not to ask information from people in a manner they find to be an invasion of privacy.

Choice of statistics. In any type of evaluation, appropriate statistics that demonstrate both the level of statistical significance and the magnitude of effects are needed. It is preferable to use simple statistical procedures, because the findings are presented to program sponsors and personnel who may not have a great deal of mathematical expertise. Nonevaluators ideally should be able to understand and to be convinced by the interpretation of the results; they should not merely be impressed by statistical sophistication. At times complicated analyses are necessary. However, it is good to keep in mind that nonevaluators are usually more comfortable with less-complicated statistics. One approach is to use statistical analyses that are as powerful as necessary, but to illustrate the conclusions using percentages or—even better—graphs.

Reporting findings. Careful thought must be given during the planning phase to how the evaluation is to be reported to the stakeholders. Often evaluators have erred in focusing on "a report." Instead, a plan for reporting throughout the evaluation better serves the interests of the stakeholders and the needs of the evaluator for constructive feedback as the project progresses. Chapter 13 contains an extended description of the variety of reporting avenues evaluators use to maintain support for the evaluation and to encourage the utilization of findings.

Present a Written Proposal

After reviewing the literature and thinking through the various methodological considerations outlined above, the evaluators are ready to prepare a written proposal for presentation to program personnel. The overall purpose is to be certain that the evaluators and program personnel agree on the nature and goals of the program, the type of evaluation desired, the measures of the program goals, and the readiness of the program for evaluation. It is psychologically important for the program personnel to understand the evaluation process, feel comfortable with it, and (if possible) be enthusiastic about it.

Some issues that were previously discussed during the initial meetings may have to be worked through once again. Program personnel may now see procedural problems that were not at first apparent. It may be necessary to delay the beginning of data collection either because they feel the program is not sufficiently operational to undergo evaluation or because the temporary presence of extraneous factors might interfere with the interpretation of data.

DYSFUNCTIONAL ATTITUDES TOWARD PROGRAM EVALUATION

Political and psychological factors can undermine an evaluation project. Some concerns simply represent a misunderstanding of program evaluation and the purpose of the project being planned. Other concerns may reflect actual conflicts within the organization that the evaluation is bringing to the surface. Effective evaluators seek to identify these concerns, discuss conflicts, and reassure stakeholders, to whatever extent possible, that the program evaluation is planned to serve their needs.

Expectations of a "Slam-Bang" Effect

Program personnel are generally enthusiastic and confident about the potential effects of their program, expecting their new program to have dramatic results—a "slam-bang" effect. They will have a tendency to feel betrayed if evaluators are able to demonstrate only a moderate improvement over the old program. The difficulties are especially likely when a new program is expected to improve on a reasonably good existing program.

One way to handle the high level of expectation is to help program personnel arrive at some rule of thumb for improvement that can reasonably be expected. For example, if elementary school students are reading at appropriate levels, a new reading program is unlikely to raise their reading levels very much. The sponsors of a new reading program should be satisfied if they raise the reading achievement just a little or if students like reading better. Furthermore, a small improvement experienced by many people could have a major overall impact (Cook and Shadish, 1986).

There are other reasons why the expected "slam-bang" effect may not occur. Whenever a group of participants is chosen for comparison with a group of participants in a new program, the comparison group will almost always be receiving some kind of service. It is rare that participants in a new program are compared to a group that receives no service at all. When evaluators are comparing two modalities of services, both of which are considered good, great differences between the group receiving the new program and the comparison group receiving the standard service are unlikely. For example, if a group of psychosomatic patients admitted to a special program in a hospital are compared to psychosomatic patients treated privately by physicians but without the benefit of the special program, both groups should improve because both groups are receiving professional treatment.

Inappropriate Pressure from Some Stakeholders

Pressure to direct the evaluation design or methods in particular directions is a potential negative side effect of working closely with stakeholders. Program personnel may feel comfortable with a particular measure of an outcome and seek to have it adopted even if there are good methodological reasons to choose something else. Worse, a stakeholder may press evaluators to use a design that is likely to produce a preordained result, either favorable or unfavorable to the program. Ideally a discussion among the stakeholders and the evaluators will reveal that better procedures are available and should be used. At times, a politically powerful stakeholder may seek to control the evaluation plan. One way for an internal evaluator to resist that influence is to seek to obtain outside help in the form of a review panel. Robin Turpin describes how she would seek to resist such pressure in Evaluator Profile 3.

EVALUATOR PROFILE 3.

Robin Turpin, Ph.D.: Reducing the Effects of Political Influences on Methodology

Robin Turpin is Program Manager for Testing Design and Evaluation for the Joint Commission for Accreditation of Healthcare Organizations. Dr. Turpin earned her Ph.D. in Applied Social Psychology from Loyola University of Chicago. Her work has included studies on the quality of life, managing multisite evaluation, health-care delivery to female veterans, and discharge planning. These comments were excerpted from her winning answer to the American Evaluation Association President's Problem of 1988.

The problem had asked for suggestions on avoiding political pressures that would cause evaluators to make less than desirable decisions in planning an evaluation. Dr. Turpin recognized the potential for pressures from powerful groups in a large organization. She recommended that instead of ignoring or working around political pressure, evaluators should assess the potential for pressure and seek to counter it. "For example, if an evaluator is being pressured to use a method that most likely would produce favorable results, insisting on a review [of the method] by a consultant or [an] expert panel would give the evaluator enough leverage to defend another [better] method." The greater the expected pressure, the more effort evaluators need to make to counter the pressure. By countering such influences, Dr. Turpin hopes to produce as credible an evaluation as possible; evaluations without credibility will not be used.

Source: Winner of 1988 President's Problem. 1989. *Evaluation Practice, 10*(1), 53–57.

Worry That Asking About Program Quality Is Unprofessional

O'Doherty (1989) described an evaluation of a mediation program. Mediation is an alternative to resolving a dispute in court; it is cheaper, minimizes hostile feelings between the protagonists, and reduces the load on the courts. O'Doherty discovered that some program directors felt that asking the people about the mediators' work would detract from their professional image. Some university faculty members seem to have a similar worry about asking students for comments on the quality of their teaching.

Fear That Evaluations Will Inhibit Innovation

Personnel in human service organizations may worry that evaluation will interfere with innovation by inhibiting them from experimenting with new techniques. In both process and outcome evaluations, the staff may feel that evaluation permits no variation in the program during the period of data collection. This is partially true insofar as there cannot be major structural changes in the program that would alter the essential goals or nature of the program. However, the need for retaining program identity does not mean that clinicians or program personnel cannot be flexible in the day-to-day operation of the program within broad structural boundaries. Every program will have variability built into it. Evaluation will not limit this. However, it is wise not to attempt to evaluate a program that is just getting started; major changes can occur as staff become clearer about their objectives.

Fear That the Program Will Be Terminated

Although it is seldom true that a negative evaluation will lead to a program's termination (Cook and Shadish, 1986), it is possible that an evaluation could result in the curtailment or elimination of a program when results demonstrate that a given approach is not working out as expected. However, before sponsors can eliminate a program designed to meet a specific problem, they are ordinarily under some pressure to decide what to put in its place. Therefore, it is more likely that an evaluation, even an unfavorable one, will result in the refinement of a program rather than its elimination.

Early in the planning stage, effective evaluators will try to have program personnel view them as valuable and needed associates. Evaluators can often achieve this goal by describing their work in terms of "documenting success." Program sponsors are inclined to demand accountability from program personnel as a condition for funding. Evaluators are there to assist program personnel in fulfilling this obligation to the sponsors.

One practice that allays some anxiety is to promise the program personnel that they will see the final draft of a report and be asked for their suggestions and clarifications before it is sent to the sponsors (see Chapter 13). Nevertheless, evaluators will not be able to eliminate anxiety completely when a program does not have the full support of the central administration or when there are valid concerns about the quality of a program.

Fear That Information Will Be Abused

In addition to the fear that a program may be terminated, there might be some concern that information gained about the performance of staff may be abused. Even competent clinicians, administrators, teachers, and other personnel are rightly concerned about merit reviews, future promotion, and career advancement. Past experience may have taught them to be wary of carelessness about divulging confidences. When procedures for access to data are clearly stated in the planning phase and then are carefully followed, evaluators build trust that may allay such worries. It is easy to lose trust and hard to regain it once it has been lost. Effective evaluators not only explicitly try to convey the idea that program evaluation is distinct from individual performance appraisal, but they carefully avoid speaking or acting in such a way that might even give the appearance that they are engaged in such an activity.

Fear That Qualitative Understanding May Be Supplanted

Service personnel rightly feel that their day-to-day observations are valuable sources of input both for improving the functioning of a program and for evaluating its effect. They may feel that the evaluators' questionnaires, complicated research designs, and statistical techniques are less sensitive than their own personal observations and evaluations. At times they are right.

The input of program personnel is a very valuable source of evaluation data. Nevertheless, their subjective evaluations can be biased; accuracy can be improved by both quantitative and qualitative data gathered from other sources. Their subjective observations will be of greatest importance when the data are being interpreted. The ideal is not to eliminate either the quantitative or qualitative approaches but rather to integrate the findings from both methodologies.

Evaluators gain the confidence of managers and staff not only by being aware of this problem but also by articulating this awareness in such a manner that program staff members are reassured that the intricacies of human services have been appropriately addressed. Early in the planning stage, the program personnel can be assured that the evaluation will not begin until they have had the opportunity to review the evaluation proposal carefully and have become assured that their concerns in this area have been addressed properly.

Fear That Evaluation Drains Program Resources

The seven concerns described thus far are focused on various aspects of evaluation but not on the concept of evaluation itself. Some objections to evaluation strike at the very idea of program evaluation. The staff may charge that program evaluation drains money that could be spent on direct service. As the statement stands, it is true. However, the main question is whether evaluation can improve service. The alternative to spending money on evaluation is to risk spending money on services that are of unknown value. Today it is hard to find a program funded either by government agencies or by private foundations that does not carry the stipulation that the activities supported are to be evaluated. Those who are not convinced by the accountability argument may be convinced by a more pragmatic one: evaluation, if done well, may help spread a good idea and may result in attracting more money and resources to a program.

Fear of Losing Control of the Program

When evaluations are conducted by consultants or internal evaluators, program managers and staff members may fear that they are losing control, and that their right to make decisions about the way the program is offered will be reduced. Such a fear may be groundless but is quite common. Staff members rightly realize that they may not be able to control the information about the program that will be available to members of the administration of the organization housing the program. Unless the staff knows that the program is grossly inadequate, this fear may be reduced by working closely with the program so that evaluation shows strengths as well as possible weaknesses. Sometimes programs can use evaluations to gain control since the evaluation will give evidence to use in presenting the case for a larger allotment of resources for the program.

Fear That Evaluation Has Little Impact

Some critics of evaluation point out that frequently evaluation has very little impact on programs. There is a good deal of validity to this objection; evaluators have often been frustrated by seeing their reports set aside and disregarded.

However, evaluators should reflect on the hard reality that evaluation is not a benign social science activity but rather a political decisionmaking tool. If relevant, evaluation results will be included among the other factors behind decisions. Because evaluators work in a political context, the results of their work must be timely and relevant to decision making (Cronbach, 1982). Well-designed and carefully executed studies are valuable only when they speak to issues that are important to the organization. When evaluators fail to show how the evaluation is relevant, they have not completed their work.

SUMMARY AND PREVIEW

Following the six steps in planning an evaluation project serves to get the evaluation off to a good start. Note that the steps are suggested to help the evaluator to be responsive to the needs of the people most concerned about the evaluation. Responsive evaluators have fewer problems with the fears outlined in the second part of the chapter, compared to evaluators who seem less concerned about stakeholder needs.

The next chapter focuses on a central concern: What are the criteria of a wisely planned, thoroughly implemented, or successful program? A thoughtless selection of criteria will negate efforts to plan a useful evaluation.

STUDY QUESTIONS

1. As an outside consultant you are invited by a large manufacturing plant to evaluate a new training program for managers called "Management Contact," which you are told applies the principles of transactional analysis to employer-employee relations. Explain the steps you would take and what you would need to know in approaching this job. What would be the major difficulties you would see?
2. Imagine that you are part of an evaluation team in the institutional research office of a major university. The chairperson of the department of psychology instructs you to evaluate a new graduate program called "Community Psychology." How would you approach this task? What would be the major pitfalls to avoid?
3. Suppose that you have been asked to evaluate the "Officer Friendly" program. You may recall from elementary school that a police officer comes to schools to talk to children about concerns such as bike safety, dealing with strangers, and how to call police. The general goals for such a program include lowered accident rates among children and a better image of police officers. List the implicit theoretical assumptions that lie beneath those goals. In other words, what must happen for the goals of this program to be achieved?

FURTHER READING

BRINKERHOFF, R. O., et al. 1983. *Program evaluation: A practitioner's guide for trainers and educators—a design manual.* Boston: Kluwer-Nijhoff.

3

Selecting Criteria and Setting Standards

What is the best measure of a good college intercollegiate athletic program? Some would say the proportion of games won, others would say the number of tickets sold; perhaps it's the devotion of the alumni to the team, the success of the student-athletes after graduation, or the favorable media attention attracted to the university through its teams. Some faculty and college presidents have argued that the criteria of a good sports program have shifted too much toward winning and away from the academic and life successes of the athletes after graduation. In fact, at some well-known schools, only a small percentage of basketball and football players actually graduate. For the few who become professional athletes, failing to complete college may not seem to matter that much in terms of earning power. For the others, not graduating denies them the vocational opportunities a degree would have offered. There are those who say that this is irrelevant; basketball and football proceeds earn enough to support the entire athletic program, and, since no one compels the students to participate, the academic administration should not disrupt a good thing ("Students cheated," 1990).

The argument at some universities between the coaches and the deans or presidents centers on the criteria to be used in evaluating an athletic department. Disputes over the choice of criteria also lie beneath many political disagreements. For example, is the overall level of a nation's economic level more important than improving economic conditions specifically for poor people? Judgments and preferences in daily life similarly depend on the choice of criteria; however, the criteria we use are often implicit. If we test drive a car, we check for degree of comfort, ease of operation, clear vision of the road, and other criteria, even though we have never written those standards down. When people disagree over the desirability of different automobiles, it is often because they are using different criteria to make their choices. For some people an attractive exterior design is more important than a reputation for reliability; for parents with several children a larger rear seat would be more important than it is for single people in their first jobs.

Whether we think about them or not, we do use criteria to make distinctions and to form preferences in our choice of foods, friends, churches, automobiles, and politicians. When conducting an evaluation of a program or a product, we need to develop or select criteria more explicitly than we do in daily life. Without the development of clear, appropriate criteria and specific standards we might never be able to agree on the value of a counseling program for students who are math phobic, food stamps for poor families, or job training for unemployed former steel workers. As mentioned in Chapter 1, the traditional model of evaluation had been a subjective assessment by the people offering or funding services. Such informal assessments are no longer acceptable, especially when programs are paid for with public funds. This chapter describes the need to specify criteria of value for program evaluation, defines different types of criteria, and illustrates a variety of evaluation questions and how they can be answered more easily after the specification of the criteria of successful programs.

IMPORTANCE OF SELECTING CRITERIA AND SETTING STANDARDS

Merely selecting a quantitative tool in order to substitute relevant numbers for a subjective reaction does not satisfy the need for a standard. The point is to choose criteria and develop standards of program quality that permit us to carry out useful program evaluations. Many evaluators have emphasized the importance of sound research design (as we do in later chapters); however, just as a chain is only as strong as its weakest link, the thoughtless selection of criteria can lead to a failed evaluation as surely as an inappropriate research design can. Ill-considered choices of standards could make it impossible to draw any conclusions from an evaluation even when the evaluation was well-planned in other ways.

Criteria That Do Not Reflect the Program's Intent

Without careful planning and a thorough understanding of the program, it is easy to select criteria that do not reflect the intent of the program. Many observers believe that the first evaluation of Head Start (Cicarelli et al., 1969), a popular, federally funded preschool program for children of poor families, was mortally wounded by the decision to use measures of the improvement of intellectual skills as the primary criterion of success. (The evaluation also suffered from a research design problem that will be mentioned later.) Lazar (1981) argued that the most important aspect of Head Start was the involvement of parents in the education of their children. It was hoped that the involvement of low-income parents, many of whom typically participate only minimally in the education of their children, would continue as their children grew. Thus, Head Start would increase the likelihood that low-income parents would encourage the development of their children, help with their children's homework, and work hard at being sure their children were in school. If parents adopted such practices, it might be that such activities would become habits and have a long-term positive effect on the children; such an effect might be far more important than the specific knowledge that the children gained in Head Start classes (Leik and Chalkey, 1990).

The manner selected to measure the achievement of a fire fighter training program suggests another example of criteria possibly not reflecting the intent of a program. A lawyer argued that a written test of fire fighter skills did not adequately measure trainee competence. The lawyer argued that many trainees could indeed perform the nonverbal skills even though they performed poorly on a written test. Good written test performance might reflect knowledge of language use as much as, or more than, actual hands-on use of the equipment. Since this is an empirical question, the argument cannot be accepted without research support. It could be that good fire fighters need to be able to do more than to set up and use the equipment currently in use. However, the point is clear: criteria of success may look valid but may not measure success in achieving the real objectives of the program.

The time an evaluation criterion is measured could fail to reflect the program's intent. A program could have a valuable immediate or short-term effect, but a marginal long-term effect. A physical fitness program can be quite effective in improving muscle tone without having an effect on the program participant's physical condition or health ten years later. On the other hand, alumni may remark how helpful a faculty member was for their development even though the faculty member was perceived as critical and overly difficult when they were in school. Here, the long-term effect seems more favorable than the short-term effect. Evaluators seek to make observations at a time that correctly reflects the objectives of the program.

Criteria That Cannot Be Measured Reliably

Physical measurements can be made reliably; that is, repeated observations will yield essentially the same values. Since it is impossible to measure without any error, reliability could be very good but not perfect. In the social sciences, observations are less reliable. Suppose we had wanted to use parental participation as a criterion in evaluating Head Start. One possible observation procedure would be to ask the children if their parents had talked with them about Head Start activities the previous night. Four- and five-year old children are not reliable sources of such information: they may have forgotten, they may not realize that their parent was talking about pre-school, or they might say what they thought the questioner wanted to hear. Even if the program had the desired effect on the parents, the unreliability of the children's answers may make it impossible to detect that effect.

On the community level, trying to measure unreliable criteria can make it hard to learn if a crime prevention program has an effect. Beyond the actual frequency of crime, official crime rates are influenced by the willingness of victims to report crimes, the way police officers record the reports, the weather and time of the year, and media coverage of recent heinous crimes. These factors could cause the apparent level of community crime to go up or down.

The Way Criteria Are Selected

The criteria for a specific evaluation are selected in close consultation between the evaluator and the stakeholders involved with the project. If the stakeholders do not accept the criteria selected, even when they are appropriate, the evaluation cannot have the impact that it would otherwise have. This does not mean that evaluators simply use whatever criteria and standards stakeholders want. Stakeholders are seldom trained in evaluation methodology; they include staff members, government officials, program recipients, and community activists. When there is disagreement over appropriate criteria and standards, evaluators spend many hours with the stakeholders to assure that all parties agree on the standards discussed. Note the comment on this process in Evaluator Profile 4.

EVALUATOR PROFILE 4.

Joseph S. Wholey, Ph.D.: Stakeholders and Evaluation Criteria

In addition to being Professor of Public Administration at the Washington Public Affairs Center of the University of Southern California, Joseph Wholey directs the *Program for Excellence in Human Services*, a cooperative effort among governments, state agencies, and universities to improve the human service system in northern Virginia. He coined the term *evaluability assessment* to describe the process of examining program plans and structure to judge whether a program can be evaluated.

During an interview in 1990, Dr. Wholey commented on the need to have stakeholders agree on the criteria of an evaluation. He said, "I recall working as an evaluator for the Tennessee Health Department, working with program [delivery] people who thought the prenatal care program objective was to deliver services, while the politicians who appropriated the money thought that the objective was to reduce infant mortality. The evaluator's role . . . was helping people at different levels (the program coordinator at the state level, local program coordinators, the bureau chief, and the deputy commissioner of health) decide what it was that their program was trying to accomplish. . . ."

"The program objective that we came to was that delivery of prenatal services would lead to [a] reduction [in the] incidence of low birth weight. Reduction of the incidence of low birth weight babies would lead to a reduction of infant mortality. [The program people and the politicians] could agree that the intermediate objective, reducing the incidence of low birth weight, was a suitable objective . . ."

Adapted from Johnson, P. L. 1990. A conversation with Joseph S. Wholey about the Program for Excellence in Human Services. *Evaluation Practice, 11*(2), 53–61.

The selection of criteria and standards also varies depending on what aspect of the program development process is to be studied. Programs go through a number of phases: proposal preparation, planning, initial implementation, actual operation, expansion, contraction, or accreditation and reaccreditation. Criteria and standards to evaluate a plan differ markedly from those used to evaluate the implementation of an operational program.

In addition, the criteria differ according to the type of program being evaluated. Programs in education, health, criminal justice, marketing, and training differ in their emphases, the relative power of different stakeholder groups, the traditional types of information found useful, and the financial support available for evaluation studies. These differences play a part in the development of standards of program success and are taken into consideration in designing a program evaluation. Many evaluators find that the opportunity to work with many different organizations is an exciting feature of their work in program evaluation.

DEVELOPING GOALS AND OBJECTIVES

In order to know how much we have achieved, we need to know what we want to achieve. We have all heard of the lost traveler who insisted on driving at 65 mph. When asked why he was driving so fast even though he was lost, he explained that although he did not know where he was going, he was making great time. If stakeholders are unable to decide what a training or service program is supposed to achieve, there is little reason to begin the program or to evaluate it. There are a number of issues related to goals that need to be addressed: Are there any clear ideas about objectives? Are there disagreements about objectives? If there are disagreements, are these disagreements mutually incompatible or could they complement each other?

How Much Agreement on Goals Is Needed?

There are times when people are very unclear on what might be accomplished by a program. Groups may sense that there is a problem and wish to provide some service, but simply saying that we want people to be educated, healthy, and happy does not permit the development of a program to assist them. In other words, stating goals only in the most abstract terms may attract supporters, but it will provide little assistance in designing a program or in evaluating a program once it is under way. Abstract goals may be called for in the U.S. Constitution or in the mission statements of organizations, but will not do once people try to produce an actual program. There really is no reason to begin to plan if no one can describe goals any more specifically than saying that "we want to empower people," "we want to provide excellent medical care," or "we want excellence in education."

When stakeholders can describe the specific goals they hold, even if the goals are dissimilar, progress has been made and negotiations may begin. Progress will be stalled if the goals conflict with each other to the extent that achieving one goal makes it impossible to achieve the other; a family cannot vacation on Baja beaches and the Canadian Rockies at the same time. Similarly, a basketball coach cannot develop a run and gun offense while demanding a tight defense, and cancer care cannot be directed at making a patient comfortable while using experimental medications. Planners can work with stakeholder groups to find mutually agreeable alternatives or to define situations in which one would use one policy over another. There might be ways to define a patient's condition that would determine when aggressive (but painful) treatment would be used versus situations when the goal would be simply to minimize pain while suspending treatment.

There are times when the goals people have are different but not incompatible. No college faculty is unified in what each member wants from students. Some teachers expect detailed knowledge, others conceptual clarity. Some are concerned about the development of employable graduates, others are more concerned that students develop a sound philosophy of life. In most colleges, these different views exist side by side while students are exposed to different points of view, a result that faculty members agree is desirable. In such a setting, mutual respect for differing points of view permits the organization to function, since no faculty group seeks to do anything that forbids others from pursuing their goals.

Different Types of Goals

Once a program has been planned and started, there are different types of goals whose achievement can be evaluated. It is important to verify whether the program has gotten underway as planned and to know whether short-term outcome goals as well as long-term outcome goals have been achieved.

Implementation goals. All programs involve some level of activity before it is possible to achieve the outcomes hoped for. For example, equipment needs to be purchased and staff members need to be hired and trained before any service is given. If these activities do not occur, there is no point in seeking to learn if the hoped-for results have been achieved. Figure 3.1 includes a number of goals that the evaluator needed to examine in an evaluation of the effectiveness of a new computerized system to keep track of the inventory of a large merchandiser. Implementation goals refer to goals that focus on the timely installation of the hardware. Other implementation goals could focus on training of employees.

Although it may seem obvious to verify that the program exists before seeking to evaluate its effectiveness, some stakeholders have ignored this step. They feel that if a program developer says that something is to be done, then it is OK to assume that it was done. One university vice-president for research challenged the assertion that the evaluation of implementation goals must be part of a program evaluation by rhetorically asking "Can't we assume that these are honorable people? Can't we assume that if they say they will do something, they will do it?" The potential evaluator responded that it is seldom a question of personal integrity. Instead, it is usually a question of unforeseen problems making it impossible to carry out plans. It is crucial to verify that program plans have been carried out before seeking to learn how the program affected the participants.

Various Types of Goals

Implementation. An example of goals that refer to the acquisition of basic hardware and personnel for computerizing an inventory control system. This is a "start-up" objective. Nothing can happen without this being achieved.

> The system will be installed in all forty-two companies in a six-year period—four in the first year, six in the second, and eight each year after.

Intermediate. The ways to recognize the inventory system as working well are included in this second level of goal statements. The achievement of Implementation goals does not guarantee achievement of Intermediate goals.

> The system can handle 15,000 inventory items.
> Items can be located using the system in an average of ten seconds, with no more than 5 percent of searches taking more than thirty seconds.

Outcome. Although achieving goals at the first two levels is crucial for the ultimate success of the project, there are additional goals that should be considered. The real reason for computerizing an inventory system is to make a difference for customers. These goals reflect whether the customers are getting better service from the company.

> Delivery times will be reduced.
> There will be 50 percent fewer items out of stock as compared to the current system.
> Formal customer complaints about out-of-stock items and slow responses to customer requests for information will be reduced by 50 percent.

FIGURE 3.1 Objectives for a program should refer to all levels of the program. Implementation, intermediate, and outcome goals are reflected in this illustration. (Adapted from Marshall, 1979)

A graduate student team sought to evaluate the effectiveness of a program in which volunteer faculty members invited ten to twelve commuter freshman college students into their homes for dinner, to help the students identify more closely with the college than was possible without such attention. The evaluators learned that 40 percent of the volunteer faculty members did not invite any students to their homes. Of the students invited, only 60 percent showed up. This means that, at best, only 36 percent of this phase of the program was implemented. The faculty members' good intentions are not in question. Scheduling problems may have come up; for some faculty members the task may have been more trouble than they had imagined; others may have misunderstood what they agreed to do; and perhaps some volunteered before checking with their spouses. Without including an implementation phase in this evaluation, the evaluators would have been unaware that the program was only one-third as strong as planned.

Intermediate goals. By intermediate goals we refer to things that are expected to occur after implementation of the program, but that do not cover the final goal intended by the program. For example, all students should have textbooks (an implementation goal) and they should read the assignments on time (an intermediate goal), but the actual criteria of success go beyond reading the assignments. In Figure 3.1 the performance of the inventory system is the focus of the intermediate goals. If the success of the organization is to be improved through the new system, the system's performance needs to meet certain standards. If it does, then there is a better chance of attaining an improvement in customer service and a reduction in complaints.

Outcome goals. Even if a system is working as planned, it is still necessary to learn whether customer service is indeed better. We cannot be satisfied with simply verifying that the equipment works: we do examine the "bottom-line" variables. If evaluators focus attention solely on the outcome goals, they have, in effect, chosen a black box evaluation model. If the outcome goals were not achieved, the evaluator would not know why and would not know what to suggest to the company to improve the performance of the system. If, on the other hand, it can be shown that implementation and outcome goals have been met, but the level of customer satisfaction has still not improved, the causes of customer complaints must be sought in aspects of the organization not involved with the inventory system. A black box evaluation cannot provide many hints of where to look when an evaluation is unfavorable.

Goals That Apply to All Programs

Critics argue that those who use objectives-based program evaluations limit the focus of evaluations to the goals of the program being evaluated and direct little attention to other factors (Scriven, 1981). If other aspects of a program were not examined, then objectives-based evaluation would have major limitations. One way to avoid this problem is to recognize that there are many goals that apply to all programs even though such goals are not stated during program planning. Program planners seldom need to state that the people are to be treated with respect, that schoolchildren are not to be treated in a way that fosters dependence, or that people are not to be discriminated against on the basis of race or gender. Since these criteria do not appear in lists of program goals, some evaluators have not treated these issues in program evaluations. One cannot measure everything; however, evaluators should strive to become sufficiently familiar with the program and participants so that they can recognize the threat of negative side effects. At times evaluators have avoided personal exposure to the program in a misguided search for objectivity, depending on surveys and records to provide evaluation data. We believe that evaluators risk serious error if they do not become intimately familiar with the program, its staff, and its customers, clients, students, or patients.

EVALUATION CRITERIA AND EVALUATION QUESTIONS

Since criteria and standards are chosen for specific programs, it is impossible to list the criteria that evaluators might use in conducting specific program evaluations. However, a number of general evaluation questions are central to program evaluation; most evaluations would include some form of these questions. The value of dealing with these questions and the costs of poor choices of criteria are illustrated in the following paragraphs.

Does the Program or Plan Match the Values of the Stakeholders?

Educational and social service programs are designed to fulfill purposes that are laced with values. For example, what should be included in sex education classes for junior high students? Should the government provide funding for abortions? Should welfare recipients be required to perform public service work? These questions cannot be answered by listing facts.

When evaluators assist the stakeholders to be explicit about their values and assumptions, evaluators fulfill a useful role. For example, most citizens believe that the U.S. Federal Income Tax should be progressive, that is, the more income people have, the greater the tax rate should be. Part of an evaluation of tax reforms would be to compare this value with the results of tax law changes. The tax reductions of 1978 and 1981 and the tax reform of 1986 reduced the maximum Federal Income Tax rate to 33 percent. Recently the maximum income on which Social Security taxes are paid (at a rate of 7.65 percent for everyone) was raised to $51,300; no income above that amount is subject to Social Security taxes. The cumulative effect of income tax and Social Security tax changes, critics say, is that the U.S. tax policies are not as progressive as they should be or were in the 1970s (Ehrenreich, 1990). Tax law changes are said to have contributed to the greater concentration of wealth among the richest Americans during the 1980s (Goozner, 1990).

Turning to a different example, public housing programs are designed to make adequate housing available to poor people at affordable costs. Most people would agree that this goal matches the values of society. However, the way public housing policies have been implemented in large cities has led to the clustering of poor people, often in high-rise buildings that neither foster a sense of community nor provide safe settings for residents. An evaluation of public housing would ideally include information on the conflict between the values on which policies were based, and the results that have occurred. While a program evaluation cannot tell anyone what values to hold, the demonstration of a discrepancy between what occurred and what was hoped for could be an important motivator for improvement.

Does the Program or Plan Match the Needs of the People to Be Served?

The unmet needs of some segment of the population usually form the basis for the development of a program. The most useful program evaluations compare the unmet needs of the people versus the services available through the program. Unemployed people need skills that lead to employment. An excellent training program for a skill that is not in demand would not fulfill a need. Programs cannot be evaluated in isolation from the problem settings and the people being served.

In order to verify that a program plan meets the needs of the people to be served, a need assessment is done as part of the development of the program (McKillip, 1987). The place of need assessment in program evaluation and an introduction to the methodology of the assessment of need are discussed in Chapter 6. At this point, we want to stress that an examination of the needs of program participants are important in all program evaluations. Since service program resources are always limited, a particularly important phase of the evaluator's job in laying the groundwork for a program is to provide some suggestions for weighing the competing needs during the program selection process.

Does the Program as Implemented Fulfill the Plans?

The plan of a program is first examined to learn if its likely outcome will match the values of the program stakeholders and meet the needs that motivated its development. The next step facing the evaluator is to examine the program in operation as compared to the plan. Observers provide numerous examples of situations in which the match between program plan and operation leaves much to be desired: the blood tests on only 8 of 31 alcoholics who were to be getting Antibuse by surgical implant showed the presence of a therapeutic level of medication (Malcolm, Madden, and Williams, 1974), teachers were not adequately trained to teach a math curriculum assigned to them (Kolata, 1977), a low-income population proved just too hard to serve so a publicly funded family planning center served nearby college students (Rossi, 1978), and shopping mall cholesterol tests were found to be exceedingly unreliable ("Cholesterol Screening," 1990). A large proportion of failures of implementation are covered by two major categories: the staff discovers that the program cannot be offered as planned, and value conflicts reduce the cooperation between major stakeholder groups.

Program cannot be implemented as planned. A program cannot be offered as planned when the population for whom the program was directed rejects the service. The community mental health system was proposed to serve chronic psychiatric patients on the community level rather than keeping the patients confined to large state mental hospitals. It was believed that antipsychotic medication would permit such patients to live independently or with family members and that the community mental health center would provide supportive care and medications. Unfortunately, most discharged patients rejected the treatment. Since people cannot be compelled to go to the centers and since funding was not as generous as expected, the program could not be implemented as envisioned. Community mental health centers broadened their concerns and sought clients who were more functional than those considered to be one of their primary targets.

Sometimes the theory behind the program was not sensitive to local conditions. The development of New Math for elementary school classes was well-planned and mathematically sophisticated. It was evaluated favorably during development. However, the teachers using the materials during development were better trained than the average teacher who tried to use the curriculum in their schools. Regular classroom teachers who had been accustomed to drilling children on multiplication tables were assigned to teach set theory. In addition, the new terminology made it impossible for most parents to offer their children any help. After a few frustrating years the new curriculum was discarded (Kolata, 1977). An objective-based evaluation that focused only on the degree to which the children learned the material would not have detected the real problem with the New Math curriculum: there was little chance that it would be effective when introduced in community schools, where many elementary schoolteachers fear or loathe mathematics.

Value conflicts can make thorough implementation impossible. People seeking to change the economic systems in Eastern Europe and the USSR were met with great resistance from people who benefited from the older centrally planned systems. Furthermore, many people who had become used to guaranteed employment and artificially maintained low food prices were skeptical of promises of better economic conditions. These two forces placed rather effective restraints on changes envisioned by national leaders. An example closer to home occurs when college deans ask faculty members to spend more time doing one-on-one academic counseling with undergraduates and to report on the counseling done. Faculty members who feel pressure to make progress with their research and who may be more interested in graduate education have found ways to appear to act in compliance with a dean's request while not changing actual behavior, perhaps by describing brief, hallway contacts as academic counseling.

Do the Outcomes Achieved Match the Goals?

Evaluations of operating programs usually examine at least some results of the programs. Developers of innovative curricula would include measures of student achievement and planners of an advertising campaign often depend on sales information. Even programmers of religious events deal with outcomes when they report the number of people who say that important behavioral changes took place as a result of participation.

The level of outcome achieved. Deciding whether the outcome observed is good or only marginal depends on what stakeholders believe should have been achieved. In other words, after a year of reading instruction, third graders read better than when they started school in September; however, school boards and parents will not be satisfied with just any level of improvement. The improvement should be commensurate with a year of instruction in third grade. Similarly, football fans may want to see their favorite team do more than improve, they want to see a victory. Thus, when evaluators and stakeholders specify goals and objectives, attention must be paid to how much improvement is expected.

When evaluators first begin to work with stakeholders to develop statements of outcome objectives, sometimes they borrow the style of writing hypotheses which they learned in statistics classes. In statistical analyses the alternative hypothesis is often presented as the mean of the experimental group exceeding the mean of the control group, $H_1: \overline{X}_e > \overline{X}_c$. In the social sciences, the amount of difference between the groups is not specified. This is not the way statistics is used in the physical sciences (Meehl, 1978, 1990). In more developed sciences the expected numerical value of an observation is compared to the actual observation in the statistical test to learn if the observed difference is smaller than sampling error (a desirable finding) or larger than sampling error (an undesirable finding). We will discuss this difference at greater length elsewhere. Statements of objectives that are modeled after hypotheses used in basic social science research are not as useful as objectives that list the actual level of achievement desired for students, patients, and trainees. For example, in Figure 3.1, intermediate goals do not only say that the new system would be faster than the old system. Instead, a minimum performance specification was given. Evaluators trained in social science research methods often have difficulty committing themselves to a specific goal because basic research in the social sciences is not carried out that way.

How to specify levels of outcome expected. Education and health are among the most well-developed areas in terms of formulating specific goals easily. Norms for academic skills are available for standardized achievement tests and normal ranges are well-known for many laboratory tests used by physicians. The outcome of on-the-job training programs could be specified in terms of the trainees' skill in carrying out the tasks needed by the employer. However, norms that have been gathered validly can be misused. Recent criticisms of the use of standardized achievement tests by school districts (Channell, 1987; Shepard, 1990) suggest that when elementary schools are repeatedly evaluated using standard tests, teachers come to tailor their teaching to the test and may even teach some aspects of the test to their students.

For programs in areas in which extensive norms do not exist, evaluators are often tempted to permit program staff members to specify the objectives of the program. Although evaluators need the contribution of staff stakeholders in all phases of evaluations, experienced evaluators frequently discover that staff members hold much too optimistic expectations of the level of success that will be observed. When the program to be evaluated is in the area of criminal justice or mental health, the observations of recent evaluations of similar programs can be used. The closer a program already evaluated parallels the program under consideration, the more relevant the previous observations will be. Regardless of the focus of the evaluation or the source of the objectives, there needs to be some rationale for the levels of achievement specified in the objectives.

Outcomes and black boxes. Readers may well feel that we are beating a dead horse when we mention the limitations of black box evaluations again; however, the ease with which staff, government auditors, and the general public fall into the black box trap leads us to continue to emphasize the issue. The Auditor General of Illinois criticized *Parents Too Soon*, a state-funded program whose objectives included reducing the rate of teenage pregnancy (Karwath, 1990). In defense the program's administrator described the difficulty of evaluating a prevention program, and mentioned the reduced number of live births to state teenagers between 1983 and 1988. (By using these figures, note that the administrator was adopting a black box evaluation.) Since the number of teenagers declined between those years and since the numbers of abortions were not known, the decreased birth rate was not seen as support for the program. In addition, there are so many influences on the rate of teenage pregnancy that the use of a black box evaluation model places incalculable limitations on the interpretation of any findings. If the program had specified implementation goals and intermediate goals as well as the final, bottom-line outcome goal, the administrator may well have been in a better position to respond to the criticism. The following section will suggest some approaches to relating implementation, intermediate, and outcome goals to each other to show that the program processes are working as hypothesized and which, consequently, will strengthen the evaluation.

Is There Support for the Program Theory?

Whenever people develop service or intervention programs, assumptions about the causes of the problems and the best ways to change problem behavior are made. Unfortunately, these assumptions are seldom spelled out (DeFriese, 1990; Lipsey, 1990a). When there is no explicit statement of the theory behind the choice of interventions or when there is no conceptual framework linking the interventions to the projected outcomes, it is hard to do as effective an evaluation as should be done.

Why a program theory is helpful. Initially many evaluations were carried out without an explicit statement of the theory behind the program design. DeFriese (1990) laments that a sizable portion of the descriptions of proposed health-related treatment programs submitted to private foundations do not include a credible description of how the intervention is supposed to work. Heller (1990) makes the same observations about community level interventions. Increasingly, it has become clear that program design is less effective without theory and, for our purposes, evaluations are less useful when carried out in a conceptual vacuum (Chen and Rossi, 1989; Lipsey, 1990a).

Specifying the theory behind the program provides assistance for planners, staff members, and people responsible for obtaining funding, as well as for evaluators. In an overview of failed social welfare programs Etzioni reminds us that people "are not very easy to change after all." Yet governments and agencies frequently propose policies that are based on the assumption that social actions can motivate people to make major changes in their life styles over short periods of time. We act as though threatening shoplifters with jail will keep them from taking clothes from stores; telling diabetics to lose weight will lead them to do so; showing teenagers how to recycle soda cans will stop them from discarding cans on the beach. Information is important, but information alone is seldom enough to change behavior (Cook, Leviton, and Shadish, 1985). There is ample evidence that such input is a very weak influence among the major influences in life, such as peer pressure, family practices, media models, and simple convenience. One potential result of thinking theoretically is to decide to focus program resources on a narrow issue rather than to dilute program funds by attempting too much.

A second value of thinking theoretically is that we can measure the intermediate results of a program rather than just the bottom line. We are also reminded that different people might respond to different forms of a program. Teenagers might respond better if a music or sports figure would participate in the program; business managers might want to see a financial-oriented approach to a social concern; most everybody needs to learn how to visualize themselves carrying out the recommended behaviors. A neighbor was overheard arguing with her husband about a newly announced community recycling program. Citizens were to place cans, bottles, and newspapers into orange-colored containers each Friday. She was not enthused and asked her husband if he were going to "sort through the garbage every night?" For decades she had put apple peels, the morning newspaper, and empty soda cans into the kitchen garbage basket, and had not yet realized that cans and apple peels could be placed in different containers. Although keeping recyclable items separate from other garbage may seem to be a small matter to some planners, the idea of separating garbage is not apparent to some residents. Publicity about a recycling program should include illustrations of how to participate in the most convenient manner. Recognizing the processes that people have to follow to make changes in their lives can prompt planners to develop more effective programs.

A third benefit of having a program theory is that theory helps us to know where to look in conducting an evaluation. Lipsey and Pollard (1989) remark that adopting "the basic two-step" in program planning and evaluation would improve current practices. Planners can specify (a) what should happen right after participation in a program and should be a prerequisite for change and (b) a more distal outcome behavior that reflects a goal of the program. Evaluators would then develop methods to measure both. Learning about success or failure while the program is ongoing is more informative than measuring whether the final outcome was achieved only. For example, suppose that the program was implemented as planned, but that neither the intermediate nor the final outcome was achieved. Particular attention would be paid to why the program did not lead to the intermediate result; perhaps additional resources are needed or the original theory was not valid. If the intermediate outcome was achieved but the final outcome was not, it would seem that the theory linking the program activities to the intermediate step was valid, but that there must be more influences on the desired final result than the program planners had considered.

How to develop a program theory. It is easier to agree with the need for a program theory than to develop one. There are a number of approaches to developing a program theory. First, evaluators talk with the staff of the program. At times the staff have a fairly clear idea of how the parts of the program affect the participants and how the intermediate stages lead to the desired final outcomes. If staff members are not too helpful, evaluators turn to the research literature on similar programs, examine correlational research that relate the characteristics of participants to program outcomes, and, if resources permit, begin to gather observations, impressions, demographic data, and outcome variables from the operational program to explore possible relationships.

The research literature contains two kinds of material that might prove helpful. First, evaluations of similar programs might provide information on program theory. Peer leadership might lead to favorable outcomes more consistently in antismoking campaigns at junior high schools than do teacher-led classes (Evans and Raines, 1990). Since junior high children are especially sensitive to the attitudes of peers, program planners might attempt to use peers in any program that attempts to influence adolescents. Another example comes from energy conservation research. Writers have noted that electricity use is not easy for people to monitor; few people ever look at their meters and, when they do, they find it hard to relate the spinning disk to kilowatts of electricity. In fact, few people know what a kilowatt is. On the basis of these observations, programs have been developed to provide new ways to give people feedback about their use of power in terms that are understandable (Seligman and Finegan, 1990). It could be concluded that anyone wanting to get a group to conserve a resource should consider how easy it is to monitor one's own behavior. Hospital administrators wanting physicians to reduce the number of unnecessary laboratory tests have experimented successfully with informing physicians of the costs of the testing they plan to order (Tierney, Miller, and McDonald, 1990).

Basic research on topics related to the interventions used is another source of ideas for program theory. Social support is often believed to be related to health and positive social behaviors in general. Approaches to help people obtain social support are discussed in social psychology and clinical psychology research studies. Some of those ideas can enrich the theory of some social service programs. Unfortunately, writers of basic research often provide only brief descriptions of the independent variable, that is, the treatment, thus making it difficult to use their work in applied settings ("The trouble with dependent variables," 1990).

A particularly good example of the development of program theory was provided by Cook and Devine (1982), who described the expected processes whereby a psychoeducational intervention helps postsurgery patients recover more quickly and experience fewer side effects. Figure 3.2 has been adapted from Cook and Devine to illustrate some of the processes that connect the nurses' teaching to the desired outcome of healthy patients being discharged sooner. Note that there are

FIGURE 3.2 Illustration of an impact model showing the intermediate steps that are expected to occur between the intervention and the desired outcome. (Adapted from Cook and Devine, 1982)

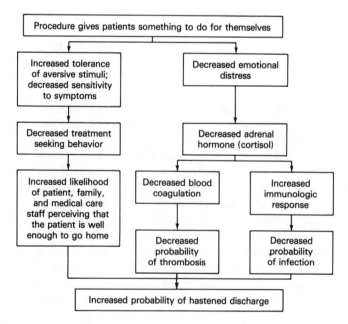

numerous criteria that may be observed by someone evaluating the program, including many intermediate variables as well as the final outcome criteria of program success.

Is the Program Accepted?

Good ideas are seldom adopted immediately. Mosteller (1981) described an incredible lag in applying the sixteenth-century finding that citrus fruits (vitamin C, of course) would protect seamen from scurvy. On some long voyages over 60 percent of the crews died. Rather than immediately implementing an action that would have reduced the loss of life, 198 years elapsed between the first of several publications of similar findings and the adoption of the knowledge by the British Navy in 1795.

Program users may also reject a program. The rejection of community mental health centers by chronically ill patients was mentioned previously. A long line of research clearly shows that physically ill patients often reject or ignore the treatment prescribed for their conditions (Posavac et al., 1985). Attempts to understand noncompliance with medical treatment suggest that better communication between physicians and patients promotes compliance. Some patients do not understand the recommended treatment; when they understand more fully, they act more responsibly. Furthermore, a means to remind patients when they are to take medications seems to help.

Although some writers in the field have dismissed client satisfaction attitude surveys as of minimal use in program evaluation, a program that cannot develop loyalty may not be effective. Clients who dislike a program or its staff are unlikely to participate fully, if at all. Marketing research firms focus on learning the preferences of potential customers and matching products to those preferences. Although human service fields cannot base service design only on what students, clients and patients think they need, program staff who are aware of client preferences have a better chance of designing and offering a service that will be accepted and utilized.

Are the Resources Devoted to the Program Being Expended Appropriately?

There are many ways in which program costs can be used in program evaluation. An introduction to procedures that relate cost to outcomes in elementary analyses are covered in a later chapter. The range of the evaluation questions that can be treated are reviewed here.

Using program costs in the planning phase. When a government program based on providing a service to all who qualify is developed, it is difficult to project the ultimate cost. However, when a specific program such as a new curriculum or a counseling service for a set number of participants is being planned, the costs can be fairly well estimated. Using the published literature, it may be possible to project the value of the results. For example, job training should result in better jobs at salaries that can be estimated. Then, the taxes those people will pay and the amount of welfare assistance they will not use can be estimated. One could ask whether that result justifies the amount of government funds needed to provide the program. If such a program succeeded in providing job skills, there may well be additional benefits to which dollar values cannot be assigned; this complicates decisions as described in Chapter 11.

A second issue in the planning phase concerns whether alternative uses of the funds would provide a more desired result. Since resources are limited, many or all stakeholders should agree that the services to be supported are needed more than other services that could be supported instead.

Is offering the program fair to all stakeholders? The use of racial origins to target educational aid is an attempt to give minorities a boost to overcome past discrimination. Many people endorse this policy; however, some writers argue that such programs primarily assist children of middle-class minority parents who do not need the assistance (Steele, 1990). Evaluations of some programs to increase the skill levels of minorities have found that the programs actually increased the difference in skills between children from low-income families and those from the middle class (Cook et al., 1975), possibly because middle-class parents made special efforts to expose their children to programs such as "Sesame Street." If so, is it fair to continue to use public funds to support the program?

A second illustration concerns support for public education. Because American public education has been funded largely through local property taxes, wealthy communities and communities with a large number of businesses and industries can spend far more per pupil than can poorer communities without industrial firms. Some critics argue that it would be more fair if school funding were dispersed on the state level so that all school districts can offer a similar quality of school programs. The evaluator cannot answer these questions of fairness using research methods. However, the use of standards of social justice in evaluation have been encouraged by some writers (Sirotnik, 1990) who argue that a value-free evaluation methodology is neither possible nor desirable.

Is this the way the funds are supposed to be spent? Another question about the use of program funding concerns whether the funds are being spent in a way that is compatible with the intention of the funding stakeholder. This question is related to the traditional accountability issue, which is designed to reduce the possibility of the misappropriation of funds. Often Congress is more interested in the question of whether funds have been spent as intended rather than the more difficult-to-answer question of whether the funds were spent wisely.

Does the outcome justify the resources spent? Once the results of a program are known, it is possible to examine the program costs to determine whether the results were worth the expenditure of funds. If it is possible to place a dollar amount on the outcome, then we can ask if the return was worth more than the cost of the program. Business-based financial analysts do this all the time. If the return on a company's investment does not exceed the investment, then there is probably something better to do with the investment next year. If there does not seem to be something better to do with the money, then the business should be sold off and the money distributed to the stockholders. Sometimes U.S. businesses are criticized for demanding a return on investment too soon; it may be that sizable returns require a long range perspective. In human service and educational fields it is quite hard to place a dollar amount on the results of programs. In this case, evaluators seek to compare programs designed to affect similar behaviors, such as developing employment skills, and to ask which program is the most efficient. Barring other restrictions, this would be the best program to offer.

Has the Evaluation Plan Allowed for the Development of Criteria That Are Sensitive to Undesirable Side Effects?

If it were possible to predict side effects, the program plans would be changed to reduce the chance of negative outcomes. Since evaluators and managers cannot foresee unanticipated outcomes, observation procedures are planned to permit side effects to become apparent. This means that evaluators will allot time for visiting program sites and talking with representatives of all stakeholders groups. An organizational consultant remarked that although management would pay him, he would not undertake the project unless the union was given equal rights in directing the project as management. There is no point in carrying out an evaluation if the evaluator only hears one view of the strengths and weaknesses of the program or the larger organization.

Although we have adopted a form of objectives-based program evaluation, we recognize that some applications of this approach have ignored unplanned results, whether positive or negative. The most egregious oversights occur when evaluators use official program plans and seek input from only one stakeholder, usually the manager, and then carry out the evaluation at arm's length. A professor of community nursing described how one evaluation group tried to evaluate a program designed to provide family physician care to poor families in suburban areas. From the comfort and security of their offices the evaluators prepared a questionnaire on the basis of official objectives presented in the grant proposal and mailed the survey to a list of participants. These evaluators never visited any of the sign-up centers, never interviewed any participants, and never contacted any of the cooperating physicians. This mechanical application of objectives-based evaluation has promoted negative reactions to evaluation in general, and objectives-based evaluation in particular.

When evaluators believe that they have detected negative side effects, they share their findings with stakeholders to obtain confirmation of their views or additional information to explain the observations. More careful observation procedures can then be developed to examine the unanticipated issue with care. Evaluators do not seek to discredit programs by finding negative side effects, but to assist programs to improve. A director of police officer training in a large city once commented that consultants sometimes used their skills to prick balloons; he called them "self-appointed pin prickers." Pin pricking is not the mission of program evaluators; program improvement is. Sometimes it helps to have an outside observer call attention to easily overlooked problems, but calling attention to a problem is merely the first step; for effective evaluators harder and more important steps follow.

SOME PRACTICAL LIMITATIONS ON SELECTING EVALUATION CRITERIA

Textbook authors have the freedom to describe ideal practices without being limited by the practical realities of particular evaluations. Three important restrictions on the selection of criteria are: the evaluation budget, time constraints, and the degree to which various possible criteria will be accepted by the stakeholders.

Evaluation Budget

Evaluation is not free; evaluators and their staffs need to be paid, surveys need to be duplicated and mailed, costs for phones and computers add up quickly, and getting around to various program sites can be expensive. Evaluators estimate the amount of time necessary to do a credible job in the light of the stakeholders' needs. It is usually necessary to negotiate the parameters of the evaluation since few stakeholders know how much time is involved in doing an evaluation or the limitations of social science research methodology to isolate causes with any degree of certainty. Since the funds for an evaluation will be fairly inflexible, the focus of the evaluation is often adjusted in these negotiations. It is better to carry out an evaluation with modest aspirations that one can trust than to plan an ambitious project that can only be done poorly within the limitations of the resources available.

Time Available for the Project

Since evaluation is an applied discipline, the use of findings are often tied into budget cycles, academic years, or the meeting schedules of governmental bodies. If an evaluation report is not available when it is needed, it may be ignored when it does come out. Some years ago the Federal government commissioned a study of an innovative approach to welfare. By the time the demonstration project and evaluation were completed the political climate had changed and Congress was no longer interested in the original idea or the evaluation. Often, projects are of a much shorter duration than expensive multisite demonstration projections costing tens of millions of dollars, but the principle is the same: there is a time when information is useful and a time after which it is no longer relevant. Majchrzak (1984) discusses a case in which decision makers were given an only partially completed project that addressed an issue being considered. Unfortunately, it contained so many unanswered questions that it was rejected by the decision makers. Majchrzak believes that the evaluators were correct in presenting the incomplete information because they knew the information would not be used if they had waited until the project was completed. A risk in presenting an incomplete project is that the last data collected may not follow the pattern that the initial observations suggest.

Before evaluators accept a project or begin to plan seriously, they ask about the project deadline. If the deadline and the stakeholders' evaluation needs are incompatible, then the evaluator must bow out or the project must be renegotiated. There is no reason to begin a project that cannot be completed when it is needed.

Criteria That Are Credible to the Stakeholders

Evaluators worry about collecting valid data in ways that permit valid interpretations; in addition, it is crucial that stakeholders accept those interpretations. Evaluators cannot carry out their work and ask others to take it or leave it. While planning an evaluation, evaluators ascertain that the stakeholders have agreed that the jointly selected criteria fit the goals of the program and are appropriate for the participants in the program. We talk about stakeholders "buying into" the criteria; it is helpful to have the agreement in writing. The stakeholders do not need to be asked to sign a statement of acceptance; however, the evaluator can keep minutes of planning meetings and distribute them to all relevant people. People who question the usefulness or credibility of one or another criterion can raise objections. Also, the evaluation team can later refer to the minutes and ask if there are changes needed before the project actually begins.

SUMMARY AND PREVIEW

The importance of the criteria selected for an evaluation is hard to overemphasize. They are the windows through which users of the evaluation see the program. If the windows distort the view, the program is misrepresented, either favorably or unfavorably. Since there are numerous phases of program development, implementation, and operation, evaluators often seek to observe more than just the final results of the program. Evaluators and their clients benefit by examining the processes whereby a social or educational service leads to the expected final results. Even a very simple program theory that includes program criteria, an expected intermediate outcome, and the final result greatly improves the evaluator's ability to understand the program.

The next chapter focuses on the specific steps that are taken to measure the criteria selected. Although a textbook separates the selection of criteria from a discussion of measurement issues, the ability to measure a criterion in a valid and reliable manner is considered at the same time as choices of criteria are made.

STUDY QUESTIONS

1. Consider a setting with which you are familiar—school, work, church, team, dormitory. Each has rules or procedures designed to meet certain objectives. Try to analyze the assumed impact model to learn how the procedures might lead to the objectives.

For example, there are required courses or area requirements for most college curricula. How might these requirements lead to educated graduates? What intermediate outcomes need to occur? How much validity does your impact model seem to possess? Drawing out an impact model often helps to detect very implausible assumptions. Try to find a few implausible assumptions underlying public policies.

2. This chapter suggested that different stakeholders have very different views of how intercollegiate athletes should be evaluated. Make a list of some public policies or programs that would be assumed to have very different purposes depending on the stakeholder group evaluating the policy.

3. Show how an evaluator might select criteria of program success that are easily measured, but that miss the central point of the program. If you have trouble, think about the criteria of success for a little league baseball team, or a volleyball coach in a junior high. Those should be easy; now work with the meaning of success for college teaching, counseling, law enforcement, or other important community activities.

FURTHER READING

Cook, T. D., Leviton, L. C., and Shadish, W. R. 1985. Program evaluation. In *Handbook of Social Psychology*, vol. 2, 3rd ed., ed. G. Lindzey and E. Aronson. New York: Random House.

Guba, E. G., and Lincoln, Y. S. 1989. *Fourth generation evaluation*. Newbury Park, Calif.: Sage.

4

Measurement Principles and Tools

Once evaluators and stakeholders agree on criteria that would indicate successful implementation and outcome, evaluators are faced with the task of measuring those criteria. There are a limited number of sources for the observations and data needed for evaluations; since each source has strengths and weaknesses, frequently more than one source is used. This chapter contains discussions of these sources and the characteristics of good measures of evaluation criteria. Last, some illustrative measurement tools are presented to illustrate the principles.

SOURCES OF DATA FOR EVALUATIONS

There are six major sources of data relevant to evaluations: (1) program records; (2) program participants; (3) staff delivering the program; (4) family members or other people with significant relationships to the participants; (5) observations made by the evaluator; and (6) community-level indexes. The characteristics of the program to be evaluated, the questions addressed to the evaluator, and the resources available determine which sources are used.

Program Records

A search of the program's records and files often provides reliable and inexpensive data for the evaluator. Archival data are most useful when the evaluation includes an examination of client characteristics, types of service provided, workload of staff members, costs of providing services, or trends across long time intervals. When archival data are objective (for example, number of visits, type of service, or identity of the care giver), the data are very valid. On the other hand, diagnoses and other subjective entries may not be quite so valid. Furthermore, Krause and Jackson (1983) found that state summary records were quite inaccurate compared to an agency's own records. Important advantages of archival data include: (1) the measurement process does not affect the program participant; (2) there can be no participant loss due to refusal or inability to participate; and, (3) it is often less costly to use existing data than to gather additional data in the field. Some aspects of archival searches used as feedback material are discussed at greater length in Chapter 7.

Maintaining confidentiality is a problem that can become acute when using the program's records. Some evaluations using public documents need not be concerned with limiting access to the data. However, many evaluations utilize hospital, school, personnel, or counselor records that are clearly confidential. Some information in files may be damaging to a person's social and financial affairs. The inadvertent release of such data could leave evaluators open to legal suits. In less sensitive situations a lack of sufficient care would make evaluators look unprofessional, and the resulting loss of credibility might result in their being denied access to records the next time it is requested. Evaluators cannot function without access to data.

Program Participants

There are several reasons to look to program participants for evaluative information. First, the person who actually receives a service is often in an excellent position to evaluate many aspects of the program. The direct contact the clients have with the staff provides them with important knowledge about the program that no one else has. Second, only the clients have access to their own feelings about the program and staff. For example, after interviewing deinstitutionalized chronically ill psychiatric patients, Shadish et al. (1985) concluded that the patients' sense of well-being was damaged by being released. Third, for many criteria the clients will be the most knowledgeable about their current state, especially at follow-up intervals. Further, they might well be the only available source of information about the use they make of additional follow-up services. A fourth advantage is that the information they provide is often relatively inexpensive to gather. Fifth, self-assessments have been found to be at least as accurate as other assessment approaches for a variety of behavioral and emotional dimensions (Shrauger and Osberg, 1981).

On the other side of the coin, certain participants may be too incapacitated to be valid sources of evaluation information. In planning an evaluation of a physical medicine and rehabilitation unit, one quickly discovers that few recent stroke victims can describe their own capabilities validly. Some are unable to talk, others have poor judgment, and others are so crushed emotionally by their impairments that it seems cruel to discuss their problems with them. Certain types of patients seeking psychotherapy cannot provide valid data; however, many others can. Also, there are surprising limitations to what people actually can communicate about themselves. For example, people have difficulty remembering what they ate the week before and people report eating "medium" sized servings even though the definitions of medium varied by 200 percent (On a diet?, 1989).

Perhaps participants can provide good data for some aspects of the program but not others. General hospital patients usually know if rooms are clean, whether nurses and resident physicians treat them politely, and how long they have to wait outside the X-ray room. However, they cannot evaluate the choice of medication or the competence of their surgeons. Similarly, college students can report on whether a teacher returned tests promptly, held classes as scheduled, and lectured or led class discussions. It is very unlikely that many undergraduates can evaluate the accuracy of the information presented. In sum, participants can validly comment on objective aspects of the services given as well as their immediate satisfaction with the services.

Evaluators are faced with the task of motivating the program participants to provide personal information about their attitudes and judgments. Participants may refuse to cooperate from fear of public disclosure. Routinely, anonymity in reports is guaranteed. Many people do not understand the social scientist's disinterest in the personal facts about individuals, nor do they understand the necessity of using overall group averages and proportions in evaluation reports. They are familiar with the case study approach often used in popular newspaper and magazine discussions of medical, correctional, counseling, and educational programs. It is not surprising then that some respondents do not believe promises of anonymity. One respondent to a survey administered in a group setting without a way to identify the respondents wrote the following: "I have tried to be honest. I hope I don't lose my job." Evaluators cannot afford to give respondents cause to question their motives for requesting information.

Even when people are not afraid of public discourse, they must still be motivated to spend time completing the forms and surveys. One approach is to appeal to an interest in improving the program being evaluated. Many people are sufficiently altruistic to be willing to share their feelings if they realize that their efforts can help improve services for others. However, they are not so altruistic that they will spend a long time or struggle with a poorly written survey.

Which program participants are most likely to cooperate? Experience shows that it is those with the most favorable impressions of a program or facility. The 86 percent who responded to a lengthy survey on a chaplaincy internship were independently evaluated by their supervisors as having performed better during the internship year than the 14 percent who did not return the survey (Posavac, 1975). However, some very angry people may well write lengthy criticisms.

Participant information may be part of an evaluation in the form of vivid illustrations of very good staff performance, or, in contrast, very bad performance. Through case studies of teenagers Love (1986) showed that troubled adolescents were unlikely to fit into the mental health and welfare systems in a large city. Although a case study cannot show the extent of problems, it can show how specific program failures do occur.

Staff

Program staff people are important sources of data for evaluations. Staff members are trained to assess the degree of the participants' impairments and are in a good position to detect improvement. Also, they are the most likely to know how well a program is managed and how well the program runs on a day-to-day basis. On the negative side, staff members can be expected to be biased toward seeing improvement. After committing their efforts to helping people improve their skills or adjustment, it may be hard to accept failure.

Over and above these concerns, the evaluators need to recognize that evaluating a program is in some ways an evaluation of the staff's performance. Few people unhesitatingly welcome an evaluation of the effectiveness of the services they provide. Most people will be concerned about the way an evaluation will be used. If they are worried, they will resist the evaluation. Some college professors refuse to permit students conducting course evaluations to enter their classrooms. Some psychotherapists argue that checklists of symptoms and rating forms are blind to the crucial but subtle changes in a client that the therapist alone can sense. Because evaluation is not a developed science with unquestioned techniques, it is easy to find weaknesses in the most carefully planned program evaluation. One way to reduce staff resistance is to provide some benefit for the staff as a by-product of the evaluation of their program. Opportunities for improvement, workshops, and individual guidance, for example, should be tied in with an evaluation so that it is a learning experience. It must be recognized that some evaluations have not been learning experiences. At times evaluators have neglected to make a presentation to the staff of the program evaluated. Sharing the findings with the staff is the least evaluators can do in return for the staff's cooperation.

Significant Others

If a program is designed to change the behavior (for example, counseling and corrective programs) or the health of a person, family members will be affected. They must adjust their own behaviors as patients or clients change. Significant others see the recipients of human services (except for inpatients and prisoners) more frequently than the staff does, and they see the participants in natural settings, not merely in the short-term, artificial setting created by the program. Family members may have biases just as staff members do; however, the direction of these biases may be hard to predict. In a comparison of nurses' ratings with spouses' ratings of the capabilities of stroke patients, we learned that nurses rated the patients as more proficient in performing daily activities (dressing, eating, grooming) than the spouses did. On the other hand, spouses rated the patients as being more proficient in cognitive tasks (speaking, reading, memory) than the nurses did.[1] In any program some family members will report more improvement than actually occurred, while others will report less. Because the focus is on program-level outcomes, not *individual* assessments, these idiosyncratic biases are less important than systematic biases such as those found with the stroke patients.

When requesting information about program participants from significant others, it is necessary to have the participants' permission beforehand. People vary in their willingness to have spouses or others provide personal information to the evaluation staff. In evaluations of hospitalized psychiatric inpatients, Ellsworth (1979) reports that 21 percent were too incapacitated to give or withhold permission, 19 percent refused to give permission, and 7 percent could not name a significant other to complete the evaluation forms. Therefore, a smaller proportion of the population can be assessed using the ratings of significant others as compared to the proportion who can provide self-ratings. The motivation to cooperate again emphasizes the long-term improvement of the program for others. Care should be taken that the request to contact a patient's or client's significant other does not imply that good treatment in the program is contingent on giving permission.

Evaluator Observations

In some settings evaluations are conducted by sending a team of evaluators to make direct observations of the program. Colleges are accredited through a process that includes a several-day site visit by college deans and other administrators. The team's direct observations are combined with other information in preparing the evaluation report. The advantage of direct observations lies in the belief that people who are experts in the services provided by the program but are not involved in the program being evaluated, are the least biased sources of information (Endicott and Spitzer, 1975). As chapter 12 points out, observations can be essential in understanding the program and making sense of the various forms of evaluative data.

Community Indexes

Some programs are planned to improve community-level variables. Examples of programs designed to influence the community include a crime-reporting program to increase citizen participation in criminal surveillance to reduce crime and raise arrest rates; a reading program to raise the achievement levels of the children in a school district; and a citizen-developed project to monitor housing code violations to increase or maintain the quality of the housing in a neighborhood. Jason and Liotta (1982) used number of busy signals, time to answer a telephone call, and seconds on hold as measures of businesses' and community agencies' responsiveness to citizen needs.

[1]For the interested reader, this finding was explained in the following fashion: Spouses, being familiar with the stroke patient, needed fewer cues for effective communication; however, like most people, stroke patients tend to perform grooming and self-care types of behaviors at a higher level for strangers than for family members.

The major difficulty with community-level indexes is that there are many steps between the program and the hoped-for end results (Cook, Leviton, and Shadish, 1985). So many nonprogram variables have an influence that an effective program may not be detectable. These influences are beyond the control of the staff. An evaluator who measures community-level indexes in an outcome study while ignoring the integrity of program implementation and intermediate outcomes may be left quite in the dark about the reasons for apparent failure or success.

Which Sources Should Be Used?

The choice of data sources depends on the cost of obtaining data, the type of decision to be made on the basis of the evaluation, the size of the program, and the time available to conduct the evaluation. If a program needs feedback information, it is likely that records, participant attitudes, and family reports may be very helpful. If a decision is planned to expand (or to eliminate) an expensive, controversial program, the judgments and observations of outside experts may be the only source of data that suffices. Such decisions must be made carefully on the basis of a widely accepted evaluation.

Regardless of the type of program or anticipated decision, evaluators should strive to use multiple measures from more than one source. In choosing multiple measures, it is especially important to select measures that are not likely to share the same biases. For example, a subjective assessment of the success of a program by a client may be mirrored by the subjective feelings of the client's spouse. If, on the other hand, a measure of subjective feelings is used with ratings of ability to function in specific settings or with objective achievement, evaluators are less likely to obtain sets of data with the same biases. When the same implication is drawn from a variety of sources, the evaluation will be treated as having greater credibility.

However, it also is possible that the multiple approaches will not agree. Shipley (1976) conducted an evaluation of a companion program for mentally ill patients. College students served as volunteer companions to discharged psychiatric patients. The volunteers, patients, and hospital staff all subjectively evaluated the program in quite glowing terms. However, more objective measures of the patients' behavior (by staff ratings and by frequency and duration of rehospitalizations) revealed highly *variable* reactions. Some patients apparently benefited; others did not. The use of multiple measures led Shipley to a different conclusion than previous studies using only subjective attitude measures. In a similar vein Sullivan and Snowden (1981) found that staff, clients, standard tests, and agency files did not agree about the problems clients had. Hougland (1987) found subjective satisfaction was not highly correlated with objective outcomes, such as income level, in evaluating publicly funded job-training programs. Evaluators need to be sensitive to the possibility that their selection of data sources and of specific measures can affect their conclusions.

The fact that evaluators frequently work with people trained in service delivery techniques, not in research methods, means that evaluators have considerable discretion in choosing the criteria of effectiveness and the analyses of those criteria. Berk (1977), Berk and Rossi (1976), and Zigler and Trickett (1978) go so far as to say that through their choice of variables and methods of analyses, evaluators can determine the results of an evaluation before it is conducted. Thus, to be fair to programs and to the consumers of program evaluations, evaluators must examine their own attitudes as they design an evaluation. Otherwise, their own biases may determine their findings. The following section describes the most important issues to consider when choosing assessment procedures.

PRINCIPLES IN CHOOSING ASSESSMENT PROCEDURES

Evaluators use several criteria in selecting methods of gathering the data required in an evaluation. Keeping these principles in mind while planning a study saves evaluators time and inconvenience later.

Multiple Variables

Evaluators usually recommend the use of multiple sources of information (Mark and Shotland, 1987). It is also recommended that evaluators use multiple variables from their data sources; the elevation of a single variable to be *the* criterion of success can obscure an effect (Lipsey et al., 1985) and will probably corrupt it (Sechrest, 1984). Elliott (1989) discussed how two school-setting variables, advancement in grade and standard-test scores, become corrupted when used as the measures of school success. If they are used repeatedly to the exclusion of other variables, teachers may promote a greater proportion of students and begin to teach the test. Barbour and Wolfson (1973) describe the difficulty of defining productivity of police officers. Concentrating on arrests may unintentionally encourage poor evidence-gathering practices; or police officers may make arrests when the interests of justice would be better served without an arrest. Turner (1977) described the effect of a poorly defined criterion for mental health workers who refer clients to other public agencies. The criterion of successful referrals was defined as "90 percent of referred clients actually make contact with the new agency." The evaluator quickly learned that the mental health workers were escorting the individuals to the other agencies. Although the workers were scoring well on the criterion of successful referral—those referred to other agencies did make contact—other aspects of their work were left unfinished. These illustrations are not presented to suggest that teachers, police officers, or mental health workers are dishonest. Behavior theory tells us that people will behave in ways that are rewarded. A short-sighted choice of variables by the evaluator can adversely affect a program; this is one aspect of the problem of reactivity, the next measurement characteristic we discuss.

One way to avoid corrupting the criteria chosen and to avoid distorting the operation of a human service system is to use multiple variables. It is especially important that the variables serve as a check on one another. Thus, both arrest rate and conviction rate should be used as the measures of police productivity. Percentage of successful referrals and number of clients served should be used as criteria for assessing the work of a mental health worker screening people in need of various services.

An additional reason to use multiple variables is that different variables are affected by different sources of error. If the multiple variables are measured in ways that are similar and if they come from the same source (for example, program participants), it may turn out that all the variables are affected by the same biases. When this happens, the extra effort is probably of little value. By using several variables, assessed by different methods from different sources of data, stakeholders can trust implications drawn from the convergence of these various sources of data (Mark and Shotland, 1987).

Nonreactive Measures

The mere act of requesting information from people or observing people can influence the behavior being studied. Measurement instruments create questions that some people have never considered before. Raising an issue may make people more aware of things they previously ignored. The test itself will bore some respondents, offend some, and please others. The greater the behavioral change created by the measurement instrument, the greater its *reactivity*. Measuring the effect of human services is not at all similar to making physical measurements of inanimate objects.

Usually evaluators do not want to select measurement procedures that influence the people studied. If the instruments have an impact, the evaluation loses some of its usefulness, because the outcomes may be different once the instruments are no longer used. Completely nonreactive measurement is an ideal seldom actually achieved. An extended discussion of reactivity has been prepared by Webb et al. (1981).

Important Variables

Because program evaluation is an applied social science, the variables to be measured must be relevant to the specific informational needs of facility management, community representatives, those responsible for budgets, and other relevant stakeholders. Thus, in planning an evaluation, evaluators must learn what questions are pressing but as yet unanswered. The variables to be measured are then chosen on the basis of their importance to the questions facing the stakeholders.

The time at which a variable is measured may determine whether it provides appropriate information. The impact of educational services can often be assessed at the end of a program. Other human services are provided with the goal of altering the course of a person's life. Thus, the success of a program for juvenile delinquents can be better judged by the degree to which participants stay out of trouble with the law over a period of time. The participant's status at the end of a program is less informative than his or her status three or six months later. Still other programs should be evaluated on the basis of their success over a period of years.

The primary way to approach selecting important and relevant variables is through discussions with staff and managers. If there is no decision to be affected by the variable, regardless of its value, or if no program standards mention the variable, then it probably is not important or relevant to the evaluation. If the location of the program participants' homes is not important to administrators, evaluators probably will not record it. However, at times evaluators may feel that a variable *should* be important and would be seen as important once summarized. Evaluators should not feel completely limited to recording just the information program managers and staff recognize as important. In other chapters we point out specific instances in which information that was not requested came as a surprise to the program staff. Furthermore, unintended negative side effects, which will certainly not be mentioned in program goals, should be considered.

Valid Measures

In an evaluation the instruments must validly measure the behaviors the program is designed to change. These behaviors may be the ultimate criteria behaviors (such as long life, better adjustment, employment) or more immediate behaviors believed to be useful in achieving the planned long-term outcomes (such as higher quality work and improved leadership practices).

In order to assure themselves of the validity of chosen measures, evaluators should discuss the measures with the program staff. If staff members have not approved the measures, they may later reject recommendations of the evaluation. However, evaluators must not depend totally on the staff members to suggest the measures, because program staff members are often inexperienced in social science methodology.

In general, the more a measurement tool focuses on objective behavior rather than on undefined or vague terms, the more likely it is to be valid. Objective behaviors (such as "late to work less than one day out of the week" or "speaks in groups") are more likely to be measured validly than less precise criteria (such as "is punctual" or "is assertive"), regardless of the specific measurement approach chosen. Mager (1972) presents an informal but thorough discussion of the usefulness of behavioral criteria rather than personality trait words in specifying the achievement of a goal.

Some variables may appear to be valid when in fact they are misleading. Campbell (1969) presented several measures of the frequencies of types of crime in Chicago plotted over time. In 1957 a liberal, highly regarded person was installed as chief of police. The year after his term began, official statistics on the number of thefts under $50 increased dramatically. Did the new chief cause a crime wave? Not likely. Instead, his reforms led to a more thorough reporting of crime and perhaps some reclassification of crimes. A check on the interpretation that the chief caused a crime wave was provided by the homicide rate. Homicides seldom go unreported and cannot be reclassified into a different crime category. When frequency of homicides was plotted over time, there was no noticeable change after the chief began. A very similar increase in crime statistics in Chicago occurred early in 1983, when reporting standards again were improved ("Good news," 1983). Evaluators try to select and interpret variables carefully in order to avoid a misleading conclusion based on a poor choice of criteria.

Reliable Measures

Social behaviors cannot be measured perfectly because such measurements are affected by the respondent's mood, attitude, and understanding of directions—things that are extraneous to the behavior of interest. The degree to which people who are theoretically equivalent on a social variable such as depression score the same on a test is the test's reliability. In somewhat oversimplified terms, a reliable test yields much the same values if administered twice within a short period of time. Reliability, like validity, is higher if the scores are minimally influenced by the passing mood of the person completing the instrument, whether that person is a program participant, staff member, or evaluator. The more reliable a measure is, the more likely it is to detect a difference between groups.

Variables referring to objective information and behavior are likely to be more reliable than subjective ratings or opinions. This does not imply that ratings should never be used, but we stress that it is harder to judge whether people are, for example, ambitious, than to record whether they have found jobs or have been promoted at work. Subjective ratings are usually less reliable since they are influenced not only by the behavior of the person being rated but also by the person doing the ratings.

Since an individual item is less reliable than a scale made up of several items, evaluators often combine items into one variable. To measure quality neighborhoods, one might combine ratings of cleanliness of alleys, degree of vandalism, repair of buildings, recreational opportunities, and number of abandoned vehicles into one measure. Such an index is far more reliable than any single rating. One often does the same thing for measures of attitudes, achievement, and skills. The concern, of course, is that the items combined must measure the criterion of interest.

Evaluators must appreciate the differences between the use of measures to estimate the general level of a *group* on some variable and their use to assess an *individual* on the variable. The greater the number of individuals whose responses are combined to estimate the level of the group, the more stable the estimate. Thus, surveys and other forms of measurement that would be rejected as insufficiently reliable to assess the views or behaviors of individuals may be very useful as measures of a group's views or behaviors. The following paragraphs illustrate the importance of the difference between estimating an individual's score and a group's score.

By using the standard deviation of a test and its reliability, it is possible to calculate a range of values that is likely to include the individual's true score. For example, assume that a person scored 105 on an IQ test with a standard deviation of 15 and a reliability of .95. The true scores of 68 percent of the people getting 105 will be between $105 \pm 15\sqrt{1 - .95}$, or between 101.6 and 108.4. The standard deviation times the square root of 1 minus the reliability is called the *standard error of estimate* and is applied when an individual's score is the question of interest (see Brown, 1983).

On the other hand, when a group's mean score is to be estimated, the *standard error of the mean* is the statistic to be used, instead of the standard deviation as in the calculation given above. If a group of 81 people scored an average of 105 on the

IQ test, the standard error of the mean is $15/\sqrt{81}$, or 1.67. We can conclude that 68 percent of such groups have true mean scores of between $105 \pm 1.67\sqrt{1 - .95}$, or between 104.6 and 105.4. Compare this range with the range calculated in the previous paragraph. Even a measure with a reliability of only .40 would yield a sufficiently precise group estimate, although a test with such a low reliability would be inappropriate for use with individuals.[2]

There are a variety of reliability indexes that are reported in test manuals. Some are very relevant to evaluation work, but others are not useful for evaluators. The classic *test-retest* approach to reliability is not as important to evaluation as it is to the area of psychological assessment. Tests that are developed to be stable over time measure well-entrenched, habitual behaviors and are precisely the sort of tests evaluators do not want. Evaluators require measures of behaviors that are subject to change.

Split-half reliability, which is found by correlating the scores respondents earned on the odd-numbered test items with the scores earned on the even-numbered test items, is quite important to evaluators. Split-half reliability gauges the extent to which a measure is homogeneous, that is, sensitive to one concept or characteristic rather than to a mixture of things. If a reading program is to be evaluated, the instrument to measure reading achievement should not include items requiring broad general knowledge or quantitative skills.

Evaluators also look for *interrater reliability,* that is, agreement between independent raters. Often the criteria of success of a program include ratings made by professionals or relatives. An instrument that yields similar ratings when used by different observers is usually better than one that yields different values. Obviously, if the observers view the rated individuals in very different situations—at home versus in school—low interrater reliability may tell us more about the differences in situations than about the reliability of the rating scale.

Sensitivity to Change

There are two general types of measures of psychological and intellectual variables. One type seeks to assess an individual's general, typical level on some variable, and the other type seeks to assess current mood or achievement. Some writers have called the first type a measure of *trait* (Spielberger, 1972). The other type of measure has been developed to assess effects that trait instruments seek to minimize. Such an instrument is called a measure of *state.* A measure of state also seeks to assess the individual's current level on a variable. This distinction is also called *psychometric* for measures of stable traits and *edumetric* for measures of variables that change more readily (Carver, 1974).

The distinction between intelligence tests and classroom tests may help to illustrate this point. Before a course few class members are expected to score well on a test covering the course material. However, after the course students are expected to do well if they have mastered the course material. The classroom test should be sensitive to the changes that have occurred in the skills of the students.

[2]Readers wishing more details on these points should examine an introductory statistics text, such as McCall (1990), and a testing text, such as Brown (1983).

Fairly stable characteristics of the students (such as intelligence) should not be primary factors leading to differences among the students' classroom test scores. In contrast, stable characteristics are expected to lie behind the differences obtained using standard intelligence tests. Although intelligence is certainly not fixed and does change in response to many environmental influences, the developers of intelligence tests sought to find test items that were minimally influenced by the individual's mood and immediate situation. It is not possible for a test to be completely unaffected by a person's habitual way of acting prior to entering the program; however, when measuring program outcome, the goal is to use instruments least affected by stable prior conditions and thus most likely to detect real changes in participants.

Evaluators usually choose measures of program output that are maximally sensitive to change, because change is what evaluators are trying to detect. This point is especially important in the evaluation of various forms of psychotherapy; therapists, who are so familiar with standardized personality tests, often approach program evaluation in the same manner as they approach individual client assessment. Individual assessment instruments are designed to measure personality and intelligence traits. Tests that show marked sensitivity to situational differences are not desirable for personality and intelligence measurement. In contrast, evaluators want a measurement instrument that is sensitive to respondents' current (hopefully improved) state. Using a trait measure to detect change raises the probability of overlooking any change that did in fact occur.

Several methods can be used to check on the expected sensitivity of a measure. Previous effective use of the dependent variables with evaluations of similar programs would give confidence that a variable is sufficiently sensitive. If the variable is to be assessed using a newly developed measure, evaluators might look for existing groups that differ on the variable to be measured. If a procedure to measure scientific reasoning does not distinguish students in a physics class from those in an English class, one would not expect it to be useful as an outcome measure for an evaluation of an innovative science curriculum (Lipsey, 1983).

A final point about sensitivity to change was alluded to in the previous chapter—very good performance is hard to improve. Just as it is harder to go from an A to a perfect paper than it is to go from a C to a C+, it is hard to improve a program participant's condition or level of satisfaction if the program is already fairly effective and well received. In such a setting the criteria of success cannot change much. Evaluations dependent on detecting such small changes usually conclude that the innovative program is no better than the old one, even when the innovative program is indeed better.

Lipsey (1990) presents a number of approaches to increasing the sensitivity of research designs. One approach is to select measures that are reliable. Criteria that are not reliable make it hard to detect the effects of a program. A second approach is to measure the program participants before and after so that an analysis of variance using subjects as a factor can be performed. In this way the degree to which participants differ from each other can be separated from error variation, making it easier to detect a program effect.

Cost-Effective Measures

In planning a program evaluation, the cost of the test materials and the costs of gathering data must not be forgotten. Several principles are usually true. First, time and money invested in making test materials attractive and easy to use reap higher response rates. Second, money spent on published forms is small relative to the costs of the evaluation staff in collecting and analyzing the data. Third, because interviews cost far more than other measurement approaches, interviews should not be used without considering all alternatives. Some evaluative questions can be answered without requiring extensive interviews. Other questions are too complicated to address in written form only. At times, respondents are unable to use written material, need prompting or encouragement to respond, do not respond to written surveys, or are defensive or misleading in answering written surveys.

Last, the effect of the instruments on participant loss must be considered. No participant would be lost to the research in a study of the program's records. Many participants, on the other hand, are lost if a lengthy survey is mailed to people after they have left the program. Thus, an instrument that is itself inexpensive may not be cost effective (1) if evaluators must spend a considerable amount of time following up on many tardy respondents; or (2) if so few respond that the results are not representative of any group.

TYPES OF MEASURES

Evaluators employ several general types of measures. The major distinction among the approaches is the degree to which they depend on self-reported impressions versus objective observations. The principles just introduced are used to describe the strengths and weaknesses of the approaches presented.

Written Surveys Completed by Program Participants

Probably the most widely used technique for evaluating programs is the written survey. The survey technique provides the most information per dollar or hour investment by the evaluation staff. Surveys are not expensive to reproduce or to buy. If they are complex and especially constructed for a particular evaluation, their cost will be higher. (Guidelines for writing survey items will be discussed later in this chapter.)

Surveys vary greatly in their reliability and validity because the topics they cover are so different. A survey asking former clients to give a global, subjective evaluation of their experience in therapy is not highly reliable; responses vary with the moods of the people responding or with the particular aspect of the service they think about. Similarly, students' evaluations of teachers may be influenced by whether a difficult assignment is due soon or whether test results have just been returned. On the other hand, a survey may yield quite reliable judgments if it focuses on current behavior, such as jobs held, further treatment sought, and source of referral.

The loss of participants to the evaluation may be large if the samples are mobile, if the survey is long, or if the participants feel ambivalent toward the program. Evaluators must be prepared to follow up a mailed survey with reminder letters or phone calls to those who do not return the survey within two weeks (Anderson and Berdie, 1975). If only a minority of the sample returns a survey, the responses of the whole sample cannot be estimated. Certainly, receiving returns from fewer than 50 percent of the sample makes the survey useless for many purposes—but not for all purposes, as will be mentioned later.

Regardless of how the survey is to be used, those who do not respond will still be different from those who return the survey. In one study the 66 percent who returned a survey about their experience in outpatient counseling participated in an average of 20.2 counseling sessions, and those who did not respond participated in an average of only 9.5 sessions (Posavac and Hartung, 1977). Experienced survey users expect to find such differences and recognize the limitations these differences impose on the certainty with which generalizations may be made.

Ratings of the Program Participants by Others

Ratings by people important in the program participants' lives can be used as measures of program success. As with surveys, ratings made by significant others may be very reliable if they focus on relatively objective behavior, such as absenteeism, participation in discussions, or physical health. On the other hand, they may be unreliable if they focus on undefined and vague variables, such as adjustment or success in the program. Our experience with forms mailed to spouses indicates that the return rate for forms mailed to significant others is similar to that of mailed self-report surveys.

The cost of ratings may be high if professional staff members are expected to perform numerous or detailed ratings. If ratings are done by nonprofessionals and are kept brief, the cost may be acceptably low. Who is expected to do the ratings is related to how complete the data will be. Members of an evaluation team usually complete nearly all the ratings planned; however, significant others may resent the intrusion of the team, and professional staff members may feel that the ratings are an oversimplification of their professional judgment. The best that evaluators can do is to keep the rating form easy to use and to stress that the focus of the study is to obtain documentation of program effectiveness—not information on personal affairs. If people are willing to take a long-range view, they will see that they have an ultimate self-interest in improving program effectiveness.

Staff members sometimes rate the progress of clients. Such ratings permit comparisons between groups of clients as well as trace the progress of individual clients. In order to make ratings routinely, an easy-to-use form is necessary. An unnamed global level-of-functioning scale was recommended by Carter and Newman (1976) for routine use in counseling or mental health centers. Figure 4.1 gives the nine levels of function ranging from nearly total dependence on others through a healthy adjustment requiring no further contact with the mental health center. The dimensions of life that would be examined by a rater can be defined according to the needs of the client population. The original scale suggested that the following areas

Nine Levels of Global Functioning

With regard to the balance among four areas of function (personal self-care, social, vocational/educational, and emotional symptoms), select the person's ability to function autonomously in the community. (Note levels 5 through 8 describe persons who are usually functioning satisfactorily, but for whom problems in one or more of the areas force some degree of dependency on a form of therapeutic intervention.)

LEVEL 1: Dysfunctional in all four areas and is almost totally dependent upon others to provide a supportive protective environment.

LEVEL 2: Not working; ordinary social unit cannot or will not tolerate the person; can perform minimal self-care functions but cannot assume most responsibilities or tolerate social encounters beyond restrictive settings (in group, play, or occupational therapy).

LEVEL 3: Not working; probably living in ordinary social unit but not without considerable strain on the person and/or on others in the household. Symptoms are such that movement in the community should be restricted or supervised.

LEVEL 4: Probably not working, although may be capable of working in a very protective setting; able to live in ordinary social unit and contribute to the daily routine of the household; can assume responsibility for all personal self-care matters; stressful social encounters ought to be avoided or carefully supervised.

LEVEL 5: Emotional stability and stress tolerance are sufficiently low that successful functioning in the social and/or vocational/educational realms is marginal. The person is barely able to hold on to either job or social unit, or both, without direct therapeutic intervention and a diminution of conflicts in either or both realms.

LEVEL 6: The person's vocational and/or social areas of functioning are stabilized, but only because of direct therapeutic intervention. Symptom presence and severity are probably sufficient to be both noticeable and somewhat disconcerting to the client and/or to those around the client in daily contact.

LEVEL 7: The person is functioning and coping well socially and vocationally (educationally); however, symptom recurrences are sufficiently frequent to necessitate some sort of regular therapeutic intervention.

LEVEL 8: Functioning well in all areas with little evidence of distress present. However, a history of symptom recurrence suggests periodic correspondence with the Center; for example, a client may receive a medication check from a family physician, who then contacts the Center monthly, or the client returns for bimonthly social activities.

LEVEL 9: The person is functioning well in all areas and no contact with mental health services is recommended.

FIGURE 4.1 Definitions of nine levels of functioning on which to base global ratings of psychological functioning. Such definitions of levels could be adapted for use in a variety of educational, rehabilitation, or training settings. (Adapted from Carter and Newman, 1976)

of life could be considered in making the rating of function: (1) personal self-care, (2) social functioning in ordinary social units and in the general community, (3) vocational or educational productivity, and (4) evidence of emotional stability and stress tolerance.

Although the scale in Figure 4.1 was prepared for a mental health setting, the principles used in constructing this scale apply to many other settings as well. The crucial characteristic is the development of behaviorally defined levels of function. For example, in a vocational setting a useful rating might concern how much supervision a trainee requires. A level of 1 might indicate that the trainee needs constant supervision with continuous oral instructions to complete the job. The highest rating might be given when the trainee can complete the job independently and can even handle major problems without assistance.

Interviews

Gathering evaluative information by personal interview is useful when evaluators need to develop an understanding of the program, when they want to obtain information from people with unique information, or when they are not at all sure what is most important to interviewees (Guba and Lincoln, 1981). Interviewing is not simply shooting the breeze with program clients or staff; it is a difficult job that requires considerable preparation. Good interviewers are thoroughly familiar with the issues to be addressed in the interview sessions. At times, specific questions are addressed to the respondents; in other situations the questions will be quite general. A more detailed discussion of interviews is given in Chapter 12 on qualitative methods.

An alternative to interviewing a participant face to face is a telephone interview (Babbie, 1989). The cost of a telephone interview is much lower since it is easy to try to reach people at many different times of the day and repeated attempts can be made with people who are not at home. A letter received before the telephone call explaining the need for the study and requesting cooperation may improve a respondent's receptivity.

Behavioral Observations

Probably the method with the most potential for providing valid information is the behavioral observation approach. The ultimate outcome of any program is expected to be behavioral change. Examples include better ways of handling anger, better performance on the job, or ability to write a theme. The goals of many psychological interventions center on emotions or attitudes that are difficult to translate into behaviors that are hard to observe, but seldom impossible.

When the behaviors are public, observations are often feasible. Actual seat belt use was measured by observers at stop signs in evaluating programs to encourage workers to use their automobile seat belts (Geller, 1990). A complex observational procedure was developed by Paul (1986) for evaluating residential psychiatric treatment facilities. By carefully defining the variables of interest, Paul and his co-workers developed a list of specific behaviors (such as pacing) that could be measured very easily. Since the definitions were objective, very reliable and inexpensive observations could be made. The effects of public policies, such as changes in state DWI laws, can often be measured by using public records, such as arrest or accident rates (West, Hepworth, and McCall, 1989). Using the actual behavior expected to be affected by a program, rather than ratings or self-reports, the measurement procedure contributes to an evaluation of high credibility.

Achievement Tests

In conducting evaluations of educational programs, measuring cognitive and intellectual achievement frequently is the method of choice. Evaluators of educational programs have a valuable resource in achievement tests. Achievement tests with high reliability are well developed and are widely accepted in educational settings (Anastasi, 1988). There is some concern about whether standard achievement tests validly measure the goals of some educational programs; however, these criticisms are mild compared to debate about measures of emotional state (Waskow and Perloff, 1975). When educational programs are assigned goals that include the development of both academic and social skills (see, for example, Datta, 1976b), evaluations of the outcome of educational programs cannot depend solely on achievement test scores. Evaluators are careful to avoid choosing measures of aptitudes or intelligence when looking for a measure of achievement. The former are constructed to measure stable cognitive traits whereas achievement tests are sensitive to specific skills or knowledge that would not be possessed just by being smart.

Published versus Specially Constructed Instruments

Published measures can be easily obtained, have probably been prepared more carefully than an individual evaluator can afford to do, and have been administered widely enough for the development of norms. However, specially prepared instruments can be fine-tuned to fit the exact nature of the program being evaluated.

Published measures are most useful when the program is designed to help all participants to achieve similar outcomes. Many education programs seek to teach skills to children of similar ages regardless of where they attend school. Thus, similar or identical measures of educational program effectiveness can be used in schools at a variety of locations. This is also true of many mental health programs because most counselors seek to help clients to reduce anxiety and depression and to cope with the problems of life. For these reasons evaluators working in educational or mental health settings often use standardized measurement instruments when they seek to learn how well a program is meeting its goals. Similarly, evaluators in medical care facilities can utilize standard laboratory tests indicating healthy physical function. Nevertheless, many programs are designed to affect behaviors that are unique to a particular social system, or, if not unique, at least the planned outcomes of the program are not measured as routinely as are academic achievement, anxiety, work satisfaction, etc. In such cases, the evaluator is required to develop a program-specific measure of impact.

The major disadvantage of published measures is easy to imagine: the program being studied may have goals and purposes not related to any currently published material. For example, there are relatively few special hospital units specifically for nonterminal cancer patients. When the authors were asked to design materials to measure patient reaction to such a new unit, we found little in the literature to help. Once the evaluators have decided that no existing measure is appropriate, a new instrument must be prepared. However, evaluators must be realistic about how much time they can afford to put into the construction of new instruments. The time pressure of work in service settings precludes the routine development of innovative research instruments.

Preparing Special Surveys

Surveys are used so widely in educational, psychological, and policy settings that we present a brief overview of the principles of survey design.

The format of a survey. The format of a survey is an important factor in gaining the cooperation of respondents, analyzing the data, and interpreting the results. If the survey is to be self-administered, the layout must be attractive, uncluttered, and easy to use. A structured answer format is preferable to an open-ended question approach. If a structured survey format is adopted, the survey might still be cluttered if the questions each have different response alternatives. For example, mixing "Yes" and "No" questions, "Agree-Neutral-Disagree" attitude statements, and "Frequently-Seldom-Never" reports of past behavior makes the survey hard to complete. The greater the proportion of questions that can be answered in the same format, the better. Figure 4.2 contains an example of a specially prepared survey that violates good practices. The respondents must repeatedly figure out what type of answer is required of them. People inexperienced in preparing surveys often construct surveys that are difficult to use. Figure 4.3, in contrast, would be easy to complete. The degree of difficulty experienced in completing a survey affects the proportion of respondents who complete it. Not only does a standard response format encourage a greater response rate, but it also increases the ease with which the results can be presented and interpreted; since the results can be summarized on one table, comparisons can easily be made among survey items. The use of an unnecessary variety of response formats can cause as much confusion for readers of a report as it does for respondents to a survey.

When an evaluator seeks the actual words of program participants, and when the range of possible reactions are not known, surveys using open-ended questions are often useful. Patton (1980) used both a structured answer format survey and open-ended questions in evaluating a performance appraisal system in an educational setting. The actual words of the respondents were presented in a way that made it impossible to ignore the unavoidably dry statistical summary of the closed-ended survey questions. At other times evaluators use open-ended questions because they do not know what specific questions to ask. Requesting personal reactions or suggestions for change are two instances in which evaluators do not want to restrict respondents' answers in any way. It is time-consuming to categorize and summarize

```
┌─────────────────────────────────────────────────────────────────┐
│                    High School Evaluation Form                    │
│                                                                   │
│  1.  How do you like attending your high school? (Circle one.)    │
│                                                                   │
│      Very much      Much        OK         Little      Not at all │
│          1           2           3            4             5      │
│                                                                   │
│  2.  How would you describe your teachers? (Check one.)           │
│                                                                   │
│          _____ 1.  Mostly excellent    _____ 4.  Mostly marginal │
│          _____ 2.  Mostly good         _____ 5.  Mostly poor │
│          _____ 3.  Half good/half marginal                    │
│                                                                   │
│  3.  To what extent would you agree with the following statement: The physical │
│      facilities of my high school (classrooms, halls, gym, lunchroom, etc.) are │
│      good.                                                        │
│                                                                   │
│      Strongly       Disagree     Neutral      Agree       Strongly │
│      disagree                                              agree   │
│                                                                   │
│  4.  Are your teachers good teachers and willing to talk with students after regular │
│      classes?    Yes _____     No _____                   │
│                                                                   │
│  5.  What is the place of interscholastic team competition in your school? │
│                                                                   │
│          _____ Not at all important                          │
│          _____ Very important                                │
│          _____ Not sure                                      │
└─────────────────────────────────────────────────────────────────┘
```

FIGURE 4.2 Example of survey items violating many of the principles of easy-to-use, self-administered surveys.

free-form answers. Potential users of open-ended questions should consult materials on qualitative methods (Guba and Lincoln, 1981; Patton, 1980) for detailed directions on analyzing these answers.

Preparing survey items.   There are a number of useful guidelines for preparing survey items. The most important principle is: remember who is expected to respond to the items. A statement that is clear to an evaluator may not be clear to someone reading it from a very different vantage point. Questions that have the best chance of being understood are written clearly, simply, and concisely. Such statements cannot be prepared in one sitting; they must be written, scrutinized, criticized, rewritten, pretested, and rewritten. Items written one week do not seem as acceptable the following week. If the first draft cannot be improved, evaluators have not learned to criticize their own work.

There are several characteristics of clear survey items. The items should avoid negatives. Negatively worded sentences take more effort to read and are misunderstood more frequently than positively worded sentences. Double negatives are especially difficult to read. Well-written items use short, common words rather than less common or longer words. Good survey items focus on one issue. An item such as "My physical therapist was polite and competent" combines two issues. In this case it is possible to interpret an affirmative answer but not possible to interpret a

A coronary patient faces many potential problems during the period of convalescence. Which issues did you encounter and how difficult was your adjustment? Circle your answers.

How much difficulty did (or do) you experience over these potential problems?	Does not apply	None	Little	Some	Much
1. Going back to work	DNA	N	L	S	M
2. Sexual activity	DNA	N	L	S	M
3. Smoking	DNA	N	L	S	M
4. Diet	DNA	N	L	S	M
5. Anxiety	DNA	N	L	S	M
6. Depression	DNA	N	L	S	M
7. Activity restrictions	DNA	N	L	S	M
8. Understanding my doctor	DNA	N	L	S	M
9. My spouse's reaction to my health	DNA	N	L	S	M
10. My family's reaction to my health	DNA	N	L	S	M
11. Other _____ (Please specify)			L	S	M

FIGURE 4.3 A section of a self-administered needs-assessment survey that is easy to use because standard alternatives are provided for each item.

negative answer. What should the director of the unit do if many people answer negatively—have a workshop on charm or on the latest physical therapy practices? Finally, we urge that survey items be grammatically correct.

Several practices can help to detect survey items that need improving. First, the sentence should be read aloud. Often awkward phrasing is more obvious when read aloud than when reviewed silently. Second, someone on the program staff should read the draft items. Third, evaluators should think critically of how to interpret each possible answer to the item. As mentioned above, sometimes one answer can be interpreted but another cannot. Fourth, if ambiguities remain, they probably can be detected if the revised draft is administered as an interview with several people from the population to be sampled.

Ordering of items.   Once survey items are prepared, they must be put into an order that is easy to use and appears logical to the respondent. The first questions should refer to interesting issues and not be threatening. The goal is to entice the potential respondent into beginning the survey. Later, questions dealing with socially controversial issues can be included. It is important to note that people like to be consistent; consequently, the first answers given may affect how people answer the following questions. If this is a severe problem, consider making two different forms of the survey so that the effect of order can be examined. The more routine demographic items (such as age, gender, and occupation) are best placed last since these are the least likely to interest respondents. Babbie (1989) points out that when conducting an interview, such demographic items are asked first in order to build rapport.

Instructions. The instructions accompanying the survey need to be clear. It is best to underestimate the effort people devote to figuring out what is wanted than to provide incomplete instructions. The more informed the respondent group, the more at ease the respondents are in answering a survey.

Pretest. Once the survey has been completed, it cannot be assumed that potential respondents will interpret the instructions and the items in the ways the evaluator intended. The best practice is to take a survey to some representatives of the population expected to complete it. Sometimes evaluators first administer the survey as an interview so that they can learn how people understand the instructions and the items.

SUMMARY AND PREVIEW

The use of multiple measures from multiple sources of information is one of the basic characteristics of valid and useful evaluations. When choosing measures of variables, evaluators should use the criteria of a good measurement instrument to evaluate the specific instruments selected. Is something *important* being measured? Is the measure *sensitive to change*, even small changes? Does the measure seem *valid, reliable,* and *cost effective*? Is *reactivity* to the instrument a problem?

The selection of appropriate criteria for evaluation studies and the use of good ways to measure those criteria are marks not only of competent evaluators, but also of ethically sound work. As applied social scientists whose findings can have practical impact on others, evaluators face a greater number of ethical dilemmas than those who study only theoretical questions. Chapter 5 deals with some of these issues.

STUDY QUESTIONS

1. The following questions violate some of the characteristics of well-phrased survey items. Improve the wording or the structured options of these questions.
   a. Would you like to continue receiving counseling at the ABC Mental Health Center? _____ Yes _____ No
   b. Is the warmth of the staff an important reason for your continued participation in the XYZ Center? _____ Yes _____ No
   c. Please rate the quality of the care you received in the recovery room after your recent surgery. _____ Excellent _____ Good _____ Fair _____ Poor
   d. Police officers do not really care about the feelings of the victims of a crime. _____ Strongly agree _____ Agree _____ Disagree _____ Strongly disagree
   e. The times that services are available during the day should be extended because people are waiting too long for appointments. _____ Yes _____ No
2. Rewrite the items in Figure 4.2 so that they have a common response format.

3. In planning an evaluation of the ALPHA County Community Mental Health Center, the Freudian counselors insist that the Rorschach Inkblot Test be administered at one-month intervals to current clients. What would your reaction be to this proposal?
4. When an evaluation of clinical services was planned, the evaluator introduced the level-of-functioning scale given in Figure 4.1. Some clinicians resisted this suggestion by saying that the scale merely refers to coping behaviors, *not* to intrapsychic growth. What would you respond?
5. Suppose an unethical evaluator wanted to stack the deck in favor of getting a favorable evaluation of a program. What types of measures would one use to achieve this? In the reverse condition, what types of variables would one choose to increase the likelihood of an unfavorable evaluation?

FURTHER READING

MUELLER, D. J. 1986. *Measuring social attitudes: A handbook for researchers and practitioners.* New York: Teachers College Press.
NUNNALLY, J. C., and DURHAM, R. L. 1975. Validity, reliability, and special problems of measurement in evaluation research. In *Handbook of evaluation research*, vol. 1, ed. E. L. Struening and M. Guttentag, chap. 10. Beverly Hills, Calif.: Sage.
NUNNALLY, J. C., and WILSON, W. H. 1975. Method and theory for developing measures in evaluation research. In *Handbook of evaluation research*, vol. 1, ed. E. L. Struening and M. Guttentag, chap. 9. Beverly Hills, Calif.: Sage.
SUDMAN, S., and BRADBURN, N. M. 1982. *Asking questions.* San Francisco: Jossey-Bass.

5

Ethical Standards of Conducting Program Evaluations

Evaluators often find themselves in ethical conflicts seldom experienced by social scientists engaged in basic research. Illustrative dilemmas are provided in two hypothetical situations. Although these scenarios are hypothetical, experienced evaluators can identify with the problems described in the following paragraphs.

A project that cannot be done well. Evelyn Marshall works for a social science research firm, Evaluation, Inc. Her firm is interested in getting a contract to evaluate an early parole program instituted by a state legislature. The question to be answered is whether early parole leads to more or less lawful behavior after release from prison, as compared to the behavior of prisoners paroled after serving the normal time. Marshall realizes that the legislature wants an evaluation that examines whether the program is causally related to a lowered arrest rate after release, and that the evaluation is needed within one year. However, she also learns that the parole board will not randomly assign prisoners to receive early parole and that there are legal reasons why random assignment may be impossible. Under these constraints Marshall knows 12 months is not enough time to test the effectiveness of the program. Should she and her firm conduct the evaluation even though they cannot do what the legislators say they want?

Advocacy versus evaluation. Morris Franklin has completed an evaluation of Central Community Mental Health Center's outreach program for high school students whose poor school performance is thought to be related to drug abuse. As typically occurs, Franklin found evidence supporting the program's effectiveness (students, parents, and school administrators like the program); evidence that does not support the program (grades of the participants did not improve); and some ambivalent evidence that could be interpreted as favorable or unfavorable depending on one's point of view (program students hold more part-time jobs than those not in the program). Franklin's report was received well by his supervisor. Meetings were scheduled to address the participants' grades and the other problems that were uncovered. Evaluator Franklin felt that he had done a good job. Later that month, however, Franklin's supervisor asked him to write a proposal to the school board supporting an extension of the program to other high schools. When the negative findings were mentioned, his supervisor told him to ignore the negative findings and "to be upbeat." Would it be unethical to write the proposal and not mention the known weaknesses of the program that the evaluation detected?

STANDARDS FOR THE PRACTICE OF EVALUATION

The need for ethical standards in research and in program evaluation has been felt by a number of organizations and individuals. Professional organizations have developed extensive statements of what it means to provide service and to conduct research in an ethical manner (see, for example, Ethical principles, 1981). The American Psychological Association (1982) devoted a considerable amount of time and resources to a detailed study of ethical and unethical research practices. This project resulted in a ten-point statement of ethical principles accompanied by a lengthy commentary describing the meaning of the principles, illustrating violations of the principles, and showing how responsible investigators protect the rights of research subjects.

This text interprets ethical standards for evaluators in a fashion that is even broader than that adopted by the American Psychological Association. Since the findings of a program evaluation may be applied in an organization, there are many more chances for the evaluator to violate ethical principles than there are for the basic researcher to do so. In recent years two statements describing principles evaluators should follow have been published. One set of principles was prepared by the Evaluation Research Society (Rossi, 1982), and one was drawn up by a committee sponsored by professional organizations, foundations, and governmental agencies interested in the evaluation of educational programs and projects (Joint Committee on Standards for Educational Evaluation, 1981). Although the latter work was prepared to improve evaluations of educational practice, the principles it sets forth apply to program evaluations in all types of settings.

This chapter includes material based on statements of ethical conduct in research, as well as descriptions of good program evaluation practices. The reason for combining these two issues lies in the authors' belief that ethics in evaluation means more than honesty with money and data and respect for research subjects.

We believe that evaluators have the responsibility to provide clear, useful, and accurate evaluation reports to the organizations for which they work. Furthermore, evaluators have a responsibility to work in a way that has the potential to improve services for people. Ethics are more complicated for evaluators working in settings designed to help people than for basic researchers working on issues with little immediate relevance to organizations because errors in basic social science research are not likely to harm people. There is a long route from a basic research study to an application; along this route are many opportunities to identify erroneous findings. In contrast, poorly done evaluations have affected the provision of services to needy people, disrupted the staffs of service organizations, and encouraged the use of harmful experimental medical treatments. For these reasons, we view ethics in evaluation as including all aspects of conducting an evaluation—from initial planning through presentation of the results to interested parties.

The beginning evaluator can use statements of ethical principles to guide the planning, conduct, and reporting of evaluations. There may well be crucial choices required at all stages of a program evaluation. As Morris Franklin learned, evaluators may perform a very careful evaluation and feel that everything has gone well, only to discover that the dissemination of their findings violates the ethical standards used to guide their work. Ethical issues for evaluators may be divided into five categories: treating people ethically, recognizing role conflicts, maintaining scientific credibility, serving the needs of possible users of the evaluation, and avoiding negative side effects of evaluations.

ETHICAL ISSUES INVOLVED IN THE TREATMENT OF PEOPLE

The first responsibility of the evaluator, as it is with the basic researcher, is to protect people from harm. Since harm can be done to people in a variety of ways, concerned evaluators guard against harm to program participants as well as to the staffs of programs evaluated.

Assignment to Program Groups

Often the first question concerning an evaluator is whether any harm can come to someone receiving the program that is being evaluated. Although medical, educational, and social service programs are offered with the purpose of helping those who participate, sometimes programs have either no impact, or a negative impact. A controversial evaluation was reported by Sobell and Sobell (1978), who designed a program for alcoholics based on behavioristic principles that theoretically should have permitted alcoholics to drink at a moderate level after treatment. The principles underlying this program contradict the traditional assumption that alcoholics cannot drink without once again becoming dependent on alcohol (Burtle, 1979). It is not unethical to conduct an evaluation of such a project; however, the evaluator working with a treatment that contradicts accepted beliefs should be sure that if the treatment fails, the program participants receive adequate additional service so that they will not have been harmed by the evaluation.

Pendery, Maltzman, and West (1982) have argued that Sobell and Sobell did not conduct sufficient follow-up research on the participants in the evaluation in order to learn whether controlled drinking worked for the participants in the program: many were back in the hospital within weeks or months of discharge from the controlled drinking therapy. Nevertheless, in the published version of the evaluation, the Sobells implied that this approach to treatment for alcoholism was a viable alternative to the traditional treatment, which emphasizes abstinence.

Informed Consent

Another way to protect the participant from harm is to obtain the prior agreement of potential program participants who are to take part in the evaluation. This is especially important when the evaluator plans an evaluation including random assignment of program participants to different forms of treatment or to a control group not receiving the treatment. When people are asked for their agreement, it is important for them to understand the request—that is, for their consent to be "informed." Informed consent means that potential participants themselves be allowed to make the decision about whether to participate, and that sufficient information about the program be provided to enable them to weigh all alternatives. If the person is misled or not given sufficient information about the risks involved, then informed consent has not been obtained, even if the person has signed an agreement to participate. Gray, Cooke, and Tannebaum (1978) reported that consent forms are often written at a level of the researcher rather than in a manner that potential program participants can understand.

Seeking to give enough information to enable people to give informed consent may create an additional ethical dilemma for the evaluator. A control group, not receiving the new service under study, may feel competition with the treatment group or, alternatively, may feel unfairly deprived (Cook and Campbell, 1979). If informed consent procedures have the potential to change the behavior of the nonprogram (or traditional program) group, then the validity of the evaluation is threatened. There is no clear way to resolve such an ethical tangle. One approach, adopted by the American Psychological Association, is to consider the costs involved to the participants being studied. For example, Mexican-American women applying for family planning services were randomly assigned to a treatment group (oral contraceptives) or to a control group (dummy, look-alike pills) (Bok, 1974). The high costs of being in the control group—ten pregnancies—argues that these women should have been given complete information about this study. Such gross violations of ethical principles in research and evaluation are far less frequent in recent years than they were in the past.

Confidentiality

Information gathered during the course of an evaluation is to be treated with the utmost care. Whether the information is about program participants, employees, or managers, evaluators violate ethical principles if they conduct the research in a manner that violates people's privacy. There are a number of ways in which evaluators can protect the confidentiality of data used in the evaluation. It is not always necessary to identify data by a person's name. At times researchers have used information to identify records that only the clients or patients themselves would recognize. For example, the first name and birthdate of a respondent's mother would provide a code for gathering all of the person's data together without using the person's name. If it might be necessary to contact the respondent in the future, the project director alone should keep a master list of the respondents' names and addresses and the associated code information. Some workers using very sensitive material have stored the names and code information in a different country. Few evaluators deal with information that sensitive; however, confidentiality is critical.

ROLE CONFLICTS FACING EVALUATORS

Evaluators gather data for the purpose of placing a value on plans for, the implementation of, or the outcome of programs. Since people serving on the staff of these programs earn their living from their work, it should not be surprising that the evaluation process creates conflicts for those involved in evaluating the quality of the services or procedures provided. The most common conflicts arise because most internal evaluators are part of the management team of the organization, but the work of evaluators involves many groups other than managers; because evaluators seek to be as objective as they can but yet are often called upon to be advocates for the organization; and because consultant evaluators need to win contracts to do research in order to maintain the financial health of their company, even when it is hard to complete the evaluation with the desirable scientific rigor. Each of these role conflicts is discussed more fully below.

The clients served by a program have a stake in the outcome of an evaluation; if the program is suspended, they may lose a needed service. The staffs of programs want their work recognized and need the income their jobs generate. A publicly funded program will have stakeholders in the government, and even the taxpaying public has a stake, regardless of whether people are aware of either the specific program or the evaluation that is being conducted. Other stakeholders can be identified by the reader. Evaluators ideally serve all the relevant stakeholders, even though evaluators are usually employed by only one of the stakeholders—the organization management, in the case of most internal or consultant evaluators. In an important sense, many of the ethical dilemmas arise from conflicts of interest among the stakeholders involved with a program. Before conducting an evaluation, it is wise to consider all the people who might be affected by the outcome. As is stated in Chapter 2, it is crucial to form a clear idea of who wants a program evaluated before beginning an evaluation. However, the evaluator has a better understanding of ethical issues if the needs of all the stakeholders are considered, whether they want an evaluation or not.

To illustrate the process of identifying the stakeholders of a program, consider the case of an evaluator charged with conducting an evaluation of a new method of sentencing convicted criminals. A state governor proposed and the legislature passed a sentencing procedure for certain crimes called *Class X crimes*. The legislation was passed because there was a widely held opinion that the sentencing practices of judges were too lenient and were quite different from judge to judge. The legislation, in effect, took the question of length of jail sentence out of the judges' hands for certain crimes: a defendant judged guilty of a Class X crime now faced a sentence determined by law. Who were the stakeholders in this situation?

First, the state legislature that commissioned the evaluation was a stakeholder, since it wrote the law that was being evaluated. The governor had a stake in the outcome of the study, since he proposed the law. The governor would want all evaluations of his work to be favorable in order to enhance his chances of reelection. Those state legislators who favored the law likewise desired a favorable finding. In contrast, some legislators who opposed the law may have preferred to see their position vindicated by a finding that the law had not had its intended effect. All the citizens who look to the courts to assist in preventing dangerous individuals from committing additional crimes had an interest in this work. Judges, too, had a stake in the findings of the study, since it was their day-to-day behavior that was being studied. Prison officials needed to be aware of evaluation findings, especially with respect to the possible influence of the new sentencing procedures on their facilities. Police officers also were interested to learn how the new sentencing procedures had been implemented. Defense lawyers, defendants, and the state attorney's office also had stakes in the outcome of the evaluation, since their strategies depend on how sentences are determined. Clearly, many groups care about the findings of program evaluations.

Effective evaluators take the range of stakeholders into account as they plan, conduct, and report their work. The conflicting expectations of different stakeholders can lead to ethical difficulties for evaluators. Anticipating these and other conflicts can spell the difference between intolerable problems—resulting in the evaluation becoming a political football—and a carefully planned, even if controversial, evaluation.

Evaluators should try to minimize conflicts among the wants of various stakeholders before the evaluation begins, since they are subject to less pressure if they can negotiate agreements on such issues as: Who will have access to results? What information is to be used? How would different patterns of data be interpreted? If the study begins without settling these issues, the probability that different groups can manipulate the evaluation to suit their own purposes increases. At times jealousies and disputes about ownership of information have made it impossible to conduct a credible evaluation. Stakeholders who do not want an evaluation conducted benefit from such an outcome; however, all others lose.

Public conflicts among stakeholders complicate the work of evaluators; however, less visible conflicts also exist. Some writers argue from a social justice ethical point of view (see Rawls, 1971) that evaluators should examine the program assumptions and outcomes in order to learn if justice is served by the program and how it is administered. It would be unethical to evaluate the degree to which a program achieved reprehensible outcomes (Ericson, 1990). Richardsen (1990) argues that it would be inappropriate for an evaluator to study a school program for "at-risk" students without carefully examining the school setting and school practices, even if the practices are widely accepted, that could be detrimental to student progress. She argues, for example, that grading the work of elementary school students contributes to failure rather than to the educational process.

THE SCIENTIFIC QUALITY OF THE EVALUATION

Once the possibility of harm to program participants is minimized and potential role conflicts are explored, the evaluator can turn to ethical issues associated with the scientific quality of the evaluation project. It is the authors' view that conducting evaluations that are invalid for the purpose for which they were commissioned is just as unethical as, for example, not protecting the confidentiality of information obtained from participants. The next sections cover the ethical ramifications of four of the most frequently found threats to the scientific validity of evaluations.

Valid Measurement Instruments

Evaluators in educational and mental health settings frequently use standardized, published tests in measuring the expected outcomes of the program being evaluated. The most well developed tests are standardized achievement tests designed to estimate a child's progress in school. Because these tests are so well developed, there is a temptation to apply them even when they may not be appropriate to measure the outcomes of a program. In other words, one cannot simply ask if a measurement tool is valid because validity also depends on the setting and the specific program participants. Choosing an inappropriate way to measure a hypothesized outcome can obscure the effects of a program (Lipsey et al., 1985; Lipsey, 1990b) or, even worse, lead to a misleading conclusion. For example, an evaluation of a school program on ecology used as an outcome measure a standardized achievement subtest on science, including topics on hygiene, biology, and earth science (Joint Committee, 1981). This subtest was not appropriate for measuring the achievement of the students in the innovative ecology course. The evaluation's negative findings did not reflect the actual results of the program.

Evaluators make mistakes, just as all people do. However, failing even to consider the specific content of the course and the actual material covered by the selected subtest can be considered unethical conduct on the part of a professional evaluator. It is unlikely that any standardized test exists to measure the achievement of students in an ecology course, because few such courses have been taught until recently: The evaluator should have recognized that. The school district would have been better off had the evaluation not been conducted at all; the program was saddled with a negative evaluation, which—although invalid—had to be explained by program supporters.

Skilled Data Collectors

It is likely that a standardized test can be competently administered by people with little training; however, many evaluations use information collected through personal interviews. Interviewing is not an easy job. Good interviewers possess skills and common sense that will permit them to obtain the information needed without injecting biases, and to maintain the good will of the person interviewed. It requires a degree of maturity and a respect for truth to be able to record and report attitudes at variance with one's own. An early study (Rice, 1929) found that two interviewers of destitute men were reporting very different answers to an interview question concerning why these men found themselves in their current condition. One interviewer reported that many men attributed their problems to alcohol; the other interviewer reported that many said they were the victims of an unjust society. The fact that the first interviewer favored prohibition while the second was a Marxist suggests that the interviewer's reports were influenced by their own political views.

It is not always easy to obtain the cooperation of the individuals to be interviewed. Guba and Lincoln (1981) note that interviewers need to exercise polite persistence as they seek to interview program participants. Carey (1974) interviewed terminally ill patients as part of an evaluation of hospital care for dying patients. It is difficult to conduct such interviews without appearing to care more about data than about the personal tragedies of the patients. Children present a very different type of problem. Interviewing children in a compensatory education program designed to improve self-confidence, study habits, and social skills requires patience and skill to gain the cooperation of the children. An interviewer without experience in working with children may learn very little about their feelings, because children do not respond to the same demands as adults do. Indeed, if young children do not feel respected, they may not say anything at all!

Appropriate Research Design

One of the themes of this book is that the research design must fit the needs of those who may utilize the information. As later chapters illustrate, different needs require more or less scientific rigor. However, once a need is articulated, it is unethical to conduct an evaluation if it is known at the outset that the planned evaluation cannot answer the questions that the sponsors of the evaluation put to the evaluator. This seems to be the ethical dilemma faced by Evelyn Marshall, as outlined in the introduction to this chapter. Although her company needs the work, and although the program should be evaluated, it seems unlikely that she can conduct an evaluation to answer the questions the state legislature has presented to her company.

At this point Marshall has at least three alternatives: (1) go ahead and do the evaluation, (2) decline to conduct the evaluation and hope that an alternative job comes by to keep her productively employed, or (3) negotiate on the actual questions to be addressed by the evaluation. The first alternative is unethical, and the second is risky for Marshall; the third may well prove productive. Frequently sponsors of evaluation are unskilled in research methods and do not know when they have given an evaluator an impossible assignment. It may be that the legislature does not really require an evaluation that traces the causes of any possible changes in parole procedures. What is actually needed may be only a careful documentation of the actual implementation of the new law. If negotiations reveal that implementation is the main issue, Marshall can conduct the evaluation; in fact, she can now do a better job than would have been possible fruitlessly trying to trace causal relationships.

Adequate Descriptions of Programs and Procedures

One of the basic characteristics of science is its public nature. Science is to be conducted in such a way that other scientists can evaluate the procedures used and repeat the same research. Only in this way can errors in research be detected. Frequently evaluations are not described in sufficient detail to permit others to fully understand either the program or the evaluation procedures. Patton (1980) illustrated the advantage of describing the program as an aspect of conducting a program evaluation. He found that an evaluation of a program to help economically disadvantaged young mothers learn parenting and financial management skills concluded that the program was ineffective—even though the program was not implemented. If the evaluators had taken the effort to observe and describe the program as put into effect (not just as planned), they would have learned that there was so much political resistance, the program never even occurred. In a review of many evaluations, Lipsey et al. (1985) discovered that a large proportion of evaluations did not address implementation issues.

Besides describing the program, the evaluation procedures should be presented in enough detail so that others can understand how the evaluator obtained and analyzed information. As will be mentioned later, all interested parties do not want to know every detail. However, such detailed reports should be available to others who want to implement the program or who want to compare evaluations conducted in different settings. If it is impossible to compare evaluations because they are inadequately reported, one might wonder if the report writers were clear in their own minds about what was done.

RECOGNIZING THE NEEDS OF ALL STAKEHOLDERS

The stakeholder concept was introduced in the context of potential role conflicts for evaluators. Considering the different stakeholders is also important for making an evaluation as useful as possible for all those who may use or be influenced by the evaluation. Figure 5.1 illustrates how stakeholders' views can lead to different conclusions, even when evaluating the same information.

Program Managers Are Concerned with Efficiency

Those who are responsible for managing an organization are concerned about the efficiency of its services and operations. Profit-making firms must produce goods and services in an efficient manner; otherwise, competing firms can serve customers at a lower cost. In time inefficient firms go out of business or are bought out by more efficient ones. Nonprofit human service agencies do not operate on the same principles as profit-making firms; however, effective managers still strive to

---

Success or Boondoggle? It Depends on How You Look at It

Differences in the views of various stakeholders are illustrated in the controversy over "workfare" programs, which require applicants for welfare to hold part-time, temporary jobs. The idea is that welfare recipients should do some work for the assistance they require. While they continue to look for steady work, they spend a week or two a month in public or nonprofit organizations doing jobs that would not have been filled by a regular employee.

Some critics say the program is shortsighted, that the people do not learn real work skills, and that the state does not adequately supervise these temporary "employees." Other critics say workfare merely requires welfare applicants to "sing for your supper," making welfare programs punitive. A public aid official counters by saying that some workfare participants need workfare to learn that holding a job requires coming to work, staying all day, not hitting anyone, and bathing before they go to work. Nonprofit service organizations report that the day-care, janitorial, and food service assistance they get through workfare has improved their services to other low-income people.

An evaluator would be hard pressed to gather data that would be acceptable to all stakeholders, because there are fundamental value conflicts that data will not resolve.

FIGURE 5.1   An illustration of how stakeholders' values can conflict. (*Source:* Brotman, 1983)

provide the maximum amount of service possible to clients, students, or patients in their agencies. The most important aspect of an evaluation in a manager's judgment may frequently be information on the efficiency of the program. A later chapter discusses the cost-benefit questions so important to managers.

An Evaluation Can Help the Staff

The needs of the staff are best served if the evaluation can provide practical guidance, improving the effectiveness with which they serve clients, students, patients, or customers. An evaluation of the flow of information through a large division of a firm may reveal inefficiencies. If the staff is provided with viable alternatives to the current procedures, they have been well served by the evaluation. An evaluation of teaching effectiveness in a college can help identify the areas in which new faculty members have the most difficulty and, thus, lead department chairs and college deans to develop preventive actions to assist new faculty before problems develop. An evaluation of a medical residency program can document not only the proportions of unnecessary medical tests ordered by residents, but the reasons for the errors in judgment. In this way the education program can be improved and the residents can serve their future patients better. Recommendations that are accompanied by a consideration of the costs to implement them are examined more carefully than those whose cost implications have not been analyzed.

Evaluators also know that an evaluation is a good vehicle for giving staff members recognition for good work. Evaluations that are unnecessarily one-sided neglect some legitimate needs of the staff—an important stakeholder group in an internal evaluation.

Clients Can Be Served by an Evaluation

An effective evaluation must also consider the program participants. Clients frequently have no voice in the planning or implementation of either programs or evaluations. Upon reflection, this fact seems almost bizarre: The group most affected by programs is the least consulted. However, clients are not unified, they seldom have spokespersons, and they do not hire evaluators. Among the ways evaluators can fulfill their responsibility to clients is to compare the needs of the program participants with the services offered, to help the staff and manager better understand the needs of participants, and to structure recommendations around the clients' needs. It is not unknown for recommendations to be made without an adequate understanding of the client population. The needs of the manager and the staff have sometimes taken precedence over those of the client.

Another aspect of the stake students, patients, or trainees have in an evaluation is their interest in continuing to receive service during the evaluation. It is usually impossible to conduct an evaluation without causing any disruption in the work of the staff and in service to participants. Ethical concerns for the needs of program participants require that service disruption be minimized.

Community Members as Stakeholders

Most service agencies receive some of their financial support from the community by way of taxation or contributions, or indirectly through reductions in property taxes. In some ways the community is in the same position as the client population: the community is dispersed and does not have easily identifiable spokespersons. Perhaps the most ambitious approach to involving the community in the evaluation process is the citizen evaluation model developed for the National Institute of Mental Health (NIMH) (Zinober and Dinkel, 1981). Following procedures and using materials prepared by NIMH, community citizens can evaluate community mental health centers themselves. This approach is one way to ensure that the stake of the community will be recognized. While this endeavor requires the commitment of citizens, it can—and has—been done (Albright, 1982).

Financial Backers

Human service agencies usually have the financial support of government bodies, charitable organizations, or foundations. These groups certainly have a stake in the success of the programs they support. Frequently governmental offices and foundations commission evaluations of programs receiving their support. In these instances their interests are probably well protected. Ethically planned internal evaluations should also reflect the interests of the groups that supply the financial backing for the service agencies.

AVOIDING POSSIBLE NEGATIVE SIDE EFFECTS
OF EVALUATION PROCEDURES

The ethical issues covered in this section are less central to the conduct of basic research; however, in the applied research arena these questions can take on immense importance both for evaluators and for the stakeholders affected by the evaluation study.

Can Someone Be Hurt by Inaccurate Findings?

Inaccurate findings can either show falsely positive findings—erroneously suggesting that the program is effective—or falsely negative findings—erroneously suggesting that the program is not effective. When such false conclusions are due to random statistical variation, the first false finding is called a Type I error, and the second is termed a Type II error. Such false conclusions can also be made when insufficient attention is paid to the design of an evaluation. Without careful thought, evaluations sometimes focus on the wrong variables or use too short a time span to show either positive or negative effects. At other times an evaluator's enthusiasm for a program may lead to falsely optimistic conclusions.

The possibly misleading work on alcoholism treatment by Sobell and Sobell (1978) has been discussed in the light of the follow-up study done by Pendery, Maltzman, and West (1982). It is possible that the treatment of alcoholics at other institutions may have been redesigned when therapists read of the apparently favorable results the Sobells claimed for the controlled drinking therapy. Basic researchers are cautioned to care for the safety and welfare of the people actually studied in an experiment. In addition, evaluators need to think about how program planners might use an evaluation of a program. Inadvertently encouraging the use of a harmful program due to insufficient care in conducting an evaluation is an ethical problem with which basic researchers need rarely be concerned; however, it is often an important issue for evaluators.

In contrast to falsely favorable evaluations, falsely negative evaluations can also harm people by encouraging the elimination of beneficial services. Lazar (1981) described one overlooked aspect of preschool programs such as Head Start. According to Lazar, Head Start, a summer preschool program for economically disadvantaged children, made its strongest contribution to the future school achievement of the children not by what it taught, but by the way it involved mothers in the education of their children. Showing mothers how to work with their children and introducing them to the school system encouraged them to develop a level of involvement with the education of their children often not found among lower income families. This involvement could have been achieved regardless of the actual content of the summer programs. Evaluations that focused only on the intellectual growth of the children during the eight-week program were too narrow. The falsely negative conclusions could have harmed other children if preschool programs had been eliminated. Comprehensive evaluations of programs such as Head Start have shown them to be effective (Darlington et al., 1980), in contrast to the initial study (Cicarelli et al., 1969).

Statistical Type II Errors

Type II errors (concluding that a program is ineffective when it is in fact effective) can occur because the sample of program participants involved in the evaluation was small or just happened to be atypical. Whenever measurements are made on a sample of people rather than on the whole population, and whenever measurement instruments are not perfectly reliable, random variation can produce Type II errors. Evaluators can seldom test whole populations, and the information sources available to evaluators are never perfectly reliable. Basic researchers worry about Type II errors because it is a waste of time to conduct research that yields inaccurate conclusions. However, Type II errors in a basic research study typically cause no harm to others. Evaluators, on the other hand, have an additional worry about random statistical errors: They do not want to conclude falsely that a valued program is ineffective. Thus, evaluators are much more concerned about Type II errors than are basic researchers (Lipsey et al., 1985; Schneider and Darcy, 1984).

Unfortunately, evaluators work in situations that make Type II errors very likely. In an attempt to reduce the demands made on program participants asked to provide data, short surveys may be used and the number of variables may be limited. To reduce the disruption of services, only a few participants may be tested. In other cases there may only be relatively few participants in an expensive program to be evaluated or the evaluator may not be given sufficient resources to measure the outcome variables on a large number of participants. In such cases the possibility of making Type II errors is increased. After reviewing 122 published program evaluations, Lipsey et al. (1985) concluded that the research design of a large proportion of evaluations was too weak to detect even a moderately sized effect, not to mention a small effect. Lipsey's (1990b) stress on the reliability of measurement tools implies that ethical evaluators exert effort in the development of measures in order to achieve as reliable measures as possible.

Pay Attention to Unplanned Program Effects

Ethical evaluators are careful to examine the programs as implemented, not just as designed. One aspect of this issue is the low level of actual implementation of programs as already discussed. A second aspect of this issue involves possible negative side effects of a program. Just as physicians are concerned about side effects of medications, evaluators work most effectively when they are alert to unexpected negative features of a program. For example, welfare procedures may demean recipients, prison regulations may cause dependency leading to more difficulty in making decisions after release, and an arbitrary method of introducing improved working conditions may alienate employees. Such outcomes, of course, are not found in the goals of the program as planned. In fact, program planners and managers might not even anticipate these results. One way to imagine possible negative side effects is to contact critics of the program. Although program supporters view such contacts as unnecessary, evaluators can do more useful work if they detect important negative side effects of programs.

Chapman and Risley (1974) described a program whereby children were paid to pick up and turn in litter. The program developers did not expect the children to bring in bags of household garbage from their homes: the program staff refused to pay for these bags. The children then threw the household garbage into nearby yards, certainly an unwanted side effect. The program was revised so that payment was made not for bags full of litter but for cleaning up specified yards. Recognizing a negative side effect led to a better program. Table 5.1 includes some additional negative side effects of policies with desirable goals.

Unexamined Values Held by the Evaluator

Conflicts between the role of program advocate and the role of evaluator have already been mentioned. The evaluation may also be rendered less valid if values are assumed by the evaluator without examination. Sjoberg (1975) suggests that evaluators typically accept the existing power structure and adopt its values with little reflection. For example, embezzlement is not treated as a major crime because, according to Sjoberg, it is a middle- and upper-class crime. He also suggests that many teenagers are labeled delinquent because they violate the norms of those who hold the power in society. Sjoberg has highlighted an important issue for evaluators, whether or not one agrees with his examples. He has argued forcefully that the needs of all groups with a stake in the evaluation cannot be met if the evaluator has implicitly adopted the values of the most powerful group involved with the evaluation. Clearly, it is difficult to recognize assumed values. One way to guard against the effects of such implicit values is to avoid working with only the individuals planning or offering the service. Trying to learn what participants seek in the program may yield insights not gained in discussions with professionals.

Other unexamined values may be hidden in statistical analyses. Ball and Bogartz (1970) examined the overall mean achievement of children watching "Sesame Street" and concluded that the series was successful in achieving some of its goals. Cook et al. (1975), however, divided the children on the basis of socioeconomic background and concluded that the program was not effective.

TABLE 5–1   Seeking to Achieve Desirable Goals Has Led to Serious Side Effects Unexpected by the Program Developers

DESIRABLE GOAL	PROGRAM	NEGATIVE SIDE EFFECT
Reduce auto pollution	Pollution control devices	Reduced gas mileage
Save energy	Burn waste forestry products for heat	Loss of nutrients currently returned to the soil
Improve food production in poor nations	Use fertilizers and farm machinery	Poor farmers who could not afford costs sold farms and became unemployed city dwellers
Test public school teacher competence	Remove incompetent and under-trained teachers	Insulted good teachers; implied that meeting the minimum standards meant someone is a good teacher

Among other things, the program was specifically designed to improve the cognitive skills of children from low socioeconomic areas. One reason the cast includes many members of minority groups is to increase the chances of children from minority groups watching the program. Nevertheless, Cook et al. learned that the cognitive skill gap between lower- and upper-class children who watched "Sesame Street" actually increased. Therefore, although watching the program had a positive impact, it did not provide the special help to disadvantaged children that was a fundamental goal of the program. Without a creative reanalysis of the evaluation, this important—but subtle—finding would have been overlooked. The social justice ethical viewpoint asserts that when benefits are uneven, the least privileged group should benefit the most (Bunda, 1983).

SUMMARY AND PREVIEW

The major ethical issues involved in conducting research fall under five topics: the protection of the people studied, the danger of role conflicts, threats to the scientific quality of evaluations, the varying needs of different groups who may be influenced by the evaluation, and negative side effects that may be related to the program or to the way of conducting the evaluation. The applied and political nature of the settings in which program evaluations are conducted is very important. The applied setting creates more ethical dilemmas than the basic research setting. Although these conflicts and limitations require evaluators to exercise considerable care in conducting evaluations, these issues make the role of the evaluator vital and exciting.

This chapter completes the general, introductory chapters. We now move into specific tasks of the evaluator. Evaluators help clarify program goals and the program's conceptual foundation by measuring the need for a program and by developing procedures to monitor a program's activities. These aspects of program evaluation are addressed in the next two chapters.

STUDY QUESTIONS

1. Analyze the different views of the various stakeholders who would be involved with a teacher evaluation procedure in a college or university.
2. Contrast the dangers of Type I and Type II errors in basic research versus those in program evaluation, with special regard to ethical considerations.
3. Some evaluators do not mention all negative or unfavorable findings in official evaluation reports, but do bring such issues to the attention of program managers during private meetings. What are the pros and cons of this practice?

FURTHER READING

JOINT COMMITTEE ON STANDARDS FOR EDUCATIONAL EVALUATION. 1981. *Standards for evaluations of educational programs, projects, and material.* New York: McGraw-Hill.

KIMMEL, A. J. 1988. *Ethics and values in applied social research.* Newbury Park, Calif.: Sage.

6

The Assessment of Need

Human service and educational programs are developed to serve people in need. Congress appropriates funds for federal nutrition agencies, towns sponsor volunteer fire departments, and school districts build and staff schools because communities have decided that needs of people will be unmet without such action. How do we decide that there is a need to be met through community action? Who decides? What information can be gathered to demonstrate the level of community need? Do people ever disagree over degree of need or whether there is a need for any community action? How does an evaluator work with planners in deciding what kinds of programs will be planned?

Informally, perceptions of need are greatly influenced by local and national media. If a local newspaper runs a series of articles on local crime, people begin to feel less safe even if they experience no direct problems themselves. The attention that national news programs devote to certain issues can fan passions increasing the outcry for attention to the problem highlighted. Groups that attract the attention of media often create the sense that their concerns are more important than those of others. Parents of a few severely ill children have gotten media attention and then obtained special care for their children while hundreds of other children with similar illnesses have continued to be treated in routine manners.

Although the opinions formed by media feed into political judgments about what is needed and what should be funded, planning agencies and organization-level planning committees usually seek more quantified, representative information on which to base their planning. When we analyze the way people use the term "need," we discover that people mean many different things when they say that they need something. In this chapter, we first develop a definition of need so that an evaluator can be clear on how the term is being used.

This chapter also includes discussions of the most widely used methods of studying the need for human services and their particular strengths and weakness. Internal evaluators seek to be part of planning committees, especially if it is likely that evaluators will be called upon to conduct a program evaluation of the project being planned. If evaluators are included in planning committees, their applied research expertise can help planning committees.

DEFINITIONS OF NEED

Many analyses of need do not include a definition of "a need." When evaluators and program staff talk about need assessments, they usually mean that a discrepancy between what is and what should be has been found. Roth (1976/1990) pointed out that there are at least five discrepancies that people could have in mind when they speak of needs. There might be a discrepancy between an actual state and (a) an ideal, (b) a norm, (c) a minimum, (d) a desired, or (e) an expected state. In social service settings, it is probably safe to assume that discrepancies from ideals are seldom being discussed. But sometimes discrepancies from a norm are used to define a need as occurs when schoolchildren of normal aptitude perform below a norm. Or, we might say that faculty members need to have convenient access to word processing facilities because it would be desirable. However, this approach permits one to conclude that people who enjoy an actual state that equals or exceeds the norm, minimum, or expected states, do not have a need (Scriven and Roth, 1978). This would lead to the odd conclusion that Americans drinking a glass of orange juice each morning do not need vitamin C since they have enough. This example shows that a discrepancy definition, if used alone, is not logical. Most assuredly, people do need vitamin C because without it we would soon become ill.

It is likely that many evaluators have been able to conduct need assessments without a clear definition of need because program planners possess an implicit understanding of what was meant; nevertheless, it seems wise to adopt a definition. Scriven and Roth's definition has merit: need refers to something *(X)* that people must have to be in a satisfactory state with regard to some aspect of experience. Without *X* they would be in an unsatisfactory state; with *X* they achieve but do not exceed a satisfactory state. For example, people need access to a health care worker when they accidentally cut themselves and require stitches, but access to a plastic surgeon to correct a slightly misshaped ear is not a need.

Assessing the level of need for planning or restructuring a social service agency means looking for potential services needed to bring people up to a satisfactory state and that are not now available. Needs will differ depending on the community and the people being studied. Most people in the world live in situations in which a liberal arts college education is not a need. However, in industrialized nations a college degree is very important and, indeed, needed. A wealthy socialite may want a car phone for status and convenience, but his life would hardly be unsatisfactory without it. However, a marketing executive may need a car phone for customer contact because without it, she may lose enough business to place her in the unsatisfactory state of unemployment.

Lurking beneath some of the confusion about the definition of need is the distinction between things people need on a regular basis (such as oxygen or vitamin C) versus things needed only once (such as a high school education). Another confusion occurs among those community resources whose use is fairly predictable (such as elementary schools) versus those whose use may be predictable for a whole community, but whose use cannot be predicted on an individual citizen basis (such as a trauma center). Individuals may believe that they will never need a trauma center (and most people will be right), but the community at large may need a trauma center.

When estimating need for any type of program, the distinction between incidence of a problem and prevalence of a problem is worth making. Incidence refers to the number of times a problem is experienced. Prevalence refers to the number of people who have the problem at a given time. For example, the incidence rate of the common cold is high: many people get at least one during a year. However, people usually recover quickly, so the prevalence at any one time is low. The distinction is important: a response to a problem will be different depending on whether the problem is viewed as widespread but temporary, or less widespread but long lasting. For example, attempts to help unemployed people will differ depending on whether it is believed that most of the unemployed are merely between jobs or that unemployed people are likely to be out of work for a long period of time.

Note that the definition developed does not rely on people knowing that they have a particular need. People may be unaware of a need (an iron deficiency), deny a need (an alcoholic denying a need for rehabilitation), or misidentify a need (adolescents desiring drugs when what they need is social acceptance). Of course, often people do know when they need assistance with housing, education, health care, or employment. Defining needs as Scriven and Roth have done implies that there is no one procedure or one source of data that leads to a valid assessment of needs.

SOURCES OF INFORMATION FOR THE ASSESSMENT OF NEED

The major sources of relevant information include objective information about the social and economic realities of a given community, information that people themselves provide in a survey, and the conclusions of experts who know the target people. Before heading out with need surveys in hand, several preliminary issues ought to be addressed. First, who are the people whose unmet needs are being studied? Second, what are the relevant resources currently available to these people?

Describing the Current Situation

Population to be studied. The population to be studied should be defined first. It might be a state, a school district, or the employees of a particular factory or business. Instead of defining the population as all the members of some group, the population whose unmet needs are to be assessed might be defined as unemployed men, home-bound elderly, or pregnant teenagers in some community. Understanding their numbers, characteristics, and home locations before beginning could be helpful. A planning committee for a governmental agency may have an easier time with this task because there are legally defined limits of responsibility and authority. Private organizations such as hospitals or businesses may have more difficulty in defining the size of the community and identifying the people they wish to serve with a new clinic or new product. A university opening a branch campus would want to know how many of its current students live in the area of the new campus, how many new high school graduates are expected in the next few years, and how many people in the area are enrolled in continuing education programs already. Such information could be easy and inexpensive to obtain, but other descriptors of the population could be difficult and costly to obtain. The need assessment report might show that part of the relevant group has great unmet needs, while other parts require no additional attention. Learning what they do now to meet needs would be helpful.

One contribution that the evaluator can make to the planning process is a concern with specificity. It is one thing to talk about juvenile delinquency and quite another to know the percentage of community male adolescents aged 16 to 19 arrested each year. Knowing that the elderly of a community lack easy access to social opportunities has less impact than knowing that 2,000 citizens over age 70 have no access to public transportation and that half of them would require public transportation in order to participate in programs for the elderly held in the town hall.

Converting problems into a quantitative form is important since people offering a service often overestimate the prevalence of a problem with which they are familiar. The decision hueristic, called availability, refers to the process whereby particularly memorable events lead one to overestimate the frequency of those events (Tversky and Kahneman, 1973).

This process was brought home forcefully to us when a hospital agreed to supply a comparison group in a study of the success of a rehabilitation unit largely serving stroke patients. Part of the motivation to cooperate lay in the expectation that the study would show that the hospital should open up its own rehabilitation unit. It became clear as the study progressed that the groups wanting a new unit had overestimated the number of stroke patients being treated. Since stroke patients are so different from other patients and have so many needs, the presence of only a few led the staff to believe that stroke victims made up a sizable number of their patients, when there actually were only a few.

Current relevant services in the area. Someone considering opening up a McDonald's in a community knows that it is unlikely that the residents have no food now, or that fast food is currently unavailable. It is important for the people involved with the new outlet to learn what restaurants are now available in the community and to mark them on a map. Similarly, community mental health planners can expect people experiencing emotional distress to have sought help not only from social workers and psychologists, but also from relatives, clergy, physicians, and even bartenders.

When examining current resources, the planning committee forms an evaluation of their value. For social support in facing normal life stresses, relatives and clergy are probably adequate. But for major psychological disturbances, more specialized assistance would be helpful.

Social Indicators of Need

Communities needing additional social services probably display many dysfunctional characteristics. Trying to measure the degree of dysfunction, or its converse, well-being, is difficult. One approach is to track social variables that are symptoms of social problems. Just as symptoms of physical illnesses can be troublesome in themselves though not the actual illness, social indicators can suggest the underlying social problems that should be addressed (Carley, 1981; Ferriss, 1988). As social problems are resolved, the social indicators used should show a lower degree of social distress and dysfunction. Some useful social indicators include divorce rate, crime rates, proportion of citizens below the poverty level, proportion of children graduating from high school, and unemployment rate. While our focus is on social problems that call out for community interventions to help resolve problems, social indicators are also used in the popular press to list the best communities in which to live (Boyer, 1989).

Where are social indicators found? The decennial federal census provides an objective approach to measuring the extent of need using social indicators. The findings of each census are divided into census tracts and enumeration districts, which are smaller than tracts. Obtaining summary data for the communities of interest permits evaluators and planners to examine many variables that could indicate unmet needs for services. Since census data may be broken down by race, gender, and age, it is possible to pinpoint areas of greatest need. Furthermore, comparing the community under study with the pattern for the whole region, state, or nation makes it easier to detect differences that reveal needs. Figure 6.1 is a list of variables used in one need assessment study to estimate the level of need for mental health services in a rural area of Illinois.

Social indicators are also available in crime rate reports from the FBI. States as well as the Department of Labor track rates of employment and unemployment. The Gross National Product and the Consumer Price Index, prepared by the Department of Commerce, are social indicators that reveal the level of economic activity and the rate of inflation. Other social indicators come from private sources. The mean SAT scores, reported by the Educational Testing Service, reveal something about the state of the American high schools and the percentage of babies born prematurely, reported by the Robert Wood Johnson Foundation, reveals something

Age distribution of population
Percentage of teenagers not in school
Percentage of working mothers of children under 18
Percentage of working mothers of preschool children
Percentage of aged persons living alone
Percentage of aged persons in poverty[a]
Percentage of extremely crowded housing units[b] without plumbing facilities
Percentage of large households[c] with low income
Percentage of disabled persons not in institutions
Percentage of disabled persons not in institutions and unable to work

[a]Based on local income levels
[b]More than one person per room
[c]Six or more persons

FIGURE 6.1 Census data used in a needs assessment study. (*Source: Community Mental Health Plan, Spoon River, Illinois.* Spoon River Community Mental Health Center, Inc., 1977)

about the health of mothers. Many organizations founded to support social and health causes compile and publicize indicators such as the amount of campaign contributions given to politicians by large organizations, the level of citizen confidence in the President, or the number of hazardous waste dumps in each state. We are awash in social indicators. Evaluators who know where to find the most useful ones can obtain inexpensive information to use in assessments of need. One could begin looking for sources of appropriate social indicators in articles related to public policy on the topic of interest.

Metro Chicago Information Center has started to organize existing community information and to administer an annual community survey for Chicago and the surrounding six-county area. Agencies planning new programs and analysts assisting government policy-making bodies have access to a rich source of information. Evaluators and planners are wise to search for such information clearinghouses before launching a need assessment.

How helpful are these indicators in planning human service programs or government policies? This is a hard question to answer. With physical health, a high temperature indicates a problem. However, the problem causing the temperature is not clear. Without a valid theory connecting a high temperature with an illness, ineffective remedies may be used. Recall that during Colonial times, a flushed face and high temperature were thought to indicate the presence of too much blood. That theory led physicians to bleed people.

Using social indicators to define community problems and to develop programs requires knowing the relationships between the indirect measures of the problem and the underlying social, educational, or economic malady. Gaining such knowledge is certainly not easy. What is the malady underlying the decline in SAT scores? Some say it is TV, a passive entertainment taking attention away from reading; others the loss of parents able to take an interest in school work; and still others unimaginative teachers. The alleged maladies suggest different remedies. Even if we agreed on the malady, sometimes one cause may suggest different responses. If teachers are not doing a good job, perhaps teachers should be paid more to attract more competent people, perhaps we need to test teachers, or perhaps teacher certification requirements are keeping out people with wide experiences who may be excellent teachers, but who lack the proper credentials.

Do these problems mean that social indicators cannot be used? No, but these difficulties do mean that social indicators cannot be the only source of information about the need of a community for a social program. Social indicators can tell us that problems exist and where they are most predominant. They cannot tell us what the fundamental problem is or what society should do about it. Other sources of information can assist evaluators and planners to be more specific about the causes of the underlying problems and the options for attacking them.

It is important to note that social indicators can be corrupted. De Neufville (1975) reports that the Nixon administration sought to suppress information showing that the rate of unemployment in urban centers was reaching 20 to 25 percent. Other nations have experienced great problems when local governments were forced or at least strongly encouraged to produce favorable reports indicating economic progress. Fraudulent social indicators are ultimately discredited, but often not until inappropriate policies have been implemented (De Neufville, 1975). As with all data, evaluators do well if they carefully evaluate the validity of social indicators before using them.

Community Surveys of Need

A straightforward way to estimate community needs is simply to ask people about their needs. The residents of a community have certain attitudes toward the development of human services and toward the particular services needed. Their attitudes can be part of the planning. If the service is relevant to all citizens, the community ideally should be surveyed systematically to obtain a representative sample of the opinions of the residents. Obtaining a truly representative sample is extremely difficult and thus expensive. Avoiding clearly biased samples, however, is possible if the planner is careful in the selection of community respondents. Interviewing only professionals, only low-income residents, or only elderly people would render the results useless. A possible compromise is to use intact groups that are likely to be fairly representative of the community. Such a course would not be expensive, because intact groups completing a survey do not require much time from a survey administrator. Public schools and church groups are two sources of respondents that may be available to a planning group. Depending on the nature of the program being planned, special groups of likely users could be sought. Thus, an interviewer gathering ideas about the needs of the elderly might use more detailed questions when a household that includes elderly people is found.

The form of a survey requires some care in preparation. When constructing a survey, remember its purposes: to assess the need for a service, the acceptability of a particular service, and the willingness of people to use the program or facility. Some surveys, however, have been set up in such a way that a very high response in favor of a proposal is guaranteed. In attitude measurement this bias is called *acquiescence,* the tendency of people to say yes to questions if the questions encourage such an answer. Some needs surveys essentially have listed various services and asked if such services "should" be available to people in the community who need it. Imagine being asked:

Do you think (your hometown) should have an emergency service that provides immediate counseling any time of the day or night for people who are having a crisis with personal or family problems?

Do you think it would be helpful to you to learn more about mental illness and where to get mental health services, or to be able to handle a specific situation?

Wouldn't you answer yes to these questions? Most people would. There is nothing terribly wrong about the questions in themselves, but there are additional items that should be added to this type of question.

Figure 4.3 was part of a need assessment survey that was mailed to discharged patients from a coronary care unit of a general hospital. Figure 6.2 is a section concerning employment taken from an illustrative community resident survey given by Warheit, Bell, and Schwab (1977) that could be administered in person or over the telephone.

If a survey does inquire about the desirability of specific community services, it seems important to ask about the respondent's intended use of possible services as well as providing an estimate of the cost of the services if charges will be involved. Without measuring intended use of services and without providing information on the costs of such services, the meaning of verbal support is difficult to interpret. People can agree that a service *should* exist but feel that the need for it is so slight that they are unwilling to devote more than a token amount of money to it. If this were the case, a marked degree of assent to a question of need would be misleading. If few are willing to pay for a service, the fact that many think it should be available is irrelevant.

Another useful approach to an assessment of need is to estimate what use people intend to make of a service. If the assessment of need concerned mental health programs, the survey instructor would be careful not to ask personal questions respondents would be unwilling to answer honestly. The survey should seek to estimate whether individuals have looked for a similar service for themselves or for someone they know.

For some services the community survey would be especially helpful. For example, many burglaries and acts of vandalism go unreported because the victims feel there is little hope of regaining the stolen goods or that it is too much trouble to report the problem. If the community survey revealed that such hopelessness was widespread, the need for a new program might be even more compelling than the crime statistics themselves.

Whether a planned program is large or small, these principles can be used in assessments of need. The need for programs within large organizations, such as faculty development, student counseling, worker safety programs, and special hospital programs are among the kinds of small-scale programs for which needs should be documented before beginning the program. For each of these programs, a survey of those offering similar services, estimates of the number of people

40. What do you consider your main job or occupation?		___	Don't know
		___	Not answered

_____

_____

(describe by title and kind of work)

41. Are you presently employed?

    ___ Yes, full time
         (*> 29 hrs.*)
    ___ Yes, part time
    ___ No
    ___ Don't know
    ___ Not answered
    ___ Not applicable

    41.A. *If yes*, For whom do you work?

    ___ Self-employed
    ___ Don't know
    ___ Not answered
    ___ Not applicable

_____

_____

    (Organization or type of industry)

    41.B. *If yes*, How many hours a week are you employed?
           (*include all jobs*)

    ___ ___ hrs./week
    ___ Don't know
    ___ Not answered
    ___ Not applicable

42. *If employed less than full time, ask*:
Are you working less than full time because of any of the following:

	YES	NO	DK	N/AN	N/AP
Retired due to age	1	2	3	4	5
Physical injury or illness	1	2	3	4	5
Mental illness or disability	1	2	3	4	5
Fired or laid off	1	2	3	4	5
Going to school	1	2	3	4	5
Have children at home	1	2	3	4	5
Pregnancy	1	2	3	4	5
Consider self homemaker	1	2	3	4	5
Unable to find suitable work	1	2	3	4	5
Not looking for work	1	2	3	4	5
Others (please list)	1	2	3	4	5

FIGURE 6.2 Section of a community need assessment survey. (Adapted from Warheit, Bell, and Schwab, 1977)

receiving similar services, and a survey of potential users would be valuable approaches to gathering information about need.

Survey data can be expensive to gather if a door-to-door survey is planned and, in some communities, the safety of the interviewer would be a serious concern. Telephone surveys have proven useful but a lower refusal rate is more likely with personal interviews. It would not be surprising for respondents to deny such problems as drug abuse or mental illness, but individuals are the best source of information concerning their own problems and level of well-being.

Residents Being Served

People with needs often seek assistance from a variety of sources that provide similar services, or they travel far to obtain what they want, or they do not get care that could benefit them. Evaluators can contrast the extent of need estimated with the level of services currently available in a community. Furthermore, a thorough analysis of the services available assures planners that services will not be duplicated.

A planning agency exploring the need for a mental health center in a rural area listed all agencies, public and private, in a four-county area that provided at least some therapy to or support for people with mental health or substance abuse problems. Thus, clinics, hospitals, Alcoholics Anonymous chapters, school drug-abuse counseling, public-health visiting nurses, church-based counseling centers, physicians and psychiatrists, and social workers were included in the search to learn about the people being treated in some way for emotional problems. At times planners may be required to work directly with agency files in order to develop a demographic description of the clients. When this is necessary, absolute guarantees of confidentiality must be made and kept. When contacting such agencies for estimates of caseloads, it would be helpful to ask for leads to additional providers of care.

A group planning day care and preschools for one-parent families and families in which both parents must work would seek out all formally organized centers, church programs and employer-supported centers. It would not be surprising to learn that many children were cared for in the private homes of relatives and neighbors. Since such baby-sitters are not organized, it would be particularly difficult to obtain estimates of the numbers and ages of the children involved without using a community survey with a sample selected to represent the community accurately.

Dividing the population served on the basis of general problem brought to the agency and by age and gender might permit the planners to pinpoint areas of particular needs. The categories in which residents would be divided varies depending on the type of needs that people have. The educational levels of people would be important if unemployment was the problem. The program might include equivalency classes if the potential clients of the program had not completed high school. If, on the other hand, the people seeking job training had recently lost jobs in a declining industry, they would more likely need additional skills to permit them to gain and hold jobs in a different industry.

Information concerning the people needing care, but not getting it, would be very hard to obtain since few in community agencies would be aware of them. Ways to learn that these people exist include agency reports of people who sought help but did not receive it because they could not pay the fees, or because their problems did not fit into the services provided by the agency. Love (1986) illustrated another way unserved people can be part of a needs assessment. Love used case studies of troubled teenagers to show how the structure of the welfare and mental health services in metropolitan Toronto made it impossible for an adolescent to get help even though his alcoholic father had thrown him out of his home. Unfortunately the unstable and, at times, aggressive 17-year-old had several recent addresses in different communities and needed several different services. It was unclear where he should have sought help, and only a few agencies could assist him with his multiple problems. Although the existence of compelling cases does not show the extent of an unfilled need, cases can show that human service reorganization or expansion may be needed to meet certain types of needs.

Key Informants

Key informants are people who know a community well and could be expected to know what community needs are going unmet. Finding informed people is not easy. Professionals whose work is the most closely related to the needs to be met by the type of program being considered and people recommended for having good ideas is the way to start. Political leaders might possess some valuable information and may be able to suggest others in the community who would have information on residents' needs. For a guidance counselor in a school concerned with adding academic skill training, teachers would be the best key informants. However, the personnel managers of local businesses might also be able to contribute ideas. For health issues, physicians, clergy, clinic managers, school nurses, and social workers would all be important. Although surveys can be mailed to such key informants, a far better response rate can be obtained if the people are visited after first making an appointment.

The reason key informants are sought is that they have the closest contact with residents in need; however, this is also the source of their most glaring weakness. Since people in need are memorable and since key informants will see a great number of such people daily, psychiatrists and psychologists are likely to overestimate the number of residents needing psychotherapy, remedial reading teachers are likely to overestimate the proportion of children needing training in reading, and personnel workers are likely to overestimate the proportion of problem employees.

A related problem with key informants is that their specialization may blind them to the reactions of others. A university English professor provides an example of the disappointing results of not realizing that a target population may not construe a problem in the same way as a professional offering a service. She reasoned as follows: (1) Many college students do not write very well, and professors in many fields agree that improvement would be desirable; (2) English professors have only limited contact with students, compared to professors in the students' major fields; therefore (3) one way to improve student writing is to improve the ability of non-

English faculty to grade, evaluate, and improve the writing done for non-English courses. She developed a series of workshops for non-English department faculty members involving a number of her departmental colleagues and obtained funds from the college dean for a guest speaker. The flaw in her plans was very basic. It was wrong to assume that people who complain want to act upon their complaints. Although many college professors complain about student writing ability, relatively few may be ready to involve themselves actively in the grading and counseling required to encourage improvement. Consequently, the attendance at the workshops and the lecture was primarily from the English department; non-English department faculty could be counted on the fingers of one hand. As a matter of fact, there were more graduate student evaluators present to observe the first workshop than there were faculty members from departments other than English. Other workshops were then canceled. Programs can be effective only when they meet real needs and when the target population agrees that it has those needs.

Focus Groups and Other Community Forums

The expense of seeking out a representative sample of community residents to interview individually suggests that information might be obtained more efficiently from groups of people. Two related approaches to group meetings are focus groups and community forums.

Focus groups. Marketing research firms use many small informal groups to discuss new products, ideas for new products, and what people think about products to learn the reasons for people's opinions on everything from plant fertilizer to automobiles. Although the questions asked of members of focus groups might be similar to open-ended questions asked in an interview, the presence of seven to ten people encourages free discussion about the product being considered. This give-and-take produces more detailed ideas about consumer reactions to the product or idea for a product than individual interviews. The focus group leader tries to remain in the background to encourage a relaxed, free atmosphere and to foster the sharing of opinions among group members (Krueger, 1988). Focus groups are usually made up of similar people. Since the goal is to foster the free exchange of honest opinion, age or educational differences would intimidate some members. Also, although the members of a focus group are similar in some ways, they do not know each other before they join the group and, most likely, will not see each other after the group meeting.

Focus groups can be used in any phase of evaluation; however, they serve particularly well in learning about the reactions to potential services of community agencies or private organizations. Krueger described using focus groups to discover why agricultural extension classes were drawing fewer and fewer enrollments among farmers in Minnesota. A mail survey suggested that farmers were interested in such classes but enrollments continued to drop. It could have been assumed that financial troubles were responsible, but the focus groups told a different story. Farmers said that they were interested and that they could afford the tuition; however, they wanted to be sure that the instructor was knowledgeable and that the classes were practical. In addition, it was learned that personal invitations would be better than the printed flyers that had been the standard way of announcing the classes. After the different approach had been implemented, attendance increased markedly.

We have noted that people's needs depend on their particular situations. Although people may not be aware of all of the needs under consideration, their views must be considered. One use of focus groups is to test the evaluator's and the planner's interpretation of the findings of community surveys. A community survey might suggest that residents would use a recycling center, but community residents might have definite ideas about the location, the hours of operation, and services of the center. A city that set up a recycling center in a centralized downtown area was forced to move it within three months because the odor of grass clippings, the noise of breaking glass, and the traffic congestion were intolerable to residents living nearby.

The questions that are used to begin focus group discussions follow the same general guidelines recommended for open-ended interview questions. These recommendations are discussed in Chapter 12. Figure 6.3 includes some questions that could have been asked in focus groups of rural business people. Plans were being made to develop an assistance program for small rural businesses as part of a state-funded project to encourage rural economic development. Extension classes for owners and managers of rural businesses were being considered, but before such classes could be developed, colleges had to identify the information needs of business owners. These questions were designed to elicit these information needs.

Community forums. A community forum is another method based on group interaction. Unlike focus groups that are selected on the basis of some common characteristics, a community forum is a self-selected group. Often a governmental agency will announce the date of a community meeting to consider some planning

FIGURE 6.3 Focus group questions to learn about the information needs of owners of rural businesses. (Adapted from Krueger, 1988)

1. Over the past few weeks, did you have an experience in your business which caused you to need information? Describe that experience and tell us where you went for the information.
2. Over the past year, think of times in which you needed help in managing your business; jot down those situations.
3. We have a list of topics suggested by some other owners and managers for programs to help them in their businesses. Please look over this list and compare it to yours. Which items are most important to you?
4. (When a topic is suggested, the leader can ask:) What makes the area of _____ important to you? {After such a question is discussed, others will also have suggestions which will then be discussed also.}
5. A topic that was mentioned by several people was _____. Where would you go to learn something about it?
6. People can get information in different forms; how would you prefer to get the information? (Probe to clarify reactions to: one-on-one, phone calls, newsletters, meetings, workshops, classes.)
7. What makes a provider of business information credible? How do you know when you can trust the information you get?

issue. Those who learn of the meeting and choose to attend may participate. Warheit, Bell, and Schwab (1977) recommend that large groups be divided into smaller groups, since only a few people will participate in a large meeting. After assembling and outlining the agenda and questions that planners want answered, the small groups would discuss the issues and report their ideas to the planners and to the large group if there is time. Needs that the groups identify should be placed in order of greatest to least need.

The advantages of community forums include the open access to anyone who wishes to participate, the very low cost, and the possibility that good ideas may be offered. One disadvantage is that self-selected groups are not representative of a community and many people cannot or will not attend such meetings. Once when a small town held an open meeting to discuss how to spend a small federal grant, only one resident attended, urging the development of a park for children along a railroad right-of-way, a location the planners viewed as dangerous. A less obvious disadvantage is the possibility that the public discussions may raise the expectations that something can and will be done to meet the needs discussed. It is also possible that assertive individuals with particular grievances can turn the meetings into gripe sessions producing little of use to understand the needs of a community.

Users of focus groups or community forums need to be cautious in drawing conclusions from the views of specific individuals. The needs of particular individuals can be quite compelling to casual viewers of TV news programs; in fact, even people trained in research methods have been known to put aside the findings of carefully conducted research and adopt conclusions based on the experiences of one or two individuals. Rook (1987) describes how case studies can influence attitudes and health-related behaviors more powerfully than more accurate, but abstract, information.

INADEQUATE ASSESSMENT OF NEED

The point of need assessment is to improve the quality of program planning. Programs designed to meet needs that are already being met are not good ways to spend resources. When needs or the context of the people in need are not assessed accurately or only partially understood, programs or services cannot be as efficient or effective as possible. Without knowing the extent of the need one cannot develop goals for programs. The findings of a need assessment can provide a basis on which to build links between needs and program services and between program services and resolution of the need. However, need assessments can be inadequate because needs may be ignored or incompletely assessed; needs may be understood, but the capacity of the community may be ignored; and the assessment may overlook the denial of need.

Failing to Examine Need

It might seem a truism to say that program designers should be sure that proposed programs are planned on basis of the needs of the people to whom the services are directed. We wish it would be unnecessary to make this point, but sometimes programs are implemented without careful attention to unmet needs. A college was concerned about the attrition of students who left the college after the freshman year even though they were in good academic standing. As tentative ideas about the college's response were described, the discussion focused on the college's desire to retain students. A listener asked an administrator: "What are the needs of the students whom we are losing?" This had not been considered in the tentative planning because the planners had focused on the college's need, but had failed to analyze why a portion of the students dropped out. Administrators had only speculated on students' unmet needs and how a program might change the students' behavior. Perhaps the attrition was caused by personal and family situations that the college could not influence, or perhaps some students developed interests in fields that the college did not support. Attempts to lower the attrition rate of such students will produce frustration and apparent failure for sponsors of a program, because no program could meet the students' needs.

Failing to Examine the Context of the Need

It is quite possible to have an accurate understanding of a community's need, but to fail to assess the community's capacity to support the program or the cultural context in which the program would be implemented. One of the tragedies of the relationship between the developed nations and the undeveloped nations during the last several decades is the repeated failure of foreign aid initiatives to consider the economic and cultural context of the people in the undeveloped nations. Many well-intentioned efforts have been misdirected. At best, such efforts do no harm; at times, such efforts have left many in the recipient nation in worse conditions. In the area of health care, a basic problem is assuming that the citizens of developing nations need Western medical services. Unfortunately, developing nations cannot support Western medical services and the foreign aid available can only provide this type of care to a small minority of the population. Inappropriate programs have weakened some indigenous systems that had provided useful care for people, but were not at the level of medical care available in developed countries (Manoff, 1985).

Bringing foreign nationals to European or North American medical schools for training means that such people will become accustomed to Western style medical practice. Partially as a result of this training, physicians returned home to practice in city hospitals with the well-to-do; 90 percent of the medical care resources of Nigeria are spent in the cities where only a small minority of the population lives. This happens while many rural children go without immunizations that would cost a pittance.

A more favorable outcome was obtained when planners examined treatment for severe diarrhea, which can lead to the death of children in poor nations if the fluids and nutrients lost are not replaced. Such fluids can be replaced using intravenous feeding; however, the cost would be staggering. Premixed packs of salt, sugars, and other ingredients were developed to make it easier to prepare an appropriate drink for the children. Widespread introduction of such premixed packages, although costing only a fraction of intravenous methods, would have been unfortunate because the packs were still too expensive to supply to everyone in need and their use would imply that people could not take care of themselves. Manoff (1985) reports that planners calculated that 750 million packs would be needed per year by 1990. A better approach was to show people how to prepare the fluids themselves using ingredients available locally. A health care program that taught people medically appropriate skills would be more effective than one that met the needs of a few but fostered feelings of helplessness among the many.

Failing to Deliver the Program to Those in Need

Sometimes a program is prepared on the basis of a good understanding of unmet needs, but the program implementation makes it difficult for people to participate. Food stamps are designed to assist poor families to purchase food at reduced costs; it is compassionate and an investment in the future of our society. Unfortunately, through local indifference and target group ignorance only about 20 percent of those eligible for food stamps were using them in the early years of the program. An advertising campaign in New Mexico tripled the number of eligible people using food stamps in six months (Manoff, 1985).

Failing to Deal with the Denial of Need

If the target population does not recognize a need, the program must include an educational effort (Cagle and Banks, 1986; Conner et al., 1985). Those screening for and treating high blood pressure deal daily with people who do not recognize a need for care. When the disease first develops, elevated blood pressure seldom produces noticeable symptoms; in addition, medication does have undesirable side effects (*Medical World News*, 1977). Because people expect to feel better, not worse, after taking medicine, many reject the treatment. A rejected treatment means program failure, even though the medication is effective in reducing the likelihood of strokes and other cardiovascular diseases.

Some people have believed that when it comes to education, health, and other social services, society fulfills its responsibility by providing the facts. These groups believe that publicly funded service providers need not attempt to persuade citizens to follow good practices. In contrast, the area of social marketing (Fredericksen, Solomon, and Brehomy, 1984; Manoff, 1985) has developed to foster the adoption of better practices by people who may not realize they have a need or who may have difficulty losing weight, stopping smoking, or providing their children with adequate nutrition and a safe environment. Social marketing is needed, Manoff (1985) argues, not only to provide basic education, but also because business interests use extensive advertising to encourage the use of products that can harm health (for example high carbohydrate and high fat foods, cigarettes).

Another aspect of getting a program to the people in need involves encouraging them to seek assistance from legitimate sources of care. People do not view care givers as interchangeable—trust develops slowly. Offering a service to meet an unmet need is not the same as offering a service that people will prefer over the way they currently seek to meet the need. The continued use of native healers by some

Spanish-American residents of U.S. cities is an example of a preference for what is known over services offered by unknown public agencies (Adler and Stone, 1979).

USING NEED ASSESSMENTS IN PROGRAM PLANNING

Once the level of need has been assessed for a particular population, then program planning may begin. Planners seek to develop a service or intervention to help the population achieve or approach a satisfactory state. This is based on the assumption that an agency has assessed needs of a population included within its mission. A hospital cannot focus attention on rehabilitating criminals or in raising the reading levels of elementary schoolchildren. Given that the unmet need fits the mission of the agency or organization, the planners begin by developing outcome goals based on the unmet needs identified. We remind readers that the probability of developing a successful program increases markedly if the important stakeholder groups are involved in the planning, working with planners and evaluators in selecting the services to be offered and the mechanisms to deliver the services. There are many ways to obtain the contributions of stakeholders, including formal representation and focus groups responding to potential plans.

Once the outcome goals have been specified, the next task is to consider the intermediate goals that need to be achieved on the way to the outcome goals. Intermediate goals refer to observable changes as the population or the organization moves from its current state to an improved state as a result of the service or intervention. Intermediate goals could include accomplishments, behaviors, physical measurements, or performance characteristics of equipment. Raising the question of intermediate goals in the planning process means that a theoretical understanding of the process of change is being developed. All too often, as mentioned in Chapter 2, programs are planned without asking what must happen to the target population, the clients, or the students as they approach the desired state described by the outcome goals.

After outcome and intermediate goals have been developed, the planning group can specify what actions the agency or organization might take to assist the target population to achieve the goals. The resources that need to be employed include the knowledge and skills of the staff members, the physical resources, financial resources needed to implement the intervention, and advertising or other outreach efforts. Since planners cannot operate with blank-check assumptions, the projected resources required are compared with the financial support that would be available to the program being planned. If the resources are not sufficient, the planners have several options. One temptation is to leave the goals intact but to reduce the intensity of the program and hope for the best. If the planning had been sound and if the conceptual basis of the plans is correct, such a decision is a prescription for failure (Rivlin, 1990). To fail in the complex task of helping people change is not a disgrace, but to continue to plan a program that planners suspect cannot work well because it is too weak is a waste of valuable resources. More useful alternatives include reducing the number of people to be served, narrowing the focus of the service, or even changing the plans to meet a different need, one that requires fewer resources.

Although this presentation seems straightforward and linear, the planning committee frequently checks back to verify that they are keeping to the mission of the organization that will sponsor the program. Furthermore, it would not be surprising that while developing intermediate goals, it became clear that some of the outcome goals were not realistic. What does not change is the need to work in a generally backward direction during the planning process, beginning with what is to be accomplished and ending with a plan to achieve those goals (Egan and Cowan, 1979; Egan, 1988a, 1988b). If there are no clear goals, rational planning cannot occur. Surprisingly often, people in agencies and organizations sense a need, but do not measure it carefully or even explore it in a qualitative manner. Instead they ignore stakeholders in the planning process and then watch helplessly as the program fails to have an observable impact on the population in need.

SUMMARY AND PREVIEW

The importance of assessing needs before beginning to plan programs must be stressed. The definition of need emphasizes that we are trying to learn what people need in order to be in a satisfactory state, not what they desire or might like to have. It is likely that we do not understand fully what it takes to satisfy our own needs as illustrated by ignorance of objective nutritional needs. Since educational, psychological, and social needs are also complex, it would not be surprising to learn that these needs are not fully understood either. Consequently, it is wise to seek information on needs from a variety of sources. Community surveys, rates being treated, social indicators, focus groups, and expert informants are sources of information about need. Once needs are clear, planning may begin. Planning has the best chance of success if the conceptual basis of the program is developed and used to set the goals and to plan the program. Once programs are in place, evaluators continue to contribute since programs must be monitored to guarantee their integrity. Furthermore, information gathered by monitoring activities serves to show what aspects of the program should be adjusted. Chapter 7 includes an introduction to management information systems and their use in program evaluation.

STUDY QUESTIONS

1. Carefully examine the daily newspapers for articles on social services or consumer products that show how a careful analysis of need for a human service or a new product was affected by an analysis of need. Note that if the example concerns a consumer product, the definition of unmet need used in this chapter may not be appropriate; in such a case, manufacturers are usually dealing with meeting wishes or preferences and sometimes offering improvements, not serving unmet needs.

2. Look for examples of agencies or producers who failed because they did not conduct an appropriate need assessment before offering a service or bringing a product to the marketplace. What kind of information might the organization have sought to avoid the failure?
3. Under what conditions would an assessment of need be threatening to an organization?

FURTHER READING

KRUEGER, R. A. 1988. *Focus groups: A practical guide for applied research.* Newbury Park, Calif.: Sage.
McKILLIP, J. 1987. *Need analysis: Tools for human services and education.* Newbury Park, Calif.: Sage.

7

Monitoring the Operation of Programs

Program monitoring ". . . is the least acknowledged but probably most practiced category of evaluation" (ERS Standards Committee, 1982, p. 10). The most basic form of program evaluation is an examination of the program itself—its activities, the population it serves, and how it functions. Program monitoring includes an assessment of how much effort in the form of human and physical resources is invested in the program and whether the effort is expended as planned. The evaluation of effort is important; a program without sufficient resources cannot be expected to influence the participants in the program, and a program planned to meet one problem will be less useful when applied to a different problem. Careful program monitoring yields "impressive results" according to Lipsey et al. (1985).

Since a well-planned, well-staffed, and well-housed program may not function effectively, evaluators commissioned to assess the quality of a program inquire into its day-to-day performance. Businesses evaluate their performance by counting cash receipts at the end of the day and by performing inventories of stock at regular intervals. Human service managers use measures of activity similar to those available to commercial firms. The problem is that the ultimate products of human service programs, well-functioning people, cannot be measured as objectively or as concretely as store inventories.

The place to begin is to ask whether the human service program has been implemented as planned. If well-designed advertisements encouraging seat belt use are not actually published or broadcast, there is no reason to evaluate the impact of the material. If drug abusers do not attend a drug rehabilitation program, there is little need to ask whether the program reduced drug abuse. Systematic methods to monitor medical care, counseling and psychotherapy, training, and other forms of human services have been developed only recently. Some of these methods assess the degree to which planned procedures are followed.

Managers need such information to facilitate their planning and decision making, to anticipate problems, and to justify the existence of the program. For example, if it is discovered that a population receiving assistance is not the one targeted, then the program is not serving the need it was designed to meet and may have to be altered. Striking differences in the contributions of different staff members or an unusually heavy client dropout rate would be other problems important to detect. Managers can act to correct problems only if they have adequate information. Thus, program monitoring usually serves a formative function for program managers. Without accurate information, problems may become apparent only when it is too late to correct them.

THE PROGRAM AUDIT AS A MEANS OF PROGRAM EVALUATION

Some evaluators have come to use the term *audit,* taken from accounting terminology, to describe the process of quantifying the amount of services rendered and the identity of program participants (Schwandt and Halpern, 1988). To distinguish the activities of evaluators from those of accountants, examinations of procedures, policies, and the structures of programs are called *operational* or *management audits* rather than financial audits.

Evaluators who conduct management audits gather information so that they can describe the program. A description of the program includes a profile of the clients coming into the program, a summary of the services given, workloads of the staff members, and sometimes clients' evaluations of the program. Program directors and staff sometimes believe they do not need quantified information to summarize the type and amount of services they provide and to whom these services are given. However, it is common knowledge among evaluators that the staff members' subjective beliefs about the program and clients are often in error.

In several studies in which the authors have participated, program staffs have been very wrong in describing the population served by the program. In an evaluation of an innovative organization of nursing on a hospital unit (Carey, 1979), the staff said that 90 percent of the patients would have one of three major problems: respiratory illnesses, diabetes, or hypertension. As part of the evaluation, the diagnoses of the patients on the unit were recorded. It turned out that only 20 percent of the patients were diagnosed as having one of these three ailments. Is it possible that service could be improved if the staff realized that they were actually serving a very heterogeneous patient population?

The description of the population served and the services rendered by a program fills several needs. First, the immediate needs of management may be most obvious. In order to manage a human service program effectively, it is necessary to know who receives what service from whom, and when the service is given. Managers fill their roles better the more they are able to anticipate and avoid crises. Second, management audit is often a necessary prelude to rigorous study of the outcome of the services since the planned outcomes will not occur if services are not or are only marginally provided. Third, knowing what is currently done provides a way to plan rationally.

A modest management audit conducted between two specific dates can serve to aid planning or as a preliminary step in an outcome evaluation. The limited approach provides a snapshot of the program; the ongoing method provides a motion picture of the program. An examination of the program's records for a limited time period answers some particular questions about the level and types of services given; such information can give the planner and manager some directions to follow in program planning. In contrast, management needs require an ongoing information system and may well require the development of a system to obtain information routinely. Repeated descriptions of a program over fairly short time periods, such as one month, permit closer monitoring and allow adjustments to be made in the way the program is run. A procedure to summarize services on a regular basis is called a *management information system,* or MIS.

As with most dichotomies, the contrast between special, limited audits and extended, routinized audits may break down in practice. However, the distinction is useful; programs have different needs at different times. If a manager needs information that is gathered repeatedly over short time intervals, an approach requiring hand retrieval of data would be overly expensive and slow. On the other hand, a small program may not require a complex information system; in such cases a simpler, less ambitious procedure would be used. Some writers in program evaluation view the development of management information systems as a major part of the role of internal program evaluators. Evaluators are expected to contribute to the development of MIS's that are useful both for management and for program evaluation purposes. Wargo (see Evaluator Profile 5) describes the importance of MIS's for evaluators.

WHAT TO SUMMARIZE IN AN AUDIT OF SERVICES

There is no standard way to select and gather the information required to describe a program. Programs differ in the types of people served, the services given, and the type of institution offering the services. Evaluators bear in mind several points as they prepare an audit of services. These points are not explicit guides as to which information to gather or which procedures to use. Rather, they help evaluators focus on the issues that need to be addressed.

Relevant Information

The information gathered must be central to the purpose of the audit. Important information can help to set staff levels, to satisfy accreditation criteria, and to plan for space needs. Effective evaluators attempt to gather only information that is

EVALUATOR PROFILE 5.

Michael J. Wargo, Ph.D.: Management Information Systems and Program Evaluation

After conducting program evaluations in consulting firms, Dr. Wargo conducted evaluations of federal government-sponsored volunteer organizations such as the Peace Corps and VISTA. In 1979, he organized the new evaluation unit of the Food and Nutrition Service of the U.S. Department of Agriculture. He earned a Ph.D. in experimental psychology (Tufts University).

Dr. Wargo was asked about the use of management information systems (MIS's) in program evaluation. Dr. Wargo responded: " . . . [E]valuators are going to become more dependent on MIS's. It's just too costly to collect new data for every evaluation. Evaluators should use their skills to help design MIS's that are useful for evaluation purposes as well as for program management."

He continued, "Five to ten years from now most of the information evaluators use will be information collected for other purposes. It's too costly to collect information the way we have in the past, and it takes too long."

Adapted from Hendricks, M. 1986. A conversation with Michael Wargo. *Evaluation Practice,* 7(6), 23–36.

---

relevant to describing the program and how it functions. Many characteristics of clients and programs are not central to program decisions. Evaluators may find many potentially interesting questions to explore while doing an evaluation, such as the relationship of birth order to the probability of becoming a juvenile delinquent or the degree that students' right/left hand preferences are related to academic success. Such questions might well be important for theories of social development or brain function. If evaluators have the time to study issues of basic research, they may seek to explore some of these hypotheses. However, every bit of additional information recorded in an audit increases the cost of data collection and analysis.

Actual State of Program

A second point is that an audit must describe the actual state of the current program. Evaluators are careful to distinguish between the program as described and the program as administered. Many programs that look very good on paper fail, not because they were designed poorly but because the staff or the participants did not actually follow the design or the procedure as planned. Reporters for the *Chicago Tribune* (Stein and Recktenwald, 1990) visited city parks during periods when activities were officially scheduled only to find field houses locked and abandoned. If the reporters had only examined the official activity schedules, they would have assumed that the programs actually were being offered. There is no excuse for an evaluator to permit written descriptions of programs, no matter how official, to substitute for on-site observations.

The information necessary to describe the services rendered include (1) the type of service offered by the program (such as job training, group therapy, immunizations); (2) the extensiveness of the program (such as hours of training or therapy, skills to be learned, location of the program, facilities); and (3) the number of people participating in the service, especially the proportion of people completing educational or therapeutic programs.

Providers of Services

The preparation of a management audit should include a description of who gives the services. In some settings many service providers—such as physicians, nurses, physical therapists, or teachers—are licensed by states for particular roles. In other human service settings, especially where pay is low, people with limited training are involved in giving the service. Counseling programs for drug addicts or former addicts are sometimes staffed by people who are neither trained nor psychologically equipped for their positions. It is also possible that the staff may be overqualified. An evaluation of a project staffed by volunteer lawyers to help ex-convicts readjust to community life found mixed results—the released prisoners looked to the volunteers for legal aid, not for general readjustment help. Thus, the legal training of the volunteers stood in the way of a truly effective program, in spite of sincere efforts (Berman, 1978).

Program Participants

A fourth major part of an audit includes a description of those who receive the services. If a program was well-planned, the population to be served would have been specified carefully and the program tailored to meet the needs of that group. An audit should document the identity and the needs of the people using the service and compare these findings to the program plans. In other words, the fit between the program and the needs of those using it can be examined. If the fit is not good, changes or redirections for the program can be considered. If the agency never actually defined the group to be served, a description of the people using the agency may be especially enlightening.

The people using the program are routinely described by gender and age. The choice of additional information to be presented depends on the specific nature of the program. Such information may include where the people live, the major problems for which they are seeking help, the source of referral, and ethnic background.

The ease or difficulty people have in obtaining the service is an aspect of the description of those receiving the service. Since this information is seldom in agency files, it would be necessary to prepare a short survey to gather it. Questions should cover how much time elapsed between initial contact and first appointment, the mode of transportation used, parking availability (if required), and time necessary to wait for care. In preparing such a survey, differences in ease of access that are related to variables such as time of day (morning versus afternoon versus evening), day of the week (workdays versus weekends), type of service, and welfare status of the individual must be considered. It is unlikely that a facility would need to gather all this information routinely. Obtaining it soon after beginning the program and at later time periods as the facility changes or expands would be sufficient.

AN APPROACH TO PROVIDING REPEATED AUDITS

When setting out to prepare a method of providing periodic reports describing the way an agency functions, the evaluator needs to have a hand in designing the agency's records. Instead of using existing files, the evaluator can help the agency design recording and filing procedures that will be useful for evaluation and for routine agency needs. When records are designed for use in evaluations, it is quite economical to prepare the type of reports described in this chapter.

Existing Records of a Program

It would be impossible to perform an empirical evaluation of effort without adequate records. However, it is no secret that the records of human service agencies are often in abysmal condition. Inadequate records are frequent even in hospitals, where sloppy handwriting has resulted in fatal drug overdoses and the amputation of a healthy leg instead of a diseased one (Dixon, 1977). Why are charts and records in such poor condition? Record-keeping is a dull and time-consuming task. Individuals attracted to human service occupations often view record-keeping as time taken away from clients, students, or patients. In the very short run, that view may be correct. Furthermore, records were less important in the recent past, when impressionistic evaluations of success and effort were sufficient evaluations in many settings. The existence of this and other books on evaluation methods shows that impressionistic evaluations are no longer sufficient for regulatory and accrediting agencies.

Evaluators helping an agency to develop an ongoing plan for documenting the provision of services will probably first ask what material is available in the current records. However, even agencies with highly detailed and carefully maintained records may not have all the information useful for program evaluation purposes. Such records often contain long narrative accounts of progress or disability that are hard to use since they lack a common frame of reference.

People adopt widely differing points of view in defining success in human services. For example, the care giver, the program participant, and the community tend to define success in mental health care quite differently. People in the local community are distressed by public acting-out behavior. Communities do not want individuals around who wear unusual clothing, argue frequently with neighbors or shopkeepers, or tell passersby about hallucinations. The larger society wants individuals to keep up their living quarters, hold jobs, and, in general, behave responsibly. If mental health counseling or the provision of tranquilizers can keep people looking and acting relatively normal, society will consider the service successful and effective.

Therapists, on the other hand, have traditionally been less interested in day-to-day responsible behavior than in personality structure and emotional health. They would not view therapy as effective if it only assisted people to cope better or to conform passively to social norms. Instead, they would desire to detect greater autonomy, greater self-actualization, less guilt, and more frequent assertiveness.

These are behaviors that are largely not observable by the community and not relevant to its evaluation of a mental health center.

Individuals receiving therapy may have an altogether different set of standards. They may evaluate therapy on the basis of whether they feel better about themselves. It is quite possible for clients to find a mode of adjustment that is acceptable to themselves but that would satisfy neither the therapist nor many members of the community. Strupp and Handley (1977) have discussed these three points of view in more detail, especially with regard to negative outcomes in therapy. When individuals differ in the relative emphasis of these three points of view, free narrative reports are not very useful to the evaluator.

Increasing the Usefulness of Records

Methods of summarizing the information must be developed to increase the usefulness of files. In different contexts, staff or managers have confidently assured evaluators that certain information was "in the files." Unfortunately, many files are incomplete, and, more importantly, in-the-files information is not useful information. Retrieving material from client folders is a time-consuming task. Further, it is a sensitive task: the privacy of the clients must be maintained. It is more efficient to develop a management information system that permits the routine summary of participant descriptors (that is, age, sex, disability) and service provided without manually going through file folders that often contain personal material important to the client and the service provider but irrelevant to the evaluator.

It is necessary for the program director and other information users to develop a list of essential information useful in managing and evaluating the program. A point repeatedly stressed in this book is that information is gathered only when it is useful. If there are legal requirements to obtain certain information, or if decisions are to be made on the basis of the information, then it should be gathered. If material is sensitive to potential negative side effects, it should be included. Information that cannot be used in an evaluation need not be gathered simply to fill folders in file cabinets. The real challenge to MIS developers is to summarize information in useful ways. Ackoff (1986) writes that managers need more information that is relevant and useful, not just more information.

How Records Can Be Used to Monitor Programs

One useful approach might be to prepare monthly summaries of all new clients. Figure 7.1 is a form that could be used when people initially request counseling at a center offering outpatient counseling. It contains much of the same information many counselors request. Regardless of the size of the facility, a sheet such as this would become the first entry in the individual's file. Notice that the center personnel add some information themselves, such as an identification number and a problem code. Otherwise, the form could be self-administered.

To use this information most easily and effectively, it is necessary to have the material entered into a computer system. In order to maintain the client's privacy, it is necessary to have some of the material in Figure 7.1 on a second copy in a form

PLEASE COMPLETE THIS FORM AND RETURN IT TO THE SECRETARY IN THE ENVELOPE PROVIDED. THE INFORMATION YOU GIVE US IS CONFIDENTIAL AND WILL BE CAREFULLY SECURED.

Name _____   Please do not write in boxes below:

Address _____   ☐ ☐ ☐ ☐ ☐ ☐ ☐

_____ Zip _____   ☐ ☐–☐ ☐–☐ ☐

Telephone _____

Marital Status: (Circle one)

   1. Never married 2. Married now 3. Widowed 4. Divorced/Annulled 5. Separated

Sex:

   1. Female   2. Male   3. Couple application

Age: _____ Age of spouse if married now: _____

Who referred you to the center? (Circle one)

   1. Myself, friend, family   4. Hospital   7. Another agency

   2. Another client   5. Physician   8. Other _____

   3. Clergy   6. Psychiatrist   _____

What problem(s) has prompted you to consider counseling at this center? ☐ ☐

_____ ☐ ☐

_____ ☐ ☐

_____ ☐ ☐

What form of counseling are you most interested in at this time? (Circle one)

   1. Individual   2. Family   3. Marital   4. Group

Who lives in your immediate family?

Adults (give their relationship to you) _____ ☐ ☐

_____ ☐ ☐

Children (give ages)   _____ ☐ ☐

_____ ☐ ☐

Have you previously received counseling from some other agency or counselor?

   1. Yes

   2. No

If "Yes" and if you do enter therapy with a counselor from the center, may we contact this person or agency about you?

   1. No

   2. Yes (Give name of counselor) _____

     Please sign _____

Where are you employed? _____

Please give the name and address of any insurance company that will meet part of your expenses at the center.

Name _____ Address _____ Ident. No. _____

FIGURE 7.1 An application form for potential clients of an outpatient counseling center.

that is not easily identifiable. A second copy can be obtained using two printed forms with carbon paper bound between the pages. Confidentiality can be maintained by making it impossible for the client's name, street address, telephone number, and other traceable material to print through. The information would be identified by the number added by the intake worker or secretary before the copies are sent to a data analyst. Figure 7.1 includes spaces to code type of problem(s) leading to a request for counseling.

The specific information to be gathered depends on the needs of the particular human service agency preparing the system. Figure 7.2 contains a list of items that agencies would want to consider in preparing forms for gathering information about new clients.

Simply having some of the information in Figures 7.1 and 7.2 summarized each month or quarter would yield a more complete description of new clients than many agencies traditionally have available. The individual reports could be combined into a yearly profile of new clients.

Figure 7.3 is an illustrative new client report for a given month. The report includes information important to a particular center. For example, one counseling center with which we are familiar seeks to be of service to community clergy when they are faced with parish members who have emotional problems that cannot be handled by brief supportive counseling. A variable included in a hypothetical report of new clients for this center would be source of referral. This center can document that it is fulfilling one aspect of its mission by showing that a large proportion of its referrals do indeed come from clergy. Age, sex, apparent problem, type of therapy desired, and location of residence are also useful in judging whether an agency is serving the population it was designed to serve.

The value of having summaries such as that shown in Figure 7.3 would be apparent to anyone who has worked in a large organization: it is necessary to let people know what you are doing. Program managers can justify the continued existence of their programs more easily if they are able to provide documentation of the number of people served, as well as brief demographic descriptions and the reasons clients give for seeking the service. Having information readily available also facilitates responding to requests for information. Frequently government agencies request material that may be available only by searching through the files. Chapman (1976) reported that the need to complete an extensive survey quickly precipitated a crisis in a mental health center because much necessary information was not easily available. The crisis ultimately led the center to prepare an information system capable of routinely summarizing client characteristics as well as much additional information.

Following the Course of Service

The course of a service can be followed by preparing standard forms with spaces in which therapists can record certain information after each client contact. This short contact report does not take the place of the therapists' process notes, which are normally for the personal use of the therapist. Figure 7.4 is an example of such a contact report. The identification number would be used to match this report

Initial Information

Name
Address
Sex
Age
Educational level
Marital status
Family description
Ethnic background
Referral source
Problem(s) leading to request for services
Previous participation in similar human services programs
Insurance coverage
Veteran's benefits
Welfare status
Dates: Of initial application
         When formal participation begun

Some information will be unique to the type of agency involved. For example:

Mental health services:	Previous hospitalizations
	Type and extent of therapy
	Current medication
	Previous diagnoses
	Alcoholism/Drug addiction
	Functional life status
	Identity of previous therapist
Criminal justice programs:	Status with court system
	Type of previous programs
	Location of programs
	Voluntary or forced participation
Job-training programs:	Jobs held, length of previous employment
	Income
	Reason for unemployment
	Types of previous job-training programs
	Location of programs
Educational programs:	School attending
	Grade level
	IQ or other standardized tests
	Location of previous programs

Ongoing Information

Amount of service rendered (hours of therapy, courses completed, skills
   mastered)
When service given
Identity of staff
Functional status or adjustment during and at termination of service
Reason for termination
Degree of self-support
Fees charged
Referral made

FIGURE 7.2   Types of information an agency might include in the basic descriptive information gathered about those seeking service, as well as the type of information added as the service is given.

MARITAL STATUS, GENDER AND AGE	FEMALE	MALE
NEVER MARRIED	28	12
MARRIED NOW	48	15
WIDOWED	3	0
DIVORCED, ANNULED	15	3
SEPARATED	4	0
TOTAL	98	30
AGE (MEAN)-YR	34	27

SOURCES OF REFERRAL	N	%
SELF, FRIEND, FAMILY	27	21
ANOTHER CLIENT	5	4
CLERGY	67	52
HOSPITAL	15	12
PSYCHIATRIST	2	2
ANOTHER SOURCE	11	9
TOTAL	127	100%

PROBLEM CODE (MORE THAN ONE MAY APPLY)	N	%
MARITAL PROBLEMS	42	33
INDIVIDUAL ADJUSTMENT ISSUES	104	81
PROBLEMS AT WORK	30	23
PROBLEMS AT SCHOOL	8	6
PROBLEMS WITH CHILDREN	62	48
ALCOHOLISM, DRUG USE	28	22
UNDIAGNOSED PHYSICAL SYMPTOMS	16	12

SERVICE SOUGHT	N	%
INDIVIDUAL THERAPY	77	60
FAMILY THERAPY	13	10
MARITAL THERAPY	29	23
GROUP THERAPY	5	4
NOT SURE	4	3

NUMBER (%) HAVING PREVIOUS PSYCHOTHERAPY 45 (35%)

NUMBER (%) EMPLOYED 92 (72%)

FIGURE 7.3 An illustrative monthly report describing new clients to a counseling center.

with other information about a particular client, such as information gathered at the beginning of therapy and from previous contact reports. The therapist identification number and therapy type are useful for documenting workload. The functional status ratings could be based on the procedure described in Chapter 4 (see Figure 4.1). Including the charges on this form would facilitate an automated billing system. Information about referral can be noted on this form, and a therapist may also indicate when a formal end of therapy has occurred.

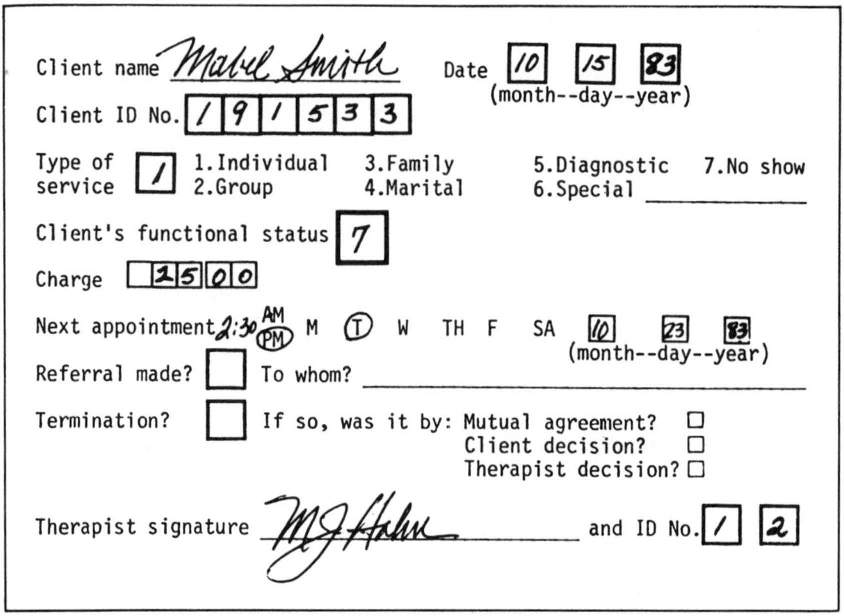

Client name Mabel Smith Date 10 15 83
(month--day--year)

Client ID No. 1 9 1 5 3 3

Type of service 1 1.Individual 2.Group 3.Family 4.Marital 5.Diagnostic 6.Special ______ 7.No show

Client's functional status 7

Charge 15 00

Next appointment 2:30 AM PM M T W TH F SA 10 23 83
(month--day--year)

Referral made? To whom? ____________

Termination? If so, was it by: Mutual agreement? ☐
Client decision? ☐
Therapist decision? ☐

Therapist signature ____________ and ID No. 1 2

FIGURE 7.4 An illustrative form for a therapist to use after each therapy session with a client. This copy would be kept by the center.

To make more efficient use of the contact report in Figure 7.4, there should be copies for the therapist, the client, and the data analyst. All three copies could be made simultaneously. The client's copy and the data center's copy would not include all the information included in the therapist's copy. The copy for data processing would not include any of the printed labels included in Figure 7.4; it would not even indicate that the report referred to a therapy session. Figure 7.5 includes just the numbers and instructions for coding. The name of the client is not included; however, the identification number is. The client's version of the form is shown in Figure 7.6. It includes the client's name and center number (to facilitate access to records if a question should occur), the charge for services, the name of a referral (if any), the time of next appointment (if any), and the therapist's signature.

A monthly report of clients who have ended their association with the center could allow a format similar to that of Figure 7.7. Information about the amount and type of service received,[1] mean functional status at the beginning and at the end of therapy, amount of charges, number of referrals, and the type of termination occurring could be summarized and related to the demographic information previously obtained. Examining just the information in Figure 7.7, the director and staff can learn that about one-quarter of the clients apparently reject the services offered. This conclusion can be drawn from the facts that 24 percent of the clients accept two units or less of counseling and that 29 percent of the clients leave without the

[1]A unit of service can be considered as one 50-minute period of individual psychotherapy or two 50-minute periods of group therapy. Other settings, of course, would require different units of service.

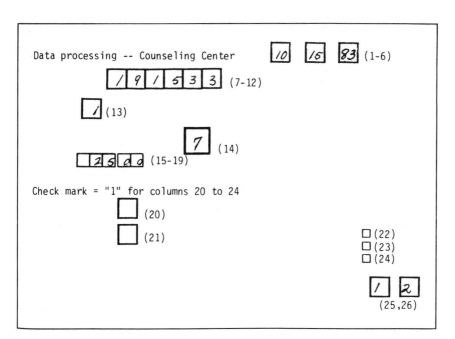

Data processing -- Counseling Center |10| |15| |83| (1-6)

|/|9|/|5|3|3| (7-12)

|/| (13)

|7| (14)

|2|5|0|0| (15-19)

Check mark = "1" for columns 20 to 24

|☐| (20)

|☐| (21)   ☐(22)
                                           ☐(23)
                                           ☐(24)

                                           |/| |2|
                                           (25,26)

FIGURE 7.5 The way the information in Figure 7.4 would be transmitted to the person responsible for analyzing the information for future use.

FIGURE 7.6 The client's copy of the therapist's form illustrated in Figure 7.4 would contain the information shown below.

Client ___*Mabel Smith*___ Date *10* – *15* – *83*

Your center no./ 9 / 5 3 3

In case a question or a need to change your next appointment arises, our number is 887-7325. Please mention your center number when calling.

The charge for today's session is
   $ 25.00

Next appointment 2:30 AM/PM   M (T) W TH F SA   *10* – *23* – *83*

Referral, if any, is to:

Therapist ___*M J Hahn*___

REPORT OF TERMINATED CLIENTS IN MAY 1991

CASES TERMINATED: 84

RATINGS OF FUNCTIONAL STATUS

LEVEL		CLIENTS AT EACH FUNCTIONAL LEVEL WHEN THERAPY BEGAN	AT TERMINATION
DYSFUNCTIONAL:	1	0 (0%)	0 (0%)
DYSFUNCTIONAL:	2	0 (0%)	1 (1%)
DYSFUNCTIONAL:	3	2 (2%)	0 (0%)
DYSFUNCTIONAL:	4	25 (30%)	3 (4%)
FUNCTIONAL:	5	41 (49%)	2 (2%)
FUNCTIONAL:	6	8 (10%)	7 (8%)
FUNCTIONAL:	7	6 (7%)	4 (5%)
FUNCTIONAL:	8	2 (2%)	21 (25%)
FUNCTIONAL:	9	0 (0%)	46 (55%)
MEAN FUNCTIONAL STATUS		5.00	8.05

TYPE OF TERMINATION AND AGE OF CLIENT

	UNDER 29	30 AND OVER	ALL
MUTUAL CONSENT	25 (76%)	32 (63%)	57 (68%)
CLIENT DECISION	6 (18%)	18 (35%)	24 (29%)
THERAPIST DECISION	2 (6%)	1 (2%)	3 (4%)
ALL	33 (100%)	51 (100%)	84 (100%)

UNITS OF SERVICE AND AGE OF CLIENT

	UNDER 29	30 AND OVER	ALL
2 OR LESS	5 (15%)	15 (29%)	20 (24%)
3 TO 6	7 (21%)	7 (14%)	14 (17%)
7 TO 15	14 (42%)	22 (43%)	36 (43%)
16 TO 30	6 (18%)	7 (14%)	13 (15%)
OVER 30	1 (3%)	0 (0%)	1 (1%)
ALL	33 (100%)	51 (100%)	84 (100%)

FIGURE 7.7 A report on the clients terminated during one month, including characteristics of services rendered to these clients.

therapist's agreement. A director would probably seek to lower these percentages. The illustrative reports offer some clues about how to approach such a goal. The lower part of the report shows that older clients rejected therapy more frequently than younger clients did. Approaches to older clients could become a topic for in-service training at this center. Material presented later in this chapter provides further suggestions for the director who seeks to lower the proportion of clients who receive little care at this center.

A monthly report can also be prepared for each therapist. Such reports would provide the therapists with information about their work compared to that of the other therapists as a group. People working in human services seldom have quantified information on how their work compares to that of others in their own field or institution. However, the value of feedback in improving one's performance has repeatedly been demonstrated. Seligman and Darley (1977), for example, showed that residential use of electricity could be reduced more than 10 percent simply by providing consumers, on a weekly basis, with information on how much electricity was used. Hospital-based physicians reduce the number of unnecessary diagnostic tests ordered when given information on the testing patterns of others (Tierney, Miller, and McDonald, 1990).

A report format that could provide information for the individual therapist is given in Figure 7.8. This hypothetical report describes the therapist's caseload and the amount of service rendered during the month in question. Note that the therapist Helper has some problems. He had a higher proportion of clients drop out during the previous month than the other therapists in the center. Of greater importance, those who quit had received less service than was given to other clients before termination. This therapist also has a relatively large number of inactive clients, that is, clients who have not received any service for 90 days or more. The report politely requests that therapist Helper terminate these clients or see if they are still interested in continuing therapy. Last, there is a frequency table of ratings of psychological function of Helper's clients who officially ended their contact with the center during the last month.

Program changes or procedural changes can be planned to remedy any deficiencies found. What sorts of questions might therapist Helper want to discuss with his director? It seems that he is losing clients after only one or two counseling sessions. Everyone has a string of bad luck once in a while. If Helper's record does not improve and he continues to lose clients prematurely, he should seek some assistance in improving his manner with clients. Perhaps he is too judgmental; perhaps new clients need more direction during the first sessions. Ideally, noting undesirable practices early in a therapist's career permits improvements in the therapist's techniques before these practices are deeply ingrained. Also, it is to a therapist's advantage to learn of problems before hearsay and rumor define his or her therapy as below average in quality (House, 1976). Prue et al. (1980) described how feedback to staff improved the performance of workers at a state hospital. Feedback on treatment activities was a cost-effective method of improving service to the patients.

A Threatening Use of Program Monitoring

Gathering the type of information requested in Figures 7.1 and 7.4 permits the presentation of information in a way that can be very controversial. No one enjoys being evaluated. Nevertheless, so long as monitoring is only on a facility-wide basis, staff members may "grin and bear it." If the information available about an individual care giver is released only to that person, the controversy may concern merely the time and expense of the information system. However, the information generated by the methods just described permits comparisons among individual therapists. Most staff members dislike having their work compared to that of others in this way. Although such evaluations will be resisted, a manager needs objective comparative information. If staff members offer different services, such comparative reports are more difficult to prepare. Crisis counselors, outpatient therapists,

REPORT FOR THERAPIST HELPER

	HELPER	OTHER THERAPISTS
TOTAL CASE LOAD ON JUNE 1, 1991	64	433
ACTIVE CASES	49 (76%)	364 (84%)
INACTIVE CASES	15 (24%)	69 (16%)
(NOT SERVED IN 90 DAYS)		

THE NAMES OF YOUR INACTIVE CLIENTS ARE:

ARCHIBALD, L.	NORRIS, M. M.
BEST, B.	OVERMAN, S.
BOULDER, M. M.	PAKOWSKI, M. M.
ERNEST, G.	RASMUSSEN, P.
GRAND, K.	THOMAS, A.
HANSEN, M. M.	TRAVERSE, P.
MORRISON, S.	WILSON, G.
NARWELL, B.	

PLEASE FILE A TERMINATION NOTICE OR A REFERRAL NOTICE, OR HAVE
AN APPOINTMENT WITH EACH OF THESE INACTIVE CLIENTS BY
JULY 31, 1991.

	HELPER	OTHER THERAPISTS
TERMINATED CASES IN MAY		
TERMINATED BY MUTUAL CONSENT	10 (48%)	47 (75%)
TERMINATED BY CLIENT DECISION	9 (43%)	15 (24%)
TERMINATED BY THERAPIST	2 (10%)	1 (1%)
NUMBER OF THERAPY SESSIONS WITH CLIENTS TERMINATED IN MAY 1991 (MEDIAN)	4.0	7.5

RATINGS OF THE FUNCTIONAL STATUS OF TERMINATED CLIENTS WERE:

LEVEL	CLIENTS AT EACH FUNCTIONAL LEVEL	
	HELPER	OTHER THERAPISTS
DYSFUNCTIONAL: 1	0 (0%)	0 (0%)
DYSFUNCTIONAL: 2	0 (0%)	1 (1%)
DYSFUNCTIONAL: 3	0 (0%)	0 (0%)
DYSFUNCTIONAL: 4	2 (10%)	1 (1%)
FUNCTIONAL: 5	1 (5%)	1 (1%)
FUNCTIONAL: 6	1 (5%)	6 (10%)
FUNCTIONAL: 7	2 (10%)	2 (3%)
FUNCTIONAL: 8	4 (20%)	17 (27%)
FUNCTIONAL: 9	11 (52%)	35 (56%)

FIGURE 7.8 An illustrative format for feedback to individual therapists.

and inpatient group leaders cannot easily be compared to one another. However, when individuals perform much the same tasks, comparisons become possible. In general, information on individual staff members should never be released in a general report. Each person can be given his/her own data, which can be compared to summary data from the whole facility; however, only the director has a right to information on all individual staff members.

In Figure 7.9 the work of each therapist is summarized in one line. Contrasts among the therapists can be made. Those with very low or very high caseloads and those with many inactive clients are easily noted. If there are particular therapists who lose a disproportionate number of clients early in the course of counseling (and thus often deliver only a minimal service to these clients), they can be readily identified. See, for example, the information on Helper.

Therapist Helper has the largest proportion of inactive clients and loses more clients than anyone else before three counseling sessions. However, Helper rates his clients as functioning higher than all other therapists except Nelson. There are at least two interpretations of these findings. One, Helper has been assigned clients who do not really need counseling. He correctly sees them as generally functioning well and does not provide unnecessary counseling. Two, Helper's counseling is not seen as helpful by the clients. Although they drop out, Helper rates their functioning as ''good'' to justify his high rate of client loss. The first interpretation is tenable if the pattern does not continue. However, if clients are assigned at random or to whomever has an opening and the pattern continues, the second interpretation appears more likely. Such a negative evaluation does not mean that Helper should be dismissed. It may mean that Helper should have some in-service training; perhaps his approach in setting the stage for counseling is not appropriate to the population utilizing this center. Such possibilities should be explored and may resolve the situation. If so, Helper will be a better counselor and his clients will be better served.

Even though initial objections to monitoring as presented in Figure 7.9 are likely to be numerous and intense, there are important advantages to preparing such materials. We believe that accurate information is better than impressionistic information of unknown accuracy. What is to be gained by giving the program director the sort of information in Figure 7.9? The director's chief responsibility is to facilitate the delivery of quality human services—psychotherapy in this example. If a therapist is performing markedly less well than others, clients are being short-changed when they are assigned to that therapist. It would be best if therapists took the initiative in approaching the director for help in improving their work. However, if they do not approach the director, the director's job requires approaching them. The reason for providing this information frequently—once a month or once a quarter—is to encourage improvement before a situation becomes intolerable.

Figure 7.9 should be supplemented with an accounting of time spent on various activities. For example, if therapists Rudov and Williams are devoting much time to community work, to administration, or to in-service training, their low caseloads are readily understandable. As an exercise, readers might try to prepare a form for therapists to use to account for their time without requiring onerous recordkeeping. Categories of activities would include individual therapy,

| | | ACTIVE CASES | | | INACTIVE CASES | | | | FUNCTIONAL STATUS | % SEEN FEWER | MEDIAN NUMBER |
THERAPIST	N	% OF CENTER CASES	FUNCTIONAL STATUS (MEAN)	N	% OF CENTER CASES	FUNCTIONAL STATUS (MEAN)	N	% ABOVE 7	THAN 3 TIMES	OF VISITS
ABRAMS	39	11	6.5	4	7	6.3	6	100	33	6
COULDER	29	8	7.2	0	0	DNA	9	89	22	7
GREGORY	43	12	6.8	9	15	5.9	4	75	25	8
HELPER	49	13	6.7	15	25	6.7	21	71	48	4
MATTHEWS	28	8	6.5	1	2	6.0	6	50	17	9
NELSON	29	8	7.0	6	10	7.2	5	80	0	6
NICOLET	36	10	6.6	8	13	6.2	8	75	12	6
PETROVICH	38	10	6.2	10	17	5.9	5	80	0	7
RUDOV	19	5	7.1	1	2	5.0	4	100	0	9
VINCENT	35	10	6.5	4	7	6.3	10	80	20	7
WILLIAMS	20	5	5.9	2	3	6.5	6	100	17	8
ALL	365	100	6.6	60	100	5.4	84	80	24	7

FIGURE 7.9 A report permitting the center director to spot problems and to suggest ways to improve services given.

group therapy, administration, education, and community service. How might such report forms be designed? How might Figure 7.9 be extended to include this new information?

As with any type of information, a report such as Figure 7.9 can be misused. Critics fear that providing summaries of information usually hidden in files allows such data to be used in a vindictive manner. Most evaluators believe that providing more information reduces the opportunities for directors to behave autocratically. Most unfair managers restrict information, just as despotic rulers control the media in the nations they govern. Nevertheless, certain precautions can be built into the system to circumvent some possible misuses of the information. For example, the system can be designed to minimize the possibility of acceptable variations in personal style appearing as deficiencies. Some therapists may encourage clients to leave therapy sooner than other therapists do. They may do this because of personal and theoretical convictions, not because of inadequate therapeutic skills. An information system should be planned in a way that does not confuse therapy designed to be short term with rejected therapy. In Figure 7.9 we sought to avoid this confusion by separating the number of clients terminating after one or two counseling sessions. Even therapists who plan on short-term therapy expect to retain clients beyond two sessions.

Implementing an Information System

The type of reports illustrated in this chapter can be produced easily by desktop computers using a database program. The software for developing tables such as those in Figures 7.7, 7.8, and 7.9 is available for less than $300. Using such programs does not require any programming experience. More complicated management information systems also can be purchased. For mental health settings, Schultz (1990) has prepared a program for organizing client information including standard diagnostic categories, progress notes, and standard government reporting forms. The program, SISYPHUS, can be altered to produce locally designed forms.

If done poorly, monitoring services can be expensive, disruptive, and unpleasant experiences for all involved. If done well, such evaluations of effort can provide feedback on performance that enhances growth. Kreitner (1977) has called such feedback *informational feedback.* Other forms of feedback, such as *corrective feedback,* also are useful in helping people improve performance. Although automated systems such as those described in this chapter provide valuable sources of feedback, managers should not permit these and similar systems to be the only source of feedback given to staff members.

AVOIDING COMMON PROBLEMS IN IMPLEMENTING AN INFORMATION SYSTEM

There are some traps that can make the development of an MIS more difficult than necessary and reduce its usefulness.

Avoid the Duplication of Records

Human service staffs will not cooperate happily with an information system that duplicates information already reported and stored elsewhere. Few agencies exist without any records. When introducing an information system, it is undesirable simply to impose the system as an addition to the existing recording procedures. Instead, integrating the information required by the old system with the automation of the new system is preferable. Staff members may question the accuracy of an automated system. The fact that staff cannot describe the population they serve in quantitative terms may mean that they will be surprised at the summaries of information gathered at times.

Avoid a Focus on Technology

To produce the most useful system, the users need to be involved in its design. The information needed, the manner of summarizing it, the frequency of reports, and other issues should all be determined with the people who will use the information. The evaluator may be enthusiastic about getting the system operating. However, learning what is useful requires patient work with the staff and administrators. Although a completed information system is not chiseled in granite, changes are expensive once the system is operational. Involving users early minimizes the possibility of producing an expensive product that no one really wants. A related danger is the temptation to use computers in a misguided attempt to monitor staff work at such a detailed level that staff members simply report fictional information.

Avoid Serving the Needs of Only One Group

People filling different roles in an organization have different informational needs because their responsibilities are different (Patton, 1986). Evaluators should know that the needs of the accounting department differ from those of the billing department, which in turn differ from the needs of service delivery staff. By working closely with only one or two such groups, the evaluator runs the risk of providing information useful only to some groups. If that happens, the information system would be seen as irrelevant by those whose needs remain unmet; such people resist giving information. The quality of information supplied can only be eroded when the system is not respected and valued. There is no substitute for understanding the organizational roles of all potential users.

SUMMARY AND PREVIEW

Human service agencies can begin an evaluation with a systematic description of their programs, the amount of service given, and the identity of those receiving the services. Such monitoring permits an accounting of how the agency's funds were expended and a comparison between the program as designed and the program as implemented. This sort of evaluation can be invaluable for showing what aspect of a program needs additional effort or why a program never had the impact intended.

Also, the need to complete accrediting agency and government surveys can be met more easily if monitoring is carried out regularly rather than developed after requests for information are made.

The two general approaches to program monitoring are a summary of effort over a given time period and a systematized information system to permit repeated summaries of effort on a monthly or quarterly basis. The former requires a manual search through existing files that are often not designed with evaluation procedures in mind. If problems are found, even this kind of evaluation can lead to plans for improvement. When records are designed to facilitate evaluations, ongoing or repeated evaluations are possible.

Monitoring is a crucial aspect of program evaluation; it is essential to keep track of program activities. However, stakeholders want to know how successful the programs are in helping participants, students, or patients to achieve the goals of the program. The following chapters focus on methods that evaluators and stakeholders use to examine the degree to which programs achieve outcome goals.

STUDY QUESTIONS

1. How does program monitoring fit into the schematic diagram in Figure 1.1.?
2. Explain the relationships between program monitoring and formative and summative evaluations.
3. People sometimes object to an evaluation of effort on the grounds that it reveals nothing about the quality of the service rendered. This statement is true. Why does this criticism not negate the reasons for doing the types of evaluations described in this chapter?
4. Suppose you managed a telephone sales office. Twenty people make telephone calls to potential buyers of educational films. If these potential buyers are interested in previewing a film, it is mailed to them. They either pay for it or return it in seven days. How would you develop a monitoring system to keep track of what your employees are doing? How would you measure their success? What type of indexes of success would be important?
5. What are some of the evaluative questions that can be answered using a management information system? What are some of the questions that an MIS cannot answer? How do these two sets of evaluative questions differ?

FURTHER READING

BANK, A., and WILLIAMS, R. C., eds. 1987. *Information systems and school improvement: Inventing the future.* New York: Teachers College Press.

8

Nonexperimental Approaches to Outcome Evaluation

A neighborhood crime prevention program, a new way of admitting patients to a hospital, and a class for diabetic senior citizens are programs that have goals that apply equally to all people using the program. Such programs are evaluated using information describing the average performance of a group of program participants. Chapters 8, 9, and 10 focus on the analysis of data gathered from groups to evaluate the outcome of human service programs. The chapters begin with the simplest approaches and progress to more complex and more scientifically rigorous ones. Each approach, regardless of its scientific rigor, has its place in program evaluation; the usefulness of a particular approach depends on the questions the evaluator seeks to answer. These chapters describe evaluative procedures that are more similar to standard educational and social science research procedures than the previous chapter or those in Part IV.

As indicated in the chapter titles, when evaluators are commissioned to confirm that a program caused an outcome, they choose a more rigorous research design than when commissioned to document that clients leave a program at a certain level of competency or health. The questions each approach can address—and the misuses of each approach—are described and illustrated. The reader should develop a sense of the purpose of careful experimental design and see how each level of control is introduced to increase the clarity of the interpretation of the data.

SINGLE-GROUP DESIGNS

One Set of Observations

When teachers, nurses, administrators, or judges inquire into the success of some social service program, they frequently use the simplest form of outcome evaluation. Basically, they want to know how the program participants are faring after the service has been provided. Do the members of a job-training group have jobs three months after receiving job skills training? What percentage of smoking-clinic participants are in fact not smoking one month after the program? The first step in deciding if a program is useful is to learn if the participants finish the program with a level of achievement that matches the program's implicit or explicit goals. This simple form of evaluation requires that a set of systematic observations be made of one group at some specified time after completion of the program. This simple posttest-only assessment of outcome can show whether participants finish the program at a low, medium, or high level of achievement. For example, the rearrest rate for released first-time felons may be 5 percent, 15 percent, 30 percent, or 75 percent. If the program is to help ex-convicts avoid further trouble with the law, but nearly all fail to do so, then there may be no need to evaluate any further. Program improvements should precede any further outcome evaluation. On the other hand, if program graduates do have a low rate of recidivism, the staff may have an effective program, which should be studied more thoroughly. With this one-observation group design, evaluators would not know whether the program participants *improved* during the program. To learn whether people improved requires a more complex design.

One Group—Two Sets of Observations

The pretest-posttest design is used when evaluators want to ascertain that the participants improved while being served by a program. The program might have caused the improvement; however, the pretest-posttest approach to data collection is not sufficient to permit such a conclusion. Case Studies 1 and 5 are both pretest-posttest designs.

The reasons causal interpretations may not be permitted have been labeled "threats to internal validity" by Campbell and Stanley (1963). *Internal validity* refers to being able to conclude that an independent variable (such as the program) caused a change in a dependent variable (such as a measure sensitive to the behavior the program was supposed to improve.) For example, showing that people who complete a reading program do indeed read well or, for that matter, better than they did a month before does not mean that the program itself led to the improvement. This caution is especially serious when only a small portion of those who began the program actually complete it. A plausible alternative interpretation is that the most motivated people learned, but the program was unsuccessful for most people. In order to evaluate the adequacy of various approaches to outcome evaluation, a detailed understanding of the threats to internal validity is critical. The posttest-only and the pretest-posttest approaches are very deficient in terms of internal validity. As more complex designs are presented, various plausible alternative interpretations are eliminated until finally the only plausible cause of change is the human service program itself.

The questions that can be answered by simple, nonexperimental approaches to outcome evaluations are summarized in Figure 8.1. This figure and other tables in the following chapters reflect the idea that the evaluation design should be based on the questions to be answered and on the resources involved with the program. Evaluation is not basic research; evaluators do not assume that an evaluation must be designed to answer the same type of questions that basic research addresses. When programs are relatively inexpensive, not harmful to participants, and fairly standard, absolutely airtight evaluations are not needed (Smith, 1981). The bulk of this chapter is devoted to the appropriate uses of the pretest-posttest design and the reasons why care must be exercised when interpreting the results of pretest-posttest evaluations.

USES OF THE PRETEST-POSTTEST DESIGN

Did the Program Participants Change?

The first level of interest in an outcome evaluation concerns whether the participants change in the direction that the program was planned to encourage. Is there less driving while intoxicated after court-ordered educational programs? Do rehabilitation patients retain their increased flexibility? These are reasonable questions, but naive applications of statistical analyses can and have often confused conclusions. Some people have acted as though a statistically significant comparison of pretest and posttest scores using, for example, a correlated groups t-test, tells whether the program caused the change. Statistical analyses do not help with this issue. When statistical tests are discussed, the concern is not about the reason for the change, but merely about the reliability of the difference between two means, such as the mean of the pretest and that of the posttest. This is called a *question of statistical conclusion validity* (Cook and Campbell, 1979).

FIGURE 8.1   Single-group evaluation designs and the questions they can answer.

Name and Symbolization of the Evaluation Design[a]	Questions That Can Be Answered
Posttest only X O	How well are the participants functioning at the end of the program? Are minimum standards of outcome being achieved?
Pretest-posttest O X O	Both of the above questions. How much do participants change during their participation in the program?

[a]Throughout this text, the notation adopted by Campbell and Stanley (1963) is used. The program is symbolized as X and an observation by O.

Second, in contrast to the above, some analysts have acted as though nonsignificant findings mean that there were no differences; that is, the participants are no different after having gone through the program. Not being able to reject the null hypothesis may be due to many factors that reduce the sensitivity of statistical analyses, such as small sample sizes or unreliably measured criteria. Lipsey (1990b) writes that one should examine carefully whether the research failed before deciding that the program failed.

Did the Participants Change Enough?

If the change from pretest to posttest is statistically significant, evaluators face another issue: did participants change *enough* to demonstrate a real effect in their daily lives? Singh, Greer, and Hammond (1977) found that the outcome of a classroom program on civic responsibility was an increase of 3 points on a 92-point attitude test. The authors concluded that the amount of change, although statistically significant, was not large enough to have a practical impact on the children's behavior.

If evaluators want their work to have an impact on decisions, they need to be sensitive to the issue of meaningful change, not just statistically significant change. Many texts on statistics do not devote much attention to determining the size of a substantial difference. Consequently, many students feel their job is complete after they have performed a statistical test and found a statistically significant difference. Applied social scientists, however, cannot stop after reporting a reliable finding. The sponsors of human services want to know if the participants are better in any *practical* way for having participated in the program. These questions are easier to raise than to answer; however, these important questions will be answered by someone—perhaps by a newspaper reporter. It is better if the evaluator and stakeholders themselves deal with the issue of the amount of change needed to label a change substantial, not trivial.

For internal evaluators performing a simple evaluation, the best approach to use in addressing the question of importance of the findings is consultation with the program's stakeholders after measures have been chosen but before data are collected. For example, would a job-training program be a success if only 10 percent of trainees found employment after three months? Would 25 percent be sufficient? Seventy-five percent? Would a mental health program be satisfied if depressed clients improved five percentile points relative to normative values? Or would a 15-point improvement be required? In addition to the program staff, other groups with interests in the achievement of a program include community groups, funding agencies, and program participants. The minimum amount of change necessary to define the outcome of a program as a success cannot be fully specified without considering the costs necessary to achieve that outcome. The relationship between the outcome and the costs of a program can be analyzed using the simple forms of cost-benefit and cost-effectiveness analyses discussed in Chapter 11.

Relating Change to Services and Participant Characteristics

The discussion of the pretest-posttest design to this point has concentrated on methods to document the possible improvement of program participants. Another approach to evaluation is to relate the amount of service received with the degree of improvement observed. Although such research may be open to the criticism that the results can be interpreted in various ways, it can be very useful in certain situations. For example, an important study in the history of medical research followed the strategy of relating the patient's condition to the amount of treatment received. In 1835 Pierre Louis (Eisenberg, 1977) reported his study comparing the amount of blood drawn from patients with their progress in recovering from inflammation (pneumonia). Early nineteenth-century medical theory led to the expectation that the more blood drawn, the better the treatment and the more likely a recovery. Louis measured the volume of blood drawn from the patients. He then compared these values to the course of their illnesses. He found that a patient's prognosis was not related to volume of blood taken. This finding was an important influence on the medical practice of that time and contributed to the eventual discrediting of bloodletting as a form of medical treatment. Louis was unable to conclude anything about the cause or the proper treatment of pneumonia, but he did identify a useless treatment.

Another reason to do an evaluation even if it is unable to identify the cause of change is to search for characteristics of the participants that might be related to achieving program goals. Do men experience better outcomes than women? Do members of minority groups complete the program as frequently as majority-group clients? Is age related to outcome? These questions can be explored, tentatively to be sure, using a simple research design. If policy-relevant relationships are found between outcome and a characteristic of participants, that variable would be involved in any future studies. The findings may even have immediate impact if a program appears to have a good effect on some segments of the target population but little effect on other segments.

Although it is quite easy to discuss the idea that personal and service characteristics may be related to success in a program, the statistical method of relating improvement to other variables is often misunderstood. The most intuitive approach is to subtract pretest scores from posttest scores, label the difference improvement, and correlate the improvement scores with age, number of units of service received, and any other variables of interest. This seemingly obvious method is not desirable. To understand this point fully requires more advanced statistical sophistication than readers of this book are assumed to have. The basic concept involved concerns the reason why improvement is more likely for some participants than for others. On the average, people who score low on a measure initially are more likely to improve than people who get high scores initially. Students know that it is generally harder to improve on a B+ than a C−. This observation is related to the concept of regression to the mean, which is discussed later.

Nunnally (1975) comments that change scores should be avoided because they are based on shaky statistical assumptions. Further, the complex methods suggested to deal with change scores are hard to explain to others and are controversial, even among experts. Nunnally makes one exception to this warning: when the evaluator is interested in relating change to a characteristic of the program participants, change scores may be used. For example, since the length of some human services, such as psychotherapy, is not standardized as is a school year, an evaluator might want to relate improvement to the amount of service received.

The best way to relate improvement or change to the amount of service received or to some characteristic of the program participant when information is available only from the group receiving the program is to use residualized change scores. Judd and Kenny (1981) call this approach *regression adjustment*. This approach is illustrated here because introductory texts do not cover the method. To calculate a residualized change score, it is necessary first to calculate a regression equation that uses the pretest to predict the posttest. Even though program participants improved on a variable, it is likely that those who were better off on the pretest will, on the average, be better off on the posttest. In other words, we usually expect a positive correlation between a pretest and posttest. Figure 8.2 includes hypothetical data that is used to illustrate the calculation of residualized change scores. Imagine a job-training program consisting of 20 training sessions. The correlation between the pretest and the posttest given in this figure is 0.47. The goal of the evaluator is to correlate job skills improvement with amount of training received.

FIGURE 8.2 Hypothetical data illustrating how change can be correlated with amount of service, adjusting for differences among program participants at the start of a program.

Program Participant	Skill Level		Change	Residual After	Training Sessions	Residual Sessions
	Before	After				
1	24	26	2	-0.54	16	-2.26
2	23	29	6	3.12	18	-0.13
3	19	26	7	2.73	20	2.40
4	18	27	9	4.39	19	1.53
5	20	19	-1	4.92	16	-1.73
6	24	31	7	4.46	20	1.74
7	25	22	-3	-5.19	15	-3.39
8	24	25	1	-1.54	19	0.74
9	21	22	1	-2.58	19	1.14
10	14	16	2	-4.01	14	-2.94
11	14	26	12	5.99	20	3.06
12	21	30	9	5.42	19	1.14
13	18	22	4	-0.61	19	1.53
14	16	15	-1	-6.31	13	-4.20
15	23	26	3	0.12	19	0.87
16	14	13	-1	-7.01	17	0.06
17	23	26	3	0.12	19	0.87
18	19	29	10	5.73	20	2.40
19	17	28	11	6.04	19	1.67
20	16	27	11	5.69	18	0.80
21	14	15	1	-5.01	14	-2.94
22	22	21	-1	-4.23	19	1.00
23	25	26	1	-1.19	19	0.61
24	23	19	-4	-6.88	15	-3.13
25	21	27	6	2.42	17	-0.86
26	22	29	7	3.77	18	0.00

To do this analysis, the pretest is treated as the predictor, or independent variable (usually denoted as X in regression formulas), and the posttest is treated as the criterion, or dependent variable (usually denoted as Y in regression formulas). The regression equation calculated to relate the two tests is

$$\text{Posttest}_i' = 10.86 + 0.65 \text{ Pretest}_i$$

The posttest score that is expected for each participant is calculated using the regression equation. For example, the value of the first person's pretest, 24, would lead one to expect a posttest score of 26.54. The difference between the actual posttest and the calculated posttest is the residualized change, -0.54. That is, on the basis of the relationship between the pretest and the posttest, person 1 showed a change 0.54 units lower than was expected.

To correlate residualized change with amount of service received, it is also necessary to use the pretest as a predictor of number of training sessions attended; that is, the service unit variable must also be adjusted for the individual differences in pretest score. In this phase of the analysis, the measure of service is treated as the dependent variable (the Y). Amounts of service received as predicted by the pretest is given by the equation

$$\text{Service}_i' = 15.08 + .13 \text{ Pretest}_i$$

Expected service is calculated for each person. Then the difference between actual service and expected service is found. The residual of number of sessions has been adjusted to reflect the fact that there was a nonzero correlation between the pretest and the number of training sessions attended. (If the correlation between the pretest and the number of sessions had been zero, this step would have had no effect on the analysis.)

Finally, a correlation is found between residualized change and the residuals of units of service. The correlation between the two columns of residuals is 0.65. This indicates that more improvement was shown by those participants who received more units of service, even after adjusting for differences in pretest scores. The same strategy can be used to correlate personality, education, or demographic information with improvements by substituting the variable of interest in place of the number of training sessions in this illustration.

This is an internal analysis to learn something about differential improvement levels. In this hypothetical program we know that improvement occurred and that, on the average, the more sessions attended, the more improvement. However, the causes of improvement cannot be discerned on the basis of this analysis. The reasons for caution in interpreting the causes of improvement are described in the balance of this chapter.

THREATS TO INTERNAL VALIDITY

When a statistically significant improvement is large enough to be nontrivial, evaluators need to eliminate explanations of the change that are not due to the program. For example, sixth-grade children do better on a task requiring precise hand-eye coordination than they did as second graders. Is this a result of primary school (the program) or maturation? Maturation is an alternative explanation that cannot be ignored here, and one that forbids attributing the cause of the change solely to the effect of grade school education. Such alternative explanations of research results are labeled threats to internal validity by Campbell and Stanley (1963). The reasons why participants achieve or fail to achieve a certain level of outcome cannot be unambiguously attributed to the program when either a posttest-only or a pretest-posttest approach is used. However, it is important to know why these single-group approaches fail internal validity considerations. As this and the next two chapters progress, different methods will be described to eliminate plausible nonprogram explanations of change. Only when the nonprogram explanations are eliminated can change be attributed to the program.

Actual but Nonprogram-Related Changes in the Participants

Two threats to internal validity refer to real changes that occur in program participants due to influences that are not part of the program. *Maturation* refers to natural changes in people due solely to the passage of time. The most obvious example is a child growing older. *History* refers to events in the community, society, or even the world that change the behavior of the participants of a program. Events such as an election, a recession, or a war may all influence the measures of program success.

Maturation. Children can perform more complex tasks as they get older; people get more tired the longer they have gone without sleep; and there are predictable patterns to the development of adults and elderly people. If an evaluation utilizes variables that can be expected to change merely with the passage of time, maturation could be a plausible explanation for the changes that occur between the time of the pretest and the time of the posttest. In other words, the evaluator may well have found that real change occurred during the course of a program; however, the reason for the change could be that the program lasted *x* number of months and thus the participants are *x* months older and *x* months more experienced—not that the participants gained anything from the program.

The existence of maturation-based changes does not mean that maturation is the only explanation of the changes observed. Nor do plausible, alternative hypotheses mean that the program had no effect. Interpretations would be easier if the evaluator could learn how much of the change was due to maturation and how much was due to the program. Using the one-group pretest-posttest design, this separation cannot be made. Methods to estimate the change due to maturation involve testing other groups of participants or potential participants as well as testing over a greater number of time periods as explained in the following chapter.

History. History refers to any specific event that occurs between the pretest and the posttest that affects the people in the program. For example, a recession may make even the most well-designed program to help people find jobs look like a dud. On the other hand, an economic recovery would make a similar but poorly run program look like a winner. These concurrent national economic changes are plausible alternative interpretations of any changes found among the participants of employment programs. All nonprogram events or series of events that affect the participants would provide plausible alternative explanations.

Some of the same approaches used to account for maturational effects can help isolate historical effects: test additional groups and test at additional times. However, maturation is more predictable and stable than is history. Unexpected events can occur at any time or may not occur at all during a given evaluation. Evaluators should be sensitive to societal or organizational changes that may affect an evaluation. In addition, Cook and Campbell (1979) discuss the influence of events occurring in a particular group under the term *local history*. Events such as staff being involved in personal feuds, the presence of a particularly influential individual in a program group, or a local community disaster cannot be accounted for by any evaluation research design unless the evaluation is replicated a number of times in different settings.

Who Was Observed

Three threats to internal validity must be considered when the participants in a program are not a random or representative sample of the people who might benefit. These three threats are called *selection, mortality,* and *regression.*

Selection. Participation in human service programs is voluntary. Even when prisoners or parolees are forced to participate, the level of meaningful participation is voluntary. Thus, the people obtaining a service are different from the typical member of the target population. In the posttest-only form of evaluation, the process of self-selection may mean that the participants were relatively well off when they began the program. The fact that the posttest detects a desirable state reveals nothing about the effectiveness of the program because the staff's implicit standard of comparison may well be the typical member of the population for which the service was designed, not the typical person who chooses to participate in the program. It is true that sometimes an evaluation is based only on the end result for the people completing the program. However, these individuals chose to complete the program and the results do not represent the effect of the program on everyone the program was designed for.

Adding the pretest permits one to make an estimate of the unwanted effects of self-selection. By measuring the participants before the program, the potential change can be documented. Centra (1977) has reported that the college teachers most likely to be involved in faculty development programs are "good teachers who want to be better." After a faculty development program, most of these teachers, the program participants, will be very good teachers. Their competence tells us nothing about the quality of the program—these teachers were better than the typical teacher from the start. However, observations of their achievements before the program permits an estimation of the amount of improvement.

Mortality. The posttest-only design is also inadequate when participant drop-out (or attrition) is a problem. People differ in whether they will begin a program (selection), and they differ in whether they will complete a program (attrition). Campbell and Stanley (1963) use the term *mortality* to refer to program attrition for whatever reason. Students drop courses they do not like or find too challenging; people in therapy quit when they learn that personal growth is hard; and, in medical settings, some patients actually do die. The longer it takes to carry out an evaluation, the more attrition is likely to take place (Keating and Hirst, 1986).

The level of achievement observed at the end of a program may indicate how well the program functioned, how good the people were when they started, or how motivated the people were who stayed until the end. As a general rule, those who stay are more prepared for the program than are those who drop out. Failing students were more likely to drop a course than are those earning B's and A's. Patients who die were probably the least likely to benefit from a health care program. Without a pretest the evaluator will not know how much attrition there was or what sort of individuals dropped out. A director of a small drug-user program informally mentioned that his program had a 90 percent success rate. Upon inquiry, however, it was learned that only 10 percent of those who start the program are there at the end. Having success with 9 out of the 100 people who begin a program is markedly different from having a 90 percent success rate.

As with selection, the pretest-posttest design handles participant attrition fairly well. By pretesting, the evaluators know who has dropped out and how they compared to those who remained. The pretest-posttest design enables evaluators to know when preprogram achievement and participant dropout are not plausible explanations for the level of outcome observed at the end of the program.

Regression. The threat to internal validity labeled regression to the mean is one of the hardest threats to understand. However, as with most basic statistics, many people already understand regression to the mean at the conceptual level, even though they may not apply it consistently.

Kahneman and Tversky (1974) report that airplane pilot trainers have a practice that illustrates how people can be misled by the effects of regression. If you think carefully about the example, you will see what regression means and why its effects are often undetected. It is said that after a particularly good landing, the trainers do not compliment the trainee, because when such a compliment is given, the next landing is usually done less well. On the other hand, the trainers severely reprimand the trainee after a poor landing in order to elicit a better landing on the next try. It is clear that the empirical observations are true—complimented exceptionally good landings are often followed by less good ones, and reprimanded bad landings are often followed by better ones. However, let us see why the compliments and the reprimands have nothing to do with the quality of the following landing.

Imagine learning a complex task. Initially, performance level fluctuates— sometimes better, sometimes worse. What goes into the better performances? At least two things: the degree of skill achieved and luck, or chance. Flight trainees know they should touch the plane down with the nose up, but they do not yet sense the precise moment to lower the wing flaps and at the same time adjust the elevators to achieve the proper touch-down angle (Caidin, 1960). Sometimes they do it a little too soon and sometimes a little too late. Because these errors are due largely to chance, the likelihood of doing everything correctly at the precise second for two consecutive landings is low. Similarly, the likelihood of badly estimating the precise instant two times in a row is low. Therefore, the probability of two consecutive good landings is low for pilot trainees. In other words, an observer (or a trainer) should not expect two consecutive good landings by a novice trainee, regardless of what is said or not said by the trainer.

The effects of regression to the mean can be further illustrated with a rather silly but instructive example. Choose 20 pennies and flip each 6 times, recording the number of heads flipped for each penny. Select the penny that produced the most "excessive" heads—five or six heads can be considered excessive. Reprimand the penny for producing too many heads. Then flip that penny six more times to see if the reprimand had the desired effect. If the penny yields fewer heads than it did during the first set of six flips, the penny is behaving in the way it was urged to behave. On the average, the reprimand will appear to have been effective 98 percent of the time if the penny originally produced six out of six heads, and 89 percent of the time if the first result had been five out of six heads. The binomial distribution permits the calculation of these percentages (Hays, 1988).

In summary, regression to the mean warns that whenever a performance level is extreme, the next performance is likely to be less extreme. This principle applies to emotional adjustment as well as to learning to fly airplanes or flipping pennies. If the people who currently are the most depressed are included in a therapy group, it is likely that in three months they will be less depressed as a group. This does not mean they will be at a healthy level of adjustment. Most likely, they will still be more depressed than the general population. However, some of the transient random events that caused the worst depression will have passed, and as a group they will be less depressed than before.

Is regression a threat to the internal validity of the pretest-posttest evaluation design? Not necessarily, but it often is. If individuals who are representative of some intact group are tested before and after a program, then regression is not a problem for evaluations following this design. For example, if all children in a school are given a special reading curriculum, regression will not be a threat to internal validity. However, if only the children reading at the lowest levels on the pretest use the special curriculum, regression will be a threat to the correct interpretation of the pretest-posttest change. Children score low in a single test because of poor reading skills; but also due to such chance things as poor guessing, breaking a pencil point, having a cold, misunderstanding directions, worrying about a sick sister, or planning recess games. A day, a week, or a semester later on a second test, these events will not be experienced by exactly the same individuals. Generally, these retest scores will be higher than those on the first test for the children who previously had scored the worst. This does not mean that all poor-scoring children will improve; it does mean that the average will go up. For the children who had scored the best, the average will go down.

Regression is often a plausible alternative hypothesis for pretest-posttest change when human service programs are aimed at those people who are in need of help. Remedial programs are not prepared for everyone, but rather for those who have fallen behind: reading poorly, earning a low income, or feeling emotional distress. Sometimes a screening test to select people for the program is also used as the pretest in an evaluation plan. For example, students scoring the most poorly on a reading test are placed in a reading improvement program, and a second administration of the same test or of a parallel form is compared to the preprogram test scores. This is a poor practice; regression is a very plausible alternate explanation for at least part of the improvement. Improvement in such an evaluation cannot be interpreted. On the other hand, if poor readers or troubled clients get worse (that is, go downhill when regression effects were likely to improve their level), then the evaluation can be interpreted. The correct interpretation is that the program has failed.

Methods of Obtaining Observations

There are two additional plausible hypotheses discussed by Campbell and Stanley (1963): *testing* and *instrumentation* effects. At times these can make the interpretations of outcome evaluations ambiguous. These threats to interpretation are generated by the evaluators themselves and by their observation methods.

Testing. The effect of testing refers to changes in behavior due to the observation techniques. First, two administrations of a test or survey may differ simply as a function of the respondent's increased familiarity with the tool at the second administration. Ability scores increase reliably on the second administration for people unfamiliar with the test (Anastasi, 1988). People interviewing for jobs gain from the experience and can present themselves better on subsequent interviews.

A second aspect of the effects of testing is called *reactivity*. People behave differently when they know they are being observed. This concept was discussed in Chapter 4; however, it is worth recalling. Clients, patients, prisoners, and schoolchildren will be affected when they know someone is recording their behavior, opinions, or feelings. Observation techniques vary in how reactive they are.

The pretest-posttest design is clearly weak in the control of testing effects. If program participants were unfamiliar with the observation procedures, scores might change on the second test. The direction of change that should be expected due to repeated testing does not seem clear except for ability and achievement tests, on which improvement is usually expected.

Instrumentation. The last threat to internal validity to be discussed refers to the use of measurement procedures themselves. Most college instructors know they are not totally consistent when grading essay examinations. There is a real potential for standards to change as the instructor becomes familiar with written examinations. The standards may become higher or lower.[1] If a pretest-posttest design uses

[1]One way to minimize these changes is to read all answers before assigning any grades. Only then are grades assigned. When there are a number of questions, there is a way to minimize the effect of the instrumentation change. Grade all answers to the first question, shuffle the papers and grade all answers to the second question, and so on. Even if standards change, the likelihood of individual total test scores being systematically affected is very low.

measures that are not thoroughly objective, it would be wise not to score the pretest until after the posttest is administered. Then shuffle the tests together and have them scored by someone who does not know which are pretests and which are posttests.

If the measures require observations that must be made before and after the program, the examiners may become more skilled as they gain experience. Thus, the posttests may go much more smoothly than the pretests. If so, a change in instrumentation becomes a viable alternative to concluding that the program had an effect. In such situations examiners who are highly experienced before the pretest is administered are the most effective.

Interactions of These Threats

Over and above the influences of these seven threats to internal validity, it is possible for our interpretations to be confused by the joint influence of two of these threats. For example, the parents who seek out special educational opportunities for their children (self-selection) may have children who are developing more rapidly than children of parents who do not seek special help for their children (different rates of maturation). This situation would be called a *selection-by-maturation interaction*. More will be said about this threat when more complex evaluation designs are discussed in later chapters.

The threats to internal validity refer to reasons why an observed change may not be caused by the program or human service that the group obtained between the pretest and the posttest. Internal validity is thus the most basic concern of evaluators who are examining whether a program was responsible for an observed improvement.[2] As noted above, obtaining strong evidence of causal relationships is not the sole reason for conducting an evaluation. However, if evidence for causality is needed, and if there are plausible explanations based on the types of influences just described, the evaluator may well avoid conducting an evaluation using these basic designs.

Internal Validity Threats Are Double-Edged Swords

When examining a comparison between means it is important to consider whether a significant effect could have been caused by an uncontrolled threat to internal validity serving to raise the value of the posttest. Although attention is usually focused on threats to internal validity masquerading as a program effect, it is also quite possible for a threat to internal validity to hide a program effect. Therefore, the appearance of no program effect, when the samples are large and the measures reliable, could be due to an ineffective program or an uncontrolled threat to internal validity serving to reduce the value of the posttest. Examples of these effects include an economic downturn, program participants being tired at the

---

[2] If there is no "improvement," there usually is nothing to explain, except in rare circumstances where a loss of function is expected without intervention. A program for arthritic patients is an example of a service in which the goal is to avoid deterioration. Such programs at best maintain abilities not cure.

posttest, successful participants being unavailable for the posttest, initially good-scoring participants regressing to the mean, and more sensitive instruments detecting dysfunction that was missed by the less sensitive pretest.

CONSTRUCT VALIDITY IN PRETEST-POSTTEST DESIGNS

When evaluators use participant self-report measures in pretest-posttest designs, it is necessary to examine whether the program might lead to changes in how the participants understand the questions. Some programs lead participants to raise the expectations they hold for themselves or to understand their problems more accurately. Spiro, Shalev, Solomon, and Kotler (1989) discovered that veterans suffering post-trauma stress described a program as very helpful, but described themselves as functioning less well and experiencing more symptoms. It seemed that the program led them to a clearer recognition of their problems and a greater willingness to acknowledge them. Evaluators have distinguished three kinds of change called: *alpha, beta,* and *gamma* change (Arevey and Cole, 1989; Millsap and Hartog, 1988).

An *alpha* change is a real change in the variable of interest. The cause of the change is a question of internal validity, as discussed above. *Beta* changes occur when respondents change their understanding of the meaning of the scale. People with increased insight may see themselves as functioning even less well than they did on the pretest; this change appears numerically as a loss, but the change may indicate an actual improvement. *Gamma* change refers to differences between the pretest and the posttest that are due to a reconceptualization of the meaning of the variable being measured. For example, a high school teacher might not see her physical symptoms as resulting from stress; once she does, her ratings of her own stress level may change because her view of the meaning of her stress has changed. Data taken from records may also be subject to these artifacts when official definitions change over time. Variables that can be measured objectively would not be subject to *beta* and *gamma* change.

For situations requiring a pretest that includes self-reported behavior, attitudes, or intentions, Aiken and West (1990) suggest several strategies to minimize these threats to construct validity, including (1) distinguishing information gathered for program evaluation from that for treatment decisions; (2) leading respondents to expect that what they report will be validated in some way; (3) using interviewers who are experienced with both the program being evaluated and the problems that the respondents have; (4) providing explicit reference groups for respondents to use to describe themselves (e.g. "How do your leadership skills compare with other managers in your division?" rather than "Rate your leadership skills from 1 [poor] to 10 [excellent]"); and (5) using behavioral anchors rather than evaluative terms (e.g. "I am so depressed that I cannot accomplish anything" rather than "Very depressed"). Some writers have argued that retrospective pretests are better than tests given before the program begins. Clearly, care must be exercised in interpreting retrospective pretests.

Taking advantage of chance and developing creative interpretations can make an evaluation appear insightful when it is not. Being aware of these misleading practices is important to producing valid evaluations.

Students and professionals not experienced in research methodology often engage in a practice that fosters inaccurate conclusions. This is the practice of "fishing" for statistically significant relationships between a large number of outcome variables and variables describing the people (such as sex, age, ethnic background). Fishing is often done by repeatedly subdividing the sample of program participants and comparing the ad hoc groups on the outcome measures. For example, if participants are repeatedly divided, first by gender, then by age, then by ethnic background, and so forth, some of the comparisons of the means of these groups will reveal differences that may indeed be significant, but just by chance. Finding significant differences by chance is a Type 1 error. If a large number of relationships are studied, some will appear to be strong, just as flipping a large number of coins six times each will reveal that certain coins appear to be biased toward heads or tails. The same coins, if retested by flipping them six more times each, will be found to be unbiased. Unfortunately, when performing evaluations, new observations cannot be obtained as easily as flipping coins several additional times.

The second reason erroneous, chance relationships are not discovered is that once the data are examined, the evaluator or the program staff can usually make sense out of the results. Once a graduate student presented a senior professor with findings that seemed markedly at variance with the professor's research.[3] The professor quickly interpreted the results in a way that coincided nicely with his work. A week later the student discovered that the computer program was malfunctioning and the initial results were meaningless. This anecdote has a happy ending: when the results were correctly analyzed, they were as originally expected, quite compatible with previous work. The point to remember is that reasonably creative people can make sense out of nearly any finding once the information is presented. This ability, coupled with the practice of gathering many variables and "fishing" for results, can result in very misleading interpretations.

A nearly foolproof manner of discovering which results are Type I errors is to repeat the research. In controlled laboratory research, replication is not difficult. However, because program evaluation often disrupts the service setting, it is seldom replicated at the same site. When only one evaluation is planned, a practical approach involves collecting only the information that can be used and having rational or theoretical reasons for the analyses. In addition, unexpected findings are best treated as very tentative, especially if they are embedded in a large number of analyses that are statistically nonsignificant. Finally, evaluators are very suspicious of surprising findings that require a number of assumptions or elaborate theorizing to understand. The professor mentioned above was able to interpret the computer-

---

[3] The first author of this book was the student, but the senior professor must remain anonymous.

generated nonsense only by making elaborate and novel, although plausible, assumptions.

USEFULNESS OF SINGLE-GROUP DESIGNS

When there are specified standards for the outcome of a human service program, and when the participants do not drop out, the pretest-posttest design may be sufficient to document the program's success. However, even when standards are not available, the reader should not gain the impression that these approaches do not have any legitimate uses. These single-group designs are less intrusive and less expensive than more ambitious designs and require far less effort to complete than the methods described in later chapters. Thus, these designs can serve very important functions in the evaluator's toolbox as first steps in planning rigorous program evaluations. Single group evaluations serve at least three purposes: (1) to assess the likely usefulness of more rigorous evaluations, (2) to search for promising variables related to success in the program, and (3) to "soften up" the facility for more rigorous evaluation in the future.

Assessing the Usefulness of Further Evaluations

Before embarking on a rigorous plan that controls for many plausible alternative interpretations, a single-group design would serve to show whether there is any improvement to interpret (Patton, 1989). If no program participants get jobs for which they were trained, it is likely that no further research is needed to evaluate a job-training program. The program failed, period. No statistical analyses are necessary. If participants finished at a good level, the pretest-posttest design may show that the people improved during the program. This finding may well satisfy some users of program evaluation reports. Also, the finding of reliable improvements may justify a more complex evaluation. Lenihan (1977) used a simple design as a first step in learning whether the use of a phone helped pretrial defendants to raise bond. Showing that 22 percent of the defendants who used a phone that was available on an experimental basis did raise bail suggested that a more rigorous evaluation could be worth the expense. Had only 2 or 3 percent been able to raise bail, the possible effect of the phone would have been very small, and no further study would have been done.

Correlating Improvement with Other Variables

The use of the pretest-posttest design and change scores permits improvement to be related to the amount of service obtained and to characteristics of the program participants. It may be that a program offered to a very needy population primarily benefits people who are relatively well-off. Thus, the good achievement found by a posttest design could be due to the already-competent people who selected themselves for the program. If so, further work is unnecessary. On the other hand, the good level at the end of the program may really indicate a general improvement in most participants. Perhaps the improvement is due to the impact of the program. Further work would be merited.

Preparing the Facility for Further Evaluation

A third reason for conducting an evaluation using only the program participants as respondents is to help staff accept the idea of evaluation. As described in earlier chapters, human service providers—from paraprofessional counselors to teachers to physicians—are beginning to recognize that their work can and will be evaluated, even though the quality of human services is hard to quantify. If evaluators begin their work with less threatening approaches, they have better chances of leading service providers to see the usefulness of evaluation and to value the contribution of evaluators.

The methods described in this and the previous chapters are among the least threatening. There is no possibility that the research could show that unserved people do as well as people who got the service. There is no possibility of learning that another program achieves the same level of success at a lower cost. If an alternative service is less expensive, a comparison of people in the two groups could create anxiety for the staff of the more expensive program. This anxiety will be manifested in roadblocks to the study, hostility, and general uncooperativeness.

Just this type of response occurred during an internal evaluation of a hospital program. The director of the program was very cooperative in initiating and implementing a study of the patients in his program. He displayed considerable openness to evaluation, saying such things as, "Maybe we don't help people as much as we think we do—we should know that"; and "If a patient is institutionalized after leaving here, we have failed." However, when the evaluators proposed increasing the rigor of the evaluation by gathering data from a neighboring hospital without a similar program, the director seemed to change his position. Such a comparison conceivably could have shown that similar patients regained as much ability as those in the director's more expensive program. He now said, "The additional data are unnecessary since the value of these programs is well known and fully documented."[4] The expanded study went on anyway. His negative attitudes dissolved when it became clear that the neighboring hospital had surprisingly few patients with the necessary diagnosis and that those who were available were much less severely ill than those served in the director's program. Because the two groups of patients were not comparable, the study could not threaten the program. Cooperation and cordial relations returned.

Rational use of resources requires that ultimately such comparative studies be done. But they should not be done in a way that leaves the staff demoralized or bitter. Internal evaluators who try to force methodologically rigorous evaluations on staff and who are unable to see the value of approaches with less-than-total experimental control will find their work undervalued and their influence on the

---

[4]Studies supporting the director's assertion were very rare and of questionable validity, a situation that is surprisingly familiar to those who carefully study support for some widely accepted practices in medicine, education, and other human services (see, for example, Eddy, 1990).

program diminished. Beginning in a nonthreatening way permits evaluators to gain the confidence of staff members. We do not intend to devalue the more rigorous approaches but to emphasize that less rigorous studies can be useful.

SUMMARY AND PREVIEW

This chapter emphasizes two major points. First, a careful understanding of the needs of the users of an evaluation may indicate that a simple research design serves quite well to answer these needs at a particular time. The second major idea concerns the conceptual tools useful to understand why simple single-group evaluation designs cannot answer certain questions often important to administrators and to those responsible for financial support of the program. These conceptual tools have been called threats to internal validity and have become part of the vocabulary of social scientists in recent decades.

The next chapter contains several approaches to clarify the interpretation of outcome evaluations. These procedures require making additional observations of the program group, of nonprogram groups, or of variables not expected to be affected by the program.

STUDY QUESTIONS

1. Not many years ago, when a child had frequent bouts of sore throat and earache, family doctors recommended removing the child's tonsils. Typically, the child's health improved afterwards. If parents and doctors attributed the improved health to the effects of the operation, what threats to internal validity were ignored?
2. Some 50 elementary schoolchildren witnessed a brutal murder on the way to school in a suburb of a large city. The school officials worked with a social worker, a school psychologist, and others in an attempt to help the children deal with their emotions, to avoid long-term ill effects, and to help parents with their children. A year after the tragedy, there appeared to be no serious aftereffects. What assumptions are necessary to call this program a success?
3. Politicians are notorious for attributing any improvements in government affairs to their own efforts and any deteriorating affairs to the policies of others. Find or recall examples. What threats to internal validity are most likely to make such an interpretation invalid?
4. Why can a smoking control clinic be evaluated using a one-group pretest-posttest study? It is also possible to gather useful follow-up data to evaluate the program. What index of success could be used to summarize effectiveness if participants could be observed only after the program?
5. Prepare some examples of pretest-posttest evaluations that would appear favorable because of threats to internal validity. Also, prepare some hypothetical examples of evaluations of programs that appear ineffective because of threats to internal validity.

FURTHER READING

COOK, T. D., and CAMPBELL, D. T. 1979. *Quasi-experimentation: Design and analysis for field settings.* Chicago: Rand-McNally.

JUDD, C. M., and KENNY, D. A. 1981. *Estimating the effects of social interventions*. New York: Cambridge University Press.

LIPSEY, M. W. 1990. *Design sensitivity*. Newbury Park, Calif.: Sage.

NUNNALLY, J. C. 1975. The study of change in evaluation research: Principles concerning measurement, experimental design, and analysis. In *Handbook of evaluation research*, vol. I, ed. E. L. Struening and M. Guttentag. Beverly Hills, Calif.: Sage.

9

Quasi-Experimental Approaches to Outcome Evaluation

The previous chapter demonstrated how very simple research designs can answer important questions for the evaluator and for users of evaluations. However, it was stressed that these designs seldom help evaluators identify the cause of changes in program participants. Whenever program administrators and governmental officials commission evaluators to discover the cause of such changes, evaluations of greater complexity must be designed. In order to show that something causes something else, it is necessary to demonstrate (1) that the cause precedes the supposed effect in time; (2) that the cause covaries with the effect; and (3) that no other alternative explanations of the effect exist except the assumed cause. It is easy to satisfy the first criterion, and the second criterion is not that difficult to test either. Both can be demonstrated using the methods described in Chapter 8. The third, however, is much more difficult and is the focus of this and the following chapters.

In this chapter various methods are presented that possess greater internal validity than the simple methods described in Chapter 8. The validity of outcome evaluations seeking to demonstrate causal relationships can be increased by (1) observing the participants at additional times before and after the program; (2) observing additional people who have not received the program; and (3) using a variety of variables, some expected to be influenced by the program and others not expected to be affected. These methods have been labeled quasi-experiments by Campbell and Stanley (1963); although these methods do not achieve the airtight control of true experiments, quasi-experiments control for many biases and can thus yield highly interpretable evaluations—if carefully planned.

DISTINGUISHING CHANGE FROM RANDOM FLUCTUATIONS OVER TIME

Increasing the number of observations across time is one approach to reducing the chances that an observed change resulted from a nonprogram source. All behaviors show random variation over time. The number of crimes on a given day or week is not a constant, nor is it a uniformly decreasing or increasing variable. Although there are some predictable influences on the number of crimes committed (for example, cold weather inhibits crime, warmer weather seems to encourage it, see Anderson, 1987), the causes of most changes in the day-to-day rate are unknown. Nevertheless, popular media often act as though such causes were known and effective remedial action well understood.

A few days after several thousand police officers were laid off in New York City, there were two days in which an abnormally high number of murders occurred: nine murders on July 8, eight on July 9. These two high-crime days were contrasted with the average for the year—four per day. Were newspapers correct in attributing the cause of these additional murders to the reductions in the size of the police force (see Egelhof, 1975)?

The first criterion necessary for a causal conclusion was met: the police were laid off before the murders. However, it is not known if murder covaries with size of police force, and alternative interpretations of the observed number of murders were not even considered. Without some information about the normal variation from day to day, it is hard to know whether eight or nine murders is unusual on a summer day. No information was provided about the weather. It may have been unusually hot. Did the murder rate stay that high after July 9? Without this additional information it is impossible to draw even the most tentative conclusions about the effect, if any, of the reduction in number of police officers on murder rate. Ignoring these threats to internal validity can lead to quite erroneous interpretations of the causal relations between two events. It is possible that an effective program will look ineffective if possible explanations of change are ignored.

A second and frequently cited example of the possibility of misunderstanding a phenomenon when given limited information occurred in Connecticut (Campbell, 1969). In 1955 there were approximately 14.2 automobile accident fatalities per 100,000 residents. This was a record rate and was especially high compared to the previous year. The governor initiated a crackdown on speeding during the following year and the fatality rate dropped to about 12.2 per 100,000. Could the governor justifiably claim that the measures he took were responsible for the reduction in fatalities? Readers might stop for a moment to develop an answer to that question.

The way to decide if the governor could take credit for the drop requires information about fatalities before the crackdown year as well as after. The number of fatalities before the record in 1955 may show that fatalities per year were systematically rising in response to the number of autos on Connecticut roads and the number of miles driven per auto. Because accidents increase when the number of cars increases, a steady increase in fatalities, while undesirable, may be unavoidable in this situation. A program to reduce fatalities would be up against strong forces and could be expected to yield few results.

A second alternative would be to consider 1955 to be a very unusual year. Perhaps a few very tragic but fortunately infrequent multifatality accidents occurred. Or perhaps especially bad weather occurred around holidays when many drivers were on the road. Because consecutive years with such unusual patterns are unlikely, a remedy for the high fatality rate is likely to appear to succeed, regardless of how well or poorly conceived. The drop would then be due to regression to the mean, not due to any remedy attempted.

The actual fatality rates for the years before and after the Connecticut speeding crackdown were reported by Campbell (1969) and are given in Figure 9.1. The reader can see that the 1955 rate does appear to be a discrepant value, even though the magnitude of fluctuations from year to year is large. This example is discussed in more detail later in this chapter. For now note that examining accident rates over a number of time periods permits a much more informed conclusion than merely examining the rates just before and just after the introduction of the treatment.

McKillip (1991) studied the effect on marriage rates in Illinois of the HIV (AIDS) Testing Law, which required couples to take an HIV test before being granted a marriage license. By examining the number of marriage licenses granted

FIGURE 9.1 Automobile accident fatality rate per 100,000 residents for Connecticut by year, before and after the beginning of a crackdown on speeding drivers. (*Source:* D. T. Campbell, Reforms as Experiments. *American Psychologist, 24* (1969): 419. Copyright 1969 by the American Psychological Association. Adapted by permission of the author.)

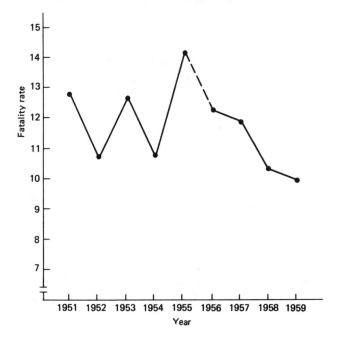

per month for 116 months, McKillip learned that the law was associated with an abrupt 14 percent drop in the number of marriages in Illinois. Adjacent states experienced a corresponding increase in marriage licenses, but other Midwestern states showed no change in the number of marriages. It appeared clear that a sizable portion of Illinois couples were being married elsewhere to avoid the law.

Time-Series Designs

In recent years considerable attention has been given to the use of information across many time intervals. These approaches have come to be called *time-series analyses*. Influences fostering this interest have come from economics at a macro level and from behavior analysis at a micro level. Economists have used information over long time periods, seeking to learn the effects of policy changes on such variables as income level, industrial output, and employment. On a very different scale, behavior analysis research has utilized objective measurement of a single individual over many time periods, during which various interventions were begun and stopped. The unit of analysis—in this case a single person—is not appropriate for most evaluations; however, the importance placed on obtaining stable base-line measurements before an intervention and on documenting both change and the maintenance of change have become concerns of program evaluators.

The data of the economist and the behavior analyst are more similar to each other than might be supposed merely by considering the units of analysis used. Whether referring to a country or to a single child, the researcher obtains one value or makes one observation for each variable during each time interval studied. For example, for the economist there is only one unemployment level in the nation per time period, one GNP, and one inflation rate. For the behavior analyst there is only one index of a specific abnormal behavior per time period. Thus, writers can refer to single subject research in both cases.

Time-series designs as applied to program evaluation received strong encouragement from the work of Campbell and Stanley (1963). Collecting data over many time periods is a way of satisfying some of the internal validity tests described in the previous chapter. Because maturation effects can be traced during the time periods before and after the intervention, the likelihood of confusing the program's effect with maturation effects is greatly reduced when using a time-series design rather than a pretest-posttest design. Similarly, the effects of history will be more easily detected using a time-series design than when an evaluation is performed using observations at only one or two time periods. By examining the reaction of the dependent variables to historical events, it is possible, at least at a qualitative level, to distinguish the effects of the program from the impact of major nonprogram influences.

A time-series approach to program evaluation minimally includes the following characteristics: (1) a single unit is defined, and (2) quantitative observations are made (3) over a number of time intervals (4) that precede and follow some controlled or natural intervention (Knapp, 1977). In the language of experimental design, the unit observed (person, group, or nation) serves as its own control.

Program evaluators, unlike economists, use time-series designs almost exclusively when a definite intervention has occurred at a specific time. The design often is called an *interrupted time series* (Caporaso, 1973) and the evaluator's job is to learn whether the interruption—that is, the human service intervention—had an impact. Figure 9.2 illustrates this design in symbols.

There are a number of possible outcomes observable in a graph of a program's outcome plotted over time intervals. Figure 9.3 illustrates some of these possibilities. Each part of the figure is plotted with time intervals along the abscissa, and magnitude of the outcome-dependent variable on the ordinate. Figure 9.3, Panel A, illustrates no effect of the intervention: there appears to be no out-of-the-ordinary change in the observations after the program. In contrast, Panel B illustrates what is usually the most-hoped-for result of an interrupted time-series analysis. The graph shows a marked increase from a fairly stable level before the intervention, and the criterion remains fairly stable afterwards. This result may be expected from an effective training program that increased the skills of employees or from the introduction of labor-saving devices. Clearly, the method can be used when the intervention is designed to lower variables (such as accident rates and failure rates) as well as to raise them.

Panels C through F all show some increase after the intervention, but their interpretations are much less clear. Panel C shows an increase in slope after the intervention. The variable being measured began to increase over time after the intervention; however, there was no immediate impact as in Panel B. An influence such as television viewing or improved nutrition, whose impact is diffuse and cumulative, might produce the result in Panel E. In Panel D there is a localized increase apparently due to the intervention superimposed on a general increasing trend.

In Panel E there appears to be an effect due to the intervention; however, it seems temporary. Many new programs are introduced with much publicity, and the deeply involved staff members want the program to work. Perhaps extra staff effort is responsible for the initial impact. However, once the program is part of the

FIGURE 9.2 Simple quasi-experimental designs for program evaluation.

Name and Symbolization	Questions That Can Be Answered Using This Design for a Program Evaluation
Interrupted time series O - O - . . . O - X - O - . . . - O - O	All the questions in Figure 8.1. Are there maturational trends that might explain an improvement? Do historical events cause the dependent variable to change?
Pretest-posttest with a nonequivalent control group O - X - O O - - O	All the questions in Figure 8.1. Is change more than the effect of history, maturation, testing, selection, or mortality?

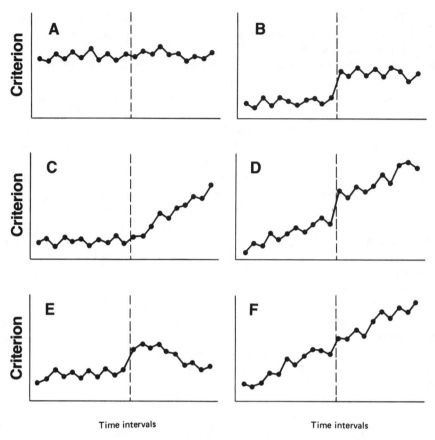

FIGURE 9.3 Some illustrative possible patterns of a criterion of program success plotted over time. Time of the program or intervention is indicated by the dashed vertical line.

regular procedure and the extra effort is no longer extended, the outcome achieved returns to its former levels. Schnelle et al. (1978) showed that a helicopter patrol decreased crime in a high-crime area. However, the authors questioned whether the effect would hold up if the experiment was to be continued beyond the initial trial period. It is possible that although the novelty of the helicopter patrol served to frighten potential thieves and thus to lower crime for a short period, the airborne patrol's inherent effectiveness is not strong.

A possible pitfall for an evaluator could exist when a pattern such as that illustrated in Panel F is found. Here a steady increase over time is observed. A naive approach to the analysis would be to contrast the mean of the time periods before the intervention with the mean of the time periods after. This contrast may be statistically significant, but it does not help in understanding the effect of the intervention.

Analysis of Time-Series Designs

Rigorous analysis of interrupted time-series design is beyond the scope of this book. The methods now accepted are described by McCleary and Hay (1980). Some steps that fall short of the most correct and complete analysis may be taken that can help in interpreting time series data.

First, when the effects of the intervention are striking, statistical analyses may be unnecessary. Case Study 2 on the effectiveness of media, illustrates a situation in which the change in the dependent measure, the criterion of success, is so strong and so closely related to the intervention that one can conclude that the program had a positive effect. Similarly, McCarthy (1978) found a strong effect from a daily posting of the number of high bobbins in a textile plant. High bobbins lead to tangles and lost production time, but their incidence can be greatly reduced by additional employee care. The feedback and the workers' attempts to meet the posted goals resulted in a dramatically reduced rate of malfunction. A graph of the number of high bobbins showed a dramatic drop after feedback was initiated. Furthermore, when McCarthy temporarily removed the feedback procedure, the number of high bobbins began to climb. Reinstatement of the feedback brought the number back down again. It is hard to argue with the interpretation that the feedback caused the results.

There are other examples of time-series records that are not as easy to interpret. The literature on medical education shows that resident physicians order more laboratory tests for hospital patients on average than do community physicians who have more experience (for example, Rich, Gifford, Luxenberg, and Dowd, 1990). To learn whether this finding held for a specified community hospital, a plot of the number of laboratory tests per month was made beginning three years before a major expansion of the hospital's residency programs and one year after. Because neither the hospital's size nor its utilization rate changed systematically during the four-year period, the influence of these variables was ignored. The most striking observation was a steady increase in the average number of laboratory tests compared to the previous month. This increase of an average of an additional 500 tests per month was observed throughout the time period. However, the increase that occurred between the month before the program was expanded and the first month of the expanded program was about 10,000. Because the steady monthly increase resumed after this big jump—that is, the graph resembled Panel D—the evaluators felt safe in attributing the increase to the fact that young residents were now ordering the bulk of the laboratory tests.[1] The effect of the residents on laboratory tests seemed clear, and the interpretation fit published reports on the topic. However, the interpretation was not as compelling as the effect of feedback on high bobbins described above. The residency program could not be introduced, removed, and then reintroduced as McCarthy did in manipulating the high bobbin feedback.

---

[1] Partially on the basis of this sudden jump, the program director instituted procedures to reduce the excessive use of laboratory tests by residents.

Finally, there are situations in which there is a valid question about the interpretation of the results of a time-series design. Figure 9.1, showing the results of the crackdown on speeding, cannot be interpreted validly using the informal examination methods described here. Cook and Campbell (1979) report that recent analyses support the belief that the program had a reliable (that is, statistically significant) effect. The methods necessary to make that interpretation require statistical skills beyond those exercised by many active evaluators. However, it is likely that the use of times series analyses will continue to grow.

One aid to visual inspection of a time-series graph has been provided by Tukey (1977). He suggests that the graph be smoothed by plotting the median of three adjacent points in place of each observation. Suppose that the following observations were made for a 15-month period: 30, 22, 40, 17, 35, 25, (Intervention), 45, 23, 55, 42, 35, 52, and 43. Plot these values. Now take the median of 30, 22, and 40. Plot 30 for month 2. Take the median of 22, 40, and 17. Plot 22 for month 3. Continue for the entire time series. When you are finished, you will see that the graph has been smoothed so that the change that was caused by the intervention can be clearly seen. This technique is most useful when the intervention leads to a lasting, large change, but the change is masked by large random fluctuations among time intervals.

OBSERVING OTHER GROUPS

Nonequivalent Control Group Designs

The simple time-series design increases the interpretability of an evaluation by extending the periods of observations over time. Another approach is to increase the number of groups observed. If the pretest-posttest design could be duplicated with another group that did not receive the program, a potentially good research design would result. So long as the groups are comparable, nearly all the internal validity tests are satisfied by this design, called the *nonequivalent control group design* (diagramed in Figure 9.2). Nonequivalent control groups may also be called comparison groups.

The evaluator expects to observe a larger improvement between pretest and posttest for the program group than for the comparison group, as illustrated in Figure 9.4. A statistical tool to analyze the data from such a design is the two groups by two time periods analysis of variance, with repeated measures over time periods (Kirk, 1982).[2] If the program was successful and the group means followed the pattern in Figure 9.4, the analysis of variance would reveal a significant interaction between group and testing period. Other analyses could also be used for this design. Reichardt (Cook and Campbell, 1979) showed how analysis of covariance can be used to compare the posttest means using the pretest to control for initial differences among students. He also showed that different analyses can bias the results in different directions depending on the pattern of data found. His discussion is beyond

[2]Other names for this design are the split-plot factorial or mixed designs.

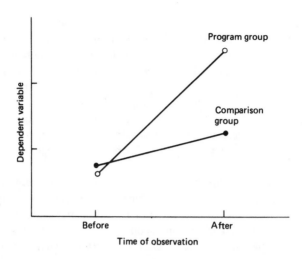

FIGURE 9.4   Hypothetical results of a nonequivalent control (comparison) group design.

the level we can present in this book. It is important that readers realize that different approaches are available; none is always correct.

Including the comparison group permits a distinction to be made between the effects of the program and the several alternative plausible interpretations of change. Because the comparison group has been tested at the same time periods as the program group, both groups have had the same amount of time to mature. Historical forces have presumably affected the groups equally. Because both groups would have been tested twice, testing effects should be equivalent. Finally, the rates of participant loss between pretest and posttest can be examined to be sure they are similar. Nonequivalent control group designs are especially useful when part of an organization is exposed to the program while other parts are not. Since selection to the program is not in the hands of the participants, and since the participants' level of need does not determine eligibility, the comparability of the groups is quite good. Unfortunately, as will be shown later, these favorable conditions are not often met. As mentioned in Chapter 8, the possibility that the meaning of the dependent variable has been affected by the program must be considered; it may be that the pretest and posttest scores have different meanings.

Problems in Selecting Comparison Groups

Comparison groups are chosen according to the evaluation question to be studied. The no-treatment group suggested previously would be used when one seeks to learn if there is an effect of the program. At other times, stakeholders want to compare different ways of offering a service. In such a case, variations in the program would be compared; a no-treatment group would not be an appropriate comparison group. If there is a suspicion that attention alone could affect that outcome, then the comparison group would be a placebo group, that is, a group that experiences a program, but not one that should affect the outcome measure used.

The major weakness in all nonequivalent control group designs is selecting a comparison group not sufficiently similar to the program group to permit drawing valid interpretations. For example, it is possible that those who choose to be in the program may be maturing at a different rate than those in the comparison group. Parents who seek out special programs for their children may also be devoting more attention to the children at home than are parents who do not seek out special programs. Another problem arises if the program participants are chosen because of extreme scores on the pretest, and the comparison group is selected from others with less extreme scores. If so, as mentioned in Chapter 8, the results may be distorted by regression effects.

A way out of the problem caused by using a nonequivalent control group research design is often sought by matching the comparison groups with the program group. People are chosen to form the comparison group because they resemble the program participants on income level, objective test score, rated adjustment, locality of residence, or other criteria. While matching often is used to select comparison groups for quasi-experiments, it is a controversial way to form such groups.

The widely cited evaluations of Head Start (Cicarelli et al., 1969) were criticized for their use of matching (Campbell and Erlebacher, 1970). Head Start, a program for disadvantaged children, is offered in the summer or during the year prior to first grade. The program was designed for the preschool children most lacking in school-relevant skills and attitudes. In addition, nutritional and medical goals were involved.

When Head Start was selected for evaluation, it was already widely accepted and offered in many communities (Datta, 1976b); therefore, the program could not be withheld from any group of children. The evaluation utilized a posttest-only design with national samples of children, some in Head Start programs and some matched samples not in Head Start. The evaluation compared achievement on standard tests of Head Start children in first, second, and third grades with similar non-Head Start children; it concluded that Head Start was largely a failure. Critics attacked the methodology utilized in this evaluation on a number of grounds; however, the focus of the present discussion is on regression effects that likely lie behind the conclusions of the Head Start evaluation.

The population of children available for the non-Head Start comparison group was less disadvantaged than the children in the Head Start group, so the children selected as matches could not be equivalent to the children in Head Start. In order to find children qualifying for Head Start who had cognitive achievement scores similar to those of children not qualifying, either or both of the following points had to have been true: (1) the comparison group was selected from among the less-able children not qualified for Head Start; or (2) the experimental group was selected from among the more able children who attended Head Start.

To understand the effects of regression toward the mean in the Head Start evaluation, it is important to understand why the previous statement is true. Once a group is selected on the basis of need for a national program, no other group exists that is just like the people in the program. There are no good comparison groups. However, on some variables (for example, family income, school grades, test scores) there will be overlap among the members of the two groups. Who will overlap? The people in the "needy" group who overlap with the "not needy" group must be among the relatively better-off among the "needy" people. Those in the "not needy" group who overlap with the "needy" children must be among the least well-off among the "not needy" people. Crano and Brewer (1986) include a numerical illustration of this principle.

Consider an artificial but illustrative example. Suppose a teacher wanted to provide a special spelling program for all the second graders. If the teacher wanted a comparison group, she could find some third graders who scored as low as the second graders. Are these groups equivalent? Probably not. These third graders would have been selected from the lower portion of a population that, in general, is more capable than the second-grade experimental group. What will happen upon retesting the groups in the evaluation? Because no spelling test is completely reliable, the low-scoring third graders in the comparison group will look as though they improved, not only because they learned some new words but also because they are regressing toward the mean of third graders. This regression will make the second graders' improvement due to the program appear smaller and less impressive than it may actually have been.

In other words, the groups of children have different influences raising their scores. The program children will probably show an improvement because the new program has affected them and because they matured a bit. The comparison children will improve because of exposure to the regular spelling classes, added maturity, and regression. Campbell and Erlebacher (1970) assert that the Head Start evaluation was biased in the same way this hypothetical teacher's evaluation would be biased. Because human service programs typically produce small improvements, the size of the regression effects might even exceed the program's effect. In fact, Campbell and Erlebacher argued that regression artifacts made compensatory education look harmful when, in fact, the programs may have had a small positive influence.[3] The moral is: the nonequivalent control group design is especially sensitive to regression effects when the groups are systematically different on some dimensions. In compensatory education evaluations a systematic preprogram difference between experimental and comparison groups is likely to be found.

The emphasis on regression to the mean does not mean that this is the only weakness of nonequivalent comparison group designs. Regression was stressed because some stakeholders may believe that selecting certain participants for inclusion in the evaluation can overcome the effects of preexisting differences between the pretest scores of the groups. There are, however, many other reasons why existing groups may differ from each other. One might compare neighboring classrooms in an attempt to learn if a novel teaching method used in one classroom is more effective. Although the children in two classrooms might seem equivalent, it might be learned later that the teacher of the nontreated class had been using methods of teaching that are similar to those used in the program. Or, when the patients of two physicians are used in an evaluation of a patient education brochure,

[3]There was no controversy over whether regression occurred in this evaluation; however, the size of the likely regression effects was hotly disputed (see Cicarelli, 1970; Evans and Schiller, 1970).

it may turn out that the physician handing out the brochure has systematically encouraged her patients to read about their illnesses and treatments. Thus, her patients are more likely to read such material than are the patients of other physicians. This preexisting difference between patient groups may make the patient education program appear more effective than would have been the case if patients of a different physician had been asked to distribute the experimental material.

If the program effect was massive and the program children improved markedly, the evaluation may reveal that the program was effective, although the size of the effect might still be over- or underestimated. On the other hand, when similar groups are available, the nonequivalent comparison group design is quite powerful and very useful.

REGRESSION-DISCONTINUITY DESIGN

There is one situation in which a comparison between nonequivalent groups can be made in a manner that is much more powerful than the methods presented so far. When eligibility for a service is based on a continuous variable, such as income, achievement, or level of disability, it may be possible to use the regression-discontinuity design. Suppose, for example, that 300 fifth-grade children are tested for reading achievement in the fall. Those scoring the lowest are defined as those most in need of extra assistance. If the program has facilities for only 75 children, it seems reasonable and most fair to take the 75 children with the lowest scores into the program. This is simply a special case of the nonequivalent comparison group design; the strength of this design lies in the fact that the evaluator knows exactly how selection into program or comparison groups was made.

If all 300 are retested at the end of the school year, what would be expected? Note that we do not expect the 75 to outperform the 225 regular class students. We would expect comparisons between pretests and posttests to show that both treatment and comparison children read better than in the fall since all children have been studying reading for the school year. If the program were effective, we would further expect that the treated children would have gained more than they would have had they stayed in regular classrooms.

The pattern of expected results for an effective program is plotted in Figure 9.5 relating the pretest to the posttest. The hypothesized program effect is shown in the discontinuity in the regression line relating the pretest to the posttest at the point on pretest axis that divides the eligible children from the ineligible. If the special program was equivalent to the regular class, one would expect a continuous relationship between pretest and posttest. If the reading program was actually (heaven forbid!) worse than the regular reading classes, we would expect treated children to read less well than expected on the basis of the pretest. In such a situation the discontinuity would be the reverse of that in Figure 9.5.

Trochim (1984, 1990) describes a variety of methods to use to estimate the effect of the program depending on the way the evaluator believes the program affects the outcome variable, that is, the posttest. The simplest alternative is to use

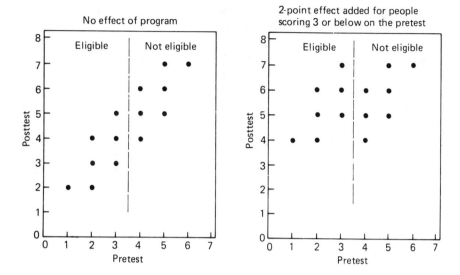

FIGURE 9.5 The relationship between pretest and posttest scores when people scoring 3 or below are eligible for special assistance to improve posttest performance. The graph on the left illustrates the case when the assistance was not effective; the graph on the right illustrates how the data would appear if the program enabled the eligible people to perform 2 points better than they would have without special assistance.

the posttest as the dependent variable in a regression analysis with two independent variables: (1) the pretest, and (2) a coded variable indicating whether the person was in the program or not in the program. This second independent variable could be coded "2" for those in the program, and "1" for those not in the program. If the regression coefficient for this second independent variable was statistically significant, one can conclude that the program was effective; there is a discontinuity in the relationship between the pretest and the posttest. If a graph of the data before analysis suggests that the slope of the regression line to the left of the eligibility cutoff point seems different from the slope to the right of the cutoff point, one is advised to obtain Trochim's book and use a more complicated analysis than is suggested here.

OBSERVING OTHER DEPENDENT VARIABLES

At this point the methods described in Chapter 8 have been expanded to include observations of the program participants at many times and to include observations of groups other than the program participants. It is possible to increase the validity of interpretations by observing additional dependent variables that are not expected to be changed by the program, or at least are expected to be changed only marginally; this design has been called the *Control Construct design* (McKillip and Baldwin, 1990).

The added dependent measures must be similar to the major dependent measure without being strongly influenced by the program. In the example above, if the children did read better, it might be expected that they would do better on a written, standardized arithmetic test than they did before the program. It is hard to imagine additional dependent measures that (1) would be affected by the same threats to internal validity as the outcome measure but (2) would not be affected by the program. Tyson (1985) used this design when he evaluated the Medicaid-required second opinion on surgical procedures by comparing the percentage reductions for ten procedures requiring a second opinion with the reductions for nine procedures not requiring second opinions. McKillip and Baldwin (1990) evaluated the effects of a media-based, health education campaign on a university campus using control constructs that were not the subject of the campaign, but were health-related.

COMBINING METHODS TO INCREASE INTERNAL VALIDITY

Time-Series and Nonequivalent Comparison Groups

The most interpretable quasi-experimental designs are those that combine the approaches mentioned above into one evaluation. If a group similar to the program participants can be found, the simple time-series design is considerably strengthened. The analysis of the Connecticut speeding crackdown mentioned earlier was made possible by examining the fatality rates of four neighboring states. Figure 9.6 contrasts the average of these four states' fatality figures with Connecticut's fatality rate. As can be seen in the figure, there seems to be a general trend toward a lower fatality rate in all five states; however, Connecticut's 1957–1959 rates are increasingly divergent from those of the neighboring states. Although regression toward the mean is a plausible alternative interpretation of the drop from 1955 to 1956, the continued favorable trend is hard to explain if the crackdown, which was kept in force during the following years, did not have an effect. Riecken and Boruch (1974) state that tests of significance are less important than a qualitative understanding of the various threats to the validity of causal conclusions about the impact of the intervention. However, methods to be used for precise analyses have been developed (see Abraham, 1980; McCleary and Hay, 1980).

A key to drawing valid interpretations from observations lies in being able to repeat the observations. If a study can be replicated, one can be more sure of conclusions than if conditions make replication impossible. The time-series design with a comparison group that receives the same intervention as the experimental group but at a later time provides additional safeguards against validity threats. Figure 9.7 illustrates the ideal pattern of results from such a study. Cook and Campbell (1979) call this design an "interrupted time series with switching replications." If the observations fit the pattern in Figure 9.7, little in the way of statistical analysis needs to be done. Case Study 2 is an example of a readily interpretable time-series design with switching replications in an evaluation of a media campaign.

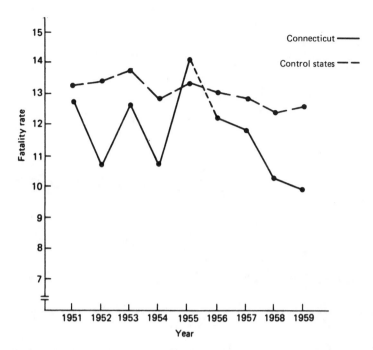

FIGURE 9.6 Automobile accident fatality rate per 100,000 residents for Connecticut and for comparable states. (*Source:* D. T. Campbell, "Reforms as experiments," *American Psychologist, 24* (1960): 419. Copyright 1969 by the American Psychological Association. Reprinted by permission of the author.)

The Patch-Up Design

By analyzing the context of a program, evaluators may be able to identify the threats to internal validity that are most likely to affect an evaluation. Evaluators then may decide to add comparison groups specifically designed to control for certain influences, until the most plausible competing interpretations are eliminated. With the use of advanced statistical procedures and an understanding of the validity of causal relationships, the patch-up design can be a powerful evaluation design (Cordray, 1986). The examples on the following pages illustrate relatively simple designs.

The dean of a college of arts and sciences in a medium-sized university requested an evaluation of a junior year abroad program sponsored and supervised by his college. The report was needed for a board of trustees meeting scheduled in six weeks. Clearly, there was no opportunity for a time-series design. (As mentioned in earlier chapters, it is not unusual for evaluators to work under considerable time pressure.) The research was planned around the obvious comparison—college seniors who had studied abroad the previous year versus seniors who had studied at the parent campus. In making this comparison, selection cannot be ignored as a threat to internal validity. Students who decide to go abroad for a year are different from those who remain at home. An approach to estimating the preexisting differ-

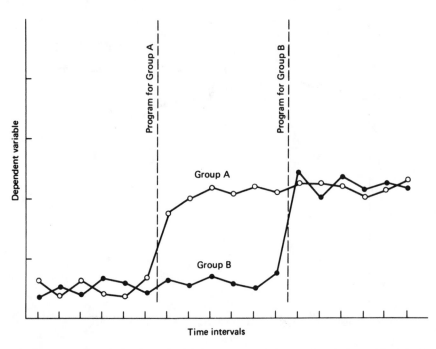

FIGURE 9.7 Hypothetical results of an interrupted time-series design with switching replications.

ences between these two groups involves testing individuals before they leave. A pretest-posttest design was impossible due to the short time allotted for the study. Because the decision to study abroad is costly and requires much planning, sophomore students sign up rather early for the program. By comparing seniors who have been abroad with sophomores arranging to go abroad, the self-selection threat is negated, because both groups have selected themselves to go abroad. However, now a second threat to internal validity becomes a problem. Sophomores are less mature than seniors. Two years in age may not be that critical for middle-aged or elderly people, but two years may make quite a difference in an evaluation of a program for college students. By adding one more group, sophomores who did not intend to study abroad, the major threats to the internal validity of this evaluation were covered.

The design is summarized in Figure 9.8. If self-selection was related to higher scores on the dependent measures, one would expect the groups in the upper row to have higher scores. If maturation led to higher scores, those in the right-hand column should have higher scores. If the program had an impact, then the upper-right-hand group, the self-selected seniors, should have especially high scores as illustrated. Unfortunately, the sophomores planning to spend the year abroad were very hard to survey, and only three were tested. Therefore, the means in Figure 9.8 are hypothetical.

		Maturation Level	
		Sophomores	Seniors
Self-Selection	Students who will study or have studied abroad	50	65 (Treatment group)
	Students who have not studied or do not plan to study abroad	40	45

FIGURE 9.8 Hypothetical mean scores on a measure of international understanding for the students in the junior year abroad evaluation. A program effect is indicated by these means.

A more complicated patch-up design was described by Lawler and Hackman (1969). They wished to evaluate the success of having custodial employees design their own incentive plan to reduce absenteeism. The authors believed that an incentive plan would work only if the employees designed it themselves. The authors had to use intact, existing work groups; therefore, some form of the nonequivalent control group design had to be used. Three intact work teams making up the experimental group developed their plans in consultation with the experimenters. The first comparison group had an incentive plan similar to that developed by the experimental group, but it was imposed upon them by management. Including this group enabled the evaluators to distinguish between the effect of an employee-designed incentive plan and the incentive itself. A second comparison group simply met with the experimenters to talk about the work and absenteeism. This group was necessary to show that any reduction in absenteeism would have been due more to the incentive plan than a positive reaction to getting attention from management. Finally, a comparison group with no incentive plan and no discussion was added.

The data were analyzed using a time-series analysis because (1) the rate of absenteeism may change slowly, and (2) absenteeism is recorded daily whether or not there is a program. Comparing the level of absenteeism for the 12 weeks before the intervention with the level during the 12 weeks afterwards showed that the participant employees improved from 12 percent absent to 6 percent, while the rates for the other groups did not change. Note that without each of the control groups (as in junior year abroad study), some alternative interpretation would have been plausible. The comparison groups were selected to counter specific, plausible interpretations of any improvement in the absenteeism rate of the experimental group.

The design does not deal with some other threats to internal validity because they were not plausible in this study. For example, instrumentation refers to possible changes in measures of outcome or success such as those that occur when staff become more vigilant or experienced because of interest in the evaluation. Because job absenteeism is a critical variable in work settings, the development of a program is unlikely to make any changes in the measurement of absenteeism.

SUMMARY AND PREVIEW

The use of quasi-experimental research designs in program evaluation is widespread. These approaches are often compatible with the need to minimize disruption in organizations and the need of evaluators to obtain sufficient information to permit the isolation of probable causes of changes in program participants. However, the use of quasi-experimental research designs is not straightforward; the evaluator needs to consider which specific threats to internal validity must be accounted for in each evaluation. Anticipating these threats can cause headaches for evaluators: there are no standard approaches to designing quasi-experimental evaluations. Often the correct statistical methods to use in analyzing a quasi-experimental evaluation are controversial. One of the most promising quasi-experimental methods, the interrupted time-series design, is receiving considerable theoretical study.

When conditions permit a controlled experimental evaluation, evaluators conduct an experiment so that they can control as many threats to internal validity as possible. When an intervention is expensive, affects many people, or might lead to serious side effects, it is desirable to conduct a controlled study. Chapter 10 describes the value and some of the limitations of experimental evaluations.

STUDY QUESTIONS

1. Explain which threats to internal validity are not covered by an evaluation of a parole program in which male parolees are tested before and after the program and are compared to a sample of men living in the same neighborhoods as the parolees.
2. Assume that reading levels in a school district were steadily declining in recent years and that a new reading program was implemented to counter this trend. After two years the reading levels continued to decline, but the superintendent announced that the program was a success because reading levels would have declined even more without the program. What would be necessary to evaluate the validity of such an announcement? Be sure to consider the cost of the information listed.
3. Suppose a new medical treatment were offered to residents of an upper-middle-class suburb. As a comparison group, similarly aged patients with the same diagnosis were found in a county hospital providing free care to welfare families. Evaluate this nonequivalent control group evaluation design.
4. A problem with quasi-experimental evaluations is that often a particular set of results can be interpreted, but a different set cannot. For example, assume a service to a disadvantaged group resulted in improved performance on some variable. If the postprogram performance of this disadvantaged group is better than that observed in the middle-class comparison group, the interpretation of the evaluation is clear. However, if postprogram performance of the disadvantaged group is lower than that of the middle-class comparison group, then there are many more possible interpretations. Explain these statements.
5. If you did not plot the time series given in this chapter, do so now and carry out the smoothing process. When some students are introduced to this technique, they object saying that the data are being replaced by medians. If this seems like a reasonable objection to you, describe what we do when we report group means instead of individual scores.

FURTHER READING

COOK, T. D., and CAMPBELL, D. T. 1979. *Quasi-experimentation*. Chicago: Rand McNally.

MCCLEARY, R., and HAY, R. A., JR. 1980. *Applied time series analysis for social sciences*. Beverly Hills, Calif.: Sage.

SECHREST, L., PERRIN, E., and BUNKER, J., eds. 1990. *Research methodology: Strengthening causal interpretations of nonexperimental data*. Rockville, Md.: Department of Health and Human Services, Agency for Health Care Policy and Research, (PHS) 90–3454.

TROCHIM, W. M. K., ed. 1986. *Advances in quasi-experimental design and analysis*. San Francisco: Jossey-Bass.

10

Analysis of Causes of Change

The previous chapter described various approaches to reducing the number of plausible interpretations of change observed in program participants. Such interpretations include many possible sources of bias as well as the desired positive effect of the program itself. These biases refer to the ideas summarized in the threats to internal validity: (1) self-selection into the program by those who would benefit; (2) general community or societal changes that overshadow all effects of the program; and (3) the reactive effects of making observations, among other factors. The ways of separating these biases from program effects involve observing the participants at a number of time intervals and observing both the relevant dependent measures and dependent measures not likely to change due to the program. In addition, observations of intact groups not experiencing the program can improve interpretability if the groups studied are similar to the program participants. Even when carefully designed quasi-experimental evaluations are conducted, there usually remains a lingering doubt that some influence other than the program led to the improvement observed or masked a real program effect. Perhaps the people forming the nonequivalent control group were different from the experimental group in some way that was not considered in planning the evaluation. Perhaps the people in the nonequivalent control group were less motivated or reacted to the observations differently than the program participants.

A way to minimize these doubts is to adopt a research strategy that best controls for threats to internal validity. The easiest way to do this is to use the classic experimental design with random assignment of participants to a program or to a control group. This chapter reviews the need for experimentation as a tool in program evaluation, describes the most opportune times to introduce experimentation, and makes practical suggestions for meeting the problems of conducting experimental research in organizational settings.

EXPERIMENTATION IN PROGRAM EVALUATION

The Value of Experimentation

Before discussing details of experimentation, a brief review of the value of randomized experimental design may be useful. A true experimental evaluation refers to an evaluation based on observations of people randomly assigned to the program group or to some control group. In the previous chapter quasi-experimental methods were presented that are useful when evaluators do not have the administrative power or when it is unethical to assign people to particular experiences. In such settings evaluators utilize preexisting intact groups; however, such intact groups were formed for reasons other than the need for an unambiguously interpreted evaluation. Because such groups exist of their own accord, it is very likely that the groups differ on many variables.

We also mentioned several approaches to making groups more comparable—matching, finding similar intact groups, or using a statistical adjustment. In some situations these approaches serve well, but often nothing suffices to control the threats to internal validity. Deniston and Rosenstock (1973) showed how a program for people with a cyclical problem cannot be evaluated without a random controlled study. In addition, if variables used to match treatment and comparison groups cannot be measured with perfect reliability, matching and statistical adjustments never can be appropriate (Campbell and Erlebacher, 1970; Cook and Campbell, 1979). Although the patch-up approach to selecting comparison groups to counter specific threats to internal validity can produce quite interpretable evaluations, it requires incredible foresight to anticipate every threat to internal validity while planning an evaluation.

Without minimizing the effort in carrying out an evaluation, there may be situations in which an experiment can be carried out without disrupting an organization's central purpose. For example, Carey (1979) conducted an evaluation of alternative approaches to providing nursing care by taking advantage of a natural random assignment of patients to hospital floors. One of two general medical floors in a large hospital used team nursing—nurses worked under one head nurse and specialized in the type of tasks they carried out. Patients see a variety of nurses each day depending on the services they need. The other floor used primary nursing, in which one nurse provides all the care for four patients during a given shift. Since patients were assigned to floor by the admissions staff without regard to type of illness or physician preference, random samples were available. Having random samples saves the evaluator from many interpretation headaches.

Experimental Designs

Figure 10.1 includes diagrams of several experimental designs. Each of the groups in the research designs is formed by randomly assigning possible participants to receive the program (the experimental group) or not to receive it (the control group). The most simple form of the true experiment, diagramed in the top section of the figure, employs observations after the program is delivered, but uses no pretests. Because the groups are formed randomly, there is no theoretical need to use a pretest to show that the groups were equivalent before receiving the program. Such pretests are advisable, if not essential, when preexisting groups are used for an evaluation, as in the quasi-experimental, nonequivalent control group design. As pointed out in Chapter 9, without pretests the evaluator and the information users would never know if the program and the nonequivalent comparison groups were indeed comparable before the program group was influenced by the program. Although this is not an issue when true control groups are used, pretests also have other uses that will be discussed below.

At times a program can be divided into two parts that might be provided separately or together as a unit. In such a case the posttest design can be enlarged, as the second entry of Figure 10.1 shows. An evaluation using this design and the best method of analyzing it will be discussed later in this chapter.

FIGURE 10.1 Evaluation designs utilizing random assignment to groups, and the questions these designs can answer.

Experimental Design	Symbolic Representation	Questions That Can Be Answered
Posttest-only control group	X O O	Did the program cause a change in the program participants?
Two-by-two factorial	O X O Y O X Y O	Did either or both of the aspects of the program cause a change in the program participants? Is there something about having the two aspects of the program given together that creates an especially favorable climate for change? Or, do X and Y interfere with each other?
Solomon four group	O X O O O O X O	Did the program cause a change in the program participants? How much change occurred?
Time series with random assignment to groups	X O O O O O O X O O O O O O X O O O	Did the program cause a change in the program participants? Did the effect of the program hold up over time?

*The program is represented by X or Y; observations are represented by O.

A brief review of the threats to internal validity can illustrate the power of random assignment to distinguish between the effect of the program and nonprogram causes of participant change. There is no reason to believe that the groups differ in maturation rate or level or that they experience different historical influences. The groups have not selected themselves into the program being evaluated. Since participants did not begin at different levels of health or adjustment, regression to the mean is not a viable threat. Both groups have equivalent testing experiences. The possibility of instrumentation changes exists in evaluation projects, especially when observations are made over an extended period of time. The possibility of the meaning of scores changing as observers gain more experience with the research instruments or get tired of the project must also be considered. The potential problems caused by participant dropout after the evaluation has begun are no worse than with other designs.

In spite of the power of randomization to assure that the control and experimental groups are not systematically different, some evaluators may feel more comfortable with pretests for both groups. Also, having pretests for experimental and control groups might help in communicating the findings to others who do not understand the advantages of randomization. For these reasons, the third design is given in the figure. The four-group design is not better in any theoretical way than the two-group design with posttests only. Flay and Best (1982), however, warn evaluators that randomization may fail in practice. If that happens, having pretest data can help to preserve the usefulness of the evaluation.

The use of pretests has a cost, however. Often the act of observation is reactive, especially in social settings. It is possible that the pretest may sensitize the program participants to the influences of the program, thus ensuring that the program works only when the pretest is given. If this is true, then the pretest becomes part of the program. There is nothing wrong with including a pretest as part of any program; however, it is easy to forget that the pretest may cause the participants to react differently than they would have had the pretest not been given. In Campbell and Stanley's terminology (1963), adding pretests to the first design weakens its external validity because the pretest may have interacted with the program to cause the observed change. If testing is expensive, it is unlikely that program designers will want to incorporate the testing procedure into the program, even though the evaluation only showed that both the pretest and the program lead to change—not that the program alone leads to change. The third design, using four groups, takes care of all these concerns.

An advantage of using pretests in experimental evaluation designs is illustrated in Case Study 3 (Majchrzak, 1986). By using pretests even though treatment and control groups were formed randomly and by monitoring program implementation, Majchrzak was able to detect the effect of different levels of implementation. Pretest observations permitted an analysis of change that would have been impossible otherwise. A further advantage of pretests is that the evaluator can adjust posttest scores for preexisting individual participant differences within each group. This can be done using just the two groups of the Solomon design that were pretested in an analysis of covariance. An analysis of covariance possesses great statistical power to detect differences between groups especially when the groups have been formed randomly. Note that the caution about comparing pretests and posttests raised by Aiken and West (1990) and described in Chapter 8 apply regardless of research design.

The advantages of time-series designs can be added to the experimental method by making repeated observations at regular intervals. In this way evaluators can learn whether the program's impact held up across time. The last design in Figure 10.1 is especially useful if follow-up assessments are desired and if the program is implemented on a staggered basis. The built-in replication provided by this design is a very attractive feature.

This discussion is not meant to imply that there are only four experimental designs. Many options are possible, depending on the needs of the evaluations. These four designs are described in order to illustrate some options available to the evaluator.

OBJECTIONS TO EXPERIMENTATION

When evaluators fail to use experimental methods, the reasons may be related to frequently voiced objections to experimental methodology. It is important for evaluators to be familiar with these objections, lest they encounter them for the first time while planning an evaluation or, even worse, after random assignment to programs has already begun.

Don't Experiment on Me!

People are not eager to have someone use them in a poorly planned experiment. Unfortunately, experimentation has sometimes been associated with the "mad scientist" of films. Moreover, the media do not use the word *experiment* in the careful way experimental design textbooks do. Consequently, it is not surprising when people not trained in social science methodology equate experiments to evaluate the effects of a social program or a medical treatment with the covert administration of dangerous drugs to unsuspecting people and other undisciplined attempts to learn about behavior. Evaluators planning an experiment will be careful to treat the question of experimentation with respect. The advantages of experimentation should be stressed and the fact that the program or service has been carefully planned by competent personnel should be made clear to possible volunteers and committees overseeing the research.

Professional Sensitivity

Often people are hesitant to become involved in experimentation because they want the best service available for their health, emotional, educational, or any other problem. They feel that because human service providers are trained and paid to choose the service most likely to help a person, random assignment to a control group means they are missing out on what they really need. In a similar fashion, service providers usually feel able to select the best care for a person in need or to select the people most likely to benefit from a service program. When they feel this way, the service provider is not likely to endorse an evaluation requiring random assignment to groups.

The fact of the matter is that in many ways people in need get a particular form of service on a fairly random basis. Different counselors follow various theories of counseling. Physicians do not follow set treatment patterns (Eddy, 1990). Different cities draw up quite different welfare programs. Judges do not assign identical sentences to people convicted of the same crimes. The reasons why a particular person experiences a particular form of counseling, medical treatment, or job training are often unrelated to valid decision processes.

It is natural for service staff to believe that they know best about the selection of treatments. The literature on professional judgment and decision making also suggests that it is not unusual for staff to believe that the selection of a particular treatment is appropriate, when in fact it is worthless or even harmful to people (Eddy and Billings, 1988; Friedman, P. J., 1990). These misperceptions sometimes occur because people remember successes and fulfilled expectations while people often explain away and forget observations that do not fit expectations (Kayne and Alloy, 1988). Highly prejudiced individuals remember incidents in which a minority member commits a social gaffe but quickly forget or sympathize with a person from a higher-status group committing a similar misstep (Allport, 1954). Partisan fans see more rule infractions by opposing teams than by their own teams (Hastorf and Cantril, 1954).

It takes a considerable amount of tact to convince service providers that their clinical judgment may not always be valid. Providing examples of nonrandomized studies that were later invalidated by randomized research may help service providers see the possibility of misperceptions and the advantages of unambiguous documentation of service effectiveness. In Chapter 2 we described the necessity of encouraging the development of an experimental orientation among program managers and staff. Campbell (1969) suggested that society should approach new human service programs as if they were experiments—treating a failure of a well-conceived program as an indication of our incomplete understanding of human nature, not as an indication of the low motivation or the incompetence of the staff. Unfortunately, some human service providers act as though a negative evaluation indicates that they are incompetent; and therefore they develop rationalizations whenever particular individuals do not seem to benefit from the service provided. Few teachers examine their own performance when a student does not pass an examination. By explaining away all failures, the program staff avoids the opportunity for growth that is provided by unfulfilled expectations. At these times evaluators feel the full force of the conflict between their skeptical role toward service programs and the providers' confidence in the effectiveness of the services given.

Time and Effort Involved

Anyone who has conducted research in an organization knows that research requires a commitment of time and effort. Evaluators should not agree to conduct a research project if they do not have the resources to carry it through promptly.

Nevertheless, it takes only a little additional work to conduct an experiment rather than a noncontrolled evaluation. Planning and obtaining approval for an experiment requires more time and perseverance than a pretest-posttest single-group evaluation. However, once approval has been obtained, data collection, analysis, and presentation require the same amount of time, regardless of the quality of the evaluation design. Some care is required by the evaluator to be sure the experiment is not corrupted. These concerns are discussed in the last section of the chapter.

THE COSTS OF *NOT* DOING AN EXPERIMENT

Performing a randomized experiment in a service delivery setting requires a lot of effort and tenacity on the part of the evaluator. In addition, the staff is inconvenienced because, at a minimum, additional forms must be completed. At worst, the staff may feel threatened and treat the evaluator with hostility. Is it worth it? Gilbert et al. (1975) point out that too often the costs of experimentation are not weighed properly. Instead of considering the costs in absolute terms, planners should compare them with the costs of *not* doing an experiment. Gilbert et al. describe several medical procedures that became widely accepted on the basis of observational, nonexperimental studies. For example, in 1964 there were approximately 1,000 treatment units being used to freeze duodenal ulcers in the United States for 10,000 patients. After a careful randomized experiment, the treatment was discarded. Although the study that finally showed the treatment to be worthless was expensive, the cost of the treatment was expensive as well. The cost of bloodletting, previously mentioned, was also high. In this case, patients did not receive a worthless treatment, but a harmful one. The cost of a small-scale experiment would have been minuscule compared to the cost of the mistreatment.

Gilbert et al. (1975) suggest that the alternative to careful clinical trials is "fooling around." A service provider trying an approach supported only by uncontrolled studies often does not inform the client/patient/trainee that the treatment is new and not thoroughly understood. Nor does the service provider seek to obtain informed consent as an evaluator would when conducting an experiment.

The costs of not doing an experiment, then, are many. Evaluations that seek to identify causes but cannot are totally wasteful. Evaluations that mistakenly purport to have found an effective program may encourage the use of ineffective programs. There are many reasons to initiate program evaluation. When the reason is to identify causal relationships between a human service and an important outcome, the cost of an experiment is surprisingly low when compared to the cost of not doing it.

THE MOST DESIRABLE TIMES TO CONDUCT EXPERIMENTS

A theme of this text is that evaluation should be built into the daily operation of all organizations. Usually such evaluation procedures are not experiments but rather the administrative-monitoring and performance-monitoring approaches described in

Chapters 7 and 8. We agree with Lipsey et al. (1985) that the experimental paradigm is not the all-purpose program evaluation methodology. There are, however, circumstances that are best served by an understanding of cause-effect relationships and that are especially well-suited to experimentation, as the following sections illustrate.

When a New Program Is Introduced

When a new program is introduced, there are several conditions likely to increase staff and manager interest in an experimental evaluation: (1) the control group can receive the old program; (2) the program may take some time to implement, thus providing time for an evaluation; and (3) there is a need to document the program's success for internal requirements, as well as to show that it might work elsewhere. Of course, the staff may need to be cautioned that most innovations, even when well planned, are not successful (Light and Pillemer, 1984).

When beginning a new program, the current form of service can be given to the control group. Whatever needs a group may have, its members receive help from somewhere. It may be from a previous program, from another agency, from family members, or from elsewhere. Because the service to be evaluated is new, it is hard for innovators to argue that randomly assigning people to continue receiving the service they have been getting is a deprivation, although people who believe deeply in the new program or are desperate may raise the argument. This occurred when new treatments for AIDS were studied (Palca, 1990).

In large organizations, many new programs go into effect in phases; evaluators can take advantage of this. Human relations seminars for managers, for example, are not given to all managers at one time. All that is necessary to conduct an experimental evaluation is to develop a random procedure to schedule the managers to attend seminars at different times. The essential aspects of this design were diagramed in the fourth entry of Figure 10.1. The delivery of the program at different times permits the formation of multiple control groups and the repeated replication of the experimental evaluation at times one through four. Furthermore, the possibility of follow-up assessment of success is possible. The most desirable outcome of the evaluation would be for the dependent variables to follow the pattern shown in Figure 10.2. If all three groups were to improve a similar amount after receiving the program, and if the groups maintained their posttraining level, alternative, nonprogram explanations of the results would be hard to support.

In order to conduct this sort of evaluation, it is important for evaluators to have access to organizational plans. All too often evaluators' services are requested after the program is in place or after its implementation is planned. People untrained in social science methods may not understand the evaluator's request for changes in implementation plans to accommodate the design needs of the evaluation. Because service personnel have worked hard to gain approval for a new program, they may resist the idea of postponing implementation for the evaluator's sake. Whenever possible, it is far better to be involved in the planning stages than to ask for a change after the staff has adopted the new program or procedure.

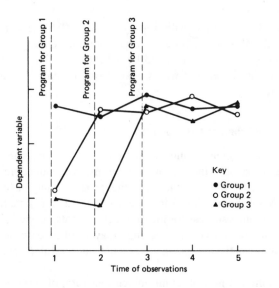

FIGURE 10.2 The most desirable outcome for a three-group design with delayed program participation for Groups 2 and 3. Group 1 received the program before the first observations; Group 2, between the first and second observations; and Group 3, between the second and third observations.

A fourth reason why new programs may be evaluated is that there may be less anxiety over the possibility of failure, as compared to a program that is widely accepted in the organization. Less is at stake if a new program does not look perfect, because fewer people have become committed to it.

When Stakes Are High

When the costs of a program or service are high or when large numbers of people might be affected, a controlled experimental evaluation would be useful. Proponents of various approaches to solving social problems support many alternative uses of resources. Since no society can carry out all that might be done, selecting the best use of funds seems wise.

When resources are scarce, many service providers strive to give the program to those most in need. There is no question that such a strategy is intended to be just; however, the ways in which eligibility is determined are often unreliable, with different service providers coming to different conclusions. In cases where the most needy are to get the program, perhaps a category of uncertain eligibility can be defined. Program participants and controls could be selected randomly from this group, and an experiment performed utilizing just the people whose eligibility is uncertain (Crano and Brewer, 1986).

When There Is Controversy About Program Effectiveness

Evaluators who work with a program of uncertain worth enjoy some advantages and must adapt to some disadvantages. While this section stresses the advantages, we must also note the disadvantages.

If service providers disagree about a program, contending factions might each seek to recruit the evaluators to their side. The evaluators' behavior may be scrutinized for signs of favoritism. In such situations evaluators would do well to keep everyone informed of plans and to carry out plans in a careful, evenhanded manner. Although such scrutiny may make program evaluation more stressful for the evaluator, the final products may actually be of high quality—unless evaluators refuse to draw any conclusions from the research. More will be said about handling controversial conclusions in Chapters 13 and 14.

Controversy provides an advantage to evaluators, because controversy over programs can be directed to support an experiment. If some influential people in an organization do not believe in the program, they are not moved by arguments that it is unjust to deprive a control group of a particular service. If there are others who strongly support the program, an institutional battle might erupt. In such a case the question of offering the program may be decided on political grounds. If, on the other hand, both sides could agree on what they would accept as evidence of the program's success, the setting for an experiment could well be excellent.

For example, welfare reform proposals have both proponents and detractors. A number of experiments have been conducted to test whether income supplements would enhance or reduce the willingness of people to seek employment (Kershaw, 1972). Some welfare recipients were randomly assigned to participate in various forms of income maintenance programs or to remain in current programs. Liberal legislators may argue that the people in the control group were being treated unfairly, while conservative legislators might argue that the new program was a giveaway. If program evaluation can supply social science observations to both groups, evaluation fills a useful role in society. Whether or not welfare is ever designed on the basis of the findings of this research, the level of debate can be raised—and the validity of arguments used can be increased—on the basis of good research (Abt, 1977).

There has been controversy over whether nutritional supplements to malnourished children in tropical areas would have long-term effects on cognitive development (McKay et al., 1978). McKay et al. randomly assigned malnourished children of low socioeconomic status from Cali, Colombia, to receive food supplements beginning at four different times before they reached school age. The four groups received the supplement for periods of forty-five, thirty-four, twenty-six, or ten months before starting school. The authors found that the younger the child was when the nutritional supplement was begun, the more impact there was on cognitive development. However, for all groups there was a positive impact lasting at least one year after the supplements were no longer given. By use of an experiment, improvement was shown to be due to nutrition, not to self-selection, regression to the mean, testing effects, or any other nonprogram effects.

When Change Is Desired

Program evaluation utilizing experimental methodology is useful when there is widespread dissatisfaction with current conditions but no consensus about what changes should be instituted. Income maintenance evaluations (Kershaw, 1972) are examples of experiments conducted in response to a desire for change in welfare policies accompanied by uncertainty about what to do. In the late 1960s the desire to prevent, or at least to reduce, the rate of school failure of disadvantaged rural and urban children led to a series of experiments with Head Start, a preschool program aimed at improving cognitive skills, health, and nutrition (Datta, 1976b). Experimentation as a conscious, rational approach to selecting among alternatives is the prime example of Campbell's concept of the "experimenting society" (1969), in which government and public alike agree to submit proposed changes in human services to experimentation, recognizing that although most innovations do not live up to expectations, the best way to choose among various possibilities is through careful program evaluation.

PRESERVING AN EXPERIMENTAL DESIGN

Up to this point this chapter has emphasized (1) the advantages of experiments over other approaches as methods to show that a program caused a change in behavior; and (2) the situations that are likely to lead to the acceptance of random assignment to experimental and control groups. However, evaluators cannot rest after planning and getting approval for an experimental design. Once begun, experiments have a way of breaking down without careful shepherding. There are some precautions that can be taken to maximize the integrity of the evaluation so that it remains an interpretable experiment (Rezmovic, et al., 1981).

Precautions Before Data Collection Begins

One of the problems with evaluations is that participants drop out of various groups. If the experimental group is receiving a service, its members are more easily followed than the people in the control group, who have nothing to gain by staying in contact with the evaluator. Participants may drop out of the experimental group also if the program makes rigorous demands. Harris and Bruner (1971) sought to measure the impact of a contract weight reduction program involving a cash deposit that would be refunded at a rate of $1.00 or $.50 per pound lost in a given week. In the first experiment 58 percent of the program participants dropped out after random assignment. In the second experiment all participants dropped out after random assignment to the program. The evaluation was not without any utility; the dropout rate clearly showed that a program requiring a cash deposit was not acceptable to these overweight people! If attrition is high and is different from group to group, even the most well-planned experiments become uninterpretable.

Perhaps one of the most thorough attempts to minimize treatment-related dropout was carried out in the selection of participants for the New Jersey Income Maintenance Study. Riecken and Boruch (1974) report that in order to minimize treatment-related dropout, the evaluators explained to possible participants all the levels of income supplement involved in the study and described the information that would be needed from them. Only those people who agreed to provide the information regardless of the group to which they were assigned were retained and randomly assigned to groups.

Few advantages are gained without some accompanying cost. Postponing random assignment until some attrition has occurred, perhaps during pretesting, introduces the possibility that the participants no longer represent the population for whom the program was designed. The people who dropped out because they would not agree to provide personal information regardless of the group they were in are likely to be different from the people who agreed to all the conditions. It is most likely that those who dropped out included some irresponsible or transient people. It is also possible that some of the most motivated obtained jobs during the initial negotiations and thus were no longer interested in the program. Income maintenance programs, if incorporated into the welfare system, would be provided to all who qualified through low incomes—not only to those who would agree to cooperate in an experiment on income maintenance. If a large proportion of possible participants refused to cooperate with the research, those who refused may have been quite different from those who agreed to cooperate. Conclusions drawn from the experiment may not apply to more than a fraction of the population. What appears to be a successful program may only be successful with some. Sound experiments whose results cannot be applied to other locations or populations are said to lack external validity (Campbell and Stanley, 1963).

A way to counter this threat to generalization is to compare those who refuse to participate with those who do participate. When evaluating a welfare program, a considerable amount of information is available about those who do and do not cooperate. If such variables as age, income, or education differ between the groups, the evaluation becomes less and less useful. If, on the other hand, the groups do not differ on such variables and only a small proportion drops out, the conclusions drawn from the experiment can be trusted.

Precautions While the Experiment Is Occurring

Even after the experiment has begun, evaluators must remain close to the data-gathering procedure in order to be sure that agreed-upon procedures are being followed. Cook and Campbell (1979) described additional threats to internal validity (not presented in Chapter 8) that can occur after an experiment has been designed and begun; each of the five serves to reduce the interpretability of an experiment.

First, *diffusion or imitation of the program* can occur when the controls learn about the program and, in effect, administer it to themselves. Straw (1978) described a weight reduction program in general terms to all volunteers before random assignment. One person who was then randomly placed in the control group (to be scheduled for the program later) used the brief oral description to design her own weight reduction program. By imitating the program, she achieved a greater weight reduction than any of the people in the experimental group.

Second, *attempts to compensate the control group* occur when staff or managers seek to give the members of the control group some special service to make up for not receiving the program. We were evaluating an information/counseling program for postcoronary inpatients. Part way through the evaluation, we learned that nurses were distributing a short book to control patients who were the most insistent about getting more information. The nurses had difficulty accepting the requirements that controls not be given the program textbook until after the predischarge assessment of knowledge and attitudes. Successful compensation of control groups results in a negative evaluation, because compensation tends to make the experimental and control groups equivalent on the outcome measures. A way to discourage such compensation is to point out that compensating the controls can serve to reduce the likelihood of finding support for the program and, consequently, discredit a worthwhile service.

Third, control groups sometimes feel a *rivalry with the experimental group*. Rahe (1978) experienced this problem in an evaluation of an exercise program for Navy fliers. The program was designed to increase the fitness of the fliers in an attempt to lower physiological stress reactions when landing on an aircraft carrier. Because the groups were all aboard a single ship, some of the controls heard about the program and were observed working out on the exercycles in order to "score" as well on the physiological outcome measures as the pilots in the experimental group.

A threat whose effects are opposite to rivalry is *resentful demoralization* of those not in the program group. It is possible that people in a control group may learn that there is a group receiving what they may consider to be a valuable service. One can easily imagine an experimental job skills program offered to some welfare applicants. Those without the program may feel that the others have an unfair advantage in obtaining work and, consequently, reduce their job-hunting efforts. The demoralization alone could make it appear that the program was effective.

The first three threats serve to make the experimental and control groups similar. The fourth may lead to greater differences between groups. *Local history* is a threat that can have either effect. Local history refers to events that occur to members of one group in an experiment. This may be a threat when participants randomly assigned to control or experimental conditions are tested in groups. One member of the group may affect the others in a way that can enhance or reduce group differences. One member of an elementary school class may act out during testing and affect the scores of the other children. If the class is part of the experimental group, group differences could be reduced. If the class belongs to the control group, the controls might appear even less accomplished due to this one student. Thus, local history could bias the evaluation to favor the control group or the experimental group. The way to avoid the effect of local history is to deliver the program and assess its effectiveness to many small groups (or even to individuals), not just to a small number of large groups.

These threats to internal validity in the context of an experimental evaluation suggest an additional concern for the evaluator. The best evaluators recognize that outcome data do not reveal much about the day-to-day functioning of the program. Thus, outcome evaluations are most effective when carried out in conjunction with program monitoring (Chapter 7) to judge the degree the program has been implemented. Furthermore, quantitative information, even when gathered in thoroughly valid ways, cannot substitute for a detailed understanding of (1) the quality of the interaction between the staff and program participants, (2) the degree the program meets the needs of the participants, and (3) how the program fits into the overall organization sponsoring the program and the community in which the program is offered. Such issues are best addressed by using qualitative methods (described in Chapter 12) to supplement the methods and evaluation designs presented so far.

SUMMARY AND PREVIEW

Whenever program evaluations are designed to determine whether or not a human service program caused any change in the people served, an experimental research design should be considered. It should not, however, be forced on a program or facility that does not support the requirements of experimental research. When implemented, program evaluations based on experimental research designs are easier to interpret and to analyze than are the less well controlled evaluations described in Chapter 9. Recall the comment that experimental designs are like aspirins; they reduce the number of headaches experienced by evaluators—reduce, but not eliminate. The most carefully designed evaluations are not interpretable if they are not carried out as planned. Evaluators recognize that many human service professionals do not fully understand the advantages of the experimental approach and could in all innocence nullify the evaluator's plans. As with all forms of evaluation, someone needs to exercise close supervision over the way the data are collected and the way individuals are assigned to research groups.

Few program outcomes are worthwhile regardless of costs and many objectives can be approached using different policies or services. Consequently, costs are frequently related to program outcomes using cost-benefit and cost-effectiveness procedures, which are described in Chapter 11.

STUDY QUESTIONS

1. If more program participants than members of the control group drop out of an experimental evaluation, what can be concluded from the evaluation? (Note: The answer "nothing" is incorrect.)
2. List the advantages and disadvantages of experimental and quasi-experimental evaluation designs. Use parallel columns so that when you are finished with the list, you have a concise way to compare these two approaches.
3. Using language that can be understood by someone without training in statistics and research methods, explain the advantages of experimentation, including random assignment to groups. Imagine you are addressing an elementary school teacher, a nurse, a police officer, or a similar human service staff person. The adequacy of your answer depends on its technical correctness and its appropriateness to the intended audience.
4. Suppose that after an experiment is described (as in question 3 above), someone asks: "If the new program is worth experimenting on, and if the staff feels that the program is good, how can you justify not letting the controls reap the benefits of the program?" What would be an appropriate answer?

FURTHER READING

Cook, T. D., and Campbell, D. T. 1979. *Quasi-experimentation: Design and analysis issues in field settings.* Chicago: Rand-McNally.
Shotland, R. L., and Mark, M., eds. 1985. *Social science and social policy.* Beverly Hills, Calif.: Sage.

11

Analysis of Costs and Outcomes

The outcomes of human service programs can be fully evaluated only when their costs are considered. Most service providers do not have training in cost accounting and thus often begin work remarkably naive about costs. However, Demone and Harshbarger (1973) assert that recommendations for programs whose costs are not estimated are simply statements of philosophy that are not taken very seriously. Similarly, conclusions about the outcome of a program are not really complete unless the evaluator has discussed the costs of obtaining that outcome. Even an evaluation accounting for all threats to internal validity and finding a highly significant degree of improvement may be a negative evaluation if the costs of obtaining the outcome are prohibitive, or if the outcome could be achieved less expensively using a different program. Being able to relate evaluation activities to cost accounting is an important aspect of the role of the evaluator (Becker et al., 1982).

Cost analysis is not a new idea to managers of businesses. The local hardware store manager counts receipts every evening and periodically records costs. By converting transactions into dollars, managers can compare input costs (salaries, inventory, and building costs) with cash receipts. A comparison of these two values tells managers whether they are making or losing money. Bookkeeping, of course, is not this simple in practice; however, the principle is straightforward and the unit of analysis, a dollar, is widely accepted. In human service settings the principles are less clear, and the benefits are usually hard to convert into dollars.

Cost analyses are done both after a program has been evaluated and in the planning stage. The topic is presented here to illustrate how outcomes are related to program costs. When cost analyses are used in planning, costs are estimated and probable levels of outcome are projected on the basis of previous evaluations of similar programs. Conducting cost analyses in the planning stage of program development helps planners to select the programs that are likely to provide the best return on investments.

COST ANALYSES

The first step in a cost analysis, whether a program is already functioning or planned, is to divide program costs into categories. It is impossible to estimate the costs of a program as a whole without this breakdown. Popham (1988) presents several ways of conceptualizing costs. His categories of costs include variable versus fixed, incremental versus sunk, recurring versus nonrecurring, and hidden versus obvious.

Variable versus Fixed Costs

All human service facilities must be housed somewhere. If the service requires special equipment, as do medical and dental care and vocational training, the facility cannot easily be used for any other purposes. Also, it is necessary in such services to have a complete set of equipment before treating the first patient or training the first student. Thus, the costs of the facilities and equipment are *fixed costs*. Because of the fixed costs of getting started, there probably is some optimal number of people to serve in order to minimize the fixed costs per person served.

Variable costs are those that change with the size of a program. The supplies used by the individuals served vary with the size of the program. The costs of maintenance, postage, custodial services, and secretarial assistance are examples of costs that will grow as a program grows to its optimal size.

Incremental versus Sunk Costs

Incremental costs are those that occur as a program continues; *sunk costs* are those that have already been expended. Thus, the distinction is useful only for decisions about continuing or terminating a program; there are no sunk costs for a planned program. Two years after installation, the General Accounting Office suggested that it would make financial sense for the Postal Service to abandon its billion-dollar automated system for sorting packages *(Chicago Tribune,* June 14, 1978). It may seem foolish to abandon a billion-dollar system after only two years. However, the decision to continue or abandon it should be made on the basis of the cost of running the system as compared to alternative systems. The money already invested (a sunk cost) is irrelevant to the new decision. Writing off the expensive system may be a big waste; however, it is cheaper than continuing to lose even more money. The GAO concluded that the incremental costs of the automated package system exceeded the benefits received; the sunk costs were not considered. Such a decision reflects the popular wisdom that there comes a time when people seek to "cut their losses" because these losses may simply grow in the future.

Recurring versus Nonrecurring Costs

Recurring costs, as the name suggests, are those that are due at regular intervals, such as salaries, rents, and utilities. The cost of purchasing equipment is a *nonrecurring cost* if the equipment is expected to last a number of years before wearing out.

Hidden versus Obvious Costs

In estimating the costs of a new building, no one forgets to include the costs of construction; less obvious costs include furniture, custodial service, lighting, heating, and maintenance. In estimating the costs of expanding staff, salaries are certainly considered; somewhat hidden but just as real are fringe benefits and liability insurance.

An Example Budget

Figure 11.1 gives the budget of a small Equal Opportunity Program for underprepared students. The proposal writers assumed that a small office could be found with furniture in an existing building. The writers did not include maintenance, custodial services, or insurance costs, because these would be the same regardless of what program the university decided to adopt and house in that space.

FIGURE 11.1 Proposed first-year budget for an Equal Opportunity Program serving 25 college students.

Director (half-time)	$18,950
Tutors (graduate student teaching assistants) 3 @ $7,500	22,500
Secretary (half-time)	8,500
Work-study tutors 3 @ $1,575 (university contribution, 33%; state contribution, 67%)	7,800
Total Salaries	$57,750
Supplies	$ 2,000
Word processor/computer	2,400
File cabinets	570
Copying	900
Phone	1,000
Total Office Support	$ 6,870
Fringe benefits @ 15%	$ 4,120
Total	$68,740

Thus, the budget is for the cost of this program operating in the space available. Note that some costs are recurring (salaries and phone), and others are nonrecurring (word processor). To make a decision on this proposal, the college administrators must compare this budget with a similar budget from alternative programs, in light of the college's values, goals, and expected benefit from the program.

Direct versus Indirect Costs

Although the terms defined above are helpful for conceptualizing the cost involved in programs, another set of terms is also frequently employed. The distinction between direct and indirect costs is important in understanding the costs of human services (Carter and Newman, 1976). *Direct costs* are those that are incurred in providing services for specific clients. *Indirect costs* are those that cannot be associated with specific clients. For example, the time a social worker spends helping a family obtain assistance from city agencies is a factor in direct costs. The wages (including all fringe benefits) make up the direct cost of the service. The salary of the secretary in the social welfare office who makes the social workers' appointments cannot be related to specific clients. Thus, the cost of secretarial assistance, as crucial as it is in maintaining a service, is not a direct cost but an indirect cost. The facility administrator's salary, telephone bills, and custodial service charges are all indirect costs. In providing a service program, both direct and indirect costs (also called *overhead*) are incurred, and both must be considered. These costs must then be related to the amount of service given.

The Necessity of Examining Costs

Public and private agencies cannot ignore costs. A rural Arkansas county instituted services for elderly residents to improve the quality of their lives and to provide services that would postpone admissions to nursing homes (Schneider, Chapman, and Voth, 1985). The evaluators discovered that although most elderly residents thought the services were a good idea, only 12 percent came to the center once a week or more often. Depending on some accounting assumptions, the cost to run the center per user was between 58 and 71 percent of the cost of the county's elementary schools per student. While those who used the services benefited, it can be asked whether this was the best use of public funds.

Although the Arkansas senior citizen center example referred to an operational program, costs should be estimated during the planning of programs; unfortunately, this is often not as easy as it might seem. Many estimates have been grossly in error. Congress passed a bill to support kidney dialysis for people suffering kidney failure and unable to obtain a kidney transplant (Culliton, 1978). When the bill was approved in 1973, the costs were estimated to be in the low millions. In 1978 the cost was $1 billion, which was half the entire budget for the National Institute of Health. By 1983 the federal government was paying $1.8 billion per year for dialysis (Wallis, 1983) and in 1987, $2.4 billion (Colburn, 1987). The failure to provide an accurate estimate of costs led to an unexpectedly large cost to the taxpayer and made it impossible to implement other programs dealing with pressing health concerns such as preventive care for poor pregnant women. Not meeting other needs raises important ethical questions for some observers (see Moskop, 1987).

COMPARING OUTCOMES TO COSTS

Once costs are calculated or estimated, the next step in a cost-benefit analysis is to develop an approach to estimating the benefits of a program. Benefits occur when goals are achieved. Surgeons save lives when they remove diseased appendixes. Because their patients lead normally productive lives afterward, there are considerable benefits to this and many other surgical procedures. Another example of a cost-effective program was a federal attempt to reduce the number of government forms. The commission set up to do this is reported to have saved 350 times as much money as the cost of the commission (Abelson, 1977). A number of cost-benefit analyses have shown the worth of education after high school. Gross and Scott (1990) report that college graduates under age 30 can expect, on average, to earn four times as much money as someone without the degree.

Another way to compare costs and benefits is based on an estimate of the benefits expected in the years after the program is completed. One begins this analysis by first calculating how much money one would have in the bank if the cost of the program were invested rather than spent. Imagine the amount one would have in the bank in 30 years if a person saved all the money that could be earned during the four years of college as well as the cost of college tuition, books, and fees. Next, using the research literature, the value of the benefits of the program can be estimated. For an economist, this is relatively easy for programs such as college education, that result in higher wages for participants. Taking into account the average additional wages earned over not going to college, one can calculate how much interest a person would need to get on the hypothetical bank account in order to make up for the expected difference in wages for high school and college graduates. In the short run, high school graduates are ahead because they are earning money during the years that college graduates attend classes. But in the long run, college graduates pull far into the lead. Over a 30-year career, estimates of the yearly interest rate needed to make up for the difference have ranged as high as 34 percent (Sussna and Heinemann, 1972). Not many investments grow at a rate of 34 percent year after year.

The Essence of Cost-Benefit Analysis

The essential characteristics of cost-benefit analyses illustrated are in a study conducted by Schnelle et al. (1978). They sought to evaluate the effectiveness of a helicopter patrol in reducing burglary in a high-crime area. Increasing the number of patrol cars seems to do little to reduce crime (Kelling et al., 1976; Schnelle et al., 1977). However, there was some speculation that a helicopter patrol with its inherently better surveillance ability might reduce burglary. The project was done in a city where most burglaries occur during daylight hours and are perpetrated by local youths. Because helicopters can repeatedly observe large areas (in daylight hours), the patrol was expected to frighten off potential burglars.

Schnelle et al. used a strategy developed in the field of behavior modification to test the effectiveness of the helicopter. The experiment was divided into five parts. First, a base-line rate of burglaries in the target area was obtained during 21 days. Second, the helicopter was introduced for 12 days. The pilot was shown the area and asked to fly low enough to be able to observe suspicious activity. Third, for 16 days the helicopter did not patrol. Fourth, the helicopter was used again for 12 days. Last, there was no helicopter patrol for 18 days. Regular car patrol continued during all phases of the experiment.

The burglary rate during the 9 A.M. to 5 P.M. shift was the outcome measure of interest. The experiment succeeded in that an average of 1.02 burglaries per day were committed during the periods of regular car patrols (base line) in contrast to an average of only 0.33 burglaries per day when the helicopter patrol was on duty. However, these data alone did not form a complete evaluation, because the helicopter patrol added to the police department's costs.

Because the helicopter pilot and hangar were already part of the police department, these costs were not considered. However, the costs of additional fuel and maintenance were calculated. These costs were compared to the benefits of a reduced rate of goods stolen. Figure 11.2 summarizes the calculation of the benefit-to-cost ratio. The cost of using the helicopter was easy to calculate. The cost of the burglaries was estimated from insurance company material. The fact that the benefit-to-cost ratio was 2.6 indicates that the program was a success. The helicopter patrol did lower crime in an efficient manner.

Several costs and benefits were not considered. Citizens' feelings of security may have increased (a benefit), but feelings of decreased privacy and irritation at the increased noise may also have occurred (costs). The benefit of lowered court costs, since it was necessary to try fewer burglars, was ignored, as was the fact that fewer burglaries permitted police officers to devote more time to other crime-preventive and investigative work (an additional benefit). Ignoring these benefits and the psychic costs of loss of privacy and of increased noise illustrates an

FIGURE 11.2 The calculation of the benefit-to-cost ratio of the helicopter patrol.

	Total	Per Day
Cost of the program (24 days)	$ 3,032	$ 126
Cost of the burglaries during no-helicopter patrol periods (55 days)	$27,171	$ 494
Cost of burglaries during helicopter patrol periods (24 days)*	$ 3,853	$ 161
Benefits (for 24-day program)	$ 8,004	$ 333
Benefit/cost ratio	——	$ 333 / 126 = 2.6

*The burglary cost figures were not supplied by Schnelle et al. (1978); however, these costs could be approximated from their report.

important principle for applied social scientists. Evaluators seek to answer practical questions directed to them in an efficient manner; once the essential question can be answered, they collect no more data. For Schnelle et al., the essential question could be answered using costs and benefits that were fairly easy to estimate. Therefore, the evaluators did not concern themselves with the very difficult task of pricing additional benefits. If they had, the benefit-to-cost ratio would have simply increased above 2.6. If the ratio had been less, say 1.1, then the additional benefits of reducing court use and freeing police time might have been priced. Because it was not necessary, it was not done. A theoretical social scientist may want to estimate the "real" benefit-to-cost ratio; an applied social scientist requires only enough information on which to base a practical decision. Case Study 4 also illustrates the use of estimates to determine benefits of a program and the practice of selecting benefits to "price" outcomes without trying to specify all the benefits.

Although Schnelle et al. chose to use costs and benefits that were fairly easy to convert into dollars, many cost-benefit studies have found it necessary to quantify costs and benefits that are hard to price. The Army Corps of Engineers has routinely used the recreational value of water projects to help justify construction plans. The dollar benefits of human services are even harder to estimate. If a service prolongs the working life of an employee, some benefits can be calculated. If a job-training program permits some to leave welfare rolls, certain savings can be quantified. But what is the dollar value of better mental health? Of reduced anxiety among cancer patients? Of a 5 percent gain on a standardized reading achievement test for sixth graders? Of increased levels of art and music appreciation? Clearly, these outcomes are worthwhile. But how much they are worth is subject to considerable disagreement.

Military planning provides an even more striking example of the limitations of cost-benefit analysis. How are the benefits of a bomb calculated? Bombs destroy. Benefits, if there are any, accrue if a war is won or averted. However, the net outcome of a war is negative, not positive, even for the victor. Instead of calculating cost-benefit ratios, one can ask how *effective* the bomb is in fulfilling its purpose. In oversimplified terms, the bigger the hole, the more effective the bomb. Thus, the concept of *cost effectiveness* was developed to use in situations in which the dollar values of benefits are very difficult to quantify.

The Essence of Cost-Effectiveness Analysis

A bomb could be rated in terms of the size of the hole it makes (expressed in cubic yards) divided by the dollar cost of the bomb. There is no way to decide if the cubic yard/$ figure is good or bad until it is compared to the effectiveness-to-cost ratio of a second bomb. By comparing the two ratios, military planners can choose the bomb with the bigger bang per buck. This same approach can be utilized in human service agencies whenever improvement can be quantified. If two or more programs effect an improvement on the same variable, the amount of improvement per dollar can be found for each program, and a cost-effectiveness evaluation can be made.

Cost-effectiveness analyses are also important in measuring the productivity of businesses. For example, a plant in Ohio that produces titanium routinely calculates three indexes based on effectiveness divided by cost measures. First, pounds of titanium produced divided by number of employees is calculated; second, pounds of titanium are divided by the total assets of the plant; and third, since energy use is so high in the production of titanium, pounds of titanium are divided by the BTU's used in production (Day, 1981). The second of these three indexes is the traditional measure of cost effectiveness; however, the other two indexes help the managers find the aspect of the plant's operation that is responsible for good or poor performance. This example illustrates that evaluators can adapt cost analyses to the needs of particular organizations. The measures of outcome and costs differ from organization to organization.

Peterson (1986) describes three approaches to using cost-effectiveness analysis in planning decisions. First, if the amount to be spent is set, an analysis can be done to see which alternative would achieve the best outcome for a specific cost. For example, one could seek to reduce highway fatalities by increasing the number of police patrols, by increasing seat-belt use through education, or by eliminating some dangerous highway curves in rural highways. Second, the costs of achieving a specified outcome can be compared for various possible approaches to a program. A school district wishing to raise the average attendance from 87 percent to 92 percent could consider a number of approaches ranging from lotteries for students with perfect monthly attendance records through a redesigned curriculum. Third, using a specified approach to a problem, the cost effectiveness of different levels of one type of program could be found. A city council, for example, might ask to what degree coronary deaths would be reduced by spending $1, 2, or 3 million dollars on paramedics and intensive care ambulances.

When Outcome Cannot Be Quantified

The size of a bomb crater can be measured directly. Quantification of improved mental health is hard, but measuring improvements in perceived environmental quality is even harder. Measuring increased art appreciation may be impossible. In these instances another approach can be used. Methods that incorporate the subjective value of the decision maker, funders, and the consumers of a program are called *cost-utility analyses* (Levin, 1983). In this case the subjective values and the costs of two or more programs are compared, and the one appearing to offer the most utility per dollar is chosen. The proposed Equal Opportunity Program (Figure 11.1) would be compared to other proposals in terms of subjective utility, not in terms of quantified effectiveness or benefits.

SOME DETAILS OF COST ANALYSIS

There are a number of issues to examine when conducting an analysis of costs, which can affect the conclusions of cost-benefit and cost-effectiveness analyses. Although some of these points are details subordinate to the major ideas presented above, these issues are extremely important, both when preparing cost analyses and when evaluating them. We present these points as issues of concern because there are no widely accepted formulas for a cost analysis in the human services.

Units of Analysis

The units of the cost analysis should be compatible with the goals of the program. Binner (1977) illustrated how use of two different units can make quite a difference in a cost analysis of inpatient psychiatric treatment. The most obvious approach might seem to be to calculate the cost per day. If there are an average of 100 patients in a facility and the cost for the year is $912,500, then the cost per patient per day would be $25. Is cost per patient-day a reasonable unit? The way to answer that question is to reflect on the reasons for institutionalizing a person. The goal is to aid patients to function in society, not simply to house them. A better unit than cost per patient-day would be cost per healthy, discharged patient. (For the moment, assume that each patient discharged is able to adjust to society and to earn a living.) The use of cost per patient-day actually encourages a departure from the true goals of institutionalization. Whatever can be done to lower the cost per patient-day would be encouraged, using this unit of analysis. The term *warehouse for people* was coined to describe the practice of developing the cheapest means of keeping people alive. On the other hand, the unit cost per patient discharged alive encourages a return to the real reason for institutionalization.

Note how the unit chosen affects the conclusion drawn from the cost-effectiveness analysis in the following example. Binner cites a state hospital that could house and feed a patient in 1901 for $2.38 per day (corrected to 1974 dollars). The cost per discharged patient in 1901 was $10,309 (1974 dollars). Comparing this hospital to 1974 averages, we find evidence for a 1300 percent increase as well as evidence for a 50 percent decrease in costs since 1901. Can both figures be true? Yes. In 1974 the average cost per patient-day was $30.86 (the 1300 percent increase), and the average cost per alive discharged patient was $5,513 (the 50 percent decrease). Should we be heartened by the decrease or alarmed at the increase? If the goals of the treatment focus on restoring patients to the community, then we should be heartened by the decrease. A comparison of these figures reflects the fact that restoring the ability to live in society requires therapy, community contacts, and medical treatment, among other things. Providing these services raises cost per day but lowers cost per discharged patient; patients are more likely to return to the community now than they were in 1901.

In recent years some nursing homes for disabled elderly people have been the subject of intense criticism for inadequate treatment—poor food, little medical care, few recreational opportunities, limited privacy. Such conditions would be encouraged by the cost per patient-day approach. Although it would not be easy to implement, relating a cost analysis of such facilities to measures of the patients' level of functioning could encourage the facility to help the patients stay healthy and alert (see Kane and Kane, 1978).

There is another complication related to the units of analysis used. At times the meaning of improvement on the variable of interest may change, depending on what level of the variable is involved. For example, it is not necessarily true that an improvement in work skills that leads to an increase in income from $0 to $6,000 is equivalent to an increase from $2,000 to $8,000. The amount of change of motivation and upgrading of skills related to these numerically equal benefits are probably markedly unequal: changing a person from being unable to hold a job to being able to hold one is probably harder than simply improving a person's skills.

Alternative Uses of Investments

A mistake often made by people informally considering costs is to ignore the component of costs called *opportunity costs*. The most expensive aspect of college education is not the tuition, even at the most exclusive private schools. The cost of tuition is less than the income students could have earned had they been employed rather than attending college. This lost opportunity is a cost of college and should be considered by potential students. Ignoring the cultural, intellectual, and social growth available to college students, people evaluating a college education on the basis of cost alone ask whether the salaries available to college graduates sufficiently exceed those of high school graduates to allow the college graduate to make up for this initial deficit of four years' wages. As mentioned above, economists report that completing college education is more cost effective than simply going to work after high school.

A person's time is part of the cost of all human services. However, the time spent waiting for a human service is often not considered a cost of the service, although it should be. Medical care that is ostensibly free is not free if waits of three or more hours are required to obtain it. If people in need of medical care do not have any employment, perhaps the oversight is understandable. However, even then, time spent waiting cannot be devoted to rearing children, preparing meals, or looking for work.

Future Costs and Benefits

A sophisticated cost analysis includes benefits expected to occur in the future. Successful rehabilitation or therapy enables a person to live with less need of special services in future years. Improvements in work skills, psychological adjustment, and physical health may well have benefits for the children of people served. The worth of these long-term benefits is, not surprisingly, hard to estimate. Viewing the human services recipient as a member of a family system and a community system is a way to become sensitive to possible secondary benefits of human services. What are some of these secondary benefits? Drug rehabilitation should lead to less crime, because addicts frequently support their habits through theft. If crime is reduced, commercial activity may be encouraged since people might now be more willing to venture into the central business district. Also, the lower the crime rate, the lower the amount the community needs to spend on detection, prosecution, and punishment of criminals.

The noneconomist faces a problem in comparing programs requiring funds and providing benefits at different times in the lives of the program. The money needed and the benefits available in the future are worth less than the same amount of money and benefits available now. This principle makes sense when you ask yourself whether you would rather have $100 now or in 12 months. Ignoring for the moment our normal preference for instant gratification, it makes economic sense to have the money now, because if it is put into a savings account, it will be worth $106 in 12 months. On the basis of this observation, some have criticized state lotteries that spread out grand prizes over 20 years. The state has the use of some of the money during those years, not the prize winner, so in a real sense, the prize is not worth as much as the promotions promise. The present value of the twentieth $50,000 payment of a million-dollar grand prize is only $10,730, because that sum invested in a readily available 8 percent savings account will yield $50,000 after 20 years.

This text does not go into the methods used to calculate the current worth of a benefit projected to occur in 20 years. The point to remember is that the cost of programs should include what could be obtained by an alternate use of resources. For example, is it worth spending $100 now in order to receive a benefit of $200 in 10 years? The answer depends entirely on the assumed rate of return for an alternative use of the $100. The amount one could obtain from this other use is the *opportunity cost*. If the rate of return for the latter were 3 percent, the answer to the question above would be yes, because $100 invested at 3 percent would be worth only $131 in 10 years. The opportunity cost is less than the benefit. If the rate of return were 8 percent or more, the answer would be no, because $100 invested for 10 years at 8 percent would equal $216. It would be better to put the money into an 8 percent savings account than to seek the $200 future benefit.

The interest rate assumed should be realistic. Critics of the cost-benefit analyses provided by the proponents of large-scale water resource projects have asserted that the rates of interest selected are unrealistically low (for example, Hanke and Walker, 1974). If so, the cost of the project would appear lower and the benefit-to-cost ratio would appear higher than they really are. For example, the opportunity cost of a $200 benefit that is 10 years away would be $134 if an interest rate of 3 percent were chosen, but it would be $179 if a more realistic figure, 6 percent, were used. It is probably obvious that fluctuating inflation rates greatly complicate these analyses.

Who Bears the Costs and Who Reaps the Benefits?

Many programs are sponsored and paid for by people who do not obtain the benefits. Clearly, the costs of primary education are borne by the whole community, while only the teachers and the children (and their parents) benefit. The community indirectly benefits by gaining a reputation for good schools that attract and hold residents. The value of homes remains high, and good employees are not likely to move away. A tax increase referendum is more likely to pass if residents believe they benefit at least indirectly by having good schools in their community. Public transit systems are often criticized by people who are required to support the systems through taxes but who never expect to benefit personally from them. Another example of this problem is seen in the development of outpatient surgery procedures. Hospitals are under intense pressure from insurance companies and from federal and state governments to lower costs or at least limit increases in costs. One response to this pressure is to develop outpatient surgical centers. A patient needing relatively minor surgery does not stay in the hospital overnight. The cost of providing the surgery is markedly lower than traditional practices. However, neither the patient nor the hospital benefits from these savings—Medicare, Medicaid, and insurance companies experience the savings (Evans and Robinson, 1980). It was hoped that society, in general, would pay lower costs for medical insurance when the costs of surgery were minimized but recent evidence suggests that surgeons have raised their fees for surgery done outside of hospitals (Millenson, 1987). This negative side effect was not an outcome that planners had in mind when outpatient surgery clinics were developed.

Evaluators conducting a thorough analysis of costs and benefits point out the problems associated with a discrepancy between who benefits and who pays the costs of programs. Whenever the benefits are enjoyed by people other than those paying for the program, special problems may exist in mobilizing political action to initiate and to maintain the program. However, it is important to note that people voluntarily enter into many contracts from which they hope to receive no dollar benefits. Home, life, health, and car insurance policies are designed to provide money to those in need after an illness or accident. The costs are borne by the majority, who benefit little in terms of dollars. The year-to-year benefit is the peace of mind gained by knowing that large expenses will be covered if a misfortune occurs. Most policy holders are satisfied with such assurances and would be delighted never to need to receive a tangible financial benefit from their insurance.

Some critics of cost-benefit and cost-effectiveness analyses argue that these techniques are flawed because they are not sensitive to long-range costs. House and Shull (1988) argue that many analyses do not reflect the cost to future generations when resource use is planned. For example, an analysis of the financial value of forests concluded that clear-cutting forests, selling the logs, and leaving the land bare is the most cost-effective use of forests for the owner. The forest's contributions to soil conservation, oxygen replacement, and ecological variety were not considered, leaving future generations to suffer when environmental damage leads to a lowered quality of life.

Using Cost-Benefit and Cost-Effectiveness Analyses

If the benefits of a program can be priced in dollars and a cost-benefit analysis can be done, one approach to program selection is to adopt the program with the largest benefit-to-cost ratio. Nagel (1983a) has shown that many decisions involve far more than simply giving or withholding support for a program. Because governmental agencies have set budgets, agency managers are not free to choose a program with the highest benefit-to-cost ratio if the cost exceeds the allotted budget. Instead, managers ideally should seek to obtain the most benefits for the resources available. Given the costs of the various programs and the size of the budget, the best program to select might not be the most efficient, when considered one at a time.

If the benefits are expressed in different units, stakeholders and managers can still use analyses relating costs with outcomes to select which programs should be maintained or expanded. The crucial technique is to list all possible courses of action and compare them to each other, taking two at a time. For example, suppose that a program to train 3,000 unskilled workers per year to fill maintenance positions could be funded for 10 years at the same cost as a road improvement project that is expected to save five accidental deaths and twenty injuries during the same 10 years. If both outcomes are equally likely (according to past research and evaluations), which course of action should a state legislature chose? This selection can be made without estimating the value of jobs or averted deaths and injuries; however, the selection would reflect the relative importance of the two outcomes for the majority of the legislators. Next, a third program could be compared to this selection. Thus, even when cost-benefit or cost-effectiveness analyses cannot be done, relating costs to outcomes illuminates the debate and allows the stakeholders to see the options more clearly than they could without such analyses. At a time when limitations on the financial resources of governments and other organizations are crucially important, analyses that help decision makers understand the impact of their decisions seem worthwhile.

Major Criticisms of Cost Analyses

There are a number of major criticisms of both cost-benefit and cost-effectiveness analyses. Users of these approaches profit by being aware of these criticisms, which point up limitations of these useful methods.

Psychic benefits. As mentioned above, improved emotional health is hard enough to price. But what about clean air? Clean streams? An unlittered park? Access to quiet places to walk? One approach would be to study what people are willing to pay to escape environmental deterioration. Another approach is to calculate what must be paid to induce workers to accept employment in dirty, dusty, noisy, or dangerous occupations. These approaches are indirect and probably will never be completely satisfactory; however, novel approaches based on local environmental conditions (such as noise, air and water pollution, and traffic) and the prices people pay for property in different locations provide some guidance (Pearce and Markandya, 1988).

The value of lives. A second criticism concerns the approach to valuing lives. Economic analyses based strictly on current or projected earning power place low values on the lives of children and the aged. The present economic value of young children is very low, because children cannot earn anything until 10 to 15 years into the future. However, people do not act as though children are to be evaluated on the basis of economic value. Nor are our moral values determined by dollar values. Considerable resources are expended on all children, and especially sick children. Very ill, premature babies may be hospitalized for months at a cost of tens of thousands of dollars. Similarly, economic analysis fails as an approach to determine the value of the elderly. Those who are unlikely to have a job in the future would have a negative dollar value. Because elderly people also have emotional value to others, this economic value does not reflect the feelings or predict the behavior of others toward the elderly.

An alternative approach to estimating the value of lives is an indirect way, similar to the approaches suggested for pricing the benefits of clean air. An examination of court settlements involving accidental deaths and the amount of money communities spend to save lives suggests the dollar values of lives. In 1977 Abt reported that in spite of widely discussed large court-determined damage awards, American society placed a $10,000 to $20,000 price tag on a year of human life. The National Research Council reported to Congress that requiring seat belts in all school buses is estimated to cost $40 million per life saved (Derby, 1989). While we don't put a price on a human life, it doesn't take much imagination to think of alternative uses of the expense of such seat belts; many pregnant, poor women do not have access to health care and many of their children do not receive recommended immunization shots. Suggesting an alternative use of the funds would not mean that a policy maker did not value the lives of schoolchildren.

Degrades life. Critics respond to an observation such as Abt's by saying that cost-benefit analysis degrades life by putting a price tag on the priceless: no amount of money can be worth a life, and attempts to put a price on life are inhumane. Social scientists often respond by saying—as Abt did—that reporting what people do does not endorse what is reported. The reporter's views, whatever they are, did not cause society's decisions. If people believe that society's actions are wrong and that lives should be worth more, then those feelings become part of the political process.

The amount that is spent on saving lives can vary markedly even within one country. Okrent (1980) cites reports that the French spent $30,000 per life saved through highway accident prevention programs, but $1 million per life saved through airplane accident prevention. Expenditures in Great Britain to save a life varied from $10,000 for agricultural workers through $20 million per life for high-rise apartment occupants. Cost-effectiveness analyses are tools to demonstrate these inequities. What is done about the inequities is part of the political process.

Requires many assumptions and estimates. Whenever cost-benefit analyses are conducted, the analyst must make assumptions about future conditions and must approximate some costs and the values of benefits. Since there is a great latitude in making these assumptions and approximations, it is not surprising that cost-benefit and cost-effectiveness analyses can be used to support predetermined opinions (Joglekar, 1984). Being open about assumptions and giving reasons behind approximations enables others to assess the validity of the analyses. Furthermore, adopting different assumptions may permit the most likely ratios to be bracketed. Many evaluators would argue that having a range of possible cost-benefit ratios would be preferable to not having any comparison of the cost of the program with its benefits.

Not complete. Sometimes cost analyses are criticized for being incomplete. This criticism was implied in material already discussed. All benefits cannot be properly priced. Those that cannot should not be assigned an arbitrary or purely speculative price (Levin, 1983). Meaningless values lead to disguised error. Such errors are bigger problems than those caused by incomplete pricing. Cost-benefit analyses are but one aspect of the evaluation of programs and only a portion of the information evaluated by managers and community representatives.

Nevertheless, costs must be considered; regardless of values, there are limitations on resources. Communities must make choices among the human services that could be offered. Some services will be offered regardless of what a cost-benefit analysis would show: the value assigned to the life of a child transcends the child's economic value. However, many other decisions and choices may be more closely related to dollar benefits. For these decisions and choices, cost analyses take on more importance, but they still are not the only inputs considered. And this is as it should be.

SUMMARY AND PREVIEW

Cost accounting is a necessary aspect of operating an organization in both the public and the private sectors. Efficient use of resources requires that costs be categorized as an aid to management and as an aid to making decisions about launching, maintaining, or terminating a service or other organizational activities. The distinctions of variable versus fixed, incremental versus sunk, recurring versus one-time, hidden versus obvious, and direct versus indirect costs all aid evaluators in conceptualizing and describing costs. Being able to measure the results of programs enables evaluators to calculate cost-benefit and cost-effectiveness indexes. To use costs in organizational and governmental decisions it is not necessary to be able to place a dollar value on the results of programs; however, it is necessary to be able to describe the expected results. Stakeholders can then select among the possible uses of governmental or organizational resources. There are several potential problems in the use of costs in program evaluation: using appropriate units of analysis, recognizing opportunity costs, and distinguishing between people who benefit versus those who pay are important issues for anyone using cost-benefit or cost effectiveness in evaluation.

This chapter ends the most quantitative portion of this book; qualitative observations are the concern of the next chapter. Note that contrasts between analyses of cost versus the integration of personal observations not only reflect different views about counting and measuring, but also different views on the use of evaluation in the decision-making processes of organizations and the degree stakeholders are included in planning and carrying out program evaluations.

STUDY QUESTIONS

1. Pretend you are involved in planning a storefront legal aid program. Draw up a budget for the first year. Take educated guesses as to costs of salaries, rent, supplies, and so on. Label each entry as to whether it is a recurring, fixed, hidden, or some other type of cost. (Some costs will have more than one label.) Then group the costs into two categories—one for direct costs and one for indirect costs.

2. Compare the following two reading programs using cost-effectiveness analysis. Program A costs $6,000 and results in an average of a six-month reading level increase. Program B costs $13,000 and results in an average gain of eight-months reading achievement. Suppose Program A serves 100 children and Program B serves 300. Which of the two programs is more efficient? (Assume that the children are randomly assigned to programs.)
3. Compare cost-benefit analysis with cost-effectiveness analysis. Think of the different types of decisions that can be made and the kind of information needed to do the analyses. Summarize your comparisons in two columns.
4. The state of medical technology is such that ill or injured people can be unable to do anything—see, hear, talk, read, walk, groom, or dress—but yet be considered alive because their hearts are still beating. While the families of such patients face very large bills, they do not really have their loved one. This problem has ethical, legal, and cost implications. What would a cost-benefit approach have to say about this problem? Think about psychic costs and benefits, opportunity costs, and alternative services to other ill patients before beginning your answer.

FURTHER READING

LEVIN, H. M. 1983. *Cost-effectiveness: A primer.* Beverly Hills, Calif.: Sage.
THOMPSON, M. S. 1980. *Benefit-cost analysis for program evaluation.* Beverly Hills, Calif.: Sage.

12

Qualitative Evaluation of Need, Process, and Outcome

"We were just about to begin collecting data on our NSF project, but Marcia and Jose tell me that they will be leaving the graduate program at the end of the semester," Dr. Lamont complained to Dr. Montrose, the Chemistry Department Chairman. "There are so many graduate students dropping out that we are in danger of losing our grant," she continued.

"Perhaps we should reevaluate our admissions decision process," Dr. Montrose suggested, "There is a university research office that might help with the job."

"I'm a little suspicious of those social science types," Dr. Lamont said, "but we need to try something."

Dr. Montrose spoke with the Graduate School Dean and together they contacted Al Gomez of the Institutional Research Office. They told Al that one-half of the new students drop out within the first two years of their graduate study. In a time of scarce resources for supporting graduate students, the faculty felt that this dropout rate was much too high. Faculty effort was wasted because just when students are ready to conduct their own research many leave, student assistantship money is wasted, and the students themselves experience frustration. They asked Al if his office could evaluate the procedure that they used in selecting students for admission from the large number of applicants.

Al is a recent graduate from a well-known and respected graduate research methodology program. His professors were very successful in obtaining sizable grants to evaluate federal and state welfare and education demonstration projects. Their practice was to conduct careful experiments as described in Chapter 10. Having participated as part of the evaluation team in some of these projects, Al had become proficient at designing and organizing the efforts to conduct such evaluations. His first suggestion to the department chair was to choose the best one hundred applicants using grades and Graduate Record Examination scores. These applicants then would be randomly divided into two groups of fifty. Ten students from one group would be randomly chosen for admission. Ten students would be chosen from the other group using the methods the faculty had been using to select the best students (such as letters of recommendation and interviews). Al wanted to follow the academic success of both groups to learn if faculty selection procedures were any more valid than using the simple numerical indexes of grades and GREs.

The faculty members were shocked by this suggestion. "Accept students randomly?" they asked. They came close to insulting Al. The chairman pointed out that it would take years before anything was learned using this approach. The department and the dean wanted a report in four months. Dr. Lamont said that she always felt social science types could not be trusted with important jobs. As a back-up plan Al suggested that the records of the selection decisions of the past ten years be examined to try to detect the way the faculty admission committee had made their selections. This would be impossible, he was told, because there were no records other than who was accepted and who was rejected. The selections were made by weighting the applicants' grades, GRE scores, the strength of the letters of recommendation (with an eye on the academic standing of the person who wrote the letter), and their general feeling for the applicant after the interview. These pieces of information were discussed, but no records of the deliberations were made beyond the accept-or-reject decision.

Reporting back to the dean, Al said that the admission procedure could not be evaluated because the faculty would not let him change the procedure to approximate valid experimental procedures nor were records available to go back to look at previous decisions. The dean explained again how much resources, time, and money were lost due to graduate-student dropout. She described the loss of faculty productivity when faculty work with students who never became proficient at conducting research. Al repeated that he understood the need, but the admission procedure could not be evaluated. The dean looked incredulous. "Surely, it can be evaluated!" she insisted.

The program can be evaluated, but not by using the methods described in the previous chapters. These methods do not apply because the admissions procedure is not based on a clearly defined policy, the decision rules of the admissions committee are not known by anyone, and the evaluative question itself may not be fully developed. Something different has to be done to conduct an evaluation in this setting. The strategies outlined in this chapter are necessary when working in an evaluative setting similar to that faced by Al. These methods have become more popular in recent years as evaluators have come to recognize that some programs cannot be studied using the methods developed to conduct quantitative social science research. This does not mean that the evaluation is not to be done rigorously; it does mean that it will be done quite differently from what has been described to this point.

EVALUATION SETTINGS BEST SERVED BY QUALITATIVE EVALUATIONS

The emphasis of this text has been on traditional evaluation methods that depend on programs having identifiable goals that can be specified and measured quantitatively. Evaluators have been encouraged to develop methods to quantify the degree to which objectives have been achieved. Furthermore, the assumption has been made that with enough care the evaluator could discover whether the influence of the program did or did not cause changes in the participants. Finding positive program effects after conducting a proper evaluation was assumed to suggest that the program could be implemented in a similar setting with some degree of confidence that the program would succeed again.

Experienced evaluators often find that they are asked to conduct evaluations when these assumptions cannot be made. In order to develop political support for a program, the goals may be vague on purpose (Cook et al., 1985). Vague goals permit different stakeholder groups to read their own goals into the program's objectives. Uncritically following the suggestions of Chapter 5 would lead the evaluator to decline to conduct the evaluation. This may not be the most advisable course of action. Vague goals have sometimes led to criticism of the evaluator's choice of the program outcomes to observe or the way to measure the outcomes observed. Evaluators who believed that they made careful choices among possible outcomes to observe, and that the most objective methods of measuring these outcomes were used, have been accused of stacking the deck in favor of (or against) finding positive results. It is also true that programs favorably evaluated in one setting were not received favorably in another setting or agency.

What do these experiences mean? Are evaluations impossible? On the contrary, evaluation is possible and needed; however, the methods outlined in the last several chapters are not applicable in all settings. There are evaluation questions and settings that require a radically different form of evaluation. Proponents of qualitative evaluation methods do not assume that program goals will be stated clearly, and they recognize that totally objective measurement is extraordinarily difficult, if not theoretically impossible (Guba and Lincoln, 1981, 1989; Patton, 1980). Qualitative evaluators, furthermore, insist that programs are highly sensitive to the specific context in which they are offered; a program working well in one setting may not work elsewhere. Therefore, great care must be taken to understand the setting of the program.

This chapter outlines qualitative evaluation approaches that are helpful when the evaluation setting is very complex or when the questions addressed by the evaluator cannot be answered by evaluation approaches based on clear goals and agreed-upon quantitative measures of outcome. Evaluating the graduate admissions procedure is a situation that cannot be approached using only the methods of

Chapters 8 through 10 and still meet the needs of the stakeholders. The following paragraphs describe some aspects of program situations for which qualitative evaluations are particularly useful.

Admission Procedure with Subjective Decision Rules

Vague goals. Although most university faculty members can identify a good graduate student when they see one, it is very hard to specify how to select the best potential students from the applicants. Graduate school performance is multifaceted, requiring ambition, creativity, a good memory, endurance, independence, and intelligence. It should not be surprising that it is hard to select the most promising applicants from a number of applicants all of whom did well as undergraduates.

Contentious, value-laden atmosphere. Neither should it be surprising to learn that faculty members disagree over what characteristics suggest that an applicant would develop into a good graduate student. Some faculty members base their expectations almost totally on standard test scores, others stress undergraduate performance in classes, while others weigh letters of recommendation most heavily.

Rich program context. Graduate school performance occurs in a very complex context. Some students do not do well because they are concerned about uncertain future job prospects. Some are not able to adapt to the degree of independent, self-initiated work required. Furthermore, the criteria of success of graduate students are far more complicated than those for undergraduate students, who merely need to accumulate passing grades in a sufficient number of properly chosen courses. To further complicate the evaluator's job, grades cannot be used easily as a measure of successful performance since range of course grades is not very wide among the graduate students.

Dissatisfaction with a Library Collection

Two additional examples may make the need for qualitative evaluative methods even more compelling. Although these examples have been prepared for this text, just as the admission procedure scenario was, the points they illustrate are not unusual. Imagine that a community library began to receive complaints about the books that have been added to the collection during the last several years. The library board was confused about the criticisms. The board members knew that something had to be done to meet these criticisms since a referendum was about to be put to the voters in order to raise funds needed to carry out extensive and necessary remodeling. Board members were afraid that if vocal critics did not feel that their concerns were being addressed, the referendum would fail and library services would have to be severely limited. After some debate the board decided to evaluate its acquisitions department. Evaluating library functions in order to find areas for short-run improvements cannot be done using experimentation.

Complex goals and potentially conflicting goals. Should the library seek to get the most critically acclaimed books or should the bulk of the collection match the intellectual level of the community? How much should be spent on meeting the needs of schoolchildren? Is the library being asked to meet school needs that the school districts should meet?

Conflicts among stakeholders. Several church groups have complained about the moral tone of some of the novels that have been purchased in recent years. They have presented a list of "inspiring" material from little-known publishers. Junior and senior high school students have requested that more than one copy of frequently used reference material be available. Residents of a local retirement community have picketed the library and board meetings over the unwillingness of the acquisitions department to buy more than a minimum number of large print books, which many elderly people need in order to read. And then there was the bitter letter from the music society attacking the board for letting the library purchase rock albums for the music department. "How can we satisfy everyone?" the board members asked each other.

A Political Campaign

Imagine a politician in a state-wide campaign who becomes dissatisfied with the voter's reaction to his campaign. Not surprisingly, he would not turn to a professional program evaluator for an experiment. A political campaign is a diffuse, complicated endeavor. Although the ultimate goal of a political campaign is very objective and quantitative, votes cast is not a useful index of campaign effectiveness if one wants to improve the campaign. An approach is needed that would provide conclusions that can be put to use very quickly.

The problem faced by this hypothetical politician is not unlike many other situations in which policy must be evaluated before the ultimate outcome index is available. Major, expensive evaluations of programs have been criticized because it took too long for the results to become available; when the evaluation was completed, it was no longer relevant to the information needs of policy makers. When, for example, the findings of the evaluation of the experimental alternative welfare system (called the "negative income tax") were published, Congress and the White House were no longer in the mood to even consider an innovative welfare reform regardless of the outcome of the evaluation (Cook et al., 1985; Haveman and Watts, 1976).

These three examples (graduate student selection procedures, library acquisitions, and political campaigns) are presented to illustrate situations that need evaluation approaches quite unlike the designs presented so far in this text. Crucial characteristics of these situations include (1) a longer cycle between program input and outcome than is expected for classroom lessons, medical treatments, or job training; (2) success indexes that are based on the whole program rather than individual variables such as lab tests or ratings of improvement; (3) a need for results in a short time; (4) multiple stakeholders perhaps with conflicting values; (5) a request for suggestions for improvement rather than just an evaluation of outcome;

and (6) a concern that the social setting of the program is unlike that of similar programs elsewhere. Every qualitative evaluation is not conducted in settings having all of these characteristics, but some of these issues are associated with every qualitative evaluation.

This chapter is divided into a section treating methods of gathering qualitative information and a section treating the validity of qualitative evaluation. The data-gathering processes include making observations of the operation of a program and conducting interviews with people involved with the program in some way. The observations can be made while actually carrying out a role in the program (called *participant observation*) or by simply being present for the sole purpose of gathering data (called *nonparticipant observation*). We begin by making the strongest argument that we can in support of qualitative evaluations. Our preference, however, is for a judicious combination of qualitative and quantitative evaluation methods, as the latter part of this chapter illustrates.

GATHERING QUALITATIVE DATA

Before we provide an overview of observation and interview techniques, the importance of the evaluator in gathering data personally must be stressed.

The Central Importance of the Data Gatherer

The single most distinctive aspect of qualitative data is the personal involvement of the evaluator in the process of gathering data. Usually measurement procedures are designed to dissociate the evaluator from the data-gathering methods. This is attempted by using written measures of the achievement of objectively defined goals. The criteria of program success are defined before the evaluation begins. Measurement instruments are administered, perhaps with little involvement of the evaluation team except to verify that the data are coming in. When this degree of automated data collection is achieved, a form of objectivity is gained. Proponents of qualitative program evaluation, however, would argue that something very important has been lost.

What is lost is the opportunity of the evaluator to respond to the data as it is gathered. In a very real sense, the qualitative evaluator is viewed as the measurement instrument. The qualitative evaluator is intimately involved in data collection so that he or she can react to the observations made. Such reactions may involve adjusting the focus of the evaluation. For example, it may become evident very early in the process of observation that the staff's expectations are incorrect or that the program sponsor's goals are quite different from the goals of the program participants. An inflexible evaluation plan based on a misconception can yield a useless report.

Some evaluators object to qualitative evaluations for fear that evaluations will become very subjective. The loss of the credibility of the evaluation process would be disastrous for evaluators who have strived to show the utility of systematic, objective evaluation for organizations. Qualitative evaluation can be rigorous; however, the meaning of research rigor in qualitative evaluation is not the same as the criteria of valid designs as described in previous chapters. Qualitative evaluations based on direct observations and interviews using the evaluator as the instrument do not mean that anything goes when conducting an evaluation. Alexander (1986) stressed that while qualitative evaluators recognize the difficulty, even the impossibility, of finding one correct point of view, this does not imply that all interpretations are equally legitimate.

The tests of validity that are used in qualitative evaluation are described throughout this chapter. At this point consider the tests of the validity of information that are used in daily life. In a mystery story you can correctly conclude that "the butler murdered the horse trainer" by gathering data from different sources and carefully combining the information in a qualitative manner. Even when a perfectly credible eyewitness is not available, defendants can be found guilty when caught in a web of evidence. Many court decisions stand on a qualitative synthesis of a great number of observations. The tests of validity of court decisions are similar to the tests of the validity of qualitative evaluations. Such tests involve corroboration of evidence from multiple, independent sources, a sense of the correctness of the conclusions, and confirmation of the conclusions by people involved in the program.

These tests are described later in this chapter; at this point we turn to the methods used to gather qualitative information for evaluations.

Observational Methods

Nonparticipant observers. Since the goal of qualitative evaluation is to understand the program, procedure, or policy being studied, it is essential for the evaluator personally to observe the entity being evaluated. Nonparticipant observers are present in the program setting, but they serve no role in the administration or delivery of the service. Case Study 5 shows the importance of nonparticipant observers in an evaluation of an educational program.

Using nonparticipant observers to gather evaluative data is practical when evaluators can be sure that their presence would not change the social system of the program. The presence of observers can lead the program staff to act in guarded ways in order to look as though they are doing their jobs effectively. Observers may make the staff nervous. The authors of this text have inadvertently distressed some staff members who had not been given sufficient warning that observations were going to be made. Defensiveness is likely to be a problem if the observation period is brief and not part of regular procedures. When observation becomes part of normal operating procedures, staff members become surprisingly relaxed to the point of doing things in front of a nonparticipant observer that could have resulted in suspension if observed by a supervisor (Licht, 1979). Nonparticipant observations would be most feasible in settings in which activities are relatively public, such as schools, libraries, many aspects of businesses, and even graduate school admissions committee meetings.

What are qualitative evaluators looking for during such evaluations? It is impossible to specify precisely what would be important before the evaluation begins. If it were possible to list all the things one would be looking for, qualitative evaluation would not be necessary. The general goals include being able to understand the critical issues in the setting and to learn how the program operates in practice. If the graduate student admission procedure can be improved, the evaluator needs to learn the weaknesses of the current method. Given that few people can describe their own decision processes clearly (Simon, 1976), having an evaluator present seems essential. It may be that some useful variables are not considered. The qualitative evaluator may discover that there is nothing wrong with the admission procedures, but that the way first-year graduate students are treated is responsible for the high dropout rate. Avoiding mental blinders and remaining open to many possible points of view is an important contribution of the qualitative approach.

Participant observation.   When the services of a program are too private to permit a nonparticipant observer to be present or when the staff members are so defensive that they would not be able to carry out their duties, it may be necessary for a participant observer to enter the system. A participant observer has a legitimate role in the program. Being a nurse in an emergency room would enable one to obtain detailed information about an emergency room. Serving as a secretary in a personnel office or as a police officer in a local police force could yield rich data about the effectiveness and the problems of the service being evaluated.

The problem with such an approach to evaluation is that the discovery that a member of the team has provided evaluative information without the agreement of the staff could be disruptive if such a person were seen as a "management spy." Certainly such an underhanded approach to evaluation is incompatible with our philosophy of evaluation. Approaching evaluation without the agreement of the people whose work is being evaluated violates the spirit of mutual trust that is important in effectively functioning agencies. Participant observation could, of course, be done with the agreement of members of the program staff. This might be a good approach in settings in which the program participants find the presence of observers unsettling. Medical patients undergoing painful or embarrassing treatments might be offended by the presence of an unnecessary person, but knowing that research on the quality of medical care is being conducted might even be a comfort to the patient.

A variant of participant observation involves a pseudo-participant to go through the system. The treatment and medication practices of mental hospitals were evaluated by Rosenhan (1973) by having people feign emotional illness to gain admission to mental hospitals. Once admitted the pseudo-patients stopped reporting any symptoms and simply participated in the ward activities. Rosenhan and his qualitative evaluators were able to provide a compelling critique of the way patients are treated by the medical and nursing staffs of the hospitals. These observations implied that the slow improvement shown by psychiatric patients may be attributed partially to the way they are treated by the staff.

Examining program traces.   Chapter 4 listed program records as a valuable, nonreactive, and fairly inexpensive data source for evaluation. The term *traces* refers to a wide variety of physical remains and outcomes of the program or policy being evaluated; records are one type of trace. In a school setting traces would include graded homework, teacher lesson plans, tests, litter in hallways, graffiti on walls, student club projects, student newspapers and yearbooks, and damage to desks and lockers. In evaluating a neighborhood improvement program evaluators might examine repairs to and painting of buildings, discarded appliances and furniture in yards and vacant lots, litter and broken glass in front yards and alleys, cars parking in front of fire hydrants, abandoned cars, and yards with carefully maintained lawns and flower beds. These traces can be observed without the cooperation of the community or anyone associated with the program. Pictures of the neighborhood might be taken before and after the program to use in an evaluation report.

Physical traces add a dimension to an evaluation that is hard to gain in other ways. Someone conducting an evaluation of a school program or a community improvement program would gain considerable understanding of the school or community by systematically examining the traces suggested above. This understanding could not be gained without the personal presence of the evaluator or members of the evaluation team.

The meaning of any one physical trace is nearly impossible to understand. It is the accumulation of evidence from many traces that leads to a conclusion. Furthermore, tentative interpretations are compared with information obtained through interviews and observations of behaviors. By seeking various forms of data as well as various data sources and then triangulating to interpretations infuses qualitative evaluations with power to explain and evaluate programs.

Interviewing to Obtain Qualitative Data

Qualitative interviewing is different from simply administering a written survey orally. A structured survey given orally is still a structured survey. Although structured surveys can be used in qualitative evaluations, they are usually used only after many observations and unstructured interviews have revealed detailed information to the evaluator. When the evaluator wants to verify tentative interpretations near the end of data collection, structured interviews may well be appropriate. However, the value of qualitative evaluation is in expanding knowledge of the program and its impact. Thus, the interviewer remains open to new information and follows leads to viewpoints that had not been considered before data collection began. Interviewers seek to help interviewees to use their own words, thought patterns, and values when responding to the questions.

Recording answers. Lincoln and Guba (1985) review the advantages of recording the interview versus taking written notes, including having complete records and having the statement in the interviewee's own words in case a dispute occurs later. But Lincoln and Guba strongly recommend written notes instead of cassette recordings for the following reasons: writing is less threatening to the interviewee, taking notes keeps the interviewer involved, technical problems with equipment can be avoided, the interviewer can record his or her own thoughts during the interview, and written notes are easier to work with than tapes. In large scale qualitative studies computer programs designed to organize verbal material are helpful (Tesch, 1990).

Preparing for the interview. Before conducting interviews evaluators make sure that the interviewee understands the purpose of the interview and has consented to be interviewed. There is no point in trying to mislead the individual as to the purpose of the interview. Such unethical behavior may well lead to controversy when the report is prepared and discredit the evaluation. It is a good idea to confirm the appointment for an interview a day or two beforehand. The interviewer should be on time, even early. One will have better rapport if the interviewer dresses according to the norms of the organization. One need not dress in a three-piece designer suit to interview an executive, but do not show up in faded jeans and a torn sweatshirt.

Developing rapport. Interviewees usually are guarded as the interview begins. A personal relationship is needed to establish rapport and a degree of trust between the interviewer and interviewee. Rapport can be fostered by asking some orientation questions and showing acceptance and friendly reactions to the interviewees. Starting out asking, "How did you first become a librarian?" gives a librarian a chance to talk and relax.

Asking questions. One of the most critical points in developing and asking questions is to avoid using questions that can be answered "Yes" or "No." Patton (1978) presents several sets of questions that could produce little information unless the interviewee spontaneously went beyond the actual question. Figure 12.1 was

FIGURE 12.1 Two possible sets of questions for a director of an Applied Social Psychology graduate program. The contrasts between the two columns are the important points of this figure. Do note, however, that the qualitative interviewer would not have an inflexible set of questions ready to use. One would have the issues clearly in mind, but the actual questions asked would develop as the interview progressed.

Questions Not Likely to Elicit Useful Information from an Interviewee	Open-Ended Interview Questions That Will Encourage the Interviewee to Provide Information
Is this a social psychology graduate program?	What is the name of this graduate program?
Are you the director?	What is your role in this program?
Is the emphasis on applications of social psychology?	Please characterize the emphasis of the program.
Do the students enter the program with interests in applications?	What are the interests of the applicants to the program?
Do the courses have an applied orientation?	How do the courses relate to the emphasis of the program?
Do the students like the applied orientation?	How do the students react to the applied orientation?
Are the theses and dissertations related to the theme?	How do the theses and dissertations fit into the program's theme?
Do the students seek teaching positions after graduation?	What type of positions do the graduates seek?
Do the graduates get good positions?	How do graduates use the skills learned from the program?

inspired by Patton's suggestions. As the questions in the figure show, qualitative interviewers use questions that encourage the respondent to talk and elaborate. The best questions begin with phrases such as "What is it like when . . . ?" "How do employees react when . . . ?," "Please tell me how . . . ," or "What goes through your mind when . . . ?" Someone can refuse to answer the questions completely or may provide misleading answers; however, the format of such questions encourages the informant to provide answers revealing important information.

Probing for more information. Taking the time to conduct a qualitative interview gives the evaluator the opportunity to react to the information. Sometimes the evaluator senses that there is something more to be said, or the interviewee has not understood the point. At these times the interviewer can probe by simply asking, "Can you tell me more about . . . ?" The interviewer may want to check on an interpretation of what was said by asking, "Let's see, if I understand you, you said that. . . . If that is correct, can you tell me what usually happens next?" It is critical to avoid using directive or leading probes. An interviewer who interprets a tone of voice as anger would be guilty of using a directive probe if the follow-up question is, "Does that make you angry?" A nondirective probe would be, "How do you feel when you think about . . . ?" In this way the interviewer has responded to the emotion and can learn about it without running the risk of labeling it incorrectly. The interviewer seeks to give encouragement to the interviewee regardless of the degree of agreement between the interviewer and the source. Such signs of encouragement can be seen during televised interviews as the journalist keeps nodding while the newsmaker talks. Obviously such a behavior can become artificial and counterproductive; the goal, however, is to show the interviewee that the evaluator is listening and wants to hear more.

Ending the qualitative interview. A structured interview ends with the last prepared question. A qualitative interview, in contrast, could go on and on. When the scheduled appointment is nearly over, when the participants are fatigued, or when the information being discussed has become redundant, it is time to quit. It usually is wise for interviewers to summarize the major points that have been made in the interview by saying, "Here is how I understand your views. You have said that (a) . . . , (b) . . . , and (c) . . . ." The advantages of summarizing include getting a chance to check on interpretations before leaving, permitting respondents to expand further on some point, and having the person on record as having made those points. Finally, interviewers thank respondents for their attention and thoughtful answers to the questions. One also might ask if it would be possible to check back for clarification if necessary.

Plan of Naturalistic Evaluations

Although naturalistic evaluations require more involvement and creativity on the part of the evaluator than do traditional evaluation methods using surveys and checklists, the essential plan of a qualitative evaluation is quite similar to careful procedures used to learn about anything. We present the plan of the evaluation in phases; however, we have erred if readers view these phases as a step-by-step recipe. The phases overlap and later phases provide feedback to earlier phases, possibly causing the evaluator to revise initial conclusions. Nevertheless, different activities predominate at different times during the preparation of an evaluation.

Phase one: unrestricted observation. Qualitative evaluations begin with an examination of the most crucial program events, settings, and documents, and observations of the most important activities of the program. If the program is part of an educational setting, observing the structured and unstructured interactions between teachers and students as well as interactions among teachers and among students would be important. The school setting, assignments, buildings, and student products would be examined. The important stakeholders, including children, teachers, administrators, parents, and school board would be interviewed. Qualitative evaluators do not seek to interview or observe a random selection of teachers or students. Instead they seek those who are likely to know more or are able to provide more information. Although the interviews and observations are unrestricted, the experience of the evaluator directs the observations to those things that are most likely to be important. Thus, school program evaluators would not examine the school furnace or the roof. The important point, however, is that the observations in this phase are to be unrestricted so that the qualitative evaluator can gather a wide range of impressions. Both observations and interpretations are recorded in extensive field notes. Van Sant (1989) points out that erroneous conclusions are likely when qualitative evaluations are based on convenient samples of settings, people, and conditions. Although he was writing in the context of the development of third-world countries, his warning to avoid using only easy-to-get samples must be heeded by anyone who conducts a qualitative evaluation.

Phase two: digest initial data. The second phase, which actually begins with the first observation, is to digest the impressions that were formed during this unrestricted observation period. From these impressions evaluators develop some specific ideas about how the teachers provide the program, how the students respond to it, and how parents feel about the program. Observations and interviews again are conducted in order to check on the accuracy of these impressions. With this additional qualitative information the evaluator refines the initial impressions. When additional observations no longer change the impressions, the major part of the data-gathering phases are completed.

Phase three: sharing interpretations. As impressions are formed, qualitative evaluators share their views with stakeholders and other evaluators. The qualitative evaluation approach has been misunderstood as subjectivity running wild. As a check on this possibility, impressions are formed and then presented to others who either know the program and have a stake in it or understand evaluation methodology. People intimately familiar with the program can correct misinterpretations by providing additional data that were overlooked by the evaluator. Experienced but uninvolved evaluators can offer suggestions based on their experiences with programs from other settings.

Phase four: preparing reports. Once checks with stakeholders and colleagues verify the impressions that have been formed, the evaluator is able to present the descriptions of the program and to draw evaluative conclusions about the program. The report is usually lengthy. One of the central goals of qualitative evaluation is to provide detailed descriptions of programs through the eyes of the stakeholders along with the insights of the evaluator. The job of the evaluator is to integrate the views of many stakeholders providing feedback on those views so that everyone understands the program better than before.

This description is not presented as a final version of the truth since different information can come to light later, conditions may change, and the membership of the stakeholder groups may change. Qualitative evaluations can be used in other settings to the extent that the other settings are similar to the one evaluated. Since qualitative evaluators are sensitive to the many specific factors that can affect program success, generalizing to other settings is done only with extreme care.

It would not be surprising if many readers reacted to this presentation with concern about the subjectivity of the process. Two comments are offered in response to such concerns. First, many years ago the first author had a conversation about research methods with a more experienced psychologist. The question concerned the issue of this chapter—traditional quantitative research procedures compared to more qualitative personal observations. When asked: "If you wanted to learn about a group you know nothing about, would you go there and live among them or would you develop and send surveys and questionnaires?" the more senior professor responded, "Go and live there." Although we both would have preferred direct involvement as the mode for personal learning, at that time neither of us was willing to give up the methods we were familiar with. Qualitative methodology is an attempt to obtain a personal understanding that cannot be obtained through predetermined surveys and checklists.

It is undoubtedly true that in an effort to be objective and to minimize bias, evaluators have planned and conducted evaluations at too great a distance from the program being evaluated; such evaluations do not reflect the richness of the program. Program stakeholders have rejected evaluations not only because they felt threatened by some negative feedback, but also because they did not recognize the program presented in the reports as their own. Only through close contact with the program can the evaluator come to understand it. When evaluators understand programs fully, evaluations have a greater likelihood of having impact.

The second response to the concern about the subjectivity of qualitative evaluations centers on the question of just how much objectivity quantitative evaluations possess. The subjectivity of quantitative evaluation is not found in the scoring of surveys or in the analyses of program records. However, the presuppositions that determine the choice of outcome variables to be measured and the decisions to ignore the less quantifiable program effects can inadvertently direct an evaluation toward certain conclusions. Although the sources of subjectivity may be different for qualitative and quantitative evaluations, evaluators must be equally wary of unexamined assumptions regardless of the form of the evaluation.

ESTABLISHING TRUST IN QUALITATIVE DATA

Approaches to establishing trust in traditional social science evaluation methods as developed in Chapters 8, 9, and 10 are fairly well-known. The criteria of construct validity, internal validity, statistical conclusion validity, and external validity have been used by many evaluators to judge the quality of the evaluation designs and sources of information. These criteria cannot be applied in a direct manner to evaluations based on qualitative procedures. This might lead to a belief that qualitative data gathering procedures are more likely to fall short of acceptable standards needed for program evaluations than are traditionally designed program evaluations. Lincoln and Guba (1985, 1989) argue that few if any quantitative evaluations meet the rigorous criteria listed by Cook and Campbell (1979). Kytle and Millman (1986) describe their experience in which the funding source wanted the proper form of evaluation, but not an actual evaluation. The use of quantitative, but superficial, procedures resulted in an evaluation containing no challenging information to disturb the program's sponsors. Although quantitative procedures are not necessarily superficial, evaluators who use qualitative procedures (e.g., Patton, 1980) believe that naturalistic approaches to describing programs are more likely to reach below surface appearances than many less than thorough quantitative evaluations. Lincoln and Guba (1985) have begun to develop the criteria by which the trustworthiness of qualitative evaluation procedures can be judged.

Because quantitative procedures have been frequently described, this discussion seeks to show how the trustworthiness criteria of qualitative procedures relate to these standards of social science research. It should be noted that proponents of qualitative evaluation methods argue that judging qualitative procedures by the criteria of quasi-experimental and experimental designs is like evaluating the qualities of a cat by criteria originally developed for evaluating a dog. Dogs and cats have different qualities; a good dog does not possess the characteristics of a good cat even though both may make wonderful pets. After examining the parallels between the criteria of good measurement and valid research designs used with qualitative methods and those used with traditional approaches, an additional criterion of good evaluations developed out of qualitative approaches is presented.

Criteria of Trustworthy Measurement Procedures

Reliability and dependability. As described in Chapter 4, measurement is reliable if a variable made up of several items measures one dimension (see Split-Half Reliability) or if different people find similar levels of a rated characteristic (see Inter-rater Reliability). Qualitative assessment, based on the evaluator's personal observations, can be trusted to the extent that other evaluators describe the situation in similar ways. However, since no two qualitative evaluators are likely to have exactly the same experiences, Lincoln and Guba (1985) suggest that observers keep detailed field notes and record their interpretations of the observations frequently. A disinterested but trained person should be able to review these materials and make the same interpretations as the original observer. This procedure is a bit like inter-rater reliability; Lincoln and Guba call this *dependability*.

Validity and credibility. Traditional measurement approaches judge measurement instruments on the basis of whether they correlate with some behavior of interest. Thus, college entrance tests should correlate with college grades, measures of psychological adjustment should correlate with ratings of adjustment made by family members or therapists, and checklists of neighborhood quality should correlate with ratings by residents or experts. Qualitative observations cannot be correlated with other measures; however, the concept of construct validity can be used with qualitative observations.

Construct validity refers to whether the instrument measures some variable that fits into a network of meaningful relations with other variables. Although qualitative observations cannot be placed into a quantitatively verified network, the observations gain credibility when they fit into an interlocking pattern of meaning with multiple checks on interpretations. Credibility thus resembles traditional definitions of construct validity. Credibility is enhanced by prolonged presence at the program site(s), by the use of a variety of sources of information, and by checking interpretations with other evaluators and participants of the setting being evaluated. The effects of the evaluator's biases and expectations are discovered by interactions with others who are likely to have different expectations; the challenge is to carry out such interactions, which might be difficult to arrange and quite possibly uncomfortable if one's views are questioned (Van Sant, 1989).

Objectivity and confirmability. Traditional measurement approaches were considered to be good if they were very objective. Attempts to achieve objectivity have resulted in sterile and misunderstood data according to critics (e.g., Patton, 1986). Qualitative evaluators would seek to establish that their interpretations can be confirmed by other disinterested evaluators after examining the original field notes and records of judgment processes. This approach to demonstrating trustworthiness is similar to that described for dependability.

Criteria of Trustworthy Evaluation Designs

Internal validity and credibility. Recall from Chapter 8 that threats to internal validity have become classic topics in the study of research design. Controlling for viable alternative interpretations of the differences between pretests and posttests are the signs of internally valid evaluation designs. As qualitative evaluators make their observations, they will be aware of these alternative interpretations, such as a general economic upturn masquerading as the positive effect of a job training program on the employment rate of trainees. Qualitative evaluators, however, do not seek to control for such a threat by designing a controlled experimental evaluation. Instead, by making varied, detailed observations and by carefully documenting their interpretations, they would expect that their overall interpretation would have credibility such as a legal case would have when made by a good detective. Qualitative evaluators would argue that their on-site observations and interviews would be more likely to detect the many influences on the program participants than would a traditional hands-off approach that depends on the research design to guarantee the internal validity of the evaluation. Evaluator Profile 6

Elizabeth Whitmore, Ph.D., and Marilyn L. Ray, Ph.D.:
The Credibility of Qualitative Evaluation Work

Elizabeth Whitmore is Assistant Professor of Social Work at Dalhousie University, Nova Scotia. She earned her doctoral degree in Human Service Studies from Cornell University. Marilyn Ray is Director of Policy and Program Planning and Evaluation at the Finger Lakes Law & Social Policy Institute in Ithaca, N.Y. She also earned her doctoral degree in Human Service Studies at Cornell.

Among their professional activities Whitmore and Ray study the trustworthiness of qualitative research and evaluation. To do this they have conducted audits of the data of several qualitative evaluations. In one audit they demonstrated *". . . the importance of making sure that interview logs contained data, not just summaries or personal impressions of the interviews."* In another audit they reported: "Although [the] evaluation design decisions made intuitive sense, the dependability of the study could not be assessed adequately because the specific logic and rationale behind design decisions had not been recorded anywhere. Such a record is essential for establishing that a qualitative evaluation is indeed more than subjective opinion based on intuition. . . . [T]his finding reinforces the importance and usefulness of comprehensive reflexive logs not only for the individual study but for enhancing the credibility of qualitative studies in general."

Source: Whitmore, E., and Ray, M. L. 1989. Qualitative evaluation audits: Continuation of the discussion. *Evaluation Review, 13,* 78–90.

includes descriptions of two evaluators who have examined the degree to which interpretations of qualitative evaluations can be supported by examining the evaluator's notes.

Statistical conclusion validity and dependability. In order to distinguish random error from differences among groups that result from the impact of the program, most evaluators use statistical significance tests. To use statistical techniques the observations must be quantified in some way. Qualitative data, thus, are unsuitable for statistical tests; however, the question of whether the information being interpreted can be trusted or is just the product of random events must still be addressed. In order to discover trends qualitative evaluators depend on the examination of detailed field notes made by independent evaluators who base their notes and interpretations on multiple sources. This independent analysis serves a function similar to that provided by statistical tests used with quantitative data.

External validity and transferability. External validity refers to the extent to which the conclusions of an evaluation can be applied to other groups of people not in the specific groups studied. The question of external validity is very important when a demonstration program is funded and evaluated for the primary purpose of learning whether it is successful and, thus, worth funding more widely. Traditional evaluators have depended on evaluating the program in a number of different settings (such as northern cities, West Coast cities, and southern rural sites) in order to develop confidence that the evaluation has external validity and, therefore, the program can be instituted elsewhere. Qualitative evaluators depend on detailed observations and descriptions to show what it is about the program, the participants, and the setting that permitted the program to work effectively. Such "thick" descriptions permit readers to learn whether a program is likely to work elsewhere since readers can determine whether proposed settings and projected participants are similar to those studied.

This brief overview cannot do justice to the detailed presentation of Lincoln and Guba (1985); however, it provides a sense of the different ways that the trustworthiness is established using the two different approaches to gathering data and describing a program.

Authenticity of Evaluation

In addition to trustworthiness, qualitative evaluators wish to apply another criterion of quality to evaluations. The criterion of authenticity is developed from the nature of qualitative research methods; it has not been applied to traditional evaluation designs. Evaluations occur in organizational contexts that are laced with stress, fear, hope, sometimes greed, at least some conflict, and lots of uncertainty. Since evaluations occur in such contexts, not in controlled laboratory settings, evaluations can be held to standards not used with laboratory research. Aspects of authentic evaluation include: (1) concerns for fairness; (2) increasing the understanding of all stakeholders about their own and other stakeholders' needs and values; (3) putting theory into action; and (4) involving all stakeholders in the evaluation so that they are empowered through the evaluation.

Lincoln and Guba (1985) do not claim to have the characteristics of authentic evaluation fully developed. Their point is that program evaluations involve important issues for the program staff, those who pay for it, and those who receive services through the program. The best evaluations, they say, treat all stakeholders and their values with respect and serve to enlarge their understanding of themselves, the program, and the other stakeholders. According to Lincoln and Guba qualitative evaluation based on intimate knowledge of the program and its stakeholders has the best chance of meeting these authenticity criteria. It is important to note that such aims go very far beyond the goals of even well-funded, traditional evaluations.

Many quantitative evaluations, we are told, are managed in such a way that some stakeholders are barred from participating in the evaluation and that frequently the findings of evaluations are not put into practice. One must ask whether these failings are due to the very nature of quantitative evaluations, as some assert, or whether quantitative evaluations can be carried out in ways that are fair, educative, sensitive to values, able to be applied, and empowering. Cook et al. (1985) support this latter position. They argue that evaluators can and should use a range of types of data and that the characteristics of authentic evaluations can indeed be met through evaluation designs Lincoln and Guba would reject. The present text, although in the quantitative Cook-and-Campbell tradition, has espoused many of the concepts said to flow only from a qualitative approach to evaluation.

The difference of opinion centers on the way stakeholder concerns, empowerment of less powerful groups, and fairness have been presented. Lincoln and Guba (1985) are correct in saying that such issues have not been viewed as central in traditional evaluation research designs. Instead, most evaluators have treated such concerns as important aspects of evaluation planning, data analysis, and followthrough after the evaluation report has been completed; that is, as independent from the internal validity of the evaluation. Nevertheless, these concerns have been viewed as important by quantitative evaluators. For example, in their evaluation of the children's television program "Sesame Street," Cook et al. (1975) displayed many of the values said to be associated with qualitative evaluations when they pointed out that although the program was initially funded to help lower economic class children, upper economic class children were more likely to watch and benefit from it. Cook et al., although using quantitative methods, were clearly concerned about the issues of empowerment and values. One contribution of qualitative evaluations has been to put the issues of fairness and conflicts among values into the focus of the evaluation design. Some observers imply that aspects of authenticity, such as empowering all stakeholders, are often not possible in the context of an evaluation (Greene, 1987; Mark and Shotland, 1985). It may be that Lincoln and Guba urge evaluators to do more than evaluations are able to do. One need not accept all of the rationale used to support qualitative evaluations in order to appreciate this contribution to the science and art of program evaluation.

MIXING QUALITATIVE AND QUANTITATIVE METHODS

Although purists from both camps would object, there is considerable agreement that the best approach is to mix qualitative and quantitative evaluation methods (see Campbell, 1987; Cook and Reichardt, 1979; Maxwell, 1985; Rossman and Wilson, 1985; Silverman, Ricci, and Gunter, 1990). Depending on the setting and the evaluation questions addressed to the evaluator, the mix of methods varies. Light and Pillemer (1984) write: "The pursuit of good science should transcend personal preferences for numbers or narrative" (p. 143).

The Setting

There are reasonable and important evaluative questions that cannot be handled using traditional evaluation methods. In contrast, someone evaluating a new medication uses quantitative measures of health improvement rather than depending only on qualitative approaches. However, it would be important for evaluators involved in medical research to keep asking questions about quality of life for the patients who may be undergoing painful treatments. It is not unknown for physicians to concentrate on the length of life and to pay minimal attention to questions about the quality of life (Illich, 1976).

Switching Between Approaches

In addition to combining methods in a single evaluation, it is quite possible for an evaluation planned as a quantitative evaluation to become a qualitative evaluation when unexpected, negative side effects are suddenly noticed. Carefully planned strictly quantitative evaluations are blind to side effects since unexpected bad effects (or good ones, for that matter) cannot be included in the planned evaluation. Evaluation procedures also change when plans for comparison and control groups cannot be carried out. In order to make any interpretations of available data it may be necessary to change to a more qualitative approach.

In a similar fashion a qualitative evaluation can become more quantitative as the evaluation questions become focused and clear. Once qualitative impressions are well developed, it might be possible to form hypotheses about the expected pattern of some quantitative measures of program outcome. In this way evaluators can verify some aspects of their conclusions. Qualitative evaluators argue that one cannot attempt to confirm hypotheses without first becoming very knowledgeable about the details of the program.

The Evaluation Question

Evaluations have been classified as evaluations of need, process, outcome, and cost effectiveness. It is hard to conduct a cost-effectiveness evaluation using qualitative methods. Certain questions are more likely to require an emphasis on one or the other form of evaluation. However, most evaluations have multiple purposes. Implementation must occur before one can expect outcomes to be affected. Evaluating implementation can be treated in a quantitative fashion. For example, "How many sessions are held? How many people are served? What is the average income of participants?" are quantitative questions. But it also might be important to know how participant questions are handled, how healthy the staff-participant interpersonal relationships are, and how the participant families make personal decisions. Fry and Miller (1975) showed that an innovative, cooperative public-private effort to assist alcoholics was so badly flawed in conception and implementation that it resulted in acrimonious interpersonal staff relationships that, in turn, led to decreased help for alcoholics, not improved care. In the area of social and health services such issues are very important in deciding how to improve programs.

Since there are so many, complex evaluative questions, it seems quite reasonable to believe that evaluations combining aspects of both qualitative and quantitative approaches would be better than methods focusing on one or the other approach.

Cost of Evaluation

How do costs of qualitative evaluations compare to traditional approaches? The extensive, on-site involvement of the evaluator can become quite expensive. The time involved created problems for some naturalistic evaluators (see Barzansky et al., 1985). The additional expense is compounded by the open-ended design of qualitative approaches. The stakeholder paying the evaluator may want to know what is going to come out of the evaluation before agreeing to support it. Lincoln and Guba (1985) agree that more trust is needed on the part of those who commission a qualitative evaluation compared to those potential funders who are given a clear description of just what variables are going to be measured and how the information is going to be presented before agreeing to support the evaluation. Since trust in the evaluator is required if any evaluation is going to be used, the difference in the methods may be more apparent than real. However, it is true that it is harder to estimate the cost of a qualitative evaluation than it is to estimate what it will cost to construct a survey, to administer it to a hundred people, and to analyze it.

SUMMARY AND PREVIEW

There are settings in which evaluators cannot follow traditional social science research methods that emphasize experimental control. Some complex programs requiring an evaluation in a fairly short time cannot be approached using strictly quantitative methods. At times direct observations are required to understand the program and quantitative information fully. Furthermore, a thorough understanding of the program is necessary if the evaluator's recommendations are to be taken seriously. Qualitative methods, while appearing simple (for example, talking, watching, and drawing conclusions), are more complicated and harder to work with than most quantitative procedures. The internal and statistical conclusion validity tests used with quantitative evaluations are not easy to translate into forms useful in qualitative work. Nevertheless, the use of qualitative methods in conjunction with quantitative procedures strengthens program evaluation.

Regardless of how an evaluator goes about gathering data, evaluations are not complete without reporting to the stakeholders. How these various reports are prepared and the various forms reports can take are covered in the next chapter.

STUDY QUESTIONS

1. Referring to Chapter 4 on measurement, what qualitative questions could be asked instead of the structured survey items given in Figure 4.4?
2. Draw up a series of interview questions that could be used for a qualitative evaluation of the program described in Case Study 1 in this book.
3. Construct a paragraph statement explaining the value of qualitative evaluation directed to someone who feels that a report of an evaluation must include tables of numbers.
4. Some larger human services facilities have program evaluation specialists on their own staff. Many observers worry that internal evaluators may be under pressure to produce overly positive evaluations of services provided by their own organizations. Why would it be especially important to have external consultants available when conducting naturalistic evaluations that might be used with community stakeholders?

FURTHER READING

Cook, T. D., and Reichardt, C. S., eds. 1979. *Qualitative and quantitative methods in evaluation research.* Beverly Hills, Calif.: Sage.

Guba, E. G., and Lincoln, Y. S. 1989. *Fourth generation evaluation.* Newbury Park, Calif.: Sage.

Krueger, R. A. 1988. *Focus groups: A practical guide for applied research.* Newbury Park, Calif.: Sage.

McCraken, G. D. 1988. *The long interview.* Newbury Park, Calif.: Sage.

Miles, M. B., and Huberman, A. M. 1984. *Analyzing qualitative data: A source book for new methods.* Beverly Hills, Calif.: Sage.

Yin, R. K. 1984. *Case study research: Design and methods.* Beverly Hills, Calif.: Sage.

13

Evaluation Reports:
Interpreting and
Communicating Findings

Communicating is a personal, interactive process; evaluators err if they assume that the end product of evaluations is a single, written report. While it would be an unusual evaluation without a summary written report, such a report is not the sole communication channel from evaluators to the stakeholders. Without careful consideration of the process of communicating with stakeholders, even well-executed evaluations that contain useful recommendations will not be understood, and, if not understood, they cannot be utilized. Communication is a complex process; just as we plan controls for threats to internal validity, evaluators need to plan to overcome threats to effective communication.

The first step in communication was mentioned in Chapter 2. Working to engage stakeholders in the evaluation is essential (Hegarty and Sporn, 1988). Involving stakeholders in formulating the evaluation questions and planning the evaluation engages stakeholders in the project. In settings in which evaluations are selected by managers, such as large organizations and in government agencies, evaluators work hard to show that they are seeking to provide useful information for the improvement of the program in question. Even if the program director cannot refuse to let the evaluation progress, the cooperation of the director, an important stakeholder, is essential. Hegarty and Sporn (1988) describe the importance of engaging stakeholders in their work in the U.S. Food and Drug Administration, stressing that effective evaluators avoid ever appearing to work behind someone's back. Following the suggestions made in the first chapters improves the chances of engaging stakeholders.

After initial negotiations, a communication plan needs to be developed that reflects the information needs of the stakeholders. This chapter stresses the importance of explicit planning for communication. Next, the principles behind the oral presentations and written reports are described. Since most stakeholders are able to understand graphs more easily than tables of numbers, evaluators should make use graphical presentations whenever possible. Some types of graphs easily produced using desktop computers are illustrated. Last, the order in which the stakeholders get information is discussed. Evaluators could offend some stakeholders if the release of information is not handled carefully.

DEVELOPING A COMMUNICATION PLAN

Analyze Stakeholder Information Needs and Potential for Input

The first step in developing a communication plan is to prepare a list of the different information needs of the various stakeholders and the points during the evaluation when the evaluators will benefit from feedback from the stakeholders. We want to emphasize that while the stakeholders have information needs and rights to information, communication is not a one-way street; a program evaluation will be better if stakeholders can respond to the plans of the evaluators and can provide insights that can come only from those intimately familiar with the program. Feedback on information gathering tools, sample selection, and initial analyses can improve the evaluation and contribute to the successful communication of the project and its eventual use to improve the program.

Plan Meetings for Reporting and for Obtaining Stakeholder Contributions

It is helpful to make a schedule of the projected meetings with the stakeholder groups. Figure 13.1 illustrates a communication plan for a hypothetical evaluation of a developmental skills program at Sanders College for students who have been admitted as part of an outreach program for underprepared high school graduates. The evaluation is a formative evaluation to gather information on how well the program is operating and is meeting the needs of the students, and to develop suggestions for improvement. Obvious stakeholders include the dean of Sanders College, the director of the program, the staff of the program, and the students served. Somewhat removed, but also important stakeholders are the parents of the students in the program and the college administration, which grants the funds for the program. This illustrative project is planned to begin in the fall and to be completed in time for the dean and director to make changes in the program for the following academic year.

As Figure 13.1 shows, the evaluators listed the times when stakeholders would need information and when it would be helpful to get feedback on tentative

Stakeholder	Information needed	Format of the communication	When information to be available	Setting
Research team	Progress to date, next step in the project	Team meetings, internal memos	Once every 2 weeks	Team meetings
	How to solve problems in the evaluation	Special meetings	As needed	Team and one-on-one meetings
Program Director	Progress updates	Oral presentations and one-page memos	Once a month	Meetings of the lead evaluator and director
	Final Report of recommendations	Oral presentation and written final report	March 15	Formal meeting
Staff advisory group	Information to be gathered	Oral presentations and discussions	During planning of the evaluation	Group meeting
	Tentative recommendations	Oral presentations and discussions	During the interpretation phase	Group meeting
Student advisory group	Information to be gathered	Oral presentations and discussions	During planning of the evaluation	Group meeting
	Tentative recommendations	Oral presentations and discussions	During the interpretation phase	Group meeting
Dean of the college	Progress updates	Copies of the one-page memos for files	When memos are given to program director	Inter-office mail
	Final Report on the recommendations	Oral presentation and the written Final Report	April 2	Formal meeting

FIGURE 13.1 An illustrative communication plan for an evaluation of a program to serve the academic needs of underprepared college students.

plans. For example, the staff of the program was felt to be a good source for comments on the information that the evaluators planned on gathering. The comments of the staff would help the evaluators plan the methods for gathering the data; however, the evaluators would retain the freedom to gather information that seemed important from their perspective as well. The illustrative plan shows that the students in the program are also to be consulted. Although the meetings with the students parallel the meetings with the staff, the content of the meetings would no doubt differ because the groups have different experiences within the program. Problems that are apparent to the students might not be apparent to the staff and vice-versa. Although this example concerns a small-scale program, regular communication throughout an evaluation is practiced in federal agencies as well (Barkdoll and Sporn, 1988).

This plan shows that the evaluators intend to keep the program director well-informed. The dean is to be kept informed through the written progress reports, but otherwise does not participate until the final report is made. Later we return to discuss the strategy of when different stakeholders learn about the report.

Fit the Communication Plan to the Organizational Calendar

Note that the dates when reports are to be made to the director and the dean are given. It would be important that the dean have recommendations to discuss with the director before the next academic year has begun. By April 2, many students have been accepted into the program; however, it is not too late to increase or decrease the number of students involved compared to the number served during the program's first year. Neither is it too late to change the level of financial support for the program or to make some changes in the composition of the staff. The dates for reporting to the director (March 15) and to the dean (April 2) are inflexible; otherwise, the communication plan can be changed if necessary. Acting as though nothing about the plan can be changed would be unnecessarily rigid.

PERSONAL PRESENTATIONS OF FINDINGS

Evaluators quickly learn that decision makers are busy and unlikely to spend a great deal of time puzzling over an evaluation report. Instead, working in ways that are compatible with the learning style of managers, evaluators plan on making personal reports of completed projects. Although the content of these reports is different from written reports, the director and the dean should have the written report before the personal presentation. Although they may have looked at it before the meeting, the evaluator does not count on their having read it thoroughly. The content of the final written report is described later.

Need for Personal Presentations

There are a number of reasons why personal presentations are required beyond the preference of decision makers for personal reports. In spite of high tech communication systems that have been developed in recent decades, people still respond more to person-to-person contact than to other forms of communication. Note in Evaluator Profile 7 how Frechtling says the personal presentation is critical in her work as an evaluator in a large school district. In a real sense the communication of evaluation findings is a form of attitude change intervention. That is, an evaluation is commissioned because people are looking for new ways of approaching the program. Ideas about the program are expected to be affected by the evaluation project. Attitudes are changed more easily through personal contact than through written material. One reason for this is that people pay more attention to a person than to the written page. Posavac (in press) discusses reporting of applied research from an attitude change perspective more fully than is done here.

The personal presentation is effective also because the presentation can be adjusted for the person being addressed. Specific questions can be asked and answered. Even facial feedback showing puzzlement or agreement provides the evaluator with information that can be used to improve the rest of the presentation. Thus, when reporting to a person with considerable responsibility, the personal presentation is more likely to be understood than any other form of communication.

Content of Personal Presentations

The personal presentation includes a short review of the background of the study. In the example in Figure 13.1, the dean has had the progress reports. Consequently, only brief reminders of the reason for the evaluation and the procedures are necessary or will be tolerated since the time allotted for a report probably will be no more than 60 minutes for evaluations of programs such as the one at Sanders College. The details of the sampling procedure and the methods used

EVALUATOR PROFILE 7.

Joy Frechtling, Ph.D.: Presenting an Evaluation Report

Joy Frechtling is the Head of the Division of Program Monitoring in the Montgomery County (Maryland) Public Schools. Previously, she had worked with the National Institute of Education. Dr. Frechtling earned a Ph.D. in Developmental Psychology (George Washington University).

A common concern among evaluators is the best way to present results to the stakeholders. She was asked the following questions: "Do you mean that to have an impact there must be a discussion? If there's only a [written] report, can it have an impact?"

Dr. Frechtling replied: "Probably not, because no report is perfect. Unless people take the time to sit down and discuss it, they're not going to act on it. They're not interested. . . . We try to keep them informed. Toward the end, we show them a draft report before it goes to the superintendent or goes public. They have a chance to review or make comments on it. If we can't reach an agreement, they can even write a rejoinder that goes forward at the same time the report does. This involvement also serves another function, because sometimes we find that program changes are made even before the report is issued."

Adapted from Wills, K. 1987. A conversation with Joy Frechtling. *Evaluation Practice*, 8(2), 20–30.

---

to analyze the data would not be discussed. The decision maker wants to hear the recommendations for improvement, thus, the presentation and discussion should focus on those.

During personal presentations, visual aids are helpful. Using an overhead projector helps make major points. Such visual aids provide information and, equally important, keep the attention of the audience on the message. A set of handouts could be prepared in which each one focuses on one major conclusion including a summary of its empirical support (Haensly, Lupinski, and McNamara, 1987). Figure 13.2 is an example of such a handout.

Audience for the Personal Presentations

It is likely that along with the dean, others present for the summary report presentation would be the program director, the assistant dean directly responsible for the program, the lead evaluator, and a member of the evaluation team. The size of the program influences the size and nature of the audience. When federal programs are described a greater number of people are present compared to small programs at Sanders College. Even with small projects, it is helpful for more than one member of the evaluation team to assist with the personal presentation. The second member can handle the handouts and visual aids, supplying information the

FIGURE 13.2   An illustrative chart that might be used as a handout during a personal presentation.

Planning Question 5. Are elderly residents underserved by the Community Mental Health Center?

Rationale.   The Center's mission is to provide needed service to all sectors of the community; however, few elderly people make use of the Center.

Core observations

- The percentage of community residents over 65 has increased to 15%; 3% are older than 75.
- Nearly half of residents over 75 live with relatives; in 45% of these families no one is home during the day time except the elderly person.
- Police officers report that they believe that there has been an increase in calls from elderly people or about elderly people having a problem when no one else is available.
- Community services to the elderly are limited to home nursing care for seriously ill elderly who qualify for Medicaid and the Central Library's Seniors & Classics book discussion program.
- Several CMHC's in the northern part of the state have developed a drop-in, informal "day care" service for ambulatory seniors; and an up-to-seven day respite care service for families with seniors needing to have assistance available at all times. Sliding scale costs are charged for each service.

Recommendation.   Plan to increase service to elderly residents by beginning with a drop-in center based on a membership fee. Develop a need assessment to estimate the community response to a respite care service and the fees that would need to be charged.

---

presenter may have forgotten, and clarify questions. Since the assistant is not responsible for the presentation, he or she has more time to assess the audience's reaction to the presentation.

Scheduling Personal Presentations

Before the personal presentation to the program director scheduled for March 15, a written draft of the final report should be available to the director. Note that this version of the report is called a *draft* and should be labeled *Confidential*. Although the interpretations and possible areas of improvements have been aired to the staff and the students involved, the recommendations are not completely set. After looking at the report, the director may be able to suggest additional recommendations or may point out errors that the evaluation team missed. A discussion of the draft is likely to result in changes in the report.

Calling this report a draft avoids offending the most senior administrator, the dean, who may feel that the final report should come to the dean's office before being released anywhere else. If any questions arose, it can be said truthfully that draft reports have been discussed elsewhere, but that the final report is being presented to the dean first. After the report to the dean and with the dean's approval, the written final report can be made available to others.

CONTENT OF FORMAL WRITTEN PROJECT REPORTS

The personal presentations to decision makers are the single most important report for a program evaluation. However there are many other channels for reporting program evaluations; this section describes the content of the written report of the whole evaluation project.

Purposes of the Formal Report

Evaluators are nearly always expected to complete a report describing the overall program evaluation. Even though major stakeholders have been regularly informed about the progress of the evaluation and an oral presentation has been made, it is necessary to provide an overall report. First, it is crucial to provide a written record that the evaluation was carried out. Those who arranged to fund the evaluation may require an overall summary for budget accountability. Second, the written report can answer questions about the findings of the evaluation or about its methodology that might come up later. Third, even when administrators make a decision on the basis of the oral presentation, the written report can back up the decision if others challenge it. Fourth, since administrators, program staff members, and evaluators take new positions and retire, their memories of the evaluation are lost. The written report remains for others to examine. Without a written report some people may propose a new evaluation in a few years thinking that the program was never evaluated. It is not unusual for members of planning committees to suggest gathering data on an issue only to learn that a study on the issue was completed a few years before. Even if planners or administrators decide that an additional study is needed, access to the written report of the previous study would be very helpful to those planning a new need assessment or outcome evaluation.

Report Outline

Figure 13.3 is a illustrative report outline; after adding page numbers to this outline, it serves as a table of contents for the report. Note that it begins with a summary. While most program staff and directors read reports carefully, many administrators read the summaries only. A summary is not the same as an abstract, which precedes many research articles. Unlike journal abstracts, summaries are

FIGURE 13.3 Sample internal evaluation report outline.

Evaluation of the Impact of the Physician Residency Program on General Medical Hospital

  I. Summary
 II. Introduction
    A. Background of the program
    B. Residency program created important changes in care
    C. Problems in conducting the evaluation
III. Procedure and Method
    A. Data collection
    B. Respondents
    C. Content of the interviews
 IV. Results
    A. How respondents evaluate the teaching function of the hospital
      1. Attending physicians' reactions
      2. Nonphysician hospital staff evaluations
      3. Residents' views of their programs
    B. Perceptions of the quality of care provided by the residents
      1. Perceptions of technical skills
      2. Interpersonal skills
        a. Staff rapport with residents
        b. Patient rapport with residents
        c. Care of dying patients
        d. Use of hospital nonmedical resource personnel
    C. Organizational changes brought about by the development of the residency program
      1. Increase in number of hospital-based physicians
      2. Development of new outpatient care unit
      3. Conflicts among residents in different specializations
      4. Effects of the program on the cost of medical care
  V. Conclusions and Recommendations
    A. Overall comments
    B. Seven recommendations

References
Appendix A.   Growth of residency programs at the hospital
Appendix B.   Interview forms used with nurses

---

longer and can stand alone. Some abstracts contain phrases such as " . . . the implications of findings are discussed" or " . . . a number of implications are drawn." A summary actually includes the recommendations; the crucial implications are given in the summary, not saved for the discussion section. Illustrative summaries are included with the case studies at the end of this text. (However, to save space the tables of contents were omitted.)

In writing a report, some beginning evaluators are hesitant to use subheadings and instead write paragraph after paragraph that provides readers little assistance in comprehending the general flow of the report. Readers of evaluations need all the help we can give them. Think about reading this text with only the major chapter breaks (those in capital letters). Without the other subheadings, the text is harder to follow and it is harder to recall the major points.

Describe the Context of the Evaluation

An overall written project report includes a description of the program setting, the program itself, and the purpose of the evaluation. These topics would be mentioned only briefly in the oral report because the audience often includes those who requested the evaluation, and they have been kept informed about the project as it was carried out. However, the audience for the written project report is more difficult to anticipate. It is written for people who know little about the program and sponsoring institution, or for those who replaced the original decision makers or program directors.

A description of the program as evaluated is also important. It is impossible to predict with accuracy how a program will evolve, how funding will change, or how directors will change it. For future readers to make sense out of the report, the program itself needs to be described. Some of these descriptions can make use of material already prepared by the program and simply placed in an appendix. It may be that other organizations have better records than universities, but it is often surprisingly difficult to find program descriptions after several years have passed or the director of a program has left the university.

It is also essential that the purpose of the evaluation be described. Although the vast majority of evaluations are formative, designed to develop ideas for program improvement, it is wise to state this in the report. The precise issues that were to be addressed should be listed. There are major differences between a project to assess the training needs of staff members and a project to provide a summative judgment about the effectiveness of current training efforts, even though the two projects might well measure some of the same variables.

Describe the Program Participants

Reports usually include a description of those who received the services of the program. Demographic information helps others to judge whether the program was particularly suited to the people served and whether the program might help elsewhere. Beyond information such as age, education, and gender, a description of the participants can include how the people got into the program. It makes a difference whether the people served represent the target population for whom the program was designed or if they learned about the service and sought it out on their own, but are different from the target population. The rate of attrition and the descriptors of those who did not complete the program would be interesting to anyone hoping to improve it.

✓ Justify the Criteria Selected

Whether the project was a need assessment or a summative evaluation certain criteria were selected to indicate unmet needs or program success. Indexes of unmet needs should be related to the subject of the need assessment; outcome criteria should be described and related to the goals of the program. In a report of an outcome evaluation this section might be an appropriate place to provide the impact model of the program. It remains true that many services are offered without demonstrating how the services are expected to lead to the desired results (DeFriese, 1990). It is also true that evaluators sometimes fail to show how the specific measures of outcome are related to the outcomes mentioned in the goals, especially when the original goals were not explicit.

Evaluators are coming to appreciate more fully how weaknesses in observation techniques, self-report surveys, community-level variables, or ratings made by observers, reduce the power of the evaluation to detect an effect of the program (Lipsey, 1990b). Evaluators may want to document that they considered these issues while they planned the evaluation; however, it might be a good idea to place technical material regarding the reliability and validity of the measurement tools in an appendix since this could get a little heavy for administrators and service delivery staff members.

Describe the Data Gathering Procedures

It is important to describe procedures used to obtain data because the way information is gathered can affect the findings. Poorly trained interviewers extract less information than well-trained ones; the 1980 census is less accurate in describing current unmet needs than the 1990 census; self-report surveys are subjected to more self-interest biases than more objective material gathered from records. The relationship of the people responsible for data gathering and the program being studied might be important also.

Provide the Findings

Use graphs. The recent availability of user-friendly software to prepare graphs has reduced the expense of having graphs drawn by a drafter. Graphs such as 100 percent Column Graph can be used like a pie chart to show the relative frequency of people in a program from different areas of the community. By placing several 100 percent Column Graphs side by side readers can compare demographic variables from various program sites or over years. Tufte (1983) argues that pie charts are difficult to interpret because they depend on a comparison of angles rather than lengths to appreciate the relative size of the groups. Figure 13.4 illustrates a set of 100 percent column graphs prepared using Graph-in-the-Box (1987) and a bar graph prepared with LotusWorks (1990). Both programs are easy to use. A book by Cleveland (1985) gives useful suggestions and conventions for preparing graphs for presentations.

Anticipate misunderstandings. There are a number of pitfalls facing evaluators and readers of evaluations in their interpretation of evaluation findings. While program evaluations share these problems with other social science research, the problem may be especially critical to evaluation because public interest in evaluations of government-funded services is sometimes intense. Inaccurate or misleading interpretations of evaluation findings can have serious implications (Friedman, H., 1990). Recognizing the possibility of such misunderstandings permits evaluators to prepare reports written so as to minimize the possibility of such misuse of findings.

Many audiences, including some well-educated ones, confuse the size of a sample with its representativeness. Large, self-selected samples responding to a survey are often overvalued, even when a small response rate really means that the findings cannot be treated as describing the population of interest. Smaller, carefully sampled representative samples yield more accurate estimates of the population values, but may be criticized unfairly simply on the basis of size.

Although many people can understand the implications of the difference between two means, variance is a very hard concept for people to understand. Readers sometimes interpret the difference between two group means to indicate that the distributions of the scores of the people in the two groups hardly overlap at all (Posavac and Sinacore, 1984). Mean differences always must be interpreted with regard to the standard deviations. However, small numerical differences that might have marked social importance must not be trivialized. Since most programs, even costly and well-implemented ones, produce only small changes in people, interpretations of groups' differences are best made in the context of the research literature on program effects (Light and Pillemer, 1985). Lipsey (1990b) has gathered nearly 200 meta-analyses summarizing the impact of thousands of individual studies. Improvements of even a fourth of a standard deviation on an *important* variable might well be a very supportive finding, although some only look at the numbers and question its relevance (see Rimland, 1979). On the other hand, if the variable used to detect success is trivial, even large differences between program and comparison groups do not help the stakeholders to estimate the success of the program.

Type II errors are overlooked so often (Frieman et al., 1978; Lipsey, 1990b) that the issue bears repeating. It may be that the resources provided to the evaluator were insufficient to perform an evaluation with enough sensitivity to detect a real effect. Although none of us enjoy pointing out that one of our evaluations might not have been designed well enough to detect a socially useful effect, recognizing this possibility is better than writing a report that implies we know the program did not achieve its goals. Report readers who only know that "p < .05" is good and

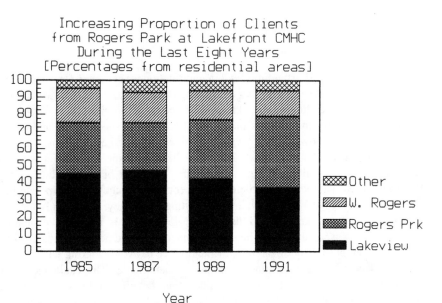

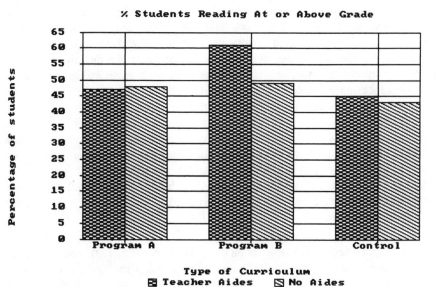

FIGURE 13.4 Illustrative 100% column graphs and a bar chart prepared with easy-to-use graph programs.

"n.s." is bad cannot examine the results to estimate the probability of Type II errors. The report should shield the program, its staff, and director from such confusion.

Deal with Hindsight Bias

A major misunderstanding, and a devastating experience for evaluators, occurs when stakeholders claim that the findings were already well-known and that the evaluation added little to their knowledge about the program. Of course, it is true that an evaluator might work independently from the stakeholders and indeed duplicate existing knowledge. If evaluators work with stakeholders as has been recommended throughout this text, it is more likely that the information was not well-known, but that the listeners are showing hindsight bias (Fischhoff, 1982; Wood 1978). Researchers have documented people's tendency to incorporate new information into what they knew, even adjusting what they knew, and sincerely believing that they "knew it all the time." Professionals receiving evaluation reports are also susceptible to the bias. This tendency should not be confused with a conscious attempt to deny threatening evaluations or to avoid working with the new ideas; hindsight bias seems quite common and automatic. The challenge to the evaluator is to demonstrate to the stakeholders that they did not know the information without damaging the interpersonal relationships between the evaluator and the stakeholders.

Some evaluators seek to get stakeholders to state explicitly what they expect the evaluation to show but the stakeholders may not like to make statements publicly that might prove to be incorrect later. We have used the following procedure: provide listeners with an empty graph, that is, a graph with axes, scales, and a title, but without any data; suggest that they privately plot the results that they expect the report to contain; and lastly provide a complete graph with all the data. In this way, they can compare their expectations with the data, minimizing hindsight bias, and not have to demonstrate in public that they were wrong. This has worked well in settings in which unit managers receive feedback on their employees' work attitudes on a variety of scales. The managers are given the scale averages for their whole division, but not those for their own units until after they have understood the meaning of the scales and committed themselves privately to how they think their own employees feel. No one knows how right or wrong the individuals are. Note also that this procedure gets the listeners involved in the feedback process rather than passively listening.

Use appendices. The description of the findings are more thorough than can be given in a personal presentation. Since the audience of the report is made up of people not schooled in research methods or statistical analyses, details such as long tables of means, standard deviations, and probability levels can be placed in an appendix. Many new evaluators do not know that appendices keep the report readable; the use of appendices is common among experienced evaluators. A liberal use of graphs to illustrate the findings documented in the appendices is desirable.

Develop Recommendations

As the communication plan in Figure 13.1 implied, recommendations are best developed in consultation with the stakeholders. Stakeholders do not dictate the recommendations, but the tentative recommendations can be suggested to groups of stakeholders to learn if the recommendations seem to be addressing the problems that stakeholders sense and if the recommendations seem workable. It may be that after the consultation, the evaluators feel that certain recommendations deserve to be considered widely even though some stakeholders do not feel that they are workable. Unresolved disagreements can be included in the report as is the practice of the Office of Inspector General of the U.S. Department of Health and Human Services (Office of Inspector General, 1990).

Recommendations need to be kept within the psychological reach of the stakeholders. Recommendations that would require major changes in the organization if adopted will simply be rejected. Even if an evaluation suggests that there are major problems with the program's plans, its implementation, or its effectiveness, the evaluator has a greater chance of having the evaluation seriously considered if only the most pressing problems are treated in the recommendations to the decision makers. If an evaluation was planned to help a program improve, then the goal of the evaluation report is not to give a grade to the program but to help it improve regardless of how well it functions.

Appearance of Formal Reports

Written evaluation reports are prepared with care both to content and appearance. In applied settings, managers are used to dealing with consultants and salespeople who present attractively prepared reports or descriptions of new products. Consequently evaluators cannot submit final reports that look like typewritten term papers.

A better report begins with a cover that includes the logo of the organization sponsoring the evaluation. A table of contents lists all the sections of the report to permit readers to find appropriate sections easily. For a price just above the lowest-priced computer printers, an evaluator can buy a printer that produces text that appears typeset like a book. We suggest that colored paper be used for the appendices. This dresses up the report and assures the reader that the text of the report does not cover all the pages in the report. Depending on the size of the reports, the binding used can vary. For short reports, an inexpensive cover with a clear front permitting the title page to show through makes an attractive appearance. For long reports, a commercial printer may be needed.

PROGRESS REPORTS AND PRESS RELEASES

Since evaluations often take at least several months to complete and since there may be some misgivings and worries about what may come out of an evaluation, crucial stakeholders should be informed about the progress of the project. Progress reports can be made when observations begin, when data collection is complete, or on some regular schedule (as shown in Fig. 13.1). Progress reports can also be used to thank people who may have assisted in carrying out a certain phase of the evaluation.

Press releases are sometimes appropriate to call attention to the evaluation among wider audiences (Ross, 1990). Before an evaluator releases information beyond the stakeholders involved, it is important to have agreement on the appropriateness of such publicity. In some settings, such as private organizations, the administrators may not permit such publicity. On the other hand, the reports of some government-sponsored internal evaluations are assumed to be public documents once the report has been approved by the director of evaluation office involved.

SUMMARY AND PREVIEW

Communicating the findings of the program cannot be treated as an afterthought; planning communication should begin when the evaluation itself is being planned. Communication is more likely to be carried out if a plan is spelled out explicitly from the beginning. A personal presentation of the findings is the most important single communication channel. A summary written report documents the details of the evaluation, serves as an official record that the evaluation did take place, and includes details of the procedures, findings, and statistical analyses. In addition, briefer progress reports and even press releases are useful forms of communication with stakeholders.

As evaluators communicate their findings, they are concerned especially with encouraging the utilization of the findings. While stakeholders are the ones deciding how to use evaluations, evaluators can exert some effort to raise the probability that good recommendations will be followed. These efforts are described in the last chapter.

STUDY QUESTIONS

1. How might communication plans for qualitative evaluations differ from communication plans for quantitative evaluations?
2. Develop a form that might be used to get stakeholders to make their expectations explicit before receiving the actual results of an evaluation.
3. Find an article describing a program evaluation in a journal. Prepare an outline of an oral presentation of the findings of the evaluation. Prepare an outline of a written report presenting the evaluation findings. Note how these outlines differ from the outline of the original journal article.
4. Prepare a summary of an article describing a program evaluation. Note how the summary differs from the abstract used in the journal.

5. List the stakeholder groups who should be part of the feedback process for the article you have been using. What are the differences in type and detail of the information these groups would want to know about?

FURTHER READING

BECKER, H.S. 1986. *Writing for social scientists*. Chicago: The University of Chicago Press.
SMITH, N.L., ed. 1982. *Communication strategies in evaluation*. Beverly Hills, Calif.: Sage.

14

A Favorable Evaluation Climate: How to Encourage Utilization

The first step in having findings utilized effectively was discussed in the last chapter: presenting reports in a manner that gets and holds the attention of the stakeholders. This chapter examines how evaluators can contribute to a climate that is conducive to having recommendations considered and implemented. This subject is discussed under five headings: (1) encouraging the proper attitude among program staff and policy makers; (2) dealing with negative findings in a constructive fashion; (3) dealing with mixed results; (4) overcoming the obstacles to effective utilization of findings; and (5) improving evaluations.

ENCOURAGING PROPER ATTITUDE IN STAFF AND POLICY MAKERS

Work with the Stakeholders

The utilization of program evaluation findings are more likely if the evaluator continues to work with the stakeholders after the evaluation is completed. This approach extends the evaluator's role beyond what characterized the field in the past. Often evaluators were called upon to gather and provide data, to present a report, and to move on. While evaluations conducted in such a manner could be useful, the probability of effective application increases if the role of the evaluator includes working with stakeholders to implement recommendations. This role is not easily filled by external evaluators; however, the role of internal evaluators can be redefined. The concept of advocacy evaluation was coined by Sonnichsen to describe his work with the FBI as described in Evaluator Profile 8.

Adopt a Developmental Interpretation

The realization that not every innovation or creative idea will be a success is the first element of a productive attitude that contributes to the effective utilization of evaluation findings. Program directors and staff must feel free to innovate; but they must also recognize failure and learn from failures. This enables individuals to work with evaluators with open minds rather than defensive attitudes that prompt them to reject attempts at evaluation at the first indication of less-than-overwhelming praise. Accepting the possibility of failure enables people to set aside less productive ideas and procedures when the evidence is not sufficiently strong to support a certain approach to a problem. Freedom to fail also enables staff to experiment with other approaches to achieve program goals.

The effects of the fear of failure in organizational development (OD) is illustrated in the writings of Argyris (1985) and in a study by Mirvis and Berg

EVALUATOR PROFILE 8.

Richard C. Sonnichsen, Ph.D.:
The FBI and the Utilization of Program Evaluation

Richard C. Sonnichsen heads the Office of Program Evaluation and Audits at FBI Headquarters in Washington, D.C. He has been an agent since 1964. He earned a B.S. in Forestry (University of Idaho) and his doctoral degree in Public Administration (University of Southern California, Washington Center). Someday, he intends to return to Idaho to get closer to nature than is possible in the Capitol.

Dr. Sonnichsen was asked about program evaluation in the FBI. He responded, "When I first started attending AEA [American Evaluation Association] meetings, people appeared reluctant to accept my explanation that I was an evaluator, and felt that I was either undercover or attending their conference for some nefarious purpose. After appearing on several panels and publishing some of my views on evaluation, I believe that the evaluation community has now accepted that the FBI does in fact conduct evaluations.

"I think that our basic approach to design and methodology is fundamentally similar to mainstream evaluation, but we do espouse a philosophical approach to evaluation that I refer to as 'advocacy evaluation.' It is an activist approach to evaluation attempting to involve the evaluators and their supervisory staff in ensuring that recommendations flowing from evaluation activities are subjected to scrutiny . . ., debated, and, if meritorious, implemented. . . . I feel that a logical extension of the evaluator's role is to participate in meetings, attend conferences, write memoranda, and actively participate in the organizational decision-making process regarding recommendations flowing from an evaluation."

Adapted from Sporn, D. L. 1990. A conversation with Richard C. Sonnichsen. *Evaluation Practice, 11,* 63–67.

(1977). Organizational development is a relatively new and developing behavioral science that aims at assisting organizations in their efforts at self-improvement. Sometimes this involves introducing complex programs designed to change the structure of an organization, its social climate, or the day-to-day behaviors of specific individuals within the organization. Because of the complexity of the situations addressed by OD programs, mistakes are unavoidable. However, because of pressure to succeed, many failures in OD efforts are ignored, denied, or unrecognized. When failures are covered up, it becomes impossible to learn from them. Problems common to OD efforts in many organizations are considered unique because they have not been publicly described. As a result, some prevailing OD practices go unquestioned and are not improved. Errors in nonroutine situations such as those faced frequently in complex and rapidly changing organizations are neither shameful nor completely avoidable, and patience and persistence may eventually be viewed as the only "right" answers in organizational development. The more fruitful approach is to measure competence not by skill in avoiding errors but by skill in detecting them and acting on the information openly. We must learn to reward those who recognize the risks involved in creating change, and yet still choose to risk, persist, and learn from their errors.

While an atmosphere that respects the freedom to fail is essential for the effective use of findings, it often is beyond the power of evaluators to foster such an atmosphere where it does not already exist. The attitude of top administration usually determines whether an organization or program is characterized by a desperate need to make a program or policy appear to work or whether there is a realistic attitude toward the possibility of failure. In healthy organizations administrators understand that innovation entails the possibility that even well-designed and fully implemented programs may fail. Where a healthy attitude toward innovation already exists, evaluators can make the most of it and use every opportunity to underscore and publicize the enlightened attitude of the administration. Where the atmosphere chokes off healthy self-examination, evaluators may request top administration to make an explicit statement to allay the anxiety of worried program personnel. In organizations where the need of success is paramount and the fear of failure is widespread, evaluators are able to do very little to bring about a change in attitude. However, evaluators rarely face this situation; organizations with a strong fear of failure are not inclined to sponsor program evaluations in the first place.

Innovations Can Be Improved

A third element of a productive attitude involves helping personnel to expect suggestions about new ways of developing and improving existing programs rather than a bare presentation of good news or bad news. It is relatively rare that an existing program is terminated or continued solely on the basis of an evaluation. In fact, evaluators are pleased when any modification in policy and procedures occurs. However, program personnel tend to be highly involved in their program and occasionally are worried about the continuation of the program in the face of a critical evaluation. As a result, they often look for a one-line answer to the question: Does the evaluation support our program or not? In other words: Does the evaluation bring good news or bad news? Evaluators have a better opportunity of seeing their findings utilized effectively when program personnel understand that every evaluation brings some good news and some bad news, and that the important question is: What concrete improvements are suggested by the evaluation that are feasible for implementation? Evaluators must encourage program personnel to see evaluation as a way to help them improve and modify their program—not as a means to enshrine it or destroy it.

For example, in conducting the evaluation of the physical medicine and rehabilitation unit in a community hospital, the health care delivery team understood from the beginning that the rehabilitation unit was going to stay intact regardless of the outcome of the evaluation. However, they were interested in finding out just how much progress the stroke patients were making during their stay in the unit, and also whether those who have improved during their hospitalization continued to improve, or at least maintained their improvement, after they left the hospital. The results of the study showed that during their hospitalization the stroke patients improved their physical skills (walking, eating, dressing) more than their cognitive skills (speaking, remembering). This information focused the attention of the health care delivery team on improving efforts to restore cognitive skills. The results also showed that the majority of patients who made progress during their hospitalization maintained their improvement after they left the hospital. The information helped the rehabilitation team to decide whether a follow-up program geared to patients who did not maintain their improvement was needed.

Applications May Be Broader Than Expected

The fourth way evaluators can promote healthy attitudes is to help program managers see connections between the findings of an evaluation and their own specific needs. For example, the chairman of a large department of pastoral care at a church-sponsored hospital commissioned an evaluation of the department to learn what patients, nurses, and physicians expected from chaplains and the extent to which patient and staff needs were being met by the chaplains (Carey, 1972). The research enabled chaplains to get a clear picture of the differences in expectations among patients of different religious denominations, ages, and marital situations. It also revealed that physicians and nurses had slightly different role expectations for the chaplains than did the patients. Furthermore, many chaplains were surprised to learn that the physicians and nurses placed a higher value on the help chaplains gave them in their work than the patients did on the more traditional role of the chaplains. This was due largely to the very active role the chaplains play at this hospital in assisting the staff to care for patients and families in times of serious illnesses and death.

These secondary findings with respect to physicians and nurses turned out to be more valuable than originally expected when representatives from Medicare and certain insurance companies resisted reimbursing the hospital for the costs of pastoral care. The representatives took the position that these expenses should be disallowed, and the cost of the chaplaincy should be underwritten by the religious organization sponsoring the hospital. They took this position because they assumed that the role of the chaplains was primarily to provide emotional support to a minority of patients who had religious needs. However, the president of the hospital was alert enough to see the application of the evaluation to defend the financing of the chaplaincy program out of patient room costs. The evaluation reported that 87 percent of the nurses and 76 percent of the physicians had said they found chaplains to be of great help to them personally in their work with patients. Consequently, it could not be argued that chaplains were assigned primarily to serve a minority of the patient population. The hospital's viewpoint prevailed, largely on the force of the evaluation. In this instance hospital administrators saw implications of the evaluation not recognized by the director of the pastoral care program. The most effective evaluators are alert to practical issues that may be peripheral to the original intent of the evaluation. If they fail to do so, the full implications may go unappreciated— even program managers cannot always be relied upon to see all the values of the evaluation findings.

Findings Are Working Hypotheses

A final aspect of engendering a proper attitude for a productive use of findings is to phrase conclusions as working hypotheses rather than as definitive generalizations. It would be very satisfying to be able to summarize an evaluation with a clear, succinct statement that settles a question or solves a problem once and for all. When much time, effort, and money are spent on an evaluation, it would be nice to have something solid to show for the results. However, those who look to an evaluation to provide definitive conclusions are almost always disappointed.

One of the reasons why conclusions are best seen as working hypotheses is that local conditions do not allow for a generalization that can be applied to every situation. Unlike research in biological and physical sciences, research on social issues is very dependent on social settings and the expectations of the people involved (Guba and Lincoln, 1989). Although we can evaluate programs and develop avenues for pursuing improvements, we cannot expect to generalize about other settings or about what would happen if conditions changed dramatically in the program's current setting. The more specific the finding or recommendation, the less likely generalization is possible. However, there are times in which the effect of some services becomes fairly clear. For example, pregnant women and their babies are healthier with adequate nutrition. In such situations evaluations focus more on documenting adequate implementation of a program and the degree to which programs meet known needs and less on showing once again that adequate nutrition is correlated with better health in an outcome evaluation.

DEALING CONSTRUCTIVELY
WITH NO-DIFFERENCE FINDINGS

When an evaluation concludes that treatment and comparison groups do not differ on criteria indicating a successful program, evaluators face challenging hurdles in working with stakeholders to implement the findings. Before facing the difficulties of helping people accept and act on an unfavorable evaluation, evaluators are called upon to analyze their methods and analyses carefully. The use of no-difference findings has often been naive; some writers have shown little regard to statistical power and sample size (Lipsey et al., 1985). The circumstances in which evaluators can conclude that the program did not have an effect are being actively debated (e.g., Julnes and Mohr, 1989; Lipsey, 1990b; Meehl, 1990; Yeaton and Sechrest, 1986, 1987).

How Can Evaluators Be Sure Groups Do Not Differ?

Although often ignored in practice it is widely known that a nonsignificant statistical test can be produced by utilizing small sample sizes, unreliable measures, and a low *alpha* level. Julnes and Mohr (1989) present three alternative approaches to avoiding Type II errors when finding that groups are similar on important criteria of program success. The first method is to raise the *alpha* level to perhaps .25, although they agree that .25 is just as arbitrary as .05 would have been.

Second, evaluators could avoid a significance test, but calculate the confidence interval of the difference between two groups. For example, one could report that the mean difference between two school groups was the equivalent of 0.12 grades with a 90 percent confidence interval of − .02 to .26. This would mean that although a traditional statistical test with *alpha* set at .05 would result in a nonsignificant test of the null hypothesis, we can be 90 percent sure that the program effect is somewhere in that range. It could be concluded that the program group did enough better than the control group to decide to offer the new curriculum to more students.

Third, using Cohen's tables (1987), the sample sizes, the desired *alpha*, and a judgment of the smallest effect size that would be of practical importance, an evaluator could estimate the power of the statistical test to detect such an effect size. If the power of the test is small, say 25 percent, then the likelihood of missing a true effect is large (75 percent in this case). Conducting studies with low power has not been uncommon (Freiman, Chalmers, Smith, and Kuebler, 1978; Lipsey, et al., 1985). If the power of detecting an effect, if it has occurred, is large instead, then the evaluator is on safe ground in arguing that the groups did not differ.

There Are Many Reasons to Continue a Program

Negative findings are disappointing. The temptation is to rationalize by saying, for example, that the program was never fully implemented or that a number of special and unusual cases in the sample affected the outcome. There are more productive ways of dealing with negative findings. One productive approach is to focus on the arguments for continuing a human service program—even if the findings are not supportive—if there are good reasons for continuing the program other than those originally proposed. For example, Waldo and Chiricos (1977) caused some consternation for policy makers who had supported the growth of a work-release program for prisoners. An analysis to determine whether members of work-release programs and those in a control group differed in recidivism showed that the programs provided no advantage on measures of rehabilitative success. Another way to look at the results is to conclude that the program, which is less expensive than incarceration, led to no harm. Thus, while work-release programs might be supported on humanitarian and economic grounds, policy makers should not implement these programs on the grounds that more prisoners are rehabilitated.

Common Sense Supports Some Innovations

Common-sense plausibility is another reason for continuing a program in the face of negative findings. When there is considerable agreement on the plausibility of a hypothesis, nonsupportive findings argue for an intensification of research rather than an abandonment of it. Ross (1975) argued in this manner after the evaluation of the Scandinavian laws on drinking and driving failed to support the hypothesis that drunken driving would be deterred by strict laws. He pointed out that even though the laws did not reduce DWI as expected, the evaluation did not lead to the conclusion that the laws have no impact. Common sense argues that the best interests of society call for reductions in DWI. However, he argued that further evaluations were needed to learn more about the effect of the laws.

Seligman and Hutton (1981) also provide an example where common-sense plausibility and prior research overrode a no-effect finding. An evaluation of the use of a feedback meter to motivate consumers to conserve energy did not provide any evidence that households with the feedback meter used less energy than households without one, but the idea of providing feedback to homeowners through instrumentation continued to be promoted. The most obvious reason is that earlier research showed that feedback was effective. Indeed, the prior research was an experimental field study that supported common sense and provided a theoretical understanding of conservation behaviors.

DEALING WITH MIXED RESULTS

When some findings support a program and others do not, proponents of a program focus attention on those findings that support the program while those who would like to see the program terminated focus attention on the negative aspects of the evaluation report. The problem of dealing with mixed results is accentuated when politics are involved, when a large number of jobs hangs in the balance, or when many people are rallied to opposing causes. Four approaches for dealing with mixed results and an assessment of the appropriateness of each are presented here.

Allowing Others to Interpret Mixed Results

First, evaluators could report the findings and leave the interpretation to the stakeholders—that is, to policy makers, administrators, or program staff. This can be accomplished by avoiding extended interpretation and discussion of the results in the written report and identifying the difficulties of interpretation only in the oral report, if at all. This approach may be appropriate when an evaluator had an explicit agreement with the sponsors of the research to keep the interpretation of findings to a minimum, and when the evaluator agreed not to deal with the implementation of the recommendations.

However, as we have argued elsewhere, evaluators ideally have a significant role in program planning. In addition, program personnel correctly expect evaluators to take a position in their analysis and discussion of the mixed results. Evaluators should seldom try to let the numbers speak for themselves. Data will be interpreted, if the evaluator does not do the interpreting, others with definite self-interest will (Richmond, 1990). Scriven (1980) argues that evaluators are commissioned to show whether a program has merit and worth. The failure of evaluators to draw interpretations and to make clear recommendations suggests incompetence or irresponsibility because program staff often are unable to interpret the data. However, they are helpful in discussing the recommendations and implications of the recommendations (Wye, 1989).

The Easy Way Out

Evaluators can choose the interpretation they feel is more favorable to the program and emphasize the results that support the favorable interpretation. When the effect was weak, evaluators can tone down unfavorable results by (1) alleging that the outcome measures were unreliable, insensitive, or inappropriate; (2) attributing the lack of statistical significance to the sample; or (3) suggesting that implementation of the program was inadequate due to lack of time, complexity, or lack of funds. These points should have been dealt with during the planning of the evaluation. Or, great weight might be placed on measures of consumer satisfaction, which are often surprisingly favorable even when more objective results are marginal.

Choosing the more favorable interpretation may be defended in some instances—for example, when the positive findings concern the more critical issues and there is hope that the program personnel will support a follow-up study to clarify the mixed results. However, espousing the more favorable position from fear of being criticized by program sponsors, to avoid hurting feelings, or merely to obtain further evaluation funding is not defensible.

The Adversary Approach

Two other ways to handle mixed results are more professionally responsible and more valuable in the long run to the evaluators and to program personnel. The evaluators can use an adversary approach to interpret the results. They can first argue one position and gather all the results that support that interpretation, and then they can take the opposite view and present the data that support that position. The evaluators can then state which view, if either, they think is stronger. If the evaluators cannot decide, they can point this out, along with their suggestions for follow-up research to clarify the ambiguity of the study.

Another form of the adversary style of presentation would be to ask two independent researchers who had not been connected with the report to study the design and the data collected and write a position paper supporting each side of the issue. These reviews can then be bound with the evaluator's own report permitting stakeholders to have all sides of debate. The adversary approach has been suggested by some writers (for example, Braithwaite et al., 1982; Datta, 1976a; Levine et al., 1978); however, this approach is likely to be relatively expensive, making it unrealistic for the evaluator working in an institution or government office.

Using the Evaluation to Improve the Program

Perhaps the best way to deal with mixed results is to emphasize that the purpose of the evaluation was not to terminate the program or provide performance appraisals of program managers but rather to help managers and staff improve the program or their conceptualization of the program. Nagel (1983b) and Leviton and Boruch (1983) suggest that utilization is often viewed simplistically because evaluators have not thought through what *might be* utilized from the study. Focusing on a simple outcome study, utilization can only be a continuation of a good program or a discontinuation of a weak one. There are other uses of evaluations, however. By thinking through alternatives and basing recommendations on those, there are many degrees of utilization. When the use of evaluations is defined broadly and sufficient time is permitted for knowledge to be used, Leviton and Boruch (1983) find that evaluations are used constructively.

To diffuse the possible negative attitudes on the part of managers and program staff, we have found a useful analogy from the medical field. Managers are asked to view evaluators in the same way physicians view laboratory and other support personnel in a hospital. Physicians are responsible for the welfare of their patients and for developing medical care plans to address their patients' illnesses. However, before developing a medical care plan, physicians order a series of laboratory tests, urine analyses, X-rays, or other diagnostic procedures. In studying the results of these tests, physicians develop a better perspective on the strengths of their patients as well as the underlying causes of their symptoms.

After prescribing a medical regimen for their patients, physicians once again have their patients undergo a similar series of medical tests to evaluate the effectiveness of the medical care. If the results of these posttests do not show improvement, physicians do not interpret the disappointing laboratory findings as attacks on their competence, nor do they harbor resentment toward the laboratory personnel for the negative evaluation reports. Rather, they conclude that the problem is difficult to diagnose and treat or does not respond quickly to treatment. After studying the implications of the reports, physicians develop alternative treatment plans to address the unrelieved symptoms of their patients. In like manner, managers and program staff can work with evaluators as partners in trying to understand the relative strengths and weaknesses of their work units or programs. Using this approach, evaluators can be viewed as auxiliary members of the program team, rather than as adversaries. Note that if groups responsible for funding programs insist on using the evaluations to determine the programs' resources, then the evaluation takes on a summative tone and healthy frankness about problems and potential solutions may well evaporate.

OBSTACLES TO EFFECTIVE UTILIZATION OF FINDINGS

In this section four of the more common obstacles to the implementation of findings are discussed. Evaluators are not always in a position to remove these blocks, but at least they can be aware of their existence and try to work around them when possible.

Value Conflicts among Evaluators

Evaluations and policy research cannot be insulated from personal values. Rigorous research methods minimize the effect of such influences; however, choice of topic and variables as well as sampling procedures can affect the results of the research. Guba and Lincoln (1989) and others who believe evaluation should follow the participatory action research approach[1] argue that a major, perhaps the central, goal of evaluation is the empowerment of less influential stakeholders. Without adopting all their positions, we agree that evaluation is best carried out when evaluators and stakeholders are explicit about their values and examine the effect of value presuppositions on evaluation procedures and interpretations.

The Weight of Nonempirical Influences

The second obstacle to the effective utilization of findings is the weight of other influences and pressures that compete with the impact of evaluations. At times it may seem to evaluators that decision makers do not pay attention to evaluation reports and do not wish to reexamine the policy decisions in view of new information received. However, decision makers may receive a report with an open mind—even with eagerness—and yet find themselves unable to act because economic realities and political pressures constrain them from making desirable improvements in programs.

Bigelow and Ciralo (1975) studied the question of what value there was in collecting information and presenting it to human service administrators. Would information improve their decisions? They studied this question in a large community health center that had thirty management and supervisory personnel. They used three different strategies to try to learn how management was using evaluation feedback. First, they conducted interviews with managers. Second, they interviewed supervisors when a substantial program modification had been made within their jurisdiction. Third, they introduced a body of data bearing on a program management issue during a meeting of supervisors and then tried to trace the effects over a two-week period. They concluded that managers were disposed to use information, that it affected their intentions to modify programs, and that it resulted in further exploration of a particular management question. The study did not demonstrate that the information resulted in improved performance for the organization. Nevertheless, in the specific instances in which information had, in fact, been introduced, the relative impact of information was appreciable.

[1]See Tesch (1990) for a concise summary of a number of viewpoints.

Preexisting Polarization of Interested Parties

A third block to the effective utilization of findings occurs when opposing factions have been strongly polarized before an evaluation takes place. Recommendations fall on deaf ears when administrators and public representatives have already chosen their position, regardless of the results of an evaluation. A clear example of the effect of polarization can be seen in the interpretations of the evaluation research conducted by Zimring (1975) on the impact of the Federal Gun Control Act of 1968. Zimring comments on this at the beginning of his report.

> The study will be of little use to the most fervent friends and foes of gun control legislation. It provides data they do not need. Each group uses the Act's presumed failure to confirm views already strongly held. Enthusiasts for strict federal controls see the failure of the law as proof that stricter laws are needed, while opponents see it as evidence that no controls will work. The picture that emerges from available data is more equivocal. There is evidence that the approach adopted by the Act can aid state efforts at strict firearms control, although other resources necessary to achieve this end have never been provided by Congress. There is also reason to believe that the potential impact of the Act is quite limited when measured against the problems it sought to alleviate (p. 133).

Zimring's comments reveal an unfortunate aspect of the way public policies are made. In order for a sufficient number of people or representatives to agree on a policy, the benefits of adopting the policy are often overstated. Should an evaluator draw unfavorable conclusions on the basis of the unrealistic expectations? Should the evaluator use a different set of expectations based on what many feel would have been more reasonable goals? Ideally, when working within a polarized setting, evaluators seek to get proponents and opponents to agree beforehand on the criteria of program success. Without such agreement, the evaluation will have little impact regardless of the findings.

Misapplied Methodology

Evaluators have tried to learn more than their resources permitted. In their view of published evaluations, Lipsey et al. (1985) showed that although many outcome evaluations were planned to investigate the causal effects of the program on the outcome, only a small fraction of the evaluations were designed in ways that would have permitted the evaluation to isolate a causal relationship. This occurs when too few program participants are observed, threats to internal validity are not controlled satisfactorily, or the outcome variables were not measured with enough reliability or validity.

Limits on resources in the context of overly ambitious or confused evaluation requests make valid experimental and quasi-experimental evaluation impossible. Frequently, people not trained in evaluation methods do not appreciate the challenge of conducting valid research in service settings. A program evaluation that cannot be interpreted validly damages the reputation of the discipline. Experimentation to isolate causes is to be reserved for situations that require an unambiguous understanding of causes. Since this is seldom needed by the stakeholders, evaluators can better help them by providing valid information on implementation or by helping the staff to develop clearer ideas about why the program is expected to influence people. Evaluators who give stakeholders a correct understanding of the benefits and limits of program evaluation have a better chance of meeting the stakeholders' needs.

IMPROVING EVALUATIONS BY USING COMPLETED EVALUATIONS IN PLANNING PROGRAMS AND EVALUATIONS

Some evaluators and planners fail to utilize information that is already available when thinking about developing a new program or evaluating an existing program. This often happens when evaluators and planners underestimate the effort and resources required to gather data for planning or to conduct an evaluation. As Wargo pointed out (see Evaluator Profile 5), many observers expect that the expense of data collections is leading evaluators to reanalyze existing information, to use management information systems, and to combine completed evaluations of similar programs to a greater degree than in the past.

Reanalyze Existing Data

At times the original data of completed projects can be reanalyzed. One approach is to request original data from someone who has published or reported on an evaluation of a program. A paper presented at the meeting of psychological, sociological, or policy organizations could refer to a program based on an idea that is similar to what is being planned in the evaluator's organization. If the data are available, the evaluator could reanalyze it to address the planning questions posed to the evaluator. This type of analysis is called *secondary analysis* (see, for example, Bowering, 1984).

Use Management Information Systems

Chapter 6 illustrated simple management information systems (MIS) that permit an agency to keep track of the services it offers to clients. An existing MIS can be used creatively to examine questions not addressed explicitly when it was implemented. Imagine evaluating a school system's efforts to improve by examining numbers of students in a grade relative to the number of children of that age in the population. If schools improve, fewer parents would be expected to send children to private schools. As another example, the quality of a college academic department could be estimated by comparing the grades of students for courses in their major with their grades in nonmajor courses. Frequently students get better grades in their major because they work harder in those courses. However, the departments for which the differences between major and nonmajor courses are the largest are probably expecting less of their students than are the departments in which this difference is the smallest.

By incorporating some additional information into management information systems it may be possible to improve the usefulness of an MIS for evaluation. In

Chapter 6 it was suggested that a rated level of psychological function, or well-being, could be included into an MIS in a facility providing psychological counseling. By incorporating a computer-based medical record system with a computer-based billing system, it might be possible to compare the effectiveness/cost ratios of different programs within one hospital.

Draw Lessons from Meta-Analyses

The term *meta-analysis* is used to describe the quantitative combination of many studies on similar topics. In program evaluation, a meta-analyst gathers program evaluations of similar programs in an effort to gain statistical power to learn whether the interventions had an effect on program participants. The use of meta-analysis in program evaluation as well as other disciplines has increased dramatically during the past decade. The use of meta-analysis to improve our understanding of research articles and program evaluation was convincingly demonstrated by Rosenthal (1984). Providing readers with a simple method of combining the findings of several articles improved their understanding of the findings compared to a group of readers who only read the set of articles without any training in meta-analytic techniques.

The focus of meta-analysis has shifted from solely asking how effective a treatment was to using meta-analyses to learn about the effect of the quality of the evaluation methods on the findings (Cordray, 1990; Lipsey, Crosse, Dunkle, Pollard, and Stobart, 1985). By comparing the methods used with the findings of evaluations it is possible to learn a considerable amount about the advisability of conducting evaluations in certain ways. For example, Lipsey et al. (1985) have shown that organizational limitations make it very unlikely for many internal evaluators to gather convincing evidence that a program *caused* any improvements in the condition of the program participants. It follows then, that the internal evaluator experiences a great deal of frustration trying to conduct an experimental evaluation of a psychological or social intervention unless blessed with considerable resources. This conclusion, based on a review of many meta-analyses, is of major importance; since evaluation resources are always in short supply, evaluators want to spend their efforts in ways that are most likely to help the organizations in which they work.

The best introduction to meta-analysis has been prepared by Light and Pillemer (1984). After getting the idea clear, one can turn to Hunter and Schmidt (1990) and Hedges and Olkin (1985), who describe the actual process of carrying out meta-analyses. Lipsey (1990) includes much that is useful for conducting meta-analyses. Using these sources, internal evaluators can develop better evaluations, ones that tackle realistic evaluation objectives.

SUMMARY AND THE FUTURE OF PROGRAM EVALUATION

Evaluators have become increasingly active in working with organizations whose programs have been evaluated. No longer do evaluators slip ten copies of a completed report into the mail after preparing a final, written report in their offices.

Instead they seek to assist the organization to make the most use of an evaluation whether the findings are mixed or even unfavorable to the program. The crucial issue is to encourage stakeholders to look upon an evaluation as a developmental tool to assist in making program improvements or for suggestions about redirecting their activities. The participation of evaluators in these discussions improves the chances for the appropriate use of social science information. Utilization is also encouraged through the use of appropriate methodology, thus improving the evaluations themselves. Using existing data and completed evaluations holds promise for assisting evaluators in their work.

The discipline of program evaluation has changed markedly from the mid-1960s when it began its period of rapid growth. There have been many evaluations carried out that were little, if any, use in improving the services of the organizations commissioning them. Evaluators have developed far more effective ways of working with organizations and decision makers. Many advances in statistical analyses and in methodology have been made, and, of even more importance, evaluators have learned how to work more effectively with stakeholders. Initially many evaluators, especially those trained in psychology and education, used simple research designs adapted from basic, experimental research, treated program participants as subjects, and expected that a single written report would suffice to communicate their findings. Today, we believe that a smaller proportion of naively planned evaluations are being conducted and that many more program evaluations are being designed and carried out in ways that improve their chances of being utilized. Evaluators are expanding their skills and the definition of their roles: the future looks promising.

STUDY QUESTIONS

1. Discuss how defensive attitudes, which can block the effective use of program evaluations, are manifested in an organization with which you are familiar.
2. Contrast the conditions under which an evaluator would recommend the termination of a program and those that would prompt an evaluator to advocate further study.
3. Contrast the advantages and disadvantages of internal evaluators compared to consultants when it comes to the effectiveness of working with an organization to change programs using evaluation-based information.

FURTHER READING

EGAN, G. 1988a. *Change-agent skills A: Assessing and designing excellence.* San Diego, Calif.: University Associates.
EGAN, G. 1988b. *Change-agent skills B: Managing innovation and change.* San Diego, Calif.: University Associates.
HAKEL, M. D. et al. 1980. *Making it happen: Designing research with implementation in mind.* Beverly Hills, Calif.: Sage.
LIGHT, R. J., and PILLEMER, D. B. 1984. *Summing up: The science of reviewing research.* Cambridge, Mass.: Harvard University Press.

Case Studies

These case studies of evaluations illustrate different styles of program evaluations. Examining these five case studies will reveal some of the forms that evaluation can take as evaluators tailor their plans to the questions that concern stakeholders.

Each case is based on a published report of an evaluation. The articles were rewritten to approximate the form that a report to a stakeholder would follow. In order to get to the heart of the points to be illustrated, many details of each report were omitted. Furthermore, a summary was written for each report that did not appear in the original.

Case Study 1 concerns the improvement of the work environment that was marked by a high level of stress threatening the quality of the performance of the staff. Although it was in a hospital setting, the principles employed can be used in any work setting. Case Study 2 measured the effect of a media campaign. It was conducted in a university setting; however, the need to show that a media campaign can get the attention of a target population is relevant to many settings. Case Study 3, carried out in an armed services base, concerned a program to improve management style and effective goal setting in organizations. Case Study 4 sought to answer the question of whether a welfare program was worth the tax money being spent on it. Last, Case Study 5 examined if an educational program was implemented in a way that fulfilled the objectives of the program. The methods used and the findings of this study can be applied in many evaluations.

A quick reading of all five case studies after reading Chapter 1 helps readers get a flavor for the field of program evaluation. Then each case study can be read carefully after reading the chapter on the evaluation method illustrated in the case study. Case Study 1 shows the usefulness and the limitations of a pretest-posttest design. In addition, it shows how a program developed out of a work-environment problem. Case Study 2 illustrates the use of quasi-experimental designs in evaluation and the value of measuring multiple outcomes. An experimental design is illustrated in Case Study 3. This evaluation also shows how important it is for evaluators to monitor the degree that program plans are actually carried out. The crucial steps in carrying out a cost-benefit analysis are illustrated in Case Study 4. Assumptions about benefits must be made when conducting a cost-benefit evaluation; some readers may well dispute the assumptions of the evaluators who conducted the fourth case study. Last, Case Study 5 demonstrates how direct evaluative questions addressed to program participants might not provide an accurate evaluation of the program. Conclusions drawn from in-person observations by these evaluators seem to be more accurate and more useful in improving the program.

Readers may benefit from examining the process of identifying the stakeholders and the evaluators' attempts to meet the stakeholders' needs. The fact that stakeholder groups differ on what they think is important in evaluating a program can create difficulties for the evaluator and can lead to continued controversy after the evaluation is completed. Note the importance that the choice of stakeholder groups makes in Case Studies 4 and 5.

CASE STUDY 1

When human service work is very stressful, staff members can experience emotional burnout, which may result in a loss of concern about the quality of the service given. The staff of a hospital burn unit began to sense that the emotional environment on the unit was threatening to hinder the delivery of high quality medical care to the patients on the unit. Notice that the need for the intervention is discussed early in the evaluation. This evaluation illustrates the evaluative attitude we have stressed in this text. Instead of simply intervening in a way that seemed reasonable, the designers of the intervention sought to show that change did occur.

In a project prepared for a single work unit, one cannot conduct an experiment. Thus, the approach to improving the unit was evaluated using a simple pretest-posttest design. Consider which threats to internal validity might be considered important in the interpretation of this evaluation. There would be a variety of ways that one could examine the possible effects of such threats, some involving unacceptable commitments from the people of the organization.

Finally, notice that the intervention did not resolve all problems that staff of the unit were experiencing. Experienced evaluators and staff recognize that evaluations will not show interventions to be cure-alls.

An Evaluation of an Intervention to Change a Work Environment: An Example of a Burn Unit[1]

SUMMARY

Staff members of a burn unit seemed to be experiencing high levels of work-related stress. The head nurse invited a hospital-based psychiatrist to explore solutions to

[1]Based on Koran, L.M.; Moos, R.H.; Moos, B.; and Zasslow, M. 1983. Changing hospital work environments: An example of a burn unit. *General Hospital Psychiatry*, 5, 7–13. Copyright Elsevier Science Publishing Co., Inc., 1983.

problems affecting staff morale and patient care. The approach taken involved assessing morale levels using the Work Environment Survey, providing feedback to the staff from that assessment, assisting in staff planning and implementing changes in the unit, and reassessing the work environment. After an initial staff meeting but before the intervention, there were large differences between the staff's view of the ideal work-setting and their actual work-setting. During the eleven subsequent meetings staff members could discuss their feelings about individual patients, staff communication gaps, and conflicts among staff and between staff and physicians. Efforts at problem solving focused on reducing tendencies toward rigid perfectionism, planning for change, and clarifying expectations for nurses, burn technicians, and physicians. Private meetings with the head nurse and medical director addressed staff-physician cooperation. Requests for help with individual patients were honored with a view to teaching additional skills in the nature and treatment of pain.

After the intervention, the readministration of the Work Environment Survey showed that staff perceptions of the unit's environment had improved; the ratings on seven of the ten dimensions had improved. Two scales improved reliably ($p = .05$) and one marginally ($p < .06$). The differences between real and ideal ratings were reduced for nine of the ten ratings. Reductions were reliable ($p < .05$ or $.01$) for the three scales. Although there was still room for improvement, the process of assessment, feedback, planning, and implementation, and reassessment was associated with positive changes in the rated work environment.

PROBLEM ADDRESSED BY THE INTERVENTION

Work-related stress has been linked to impaired performance and high rates of turnover and absenteeism among nursing and other health center staff. Responsibility for acutely ill patients and the tense emotional climate associated with serious illness can lead to high levels of emotional stress and the loss of motivation. Staff of burn units run the risk of exceptional stress due to the nature of the patients' problems and the intense pain involved in burn treatments. Understandably, unlike many other patients, burn patients cannot express appreciation for the care they receive from nurses and technicians. Relatives of patients frequently place impossible demands on the staff. Last, work on a burn unit, like other intensive care settings, involves hard work requiring lifting of patients, exposure to severely damaged patients, and guilt feelings when patients die.

On this particular burn unit the staff felt that communication patterns had broken down. The staff felt that they had difficulty cooperating on matters of patient care and felt only minimal support from supervisors and resident physicians who seemed to be unavailable to help with decisions involving patient care. Many felt frustrated in dealing with hostile patients and relatives.

BRIEF DESCRIPTION OF THE INTERVENTION

The intervention took place in the burn unit of a 425-bed county general hospital affiliated with a medical school. The full- and part-time staff consisted of eighteen nurses, three burn technicians, eleven attendants/orderlies, and two unit clerks caring for five acute patients and six patients recovering from plastic and reconstructive surgery. Physical therapy, dietary, and social work services were available on a consultative basis. The average length of hospital stay was about twenty days, although some patients stayed more than sixty days.

The head nurse contacted a hospital psychiatrist whose job entailed assisting with psychosocial problems interfering with quality of patient care. The intervention was based on (1) a systematic assessment of the work environment; (2) feedback to staff emphasizing differences in real versus ideal work settings; (3) planning and instituting specific changes; and (4) a reassessment of the work environment. The psychiatrist agreed to meet with the staff for an hour every other week to attempt to resolve issues affecting the quality of care. Such issues could include problem patients, insufficient support from physicians, and personal conflicts affecting patient care. Personal conflicts could be discussed only if all parties to the conflict were present. It was believed that if staff could air these sources of stress, morale would improve. Furthermore, the problem-solving process and the solutions developed were expected to create a more healthy work environment that would result in the maintenance of good patient care.

The intervention was delivered in eight group meetings held at the time of the change between day and evening shifts, two group meetings during the day shift, and two group meetings during the night shift. In addition, requests to assist with particular problem patients were honored. These consultations centered on dealing with acute and chronic pain, management plans for patients with personality disorders, and the management of severe depression. Such patient-specific training and several teaching lectures were designed to raise the level of staff competence, increase independence of staff, decrease pressure and time urgency, and promote innovation in patient care.

PLAN OF THE EVALUATION

The Work Environment Scale (WES) was administered before the beginning of the intervention and six months afterwards. Assurances of confidentiality for individual answers were given. The WES consists of ten dimensions of the social environments of work settings. These ten dimensions fall into three general categories: (1) *relationship* dimensions—how involved people feel in their work and the support they give their coworkers; (2) *goal orientation* dimensions—how much autonomy people have, the emphasis on planning and efficiency, and how much time pressure there is; and (3) *system maintenance and change* dimensions—clarity of expectations, the extent rules are used to control behavior, the degree innovation is encouraged, and the pleasantness of the physical setting. There are two forms of the WES, real and ideal. Differences in the ratings of both forms from the mean ratings of norms are indicated in the feedback of the ratings.

It was expected that at the pretest there would be sizable differences between the real and the ideal work environments. In addition, it was expected that the real ratings would be less favorable than the norm values. A successful intervention was expected to show decreased differences between the real and ideal rated work environments as well as real ratings that were closer to the mean norm values.

EVALUATION FINDINGS

Preintervention Work Environment Ratings

The preintervention WES real and ideal ratings are summarized in Figure C1.1a and the postintervention ratings in Figure C1.1b. The ratings were converted to standard scores with 50 equaling the mean of the norm population and 60

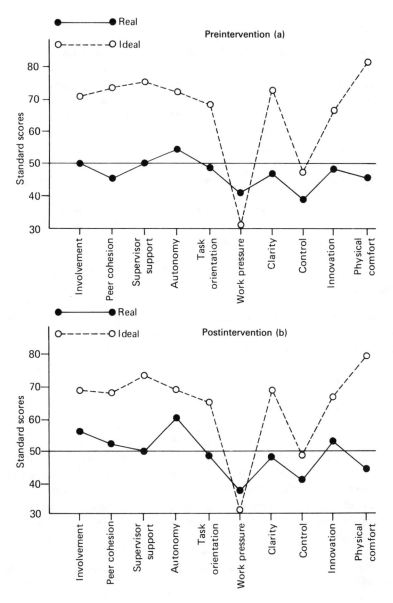

FIGURE C1.1   Preintervention and postintervention WES profiles for burn unit staff.

equaling a rating one standard deviation above the mean of the norms. Before the intervention the problems described by the staff were reflected in the WES ratings. The preintervention survey was completed by 72 percent of the nurses and 75 percent of the other members of the unit staff. Poor communication patterns were seen in the large differences between real and ideal ratings of *Peer Cohesion*. Supervisor support also was said to be needed. A very sizable discrepancy was observed between ideal and real levels of the *Clarity* (of rules and policies) dimensions.

Postintervention Work Environment Ratings

The response rates for the WES administration after the intervention was 72 percent for nurses and 94 percent for other staff members. The postintervention work environment survey is shown in Figure C1.1b. The figure reveals somewhat smaller discrepancies between real and ideal ratings compared to the preintervention ratings. There are several ways the two halves of Figure C1.1 can be compared. It is of interest, first, to learn whether the staff's views of the quality of the work environment improved. Second, since discrepancies between ideal and real ratings would indicate that staff members were stressed by their work, the discrepancies between the preintervention and the postintervention ratings were examined.

Comparing ratings of actual work environment. Of the ten WES scales, seven of the real environment ratings changed in a favorable direction. Two did not change and *Physical Comfort* changed for the worse. The increase in *Autonomy* was statistically significant ($t(47) = 2.17, p < .05$)[2] while the increases in *Involvement* ($t(47) = 1.65, p < .06$) and *Peer Cohesion* ($t(47) = 1.68, p = .05$) were marginally significant.

Comparing real and ideal ratings. Real and ideal discrepancies were reduced in nine of the ten WES scales; there was no change in *Physical Comfort*. The real-ideal discrepancies decreased significantly for *Involvement* ($t(47) = 2.17, p < .05$), *Peer Cohesion* ($t(47) = 2.79, p < .01$), and *Autonomy* ($t(47) = 3.85, p < .01$).

CONCLUSIONS

The favorable changes in the ratings of the work evaluation matched the perception of the head nurse and the medical director that morale on the burn unit had improved during the intervention. Although there still was room for improvement and although it would be helpful to clarify how an improved work environment affects patient care, the intervention was accompanied by positive changes in the burn unit. Benefits of the assessment, feedback, consultation, and reassessment process included:

1. Staff members were encouraged to think about many dimensions of the work setting, not just high or low stress.

[2]All *t*-tests were directional.

2. Important, but often overlooked qualities of work-setting, such as clarity of expectations, became explicit.
3. Involvement was increased simply because staff members were working together to change the work setting.
4. Staff members were given a chance to expand their concerns from care for individual patients to considering the impact of the setting on all the patients and the staff as well. Being considered competent to participate in program planning was a boost to their morale.

Since these changes accompanying the intervention were positive, it seems advisable to recommend that similar interventions be considered in other hospital units whose staff members report high levels of work stress.

CASE STUDY 2

Residents of industrialized societies are bombarded with seemingly countless messages encouraging us to buy something, do something, believe something. These messages come over the radio and television, are printed in newspapers and magazines, appear on billboards, and seem to generate spontaneously in our mailboxes. It is not surprising that most people try to ignore ads and slogans. Anyone trying to get the attention of a population considers whether the message is likely to get through. This evaluation sought to answer the question of whether messages encouraging college students to use alcohol wisely would be noticed. Regardless of how noble the cause is, messages that are ignored cannot influence people for good.

Note how the program designers explored the need for the program before implementing a program. This evaluation illustrates the use of an interrupted time series design with switching replications, a particularly powerful quasi-experimental design. Note percentages of students claiming to have seen the media messages before the campaign began. These students could have been mistaken, could have seen a similar message off-campus, or could have just been saying what they thought the interviewer wanted to hear. Regardless of the reason, evaluators seek to use research designs that permit the effect of the program to be found in spite of such a source of error.

Responsible Alcohol Use Media Campaign: Can We Get College Students' Attention?[1]

SUMMARY

Responsible alcohol use was encouraged by a program sponsored by the Alcohol Education Project at Southern Illinois University. A needs assessment showed that students endorsed moderate drinking, but believed that their friends expected them

[1]Based on McKillip, J.; Lockhart, D. C.; Eckert, P. S.; and Phillips, J. 1985. Evaluation of a responsible alcohol use media campaign on a college campus. *Journal of Alcohol & Drug Education 30*, 88–97. Copyright 1985 by the *Journal of Alcohol & Drug Education.*

to do more heavy drinking. The experiences of the Alcohol Education Project (AEP) staff suggested that another problem on campus was drinking and driving. A campaign was planned to encourage students to resist peer pressure to drink heavily and to stop friends from driving while drunk. Posters, newspaper ads, an information booth, and a radio call-in show were used by the AEP staff to stress these two themes. There is evidence that students still forming their drinking habits can be influenced by appropriate information; however, information will not be received if the media used to provide the information do not attract the attention of the target audience.

Since the effectiveness of posters, ads, and other methods in attracting student attention was not known, an evaluation was conducted during a ten-week period. A two-week baseline period (with no AEP posters or ads in place) was followed by a two-week emphasis on resisting peer pressure to drink. A second two-week baseline period was followed by a two-week emphasis on keeping friends from driving while drunk. The evaluation ended with a third two-week baseline period. During the two intervention periods, posters, ads, and a radio show stressed one of the themes. For the first four periods (eight weeks) the information table was set up in the student union on Thursdays during the lunch honor. No AEP materials were available during the last two-week period.

Interviews during the ten-week evaluation showed that students were aware of the campaign and its themes, student recognition of theme one increased abruptly during week three, but the level of recognition of theme two did not change. When theme two materials were available (during weeks seven and eight), recognition of theme two increased abruptly. The conclusion that students were aware of the messages was also supported by the numbers and types of material taken from the information table during the weeks of the campaign. Last, a mailed survey during weeks nine and ten showed that the two themes targeted by the campaign were recognized more frequently than the other AEP themes not stressed in this media program.

It was concluded that the media campaign was effective in attracting student attention. Although getting student attention is merely a first step in a chain of events that is hoped to result in responsible alcohol use, it is an essential step. Student services staff members can be confident that using well-placed posters and providing alcohol-related information is an effective use of educational resources.

NEEDS TO BE MET BY THE PROGRAM

Widespread evidence indicates that the rate of abuse of alcoholic beverages on U.S. college campuses is a current problem with implications for the future health of students. Informal observations suggested that alcohol abuse is a problem at Southern Illinois University as well. In addition, answers to mailed surveys to students indicated that although the majority of SIU students viewed moderate drinking as desirable, they believed that their peers expected them to drink heavily. It seemed important for students to be encouraged to hold to their belief in moderate drinking by helping them to resist peer pressures to abuse alcohol. Drinking and driving was also found to be a frequently encountered alcohol-related problem on campus. On the basis of this needs assessment, the SIU Alcohol Education Project staff designed a media-based education program to address alcohol use as related to peer pressure and driving.

PROGRAM DESCRIPTION

Target Population

SIU students, approximately 18,700 undergraduates and 3,300 graduate students, made up the target population of a multimedia campaign to encourage responsible alcohol use.

Intervention

Previous research (Ray, 1973; Rothchild, 1979) has implied that students who are not heavily involved in alcohol abuse, those just forming their alcohol-related attitudes, can be influenced by material strengthening inclinations toward responsible alcohol use. Therefore, the staff of the Alcohol Education Project (AEP) expected that a media-based education project could have positive effects. (Heavy drinkers and those whose drinking patterns are well practiced would probably not be influenced by this approach.)

The two themes for the intervention were selected on the basis of the needs assessment. Theme one was: "It's not rude to refuse a drink." Theme two was: "Friends don't let friends drive drunk."

The program sought to increase student awareness of these themes by (1) putting posters in public places throughout the campus (307 were used for the first theme and 203 for the second); (2) placing half-page ads identical to the posters in the Tuesday and Thursday issues of the campus newspaper; (3) creating a 9.8 ft.^{2} window display in the student union concerning the theme being publicized; (4) having an AEP staff member on a radio call-in show during the first week each of the themes was stressed; and (5) providing an information table in the student union during the noon hours of each Thursday stocked with written material on responsible alcohol use with an AEP staff member available to answer questions.

EVALUATION QUESTIONS

The materials could be ignored or they could be attended to by students. Thus, the evaluation sought to assess the degree that the media campaign attracted student attention. Interviews, surveys, and behavorial measures were used to judge whether students were aware of the campaign.

EVALUATION DESIGN

To permit an evaluation of the program, the campaign was divided into five two-week periods as shown in Table C2-1. The five periods included:

1. A two-week baseline period that only involved the informational table in the student union.
2. A two-week period, weeks three and four, during which the first theme was emphasized using posters, newspaper ads, the window display, and the radio call-in show.
3. A two-week baseline period during which all materials for the first theme had been removed except for the materials at the information table.
4. A two-week period, weeks seven and eight, during which the second theme was emphasized in the same ways used with the first theme.
5. A two-week baseline period in which all campaign materials were removed including the information table.

The use of baseline periods is frequently used in some forms of psychotherapy in order to show that the treatment had an effect. If the present program had an effect, one would expect students to be more aware of the themes of the campaign after the posters, ads, display, and radio show were in place compared to the weeks before. The use of two interventions permitted a replication of the design. That is, if any apparent effects of the first theme of the program were detected by comparing the first period with the second, the pattern could be verified by comparing the first six weeks of the program with the fourth period (weeks seven and eight) using student reactions to the second theme. If the patterns were very similar, one could conclude confidently that the AEP media campaign was responsible for student awareness of the themes. Possible alternative interpretations based on national news reports or alcohol industry ads could be rejected as implausible.

EVALUATION FINDINGS

Interviews

Of the 371 students interviewed over the ten weeks, 60 percent were male and 40 percent were female, approximating the composition of the student body. No student was interviewed more than once. During each of the ten weeks approx-

TABLE C2–1 Time-line for Media Campaign and Evaluation Activities

	WEEK OF SEMESTER									
	1	2	3	4	5	6	7	8	9	10
Media[a]:										
Theme 1	O	O	X	X	O	O	O	O	O	O
Theme 2	O	O	O	O	O	O	X	X	O	O
Measurements:										
Interviews	+	+	+	+	+	+	+	+	+	+
Mailed Survey	a	a	a	a	a	a	a	a	+	+
Media Booth	+	+	+	+	+	+	+	+	a	a

[a]Includes posters, newspaper advertisements, window displays and radio appearance.
Note: "O" indicates that media related to the theme were not available and "X" indicates that media were available, "+" indicates measurements were taken and an "a" indicates that measurements were not taken. All measurements were relevant to both campaign themes.

imately 40 students were selected at random during the lunch hour from students at the library, a student union cafeteria, and busy outdoor walkway. AEP staff members interviewed students concerning the recall of the poster and the newspaper ad. Respondents were shown a facsimile of the newspaper ad/poster for both campaign themes and were asked if they had seen them in the university newspaper or as a poster.

Figure C2.1 includes the percentage of students reporting that they recalled seeing the poster and the newspaper ad for each of the ten weeks of the campaign. The upper panel of the figure shows the pronounced jump in awareness for the first theme in week three. Note that the lower panel shows that the second theme was not recognized by as many students during weeks three and four as was the first theme. Since only the first theme was being publicized, these patterns support the interpretation that the campaign was effective in attracting student attention. The difference in the students' reactions to the two themes shows that students were not simply saying that they saw the posters/ad because they thought that is what the interviewer wanted them to say.

In week seven the materials for the second theme appeared. As expected, awareness of having seen theme two material increased abruptly. Recall of theme

FIGURE C2.1 Record of percentage of students interviewed reporting recall of poster and newspaper ad containing media campaign themes. *Baseline*—period before theme's posters or ads were introduced. *Campaign*—two weeks period in which posters and ads for particular theme were displayed about campus and published in campus newspaper. *Post-theme baseline*—period following campaign, ads for theme were not published and posters for them were taken down.

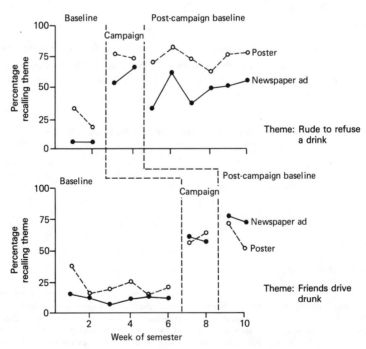

one material did not drop to the baseline level since students could remember having seen theme one material earlier. This replication gave credibility to the interpretation that the multimedia campaign was responsible for student awareness of the program's themes.

Mailed Survey

During the final two-week period, a twelve-page survey on alcohol use was mailed to a random sample of 1,113 students. Usable questionnaires were received from 56.7 percent of this sample. Answers to demographic questions indicated that the respondents accurately reflected the characteristics of the student body.

In addition to questions about alcohol consumption, students were asked which of the seven AEP posters, two from the campaign themes and five not used in this campaign, they had seen. All posters were identified only by their textual content and had been available from AEP since the spring semester prior to this fall semester study. The percentage of respondents who recalled having seen each of the posters "more than once" was the measure of program effectiveness. Theme one was recalled by 62 percent of the respondents and theme two by 83 percent. In contrast, the other five AEP (noncampaign) posters were recalled by only 12 to 48 percent of the respondents. The difference between the campaign themes and the other messages was statistically reliable ($p < .05$). The level of recall was not related to respondent gender, reported college class, or self-described level of alcohol consumption.

Media Information Table

During weeks one through eight the information table was maintained during the Thursday lunch hours in the student union. An AEP staff member answered questions and seven different posters (two campaign theme posters and five others) as well as other materials were available for student use. Overall, more responsible alcohol-use literature was taken during the weeks of the campaign compared to baseline weeks. During the campaign weeks (weeks three, four, seven, and eight) an average of 13.00 campaign theme posters were taken per day compared to an average of 5.33 during the baseline weeks ($t(14) = 2.38$, $p < .025$, one-tailed). Furthermore, during the four weeks of the campaign an average of 75 pieces of material were taken compared to 51 pieces during the baseline weeks. This difference is in the direction that one would expect if the campaign had been successful; however, the difference was not reliable.

CONCLUSIONS AND IMPLICATIONS

These findings support the use of media, especially multiple media, to publicize responsible alcohol use. Attracting student attention is the essential first step in providing information that may be internalized and may, in turn, result in the development of responsible alcohol use habits. The staff of the Alcohol Education

Project can feel confident that media programs are effective uses of educational resources.

REFERENCES

RAY, M. 1973. Marketing communication and the hierarchy of effects. In *New models for mass communication research*, ed. P. Clarke. Beverly Hills, Calif.: Sage.

ROTHCHILD, M. L. 1979. Advertising strategies for high and low involvement situations. In *Attitude research plays for high stakes*, ed. J. Maloney and B. Silverman. New York: American Marketing Association.

CASE STUDY 3

Employers in many sectors of American society complain about absenteeism. It may be a surprise, but absenteeism is also a problem in the American Armed Services. A social science research firm was asked to examine the problem of absenteeism in the Marine Corps and to develop an approach to reduce the extent of the problem. Preliminary studies suggested that absenteeism problems were due in large part to leader actions, that leaders rarely monitored absenteeism over time, and that rewards for units achieving low absenteeism were infrequent and arbitrarily administered.

There are three particular points illustrated in this case. First, this case study shows how the program was developed on the basis of organizational theory rather than on implicit, atheoretical ideas about the process of bringing about the needed change in behavior. Unfortunately, the use of explicit conceptualization is still rather rare in the design of organizational interventions. Second, note that the setting and the number of the individuals available for the program permitted the use of true experimental design. Third, the value of careful monitoring of the implementation of the program illustrates how the planned analysis had to be adjusted to reflect the varying degrees to which the program was implemented.

Keeping the Marines in the Field[1]

SUMMARY

Unauthorized absences (UAs) of Marines creates problems for unit effectiveness and morale. Preliminary analysis showed that the most common reason for UA was an attempt by the Marine to deal with a problem that the chain of command did not

[1] Based on Majchrzak, A. 1986. Keeping the Marines in the field: Results of a field experiment. *Evaluation and Program Planning* 9, 253–265. Copyright 1986 Pergamon Journals Ltd.

handle well. A study of the practices of Marine commanders showed that rate of UAs was related to leadership practices. A program to deal with UA was developed on the basis of these preliminary studies and published research on the behavior of effective leaders.

The program consisted of (1) setting UA objectives at the company level rather than at the battalion level; (2) developing a method to monitor and graph UA rates; (3) clarifying and communicating the battalion policies to company commanders; (4) discussing UA trends in sessions that also served to clarify policies; and (5) rewarding platoons for meeting UA objectives. This program was planned to affect UA rate, commander behavior regarding UA, and individual Marine's understanding of UA policies.

Eight battalions were divided randomly into a treatment group and a control group of 20 companies each. The degree of implementation of the UA program was carefully monitored by the evaluators. A randomly selected group of Marines answered a pretest while a second randomly selected group answered a posttest six months later. An average of 78 Marines from each company answered the pretest or the posttest. Differential degrees of the use of the program suggested that the 20 treatment companies should be divided into 10 companies in a strong treatment group and 10 in a weak treatment group.

The program did not seem to affect commander behavior. Marine attitudes, on the other hand, did differ across levels of treatment; however, not always in the ways expected. UA in the control companies seemed to get worse while it remained relatively stable in the treatment groups. The higher levels of Marine turnover in the control companies indicated that length of time in the Marine Corps needed to be considered in the analysis. An examination of the degree to which changes in UA policies were noticed by Marines in the treatment companies showed differences between companies. In those companies whose members did not report a change, UA actually went up. Among the companies whose members noticed the most change, the UA rate dropped from being higher than the control companies at the beginning of the program to being below the control companies at the posttest. Although the findings do not permit one to specify which of several possible processes accounted for the program's effectiveness, a 50 percent reduction was obtained when the program was implemented and communicated to the Marines. This reduction occurred with only minimal changes in commander behavior.

NEEDS ASSESSMENT AND THE SPECIFICATION OF THE PROBLEM

Although all members of the Marine Corps are expected to be present for duty every day, illness, personal problems, and cases of maladjustment can result in cases of UAs. Some studies have shown that the rate of UA has been over 10 percent in some units. Absences occur for different reasons. Nicholson (1977) suggested three types of absenteeism for industry in general: a rational decision involving a weighting of the sanctions against personal preferences; second, an impulsive pain avoidance reaction by those who cannot cope with the stresses of the military; and, third, a way to resolve a problem that is not handled well by the military commanders.

Distinguishing among these possible causes is important since an approach addressing one reason may not be appropriate to deal with a different one. For example, if UA is due to individual maladjustment to the military, the approach most likely to reduce rates of UA would center on selection of volunteers for the Corps. There would be little that officers could do once the UA-prone person was in the Corps.

Interviews with 34 Marines, some with UAs and some without, suggested that Nicholson's third possible cause of UAs was the most frequent: going UA was a method of handling a problem that the Marine felt was not being handled well by the chain of command. For example, if a Marine private was not given time off to take his sick child to the doctor, he might go UA, especially if he was aware of other Marines being given time off for less pressing reasons.

These interviews also suggested that the commander's actions may be related to UA behavior. To verify this impression, surveys with 267 commanders (battalion and company commanders in the U.S.) were conducted to learn about their attitudes, actions, and policies concerning UAs. Comparing the survey rates with the actual battalion-level UA rates showed that leadership activities were indeed correlated with UA. Taking both sources of data together suggested that a program focusing on leadership behavior might reduce the rate of UAs.

UA PREVENTION PROGRAM

Previous research on leadership behavior yielded five tentative conclusions about the behavior of effective leaders. According to Bass (1981) effective leaders clarify the purposes and objectives of performance, spell out the criteria of evaluation, explain how to meet the criteria, provide feedback about the degree the objectives are being met, and allocate rewards contingent on meeting the objectives. A program was designed to assist Marine officers to follow these principles in dealing with UAs.

To develop a program for use in the Marine Corps it was necessary to integrate the program into the existing chain of command. A battalion, the largest Marine fighting unit, ranges in size from 600 to 1,000 members. Battalions are divided into five companies (for infantry units) or five batteries (for artillery units). Daily activities generally occur among members of the same companies or batteries. Thus, although company and battery commanders report to the battalion commander, they have a fair amount of discretion in the ways in which they supervise. Any policies toward UA had to be carried out at the company or battery level while simultaneously being compatible with the policies of the battalion commander.

Setting Objectives

The first part of the program involved setting objectives. In the past, UA objectives had been set; however, they were typically unattainable since a goal of 0% UA was usually set. The criterion was also flawed in that individual company commanders deal with UA policy but the 0% UA objective referred to the larger battalion level. To correct these problems, commanders were taught how to set realistic objectives. New monthly UA objectives were to be based on the previous month's UA rate, subordinate commanders were to be involved with setting objectives, and methods to monitor false reports were mentioned. [*Note:* The term *company* is used for the rest of this report to refer both to companies and batteries.]

Monitoring UA Rates

UA had been reported daily; however, no methods had been used to track trends of UA rates. The UA Prevention Program (UAPP) provided forms and graphs so that each unit could calculate and post UA rates with comparisons to unit objectives. Individual Marines could monitor the progress of their own units in meeting objectives.

Clarifying and Communicating Commanders' Policies

Clarifying policies was approached by having battalion commanders examine issues that seemed to be related to an individual's propensity to go UA. The battalion commander reported what UA policies were acceptable. The commander could indicate that from 30 minutes to one-half day time off for each of 16 personal situations was acceptable in the battalion. The commander was then to write a two-sentence description of a situation in which the policy would be appropriate. After the commander described acceptable UA policies, these policies were communicated to the company commanders in the battalion. The company commanders were responsible for communicating the policies to the Marines in each company.

Monitoring Command Actions

By using the trend graphs, the written policies, and example cases in weekly discussions among commanders and between commanders and Marines, policies were clarified and communicated and command actions were monitored.

Providing Small Units with Rewards

Performance-contingent rewards were included in the UAPP. A period of time off was to be awarded to the members of any platoon, the smallest unit in a battalion, that had no cases of UA in a month.

Implementing the Use of UAPP

Throughout the development of the program, field commanders were consulted about all decisions of the program planners. To assist further in implementation, a handbook was developed to help commanders use the five parts of the UAPP. The handbook dealt very specifically with the five phases of the program and the battalion and company commander activities. The contrast between this approach and standard management training is worth noting: most management training consists of generalized management training apart from the actual management setting while this program dealt with specific activities and very clearly defined problems.

UAPP was pilot tested for six weeks with a battalion that was scheduled to be deployed overseas before the actual evaluation of the program. This battalion was used for the pilot test so that members of the other battalions were less likely to learn of the program before it was implemented in their own battalions.

EVALUATION DESIGN

Eight battalions were used in the evaluation design. Three pairs of battalions were matched on variables that could affect UA, for example, tenure of commander. Matched battalions were randomly assigned either to the UAPP or control. Two unmatched battalions were also randomly assigned to treatments. This approach resulted in twenty treated companies in the program and twenty control companies.

Although the Divisional Commanding General wrote all twenty treatment company commanders strongly supporting the program, individual company commanders did not have to adopt the UAPP. Thus, careful implementation checks were built into the design. Site visits by the evaluators, checklists of UA activities, and a survey of Marines were all used to check on implementation. These checks showed that some commanders needed clarification of the instructions while some others were hostile toward attempts to encourage the adoption of the program.

Outcome Variables

Three types of effects were expected if UAPP had been fully implemented: effects on UA rates, on commanders, and on unit members.

UA rates. The UA rate among the first-term Marines for each of the forty companies was obtained using a specially designed procedure for identifying each unit's UA individuals without the unit's knowledge. Since reports of UA for longer than 24 hours are reported more reliably than shorter UA periods, the former were the focus of this report and the dependent variable used. The rates were computed as the number of different individuals going UA in a month divided by the number of first-term Marines in each company averaged across each day of the month.

Commander variables. If the commander used the UAPP materials, it was anticipated that the UA standards for unit members would become more clear. Increased consistency in the battalion's chain of command was expected to follow, and the commander was expected to have better information about UA rates.

First-term Marines. Increased knowledge among Marines of the commander's expectations was a third anticipated result of UAPP. Clearer policies were expected to change the way Marines learn about UA policies. Instead of grapevine and other informal sources, UAPP was expected to lead to more announcements of policy and the perception that UA policies were more equitable in the treatment compared to the control battalions. Finally, the use of UAPP procedures was expected to lead to more commander attempts to solve the problems that lead to Marines going UA.

Effects on commanders and Marines were assessed using questionnaires. These questionnaires were given to forty-eight commanders and random samples of Marines prior to the program and at the termination of the six-month program. On the average, thirty-nine marines per company answered the questionnaire for the pretest or for the posttest. A random sample of Marines was chosen to answer the pretest. An independent sample was chosen to answer the posttest since few Marines stayed in the same company for more than the six-month period.

EVALUATION FINDINGS

The observations of the degree to which UAPP was implemented revealed that the twenty companies in the treatment group should be divided into strong treatment (ten companies) and weak treatment (ten companies) groups. Without the efforts to learn how company commanders implemented the program, these differences in the degree of implementation would not have been recognized.

Effects on Commanders

Although there were some differences among the three groups of commanders, UAPP did not produce the expected changes in the behavior and knowledge of the commanders. [*Note:* The description of the analysis of the commanders' surveys have been omitted from this condensation to save space.]

Effects on Marines

The pretest and posttest samples were compared on various demographics to assess their equivalence. Posttest Marines had spent less time in their units than pretest Marines ($t(1783) = 3.72$, $p < .001$). This difference accurately mirrored changes among the Marines at the base. Furthermore, the turnover rate was higher in the control group than in the treatment group. These differences made it important to control unit tenure statistically by using analyses of covariance.

Marines were asked to name UA policies in their company. On the average they were able to name 2.14 ($sd = 1.17$) out of four policies. The means for the three groups are given in Table C3-1. The number of policies rated as fair was a second variable, the overall mean was 1.08 ($sd = 1.27$). Since UAPP was designed to enable commanders to reduce UA rate, Marines were asked for their own level of agreement with the statement: ''The chain of command can do little to prevent a Marine from going UA.'' Also, they were asked how much they thought their commanders would agree with the statement. Both ratings averaged close to the scale midpoint (2.90 ($sd = 1.51$) out of 5) for Marine attitudes and 3.14 ($sd = 1.47$) for perceived commander attitudes. Marines were asked to indicate the number of formal methods they used to learn about UA policies. The maximum possible was three. The overall mean was 0.73 (sd = 0.93). Last, Marines were to indicate how frequently they discussed personal problems with their leaders; one indicated "1 or 2 times per month" while six indicated "nearly every day." A grand mean of 2.4 (sd = 1.47) was found.

If UAPP was effective, the treatment groups (strong and weak) were expected to show changes between the pretest and the posttest, but the control battalions were expected to show no systematic change. Table C3-1 contains the means and standard deviations for the three groups at the pretest and the posttest for the five variables. Each dependent variable was analyzed using a two (pretest vs posttest) by three (strong, weak, control) analysis of covariance using time in unit as the covariate. Support for the expectations for the program would be reflected in interactions between time of test and type of treatment.

As the table shows, four variables showed the expected interaction; however, not in the form that had been expected. Instead of showing no change, the control group showed a decrement in good UA management from the pretest to the posttest, while the treatment groups showed more stability or slight improvement. For example, examine the means of "discussing problems with leaders." Marines reported that discussion frequency dropped in the strong treatment condition, stayed the same in the weak treatment condition, but dropped markedly in the control battalions. It is possible that the high turnover among the Marines made it impossible for them to notice improvement. It seemed that the impact of UAPP was to counteract the deleterious effects attributable to being in the unit a short period of time.

Effects on UA

Table C3-2 contains two sets of mean UA rates. When divided by the three groups, UA rate went down in both the strong and weak treatment battalions, but increased in the control battalions. Although this pattern of changes was supportive of the program, the results were not statistically significant, and the weak treatment battalions had higher UA rates than the control battalions.

The lower part of Table C3-2 divides the battalions on the basis of number of changes in UA policies as perceived by Marines. The data in Table C3-2 were reanalyzed for each battalion separately. The seven treatment battalions whose data produced no statistically significant changes were grouped together. The six treatment battalions showing one significant change from pretest to posttest were grouped together. Seven treatment battalions showed two or more statistically significant changes. Preprogram and postprogram UA rates were calculated for each of these three groups. As shown in the lower part of Table C3-2 the greatest decrease in UA rate occurred in the battalions whose members detected the greatest number of positive changes. Those treatment battalions in which no change was detected actually showed an increase in UA. Furthermore, in spite of beginning the program with UA rates higher than the control battalions, the battalions in which change was detected showed lower UA rates after the program. Several approaches to the analysis of the lower half of Table C3-2 to rule out such alternative interpretations as regression to the mean [omitted from this condensation] showed

TABLE C3–1 Effects of UAPP on Unit Marines

EXPECTED EFFECTS	STRONG TREATMENT		WEAK TREATMENT		CONTROL	
	$\overline{X}(SD)_{Pre}$	$\overline{X}(SD)_{Post}$	$\overline{X}(SD)_{Pre}$	$\overline{X}(SD)_{Post}$	$\overline{X}(SD)_{Pre}$	$\overline{X}(SD)_{Post}$
1. Number of policies known (Range: 0–4)*	2.15(1.6)	2.20(1.5)	2.14(1.1)	2.19(1.2)	2.18(1.2)	2.03(1.1)
2. Number of policies unfair (Range: 0–4)	0.89(1.2)	1.02(1.3)	1.14(1.3)	1.17(1.3)	1.03(1.2)	1.17(1.3)
3. Own attitudes about leaders preventing UA (Range: 1–5; 5 = most positive)	2.97(1.5)	2.89(1.5)	2.65(1.5)	2.78(1.5)	3.06(1.5)	2.97(1.5)
4. Perceived attitudes of leaders (Range: 1–5; 5 = most positive)**	3.00(1.5)	3.30(1.5)	3.00(1.5)	3.21(1.5)	3.13(1.5)	3.14(1.5)
5. Number of formal methods to learn policies (Range: 0–3)†	0.83(0.9)	0.75(0.9)	0.69(0.9)	0.81(0.9)	0.74(0.9)	0.64(0.9)
6. Frequency of discussions with leaders about problems‡	2.56(1.5)	2.45(1.5)	2.59(1.4)	2.60(1.6)	2.52(1.5)	2.16(1.3)

*$F_{(2,3096)}$ = 4.2, $p < .01$
**$F_{(2,2747)}$ = 2.8, $p = .06$
†$F_{(2,3096)}$ = 4.5, $p < .01$
‡$F_{(2,2746)}$ = 3.1, $p < .05$

TABLE C3–2 Effects of UAPP on Unit UA Rates

A. UNITS GROUPED BY IMPLEMENTATION

STRONG TREATMENT (N = 10)		WEAK TREATMENT (N = 10)		CONTROL (N = 20)	
$\overline{X}(SD)_{Pre}$	$\overline{X}(SD)_{Post}$	$\overline{X}(SD)_{Pre}$	$\overline{X}(SD)_{Post}$	$\overline{X}(SD)_{Pre}$	$\overline{X}(SD)_{Post}$
2.59(.7)	1.86(1.4)	3.04(1.4)	2.23(1.4)	1.89(1.2)	2.09(1.2)

B. UNITS GROUPED BY CHANGES TO MARINES

TREATMENT: ≥ 2 CHANGES (N = 7)		TREATMENT: 1 CHANGE (N = 6)		TREATMENT: NO CHANGE (N = 7)		CONTROL (N = 20)	
$\overline{X}(SD)_{Pre}$	$\overline{X}(SD)_{Post}$	$\overline{X}(SD)_{Pre}$	$\overline{X}(SD)_{Post}$	$\overline{X}(SD)_{Pre}$	$\overline{X}(SD)_{Post}$	$\overline{X}(SD)_{Pre}$	$\overline{X}(SD)_{Post}$
3.10(1.6)	1.57(1.1)	2.52(.7)	1.27(.8)	2.78(.8)	3.19(1.3)	1.89(1.2)	2.09(1.2)

that only the battalions whose members detected changes showed reductions in UA rates. The reduction in UA rates was approximately 50 percent.

In summary, the UAPP seemed effective in its overall goal of reducing UA rates. However, the process of changing UA rates is not clear. Several of the expected changes in leaders' behaviors were not found. It appears that the rates were reduced in those units whose members experienced a greater opportunity to learn about the commander's policies, were able to test those policies through discussions, and had the policies periodically reviewed. Since the unit members knew that a policy existed, punishment for UA would not be unexpected. Even though the Marines were not less likely to view the policies as fair, knowing about the policies made it more likely that they would be obeyed. An important point is that the 50 percent reduction in UA was achieved with relatively minimal changes on the part of the commanders who agreed that the changes were "good management practices."

REFERENCES

BASS, B. M. 1981. *Stodgill's handbook of leadership*. New York: The Free Press.
NICHOLSON, N. 1977. Absence behavior and attendance motivation: A conceptual synthesis. *The Journal of Management Studies 14*, 231–252.

CASE STUDY 4

Welfare policies continue to be a source of controversy. Some people say that welfare is essential in a complex, humane society. Others argue that welfare is misused and encourages passive, unproductive behavior. The provision of family planning services is particularly controversial. An evaluation cannot resolve disagreements over philosophical and value-related issues. However, one could ask if public tax money is being spent in a way that achieves the short-run goals of the program. And, in the case of welfare services designed to prevent future problems, one could ask if the probable cost of the prevented problems exceeds the cost of the preventive welfare services.

Case Study 4 sought to answer the question of whether publicly funded family planning services were saving tax dollars by estimating what the welfare costs of users of the services would have received if the family planning service had been unavailable. Estimating what did not occur is a problem for an evaluation of any preventive service whether in a medical, criminal justice, or education setting. Note how the evaluators made estimates of what could have been expected if the services had not been available. They then converted these estimates into estimated additional welfare costs and compared them to the costs of the preventive program.

The Costs and Benefits of Title XX Funding for Family Planning Services in Texas[1]

SUMMARY

Through the Title XX program the Texas Department of Human Resources funded family planning services for 227,253 women in Fiscal Year 1981. A cost-benefit

[1]Based on Malitz, D. 1984. The costs and benefits of Title XX and Title XIX family planning services in Texas. *Evaluation Review 8*, 519–536. Copyright, 1984. Sage Publications, Inc. Adapted by permission of Sage Publications, Inc. This condensation omits references to Title XIX programs, which were included in the original.

analysis of the program was conducted to learn whether this use of state funds was effective. The outcomes of a program designed to prevent something from occurring are especially difficult to determine. The approach chosen was based on making estimates of births that would have occurred among the women served by this program in its absence. These estimates were made by using national data giving the typical effectiveness rates of the various contraceptive methods used by the women who sought services from the seventy-eight providers funded by Title XX. Information on the contraceptive methods used before entering the program and after receiving services was gathered from the providers for randomly selected samples of 1,606 adolescents (< 20 years old) and 1,605 adults (> 19 years old). Information was provided by sixty-five out of the seventy-eight providers yielding rates of 78.0 percent of the adolescent sample and 79.9 percent of the adult sample. The biggest changes were in the percentages of women changing from "no method" to using the pill. The number of births that would have been expected in the next twelve months were compared with similar estimates of the number of births expected during the twelve months after the women received the services of the funded centers. These estimates were converted into the number of births averted through the services funded by Title XX. On the average, 99 births were estimated to have been averted for each 1,000 patients served.

Estimates were then made for the welfare costs that the state would have incurred during the next 12-month period. Hospital care for mothers and infants eligible for Aid to Families of Dependent Children (AFDC) would have averaged $2,111 per birth. Welfare maintenance for twelve months would have averaged $2,038 for AFDC-eligible mothers. Last, additional food stamp allotments would have totaled $475 for twelve months. These total $4,624 saved for each birth to a family that would have qualified for AFDC. Using state-wide data it was estimated that 30.4 percent of the women served would have qualified for AFDC. The 69.6 percent of the patients who would not have qualified for AFDC would have received an additional $82 in food stamps if a child had been born. Combining these projected costs with the percentage of AFDC-eligible families yielded an average saving to the Department of $1,463 per birth averted. Since 99 births per 1,000 women were averted, the average savings per client patient was $145. Cost per woman served was $75, yielding a cost-to-benefit ratio for the 12 months after treatment in the funded clinics of 1 to 1.93. In other words, the department saved nearly $2 for each dollar spent within the first year. The report describes the estimation methods and divides the patients by adolescents and adults.

PROGRAM BEING EVALUATED

Family planning services funded by the State of Texas (Title XX) are administered by seventy-eight providers throughout the state. In Fiscal Year 1981 227,253 women were served by these programs. Many of the women served and their children would be qualified to receive welfare support including Aid to Families of Dependent Children (AFDC), Food Stamps, and Medicaid.

THE EVALUATION QUESTION

All government-funded programs face the issue of relating their costs to their benefits. Welfare programs are especially scrutinized since the beneficiaries of the programs do not pay for the services provided. Services purchased directly by consumers are not subject to a similar scrutiny since the purchaser and the consumer are identical, and consumers are presumably doing their own evaluations. The present report focused on the question of the costs and benefits of family planning services funded by the Texas Department of Human Resources (TDHR) for women qualified for public assistance. The costs of the programs funded by Title XX are easy to ascertain; however, the benefits are much more difficult to determine. Conducting a cost-benefit study is especially difficult when the program is preventive in nature. It is necessary to estimate the frequency of what would have happened had the program not been available.

EVALUATION METHOD

To conduct a cost-benefit analysis it is necessary to define what benefits are to be included in the analysis and which benefits are not. It was decided to limit the benefits analyzed to the cost savings to TDHR due to lower demands on AFDC, Food Stamp, and Medicare programs in the year following contact with a supported family planning agency. There are other benefits from Title XX that were not considered. Some women benefited from health screening, which is part of Title XX services. Some patients benefited by avoiding the adverse effects of adolescent pregnancy; however, these benefits were not considered either. Last, limiting births may have helped some of the patients to avoid long-term welfare dependency, a benefit to the women and TDHR. The difficulty of estimating the value of such a benefit suggested that it not be used. By ignoring these benefits, the value of Title XX services was underestimated. However, by focusing on more objective outcomes, cost-benefit analyses are less controversial as long as benefits exceed costs. If the analysis were going to be used to argue that the program was inefficient and should be curtailed, then it would be important to search for every possible benefit.

Calculating the amount saved in welfare costs required an estimate of the number of births averted through Title XX. To estimate the number, the proportions of patients using various contraceptive methods before they entered the program (premethod) were compared to the proportions using various methods at their last visit (postmethod). The degree to which the patients began to use more effective methods would indicate the degree of program effectiveness. Use-effectiveness rates are available for methods of contraception. The number of pregnancies expected during the twelve months following entry into the program could be calculated using these use-effectiveness rates. It was assumed that without the program, the women's choices of contraception methods would not have changed. Similarly, the pregnancies expected for the twelve months following the last visit were also estimated from the use-effectiveness rates. The difference between these two estimates is the number of pregnancies averted through the services of Title XX.

Data Collection

Patients were stratified by provider and age: adolescents (19 years and younger) and adults (20 years and older). Based on this stratification and expected rate of return from providers, random samples of 1,606 adolescents (about 2.5 percent of the Title XX adolescent population) and 1,605 adults (1.0 percent of the adult patients) were defined. Surveys were prepared for each of the women sampled and sent to the appropriate providers. These surveys asked the provider to report the date when the patient first came to the center, the date of the last visit, and the methods of contraception used at both times. Staff were assured that patient confidentiality would be respected. In fact, the forms were designed in a way that permitted the names of the patients to be readily removed.

FINDINGS

Pregnancies, Births, Abortions, and Miscarriages Averted

Contraceptive method and averted pregnancies. Survey forms were returned by sixty-five of the seventy-eight providers. Overall, 1,252 complete and usable survey forms for adolescents (78.0 percent) and 1,283 for adults (79.9 percent) were returned.

Table C4-1 summarizes the contraceptive use rates for adolescents and adults. When the surveys indicated that a patient used multiple methods, the most effective method was coded. In addition, the table gives the expected number of pregnancies expected in 12 months among sexually active women using the various methods.

For both adolescents and adults, the table shows a dramatic drop in the percentages of women reported to be using no method. For example, when entering the program over two-thirds of the adolescents did not use any contraceptive method, but when leaving only 14 percent were still not using any method. The method most often used when leaving the program was the pill for both age groups. These percentages were roughly comparable to the findings of other surveys of contraceptive use.

One might consider the women leaving the program not using a contraceptive method to be program failures. Clinic personnel, however, report that some women seek pregnancy tests at the centers and that some others did not receive any method for medical reasons. It is not possible to distinguish these patients from true program failures.

The lower section of Table C4-1 is based on the rates of use data across methods. The numbers of expected pregnancies per 1,000 users for each method was projected to be the number of expected pregnancies in 12 months among 1,000 patients of the clinics supported by Title XX funds. These expected values are calculated for patients if they had continued with the methods they used when they

TABLE C4–1 Contraceptive Method Use Patterns and Expected Number of Pregnancies Averted Among Title XX Patients Served

CONTRACEPTIVE METHOD	EXPECTED NUMBER OF ANNUAL PREGNANCIES PER 1,000 WOMEN	ADOLESCENTS Pre	ADOLESCENTS Post	ADULTS Pre	ADULTS Post
Pill	25	21.4	74.7	42.9	62.9
IUD	71	0.8	1.8	3.7	6.7
Diaphragm	172	0.3	1.1	0.6	1.9
Foams, creams, jellies	184	1.9	0.8	2.3	2.4
Rhythm	250	0.2	0.0	0.2	0.2
Sterilization	0	0.0	0.1	1.7	6.9
Condom	123	5.9	6.5	4.8	7.9
Other	189	0.8	0.6	1.1	1.2
None	490 to 640	68.7	14.4	42.6	9.9
Total	—	100.0	100.0	100.0	100.0

EXPECTED NUMBER OF ANNUAL PREGNANCIES PER 1,000 PATIENTS	ADOLESCENTS Pre	ADOLESCENTS Post	ADULTS Pre	ADULTS Post
Low estimate	357	103	237	90
High estimate	460	124	301	104
Midpoint estimate	408.5	113.5	269.0	97.0
Pregnancies averted	295		172	

Note: Based upon surveys of contraceptive failures among married women using the methods listed. The estimates of pregnancy rates among users of no method are based upon surveys of unmarried, sexually active adolescents.

Source: Forrest, Hermalin, and Henshaw (1981) for expected number of annual pregnancies per 1,000 women.

came to the clinics (''pre'' columns) and if they continued with the methods in use when they left the program (''post'' column). Since the estimates for ''no method'' vary widely, both a high and a low number of estimates of pregnancies per 1,000 women for a year are given. For purposes of this study, the midpoint between the high and the low estimates was taken. The differences between the number of pregnancies expected for women using the preclinic methods and for women using the postclinic methods are the numbers of pregnancies averted for adolescents and adults, 295 and 172 per 1,000 patients per year, respectively. Table C4-2 converts these pregnancy rates into number of pregnancies averted for the entire patient population of Title XX programs.

Births averted. The number of pregnancies averted, however, is not the same as the number of births averted. On the basis of national data for low-income

TABLE C4-2 Estimated Number of Pregnancies, Births, Abortions, and Miscarriages Averted by the Title XX Family Planning Program

AGE GROUP	NUMBER IN PROGRAM	PREGNANCIES AVERTED	TOTAL BIRTHS, ABORTIONS, AND MISCARRIAGES AVERTED			BIRTHS AVERTED PER 1,000 PATIENTS
			Births	Abortions	Miscarriages	
Adolescents	63,176	18,637	6,784	9,542	2,311	107
Adults	164,077	28,221	15,614	8,592	4,015	95
Total	227,253	46,858	22,398	18,134	6,326	99

U.S. PREGNANCY OUTCOMES AGE GROUP	PERCENT DISTRIBUTION OF UNINTENDED PREGNANCIES BY OUTCOME		
	Births	Abortions	Miscarriages
Adolescents	36.4	51.2	12.4
Adults	55.3	30.4	14.2
Total	47.8	38.7	13.5

Note: Pregnancies averted are calculated by multiplying program counts by Title XX rates in Table C4-1.
Source: Dryfoos (1982) for distribution of unintended pregnancies by outcome.

women, the numbers of pregnancies averted were divided into numbers of averted births, abortions, and miscarriages. The assumption had to be made that these national rates are applicable to the women who attended the Title XX clinics. On the basis of these estimates, it was concluded that the clinics were responsible for averting 22,398 births, or 99 per 1,000 patients, per year. In other words, the program averted almost one birth for every ten patients served.

Estimate of the Benefit of Title XX

Births to Title XX women create costs to TDHR in several ways. Some women qualify for Medicaid payments for some delivery expenses. TDHR pays AFDC and Medicaid benefits for each mother and her child for one year. Last, a birth qualifies some women for additional food stamps. Births to women who qualify for AFDC are called "AFDC births." Women who do not qualify for AFDC will still qualify for increased food stamps. Births to these women are called "non-AFDC births."

Costs of AFDC Births to TDHR. The average direct cost of births to TDHR in FY 1981 was $1,304 for each delivery and $807 for inpatient care for premature babies and treating birth defects. Thus, the average cost associated with each birth was $2,111.

An AFDC mother with one child received $86/month, or $1,032 for 12 months. In addition, non-birth-related Medicaid benefits were estimated to be $1,006 for each AFDC mother and child. Welfare maintenance, thus, totals $2,038 for a year.

The maximum food stamp allotment for increasing the family size from one to two members is $50/month. However, only 87 percent of AFDC cases receive food stamps, and the average case receives 91 percent of the maximum allowed. Therefore, the average AFDC birth was estimated to lead to an additional cost of $50/month × 12 months × 0.87 × 0.91, or $475 for the first year.

In total then, the average AFDC birth was expected to lead to an increase of $2,111 plus $2,038 plus $475, or $4,624, during the 12 months after the birth.

The percentage of births to clinic patients who will become AFDC cases. Since not all of Title XX patients would have qualified for AFDC, these costs must be reduced to reflect only the proportion of mothers who would have qualified for AFDC. It was believed that the percentage of Title XX patients who were already mothers and were qualified for AFDC would be the best estimate of the proportion of child-bearing Title XX women who would have entered AFDC if a child had been born. These percentages are 35.8 percent and 28.3 percent for adolescents and adults, respectively.

Combining the costs of an AFDC birth and the proportion of Title XX patients who probably would have qualified for AFDC yielded the following average expected benefits for each averted Title XX birth: for adolescents, 0.358 × $4,624, or $1,655; for adults, 0.283 × $4,624, or $1,309.

TABLE C4–3   Costs and Estimated Savings Associated with the Title XX Family Program for Adolescents and Adults

	ADOLESCENTS ONLY (19 AND UNDER)	ADULTS ONLY (20 AND OVER)	ALL PATIENTS
Savings			
Total estimated savings per birth averted	$ 1,708	$ 1,368	$ 1,463
Births averted per family planning patient	0.107	0.095	0.099
Savings per family planning patient	$ 183	$ 130	$ 145
Costs			
Average Title XX expenditure per family planning patient (including sterilizations)	$ 75	$ 75	$ 75
COST-BENEFIT RATIO	1:2.44	1:1.73	1:1.93
Total cost and savings in FY81			
Number of patients	63,176	164,077	227,253
Total cost	$ 4,778,000	$12,410,000	$17,188,000
Total estimated savings	$11,658,000	$21,469,000	$33,127,000
Net estimated savings	$ 6,880,000	$ 9,059,000	$15,939,000

Costs of non-AFDC births to TDHR.   The maximum food stamp allotment was $600/year. However, only 27.4 percent of Title XX patients qualify for food stamps, and the average non-AFDC case only qualifies for 50 percent of the maximum allotment. Therefore, the average yearly increase in food stamp allotments for each non-AFDC birth will be about $82, i.e., $600 × 0.274 × 0.50.

Percentages of non-AFDC Title XX Patients.   Since the percentages of AFDC cases were estimated above, the percentages of non-AFDC Title XX cases will simply be 100 percent minus 35.8 percent, or 64.2 percent for adolescents and 100 percent minus 28.3 percent, or 71.7 percent, for adults. Applying these percentages to the $82 figure yields the second component of the cost of the average Title XX birth for adolescents of $53,[2] and $59 for adults.

As shown in Table C4-3, the total benefit to TDHR for each Title XX birth averted was $1,655 plus $53, or $1,708, for adolescents and $1,406 plus $59, or $1,368, for adults.

[2]The published article erroneously gave this figure as $43.

Cost-Benefit Analysis of Title XX

Since each patient could not be considered to have a birth averted through the services of the Title XX-supported clinics, the benefits need to be scaled down from the benefit of each birth averted to the average for each Title XX patient. Table C4-3 includes the average saving for each adolescent and adult family planning patient.

The balance of the analysis is easy to complete. In FY 1981 227,253 patients were served at a cost of $17,187,782; an average cost per patient of about $75. The cost-benefit ratios can then be readily calculated by dividing the benefits by costs. For example, $183 divided by $75 yields a cost-benefit ratio of 1 to 2.44. For each dollar spent on Title XX services, TDHR is estimated to have gained a benefit of $2.44 in the 12 months following the provision of services to adolescents. For adults the ratio was 1 to 1.73.

Final Comments on the Method

Many potential benefits of Title XX family planning services were not included in this analysis. There were benefits from avoiding nearly 22,000 abortions and over 7,000 miscarriages that were not included. Some of the expenses of the averted births that would have been covered by counties and cities (not TDHR) were ignored since the focus was on the benefits of savings to TDHR, not on benefits to cities and counties. Last, when possible, estimates were compared to other studies of family planning clinics. These comparisons [largely omitted from this condensation] generally supported the findings of the study.

REFERENCES

DRYFOOS, J. G. 1982. Contraceptive use, pregnancy intentions and pregnancy outcomes among U.S. women. *Family Planning Perspectives 14*, 81–94.
FORREST, J. D.; HERMALIN, A. I.; and HENSHAW, S. K. 1981. The impact of family planning clinic programs on adolescent pregnancy. *Family Planning Perspectives 13*, 109–116.

CASE STUDY 5

Many evaluations rightfully focus on the reactions of the program participants as a major aspect of an evaluation. There are times, however, when the views of the participants cannot reflect crucial aspects of the quality of the program. Furthermore, the self-interest of the participants may not coincide with the interests of other important stakeholders. The authors of this case study found that the program participants (medical residents) were quite pleased with their training. The observations of the evaluators, on the other hand, indicated discrepancies between the goals of the program and the actual training the residents received. Inadequacies in training could result in less competent performance as the residents complete their programs and began to function as independent physicians. By identifying the residents' future patients as an important stakeholder group, the evaluators concluded that the residency program had many deficiencies that were not recognized by the residents themselves.

Crucial points to note in this case study include the contrast between the participants' and evaluators' views of the quality of the training, the evaluators' concern to identify the stakeholders more broadly than just those groups immediately involved in the program, and the use of naturalistic research methods as described in Chapter 12.

An Evaluation of a Family Practice Residency Program Using a Naturalistic Inquiry Paradigm[1]

SUMMARY

Naturalistic observations and ratings of quality of education were used to evaluate a residency program for family practice physicians. The curriculum committee of the

[1]Based on Bussigel, M., and Filling, C. 1985. Data discrepancies and their origins: An evaluation of a family practice residency program using a naturalistic inquiry paradigm. *Evaluation & the Health Professions 8*, 177–192. Copyright 1985 by Sage Publications, Inc. Adapted by permission of Sage Publications, Inc.

program requested an evaluation in order to identify curriculum areas in which improvements could be made and themes that could be used in faculty development. This concern was important since (1) family practice is a new, still developing, specialty, (2) family practice residents serve rotations, gaining hands-on experience and instruction from specialists in internal medicine, pediatrics, and obstetrics/ gynecology, and (3) greater emphasis is placed on the development of interpersonal skills in family practice residencies compared to other specialties.

Program expectations were developed with the curriculum committee, the director, two family practice physicians, and the psychologist associated with the residency. The degree to which these expectations were carried out was examined through structured interviews with eleven of the twelve family practice residents and through nine days of observations of the activities of the residents and their supervising physicians and program faculty.

Residents rated their experiences in quite favorable terms. However, the evaluators observed may examples of poor teaching strategies among the faculty from non-family-practice specialties, inadequate feedback from supervising physicians, and low interest on the part of residents in psychosocial issues related to patient care.

Possible reasons for these discrepancies include different implicit standards for teaching and different implicit views of the primary stakeholder group. Residents seemed to be basing their ratings of the quality of instruction on their experiences with medical education. It seems unlikely that they could recognize the need for a better quality of instruction without appropriate experience with other, more effective instructional methods. Second, residents may have been making the favorable ratings because they were comfortable with the learning climate rather than on the basis of the amount of learning taking place. The evaluators felt that future patients should be viewed as the primary stakeholder in evaluations on the quality of residency programs. This orientation made the evaluators especially sensitive to lost opportunities for training.

PROGRAM DESCRIPTIONS AND EVALUATION QUESTIONS

Residency programs for physicians are hands-on training programs to be completed by graduates of medical school before becoming licensed medical doctors. Hospitals sponsor residency programs in which the residents provide the primary patient care under the direction of attending (i.e., licensed) physicians. [Note: Family practice residencies are for medical school graduates who plan to offer "primary" medical care to children and adults whose problems do not require the attention of specialists. Family practice physicians also treat patients with chronic conditions requiring monitoring and periodic medical assessments.] Residents work under attending family practice practitioners as well as serving rotations (for example, three months) in such specialties as obstetrics/gynecology and internal medicine. Since family practice is a fairly new form of medical care, many family practice residencies are rather new. This evaluation was part of a larger project aimed at improvement and expansion of a new residency program.

The curriculum committee contacted the evaluators for help in identifying those curriculum areas in which modification was most likely to improve the program and for suggestions of promising themes for faculty development. To carry out this evaluation, explicit statements of program expectations were developed. Since family practice physicians are responsible for initial diagnosis of illnesses, routine medical care for children, and on-going care of chronic illnesses, their interpersonal relations with their patients are more important than for other specialist physicians. Specifically, the evaluation was designed to (1) identify the fit between expectations and program components, (2) identify the major learning experiences of the residents, (3) identify major strengths and weaknesses of the program with a particular focus on areas in which expectations and what actually occurs do not match, and (4) offer preliminary suggestions for improving the residency program.

THE INQUIRY PROCEDURE

Four data sources were used. One, documents describing the program structure were reviewed. Two, key faculty members (specifically, the curriculum committee, program director, two family practitioners, and one psychologist) were asked to describe the program components and how each one contributed to achieving specific program goals. This group later responded to the initial draft of the findings and their interpretation. Three, one resident from each of the three classes was observed for three full days to gain insight into the learning experiences of the residents. Observations were conducted in the out-patient clinic as well as in patient hospital rooms. Both family practitioner settings and specialty rotations were observed. Four, all residents (except one who could not be reached) were interviewed. They were asked to evaluate various aspects of the program and to list major strengths and weaknesses.

EVALUATION FINDINGS

[*Note*: Many of the findings of this evaluation have not been included in this condensation, which stresses the way qualitative observational data changed the interpretation of the interviews.]

Areas for program improvement were considered to be most promising when program expectations and the residents' reports were most discrepant with the evaluators' direct observations.

Comprehensive Care and Continuity of Care

A major goal of the family practice residency was to provide training that emphasized care for the whole person and care that followed the patient throughout the treatment. Since major portions of the residency are spent in rotations outside the family practice department, it was necessary to learn whether the goals of family practice were carried out in all rotations included in the residency. When interviewed, residents affirmed that comprehensive care and continuity of care were stressed in all rotations. Residents reported that these goals were most in evidence in family practice settings, but had little criticism for the training in other settings. The observations of the evaluators contrasted with the residents' views about the non-family-practice rotations. Since all agreed on the goals, the disagreement reflected different standards for measuring adequacy. For example, since no attempt was made to be sure that patients would see the same resident at each visit, the evaluators felt that continuity of care, a major family practice goal, was being ignored.

Formal Teaching Sessions

Besides the hands-on training in clinics and patient rooms, two formal teaching seminars focusing on patient-physician relations and psychosocial topics were held weekly. [These training experiences are especially important to this residency since family practice practitioners are physicians who need to distinguish between medical diagnoses and problems of a psychological origin or health problems compounded by psychological issues.] The residents again described the sessions as very valuable. All but one of the eleven residents claimed to attend usually and seldom to have a schedule conflict with the sessions. However, of the three teaching sessions observed, two were attended by only six or fewer of the residents. One resident mentioned that average attendance was up from the former level of two or three residents per session. In addition, the residents described the sessions as very interesting, a marked contrast to the observed low level of engagement in the discussions of the case studies. It appeared that the residents were describing their interest in positive terms compatible with what they thought the ideal family practice resident ought to believe.

Quality of Clinical Teaching and Training

Residents were asked to rate the quality of teaching and opportunities for hands-on inpatient and outpatient contact.

Obstetrics/gynecology rotation. Residents were quite positive about the degree of patient contact and mildly critical to very positive about the quality of the teaching. Overall, residents evaluated the Ob/Gyn rotation in favorable terms. In contrast, the evaluators concluded that the residents received virtually no feedback on their work. Although contact between residents and Ob/Gyn attending physicians was mandated by a sign-off procedure, this contact was not used for teaching. Moreover, attending physicians were not found to express much concern about the development of interpersonal skills among the residents.

Internal medicine rotation. A similar contradiction between resident assertions and evaluator observations occurred for the internal medicine rotation. Residents rated teaching in internal medicine as good to excellent. There was some concern about the limited opportunity to do "procedures." This point did match the evaluators' view in that the patient load was light and included contact with only a limited variety of problems. Observations suggested that attending internal medicine physicians were motivated to teach; however, they displayed undeveloped teaching skills. Cases presented for discussion seemed to be chosen on an ad hoc basis, and teaching sessions were poorly structured.

In general, although the residents rated their experiences in favorable terms, the qualitative observations of the evaluators were quite unfavorable.

INTERPRETATIONS OF THE FINDINGS

Contrast between the residents' views and the evaluators' conclusions based on their observations requires interpretation. Two likely reasons were suggested to lie behind the discrepancies.

Variations in Standards

Asking residents about the quality of their educational experiences assumes that the residents know what a good residency would be. This assumption is not valid since residents have been exposed to many nonoptimal educational situations for several years. In fact, their experiences in the residency may be similar to many instructional settings in medical school during past years. Second, there is no reason to believe that residents should be able to intuit a medical educational system better than the systems they have known.

Variations in Definitions of Goals and Clients

The evaluators became aware that they may have held different goals for the residents than the residents held for themselves. Furthermore, the evaluators discovered that they often identified with patients and thus viewed future patients of the residents as the primary stakeholder group of the evaluation. It is likely that residents saw themselves as the primary beneficiaries of the residency program. Thus, residents may have responded to the interview questions in terms of their own level of comfort with the form of instruction they experienced.

RECOMMENDATIONS[2]

In the light of the findings it is recommended that instructional methods be given close attention by the residency curriculum committee. The expectations for the

[2]Recommendations were not part of the published report. These recommendations were added to make this condensation conform to the style of an evaluation report.

residency seemed well known by all, but attending physicians not in family practice do not seem to be tailoring their teaching to meet family practice expectations. In some cases, teaching itself needs to be instituted since it isn't occurring.

Second, the focus of the family practice curriculum committee on the importance of psychological and sociological issues is not shared by the residents. Psychosocial issues may become more important to the residents if they see such issues being taken seriously by attending physicians in all of the rotations in which family practice residents serve.

Epilogue

This text has sought to provide the groundwork for the development of the technical skills necessary to conduct program evaluations in human service and business settings. The evaluator's attitudes and orientation toward the role of program evaluator is as important as technical skills are. While these are referred to throughout this book, it may be of help to draw these themes together in this section.

Humility won't hurt. Evaluators work in service settings. These settings are not designed to facilitate the conducting of research. Because this is true, the evaluator can expect to be seen as filling a marginal role in the service delivery setting. Because the evaluator is always working on someone else's turf, arrogance will effectively block the exercise of even superb technical skills.

Impatience may lead to disappointment. Program and facility administrators have many constituencies, all expecting attention. Program evaluation is only one source of information on which decisions and plans are based. Financial concerns, community pressures, political realities, and bureaucratic inertia are all powerful influences on program planners and administrators. Evaluators who have patience are less likely to feel ignored and unloved when their recommendations do not receive immediate attention.

Recognize the importance of the evaluator's perspective. Service staffs focus on individuals and often do not understand the overall program; evaluators have a social orientation that can provide the staff with a new viewpoint. In contrast to service staff, administrators seek an overall perspective and have a far better grasp of financial and other tangible matters than of social variables affecting the patient/client/student/trainee population served. Evaluators can provide information to administrators on social variables that are usually unavailable to administrators.

Focus on practical questions. People working in human service organizations are seldom concerned about matters of only theoretical interest. Evaluators can work more effectively when they are oriented toward practical questions about the program being studied. Try not to forget that seeking to initiate and sustain change in people's lives is hard work. Faced with pressing human needs and with criticism from governmental bodies or insurance companies for excessive costs and alleged inefficiencies, agency staff and management desire practical assistance.

Work on feasible issues. If an evaluation is not feasible, do not attempt it. Do not waste your time and that of the staff. However, although it may not be feasible to work on a particular issue, it might be feasible to work on a less ambitious question. For example, if outcomes cannot be handled, it may be possible to develop a procedure to monitor the delivery of service.

Avoid data addiction. It is tempting to seek to gather a great amount of information about the program or about those served by the program. It might be nice to know everything possible about the program, but there are two compelling reasons to limit the amount of data sought to that which is essential. First, asking for too much information increases the percentage of potential respondents who refuse to cooperate and consequently provide no information. Second, evaluators often find themselves under too much time pressure to analyze all the data gathered. Thus, the effort of the cooperative respondents is wasted. If the information is not essential to the evaluation, do not try to gather it.

Evaluators are information channels. There are many things that can get in the way when new information is presented to potential users. Social science jargon and esoteric analyses can reduce the flow of information to those not acquainted with the jargon or schooled in statistics. Readers and listeners are bored with presentations that seem planned to display the evaluator's knowledge and technical skills. Save that for meetings of professional societies. To be effective, presentations to staff should be relevant to the program, and recommendations should be practicable.

Encourage an evaluation orientation. Ideally, evaluation encourages honest relations among staff, clients, administrators, and program sponsors. These groups often act as though all failures could have been avoided. Although failures cannot always be avoided, people can always learn from failures. The essence of the concept of the experimenting society is the recognition of the inevitability of failure.

Instead of hiding failures or condemning them, help staff and administrators to treat honest attempts as experiments and to learn from failures as well as successes.

Adopt a self-evaluation orientation to your own work. When evaluation results and recommendations seem to be ignored, evaluators will benefit by asking themselves: Was my presentation clear? Did I address the right questions? Were my answers right? At times the honest answer to these questions will be "No." Evaluators are like service staff people in some ways: neither can always avoid failures, and both can learn from their errors.

References

ABELSON, P. H. 1977. Commission on federal paperwork. *Science 197:* 1237.
ABRAHAM, B., 1980. Intervention analysis and multiple time series. *Biometrika 67:* 73–78.
ABT, C. C. 1977. Applying cost/benefit paradigms to social program evaluations. Paper presented at the meeting of the Evaluation Research Society, October, Washington, D. C.
ACKOFF, R. L. 1986. *Management in small doses.* New York: Wiley.
ADLER, N. E., and STONE, G. C. 1979. Social science perspectives on the health system. In *Health psychology: A handbook,* ed. G. C. Stone, F. Cohen, and N. E. Adler. San Francisco: Jossey-Bass.
AIKEN, L. S., and WEST, S. G. 1990. Invalidity of true experiments: Self-report biases. *Evaluation Review 14:* 374–390.
ALBRIGHT, J. 1982. Citizen evaluation from the inside. Paper presented at meeting of the Evaluation Research Society, October, Baltimore.
ALEXANDER, H. A. 1986. Cognitive relativism in evaluation. *Evaluation Review 10:* 259–280.
ALLPORT, G. W. 1954. *The nature of prejudice.* Reading, Mass.: Addison-Wesley.
AMERICAN PSYCHOLOGICAL ASSOCIATION. 1982. *Ethical principles in the conduct of research with human participants.* Washington, D.C.: Author.
ANASTASI, A. 1988. *Psychological testing.* 6th ed. New York: Macmillan.
ANDERSON, C. A. 1987. Temperature and aggression: Effects on quarterly, yearly, and city rates of violent and nonviolent crime. *Journal of Personality and Social Psychology 52:* 1161–1173.
ANDERSON, J. F., and BERDIE, D. R. 1975. Effects on response rate of formal and informal questionnaire follow-up techniques. *Journal of Applied Psychology 60:* 225–257.

ARGYRIS, C. 1985. *Strategy, change and defensive routines.* Boston: Pitman.

ARVEY, R. D., and COLE, D. A. 1989. Evaluating change due to training. In *Training and development in organizations,* ed. I. Goldstein & Associates. San Francisco: Jossey-Bass.

BABBIE, E. 1989. *The practice of social research.* Belmont, Calif.: Wadsworth.

BALL, S., and BOGARTZ, G. A. 1970. *The first year of Sesame Street.* Princeton, N.J.: Educational Testing Service.

BANK, A. 1987. A case study: The review of the Los Angeles Bureau of Jewish Education. *Evaluation and Program Planning 10:* 169–178.

BANK, A., and WILLIAMS, R. C., eds. 1987. *Information systems and school improvement: Inventing the future.* New York: Teachers College Press.

BARBOUR, G. P., and WOLFSON, S. M. 1973. Productivity measurement in police crime control. *Public Management 55:* 16, 18, 19.

BARKDOLL, G. L., and SPORN, D. L. 1988. Federal government in an executive environment: Two programmatic principles. In *Timely, low-cost evaluation in the public sector.* New Directions for Program Evaluation, No. 38, ed. C. G. Wye and H. P. Hatry. San Francisco: Jossey-Bass.

BARZANSKY, A.; BERNER, E.; and BECKMAN, C. R. R. 1985. Evaluation of a clinical program: Applying the concept of trustworthiness. *Evaluation & the Health Professions 8:* 193–208.

BASS, B. M. 1981. *Stodgill's handbook of leadership.* New York: The Free Press.

BAUER, S. M. and TOMS, K. 1989. Will there be any scientists in the class of 2000? [summary]. Proceedings of the Annual Meeting of the American Evaluation Association, 26.

BECKER, H.S. 1986. *Writing for social scientists.* Chicago: The University of Chicago Press.

BECKER, H.; HARRELL, W.; and KIRKHART, K. 1982. Evaluators in grey flannel suits: Implications of changes in roles and evaluation priorities for training evaluators. Paper presented at the meeting of the American Psychological Association, August, Washington, D.C.

BERK, R. A. 1977. Discretionary methodology decisions in applied research. *Sociological Methods and Research 5:* 317–334.

BERK, R. A., and ROSSI, P.H. 1976. Doing good or worse: Evaluation research politically re-examined. *Social Problems,* February, pp. 337–349.

BERMAN, J. J. 1978. An experiment in parole supervision. *Evaluation Quarterly 2:* 71–90.

BIGELOW, D. A., and CIARLO, J. A. 1975. The impact of therapeutic effectiveness data on community health center management: The systems evaluation project. *Community Mental Health Journal 11:* 64–73.

BINNER, P. R. 1977. Outcome measures and cost analysis. In *Emerging developments in mental health evaluation,* ed. W. Neigher, R. Hammer, and G. Landsberg. New York: Argold Press.

BOK, S. 1974. The ethics of giving placebos. *Scientific American,* 231(5), 17–23.

BORUCH, R. F., et al. 1983. Recommendations to Congress and their rationale. *Evaluation Review 7:* 5–35.

BOWERING, D. J., ed. *Secondary analysis of available data bases.* New Directions for Program Evaluation, no. 22. San Francisco: Jossey-Bass.

BOYER, R. 1989. *Places rated almanac: Your guide to finding the best places to live in America.* New York: Prentice Hall.

BRAITHWAITE, R. L.; PATTON, J. M.; and FANG, W. L. 1982. Evaluating a human service program: Employing the judicial evaluation model. *Evaluation and Program Planning 5:* 81–89.

BRINKERHOFF, R. O., et al. 1983. *Program evaluation: A practitioner's guide for trainers and educators—a design manual.* Boston: Kluwer-Nijhoff.

BROTMAN, B. 1983. "Workfare": What state terms success others call boondoggle. *Chicago Tribune,* January 2, sec. 3, pp. 1, 4.

Brown, F. G. 1983. *Principles of educational and psychological testing*. 3rd ed. New York: Holt, Rinehart and Winston.

Bryk, A. S., ed. 1983. *Stakeholderbased evaluation*. San Francisco, Calif.: Jossey-Bass.

Bunda, M. A. 1983. Alternative ethics reflected in education and evaluation. *Evaluation News 4* (1): 57–58.

Burtle, V., ed. 1979. *Women who drink*. Springfield, Ill.: Charles C. Thomas.

Bussigel, M., and Filling, C. 1985. Data discrepancies and their origins: An evaluation of a family practice residency program using a naturalistic inquiry paradigm. *Evaluation & The Health Professions 8:* 177–192.

Cagle, L. T., and Banks, S. M. 1986. The validity of assessing mental health needs with social indicators. *Evaluation and Program Planning 9:* 127–142.

Caidin, M. 1960. *Let's go flying!* New York: Dutton.

Campbell, D. T. 1969. Reforms as experiments. *American Psychologist 24:* 409–429.

Campbell, D. T. 1983. The problem of being scientific in program evaluation. Paper presented at the meeting of the Evaluation Research Society, October, Chicago.

Campbell, D. T. 1987. Guidelines for monitoring the scientific competence of preventive intervention research centers. *Knowledge: Creation, Diffusion, Utilization, 8:* 389–430.

Campbell, D. T., and Erlebacher, A. 1970. How regression artifacts in quasi-experimental evaluations can mistakenly make compensatory education look harmful. In *Compensatory education: A national debate*, ed. J. Hellmuth, pp. 185–210. Vol. 3 of *Disadvantaged child*. New York: Brunner-Mazel.

Campbell, D. T., and Stanley, J. C. 1963. *Experimental and quasi-experimental designs for research*. Chicago: Rand-McNally.

Caporaso, J. A. 1973. Quasi-experimental approaches to social science: Perspectives and problems. In *Quasi-experimental approaches: Testing theory and evaluating policy*, ed. J. A. Caporaso and L. L. Roos. Evanston, Ill.: Northwestern University Press.

Capper, J. 1983. Marketing evaluation skills and services. *Evaluation News 4*(2): 57–60.

Carey, R. G. 1972. *Hospital chaplains: Who needs them?* St. Louis, Mo.: Catholic Hospital Association.

Carey, R. G. 1974. Emotional adjustment in terminal patients. *Journal of Counseling Psychology 21:* 433–439.

Carey, R. G. 1979. Evaluation of a primary nursing unit. *American Journal of Nursing 79:* 1253–1255.

Carey, R. G., and Posavac, E. J. 1977. *Evaluation of the Medical Ecology Program*. Park Ridge, Ill.: Lutheran General Hospital.

Carey, R. G., and Posavac, E. J. 1978. Program evaluation of a physical medicine and rehabilitation unit: A new approach. *Archives of Physical Medicine and Rehabilitation 59:* 330–337.

Carley, M. 1981. *Social measurement and social indicators*. London: George Allen & Unwin.

Carter, D. E., and Newman, F. L. 1976. *A client-oriented system of mental health delivery and program management*. Rockville, Md.: National Institute of Mental Health.

Carver, R. P. 1974. Two dimensions of tests: Psychometric and edumetric. *American Psychologist 29:* 512–518.

Centra, J. A. 1977. Plusses and minuses for faculty development. *Change 9*(12):47, 48, 64.

Cannell, J. J. 1987. *Nationally normed elementary achievement testing in America's public schools: How all states are above the national average*. Daniels, W.Va.: Friends for Education.

Chapman, C., and Risley, T. R. 1974. Anti-litter procedures in an urban high-density area. *Journal of Applied Behavorial Analysis 7:* 377–383.

Chapman, R. L. 1976. *The design of management information systems for mental health organizations: A primer*. Rockville, Md.: National Institute of Mental Health.

Chelimsky, E. 1978. Differing perspectives of evaluation. In *New Directions for Program Evaluations*, no. 2, ed. C. C. Rentz and B. R. Rentz. San Francisco: Jossey-Bass.

CHEN, H., and ROSSI, P. H. 1990. Issues in the theory-driven perspective. *Evaluation and Program Planning 12:* 299–306.

Chicago-Tribune. 1978. Postal Service may dump billion-dollar parcel plan. June 14, sec. 4, p. 1.

Cholesterol screening. 1990. Washington, D.C.: Office of Inspector General, U.S. Department of Health and Human Services.

CICARELLI, V. G. 1970. The relevance of the regression artifact problem to the Westinghouse-Ohio University evaluation of Head Start: A reply to Campbell and Erlebacher. In *Compensatory education: A national debate,* ed. J. Hellmuth, pp. 211–216. Vol. 3 of *Disadvantaged child.* New York: Brunner-Mazel.

CICARELLI, V. G.; COOPER, W. H.; and GRANGER, R. L. 1969. *The Impact of Head Start: An evaluation of the effects of Head Start on children's cognitive and affective development.* Westinghouse Learning Corporation, OEO Contract No. B89–4536.

CLEVELAND, W. S. 1985. *The elements of graphing data.* Monterey, Calif.: Wadsworth.

COHEN, J. 1987. *Statistical power analysis for the behavioral sciences.* Rev. ed. Hillsdale, N.J.: Lawrence Erlbaum.

COLBURN, D. 1987, Jan. 20. Who pays? Insurance coverage varies widely. *Washington Post, Health: A weekly journal of medicine, science, and society,* p. 18.

Community Mental Health Plan. 1977. Spoon River, Ill.: Spoon River Community Mental Health Center.

CONNER, R. F., et al. 1985. Measuring need and demand in evaluation research. *Evaluation Review 9:* 717–734.

COOK, T. D., APPLETON, H., CONNOR, R., SHAFFER, A., TAMKIN, G., and WEBBER, S. J. 1975. *Sesame Street Revisited.* New York: Russell Sage.

COOK, T. D., and CAMPBELL, D. T. 1979. *Quasi-experimentation.* Chicago: Rand-McNally.

COOK, T. D., and DEVINE, E. C. 1982. Trying to discover explanatory processes through meta-analysis. Paper presented at the National Meeting of the American Educational Research Association, March, New York.

COOK, T. D.; LEVITON, L. C.; and SHADISH, W. R. 1985. Program evaluation. In *Handbook of Social Psychology,* 3rd ed. ed. G. Lindzey & E. Aronson. New York: Random House.

COOK, T. D., and REICHARDT, C. S., eds. 1979. *Qualitative and quantitative methods in evaluation research.* Beverly Hills, Calif.: Sage.

COOK, T. D., and SHADISH, W. R. 1986. Program evaluation: The worldly science. *Annual Review of Psychology 37:* 193–232.

CORDRAY, D. S. 1986. Quasi-experimental analysis: A mixture of methods and judgment. In *Advances in quasi-experimental design and analysis,* ed. W. M. K. Trochim. San Francisco: Jossey-Bass.

CORDRAY, D. S. 1990. Strengthening causal interpretations of nonexperimental data: The role of meta-analysis. In *Research methodology: Strengthening causal interpretations of nonexperimental data,* ed. L. Sechrest, E. Perrin, and J. Bunker. Rockville, Md.: U.S. Department of Health and Human Services, Agency for Health Care Policy and Research, (PHS) 90–3454.

CORNES, R. 1990. *Business systems design and development.* Englewood Cliffs, N.J.: Prentice Hall.

CRANO, W. D., and BREWER, M. B. 1986. *Principles and methods of social research.* Newton, Mass.: Allyn and Bacon.

CRONBACH, L. J. 1980. *Toward reform of program evaluation: Aims, methods, and institutional arrangements.* San Francisco: Jossey-Bass.

CRONBACH, L. J. 1982. *Designing evaluations of educational and social programs.* San Francisco: Jossey-Bass.

CULLITON, B. J. 1978. Health care economics: The high cost of getting well. *Science 200:* 883–885.

DARLINGTON, R. B., et al. 1980. Preschool programs and later school competence of children from low-income families. *Science 208:* 202–205.

DATTA, L. 1976a. Does it work when it has been tried? And half full or half empty? *Journal of Career Education 2:* 38–55.

DATTA, L. 1976b. The impact of the Westinghouse/Ohio evaluation on the development of project Head Start. In *The evaluation of social programs,* ed. C. C. Abt. Beverly Hills, Calif.: Sage.

DAVIS, D. D. 1982. *Primary prevention through organizational change: Improving program evaluation practices.* Paper presented at the meeting of the American Psychological Association, August, Washington, D.C.

DAVIS, D. F. 1990. Do you want a performance audit or a program evaluation? *Public Administration Review, 50:* 35–41.

DAY, C. R., JR. 1981. Solving the mystery of productivity measurement. *Industry Week,* January 26, pp. 61–66.

DeFRIESE, G. B. 1990. Theory as method. In *Research methodology: Strengthening causal interpretations of nonexperimental data.* ed. L. Sechrest, E. Perrin, and J. Bunker. Rockville, Md.: Department of Health and Human Services, Agency for Health Care Policy and Research, (PHS) 90-3454.

DEMONE, H. W., JR., and HARSHBARGER, D. 1973. *The planning and administration of human services.* New York: Behavorial Publications.

DE NUEFVILLE, J. I. 1975. *Social indicators and public policy.* Amsterdam: Elsevier Scientific Publishing Company.

DENISTON, O. L., and ROSENSTOCK, I. M. 1973. The validity of nonexperimental designs for evaluating health services. *Health Services Reports 88:* 153–164.

DERBY, A. 1989. Equating death and dollars on the highway. *Business and Society Review, 71* (Fall): 47, 48.

DIXON, M. G. 1977. Medical records guaranteed to ruin any malpractice defense. *Medical Economics 54:* 79–83.

DRYFOOS, J. G. 1982. Contraceptive use, pregnancy intentions, and pregnancy outcomes among U.S. women. *Family Planning Perspectives 14:* 81–94.

EDDY, D. M. 1990. Practice policies: Where do they come from? *JAMA, 263:* 1265, 1269, 1272, 1275.

EDDY, D. M., and BILLINGS, J. 1988. The quality of medical evidence: Implications for quality of care. *Health Affairs, 7*(1): 19–32.

EGAN, G. 1988a. *Change-agent skills A: Assessing and designing excellence.* San Diego, Calif.: University Associates.

EGAN, G. 1988b. *Change-agent skills B: Managing innovation and change.* San Diego, Calif.: University Associates.

EGAN, G., and COWAN, M. 1979. *People in systems.* Monterey, Calif.: Brooks/Cole.

EGDAHL, R. H. and GERTMAN, P. M. 1976. *Quality assurance in health care.* Germantown, Md.: Aspen Systems.

EGELHOF, J. 1975. Cop layoffs spur slayings. *Chicago Tribune,* July 10, sec. 1, p. 2.

EHRENREICH, B. 1990. A conservative tax proposal. *Time,* Aug. 27, p. 70.

EISENBERG, L. 1977. The social imperatives of medical research. *Science 198:* 1105–1110.

ELLIOTT, E. J. 1989. Accountability in the post-Charlottesville era. *Evaluation Comment* (UCLA Center for the Study of Evaluation), December, pp. 1–4.

ELLSWORTH, R. B. 1975. Consumer feedback in measuring the effectiveness of mental health programs. In *Handbook of evaluation research,* vol. 2, ed. M. Guttentag and E. L. Struening. Beverly Hills, Calif.: Sage.

ENDICOTT, J., and SPITZER, R. L. 1975. Designing mental health studies: The case for experimental designs. *Hospital & Community Psychiatry 26:* 737–739.

ERICSON, D. P. 1990. Social justice, evaluation, and the educational systems. In *Evaluation and social justice: Issues in public education,* ed. K. A. Sirotnik. San Francisco: Jossey-Bass.

ERS STANDARDS COMMITTEE. 1982. In Standards for practice, ed. P. H. Rossi, pp. 7–20. No. 15 of *New Directions for Program Evaluation.* San Francisco: Jossey-Bass.

Ethical principles of psychologists. 1981. *American Psychologist 36:* 633–638.

EVANS, J. W., and SCHILLER, J. 1970. How preoccupation with possible regression artifacts can lead to a faulty strategy for the evaluation of social action programs: A reply to Campbell and Erlebacher. In *Compensatory education: A national debate*, ed. J. Hellmuth, pp. 216–220. Vol. 3 of *Disadvantaged child*. New York: Brunner-Mazel.

EVANS, R. G., and ROBINSON, G. C. 1980. Surgical day care: Measurements of economic payoff. *CMA Journal 123:* 873–880.

EVANS, R. I., and RAINES, B. E. 1990. Applying a social psychological model across health promotion interventions. In *Social influence processes and prevention*, ed. J. D. Edwards, R. S. Tindale, L. Health, and E. J. Posavac. New York: Plenum.

FAIRWEATHER, G. W., and DAVIDSON, W. S. 1986. *An introduction to community experimentation*. New York: McGraw-Hill.

FERRISS, A. L. 1988. Uses of social indicators. *Social Forces, 66:* 601–617.

FISCHHOFF, B. 1982. For those condemned to study the past: Heuristics and biases in hindsight. In *Judgment under uncertainty: Heuristics and biases*, ed. D. Kahneman, P. Slovic, and A. Tversky. Cambridge: Cambridge University Press.

FLAY, B. R., and BEST, J. A. 1982. Overcoming design problems in evaluating health behavior programs. *Evaluation & the Health Professions 5:* 43–49.

FORREST, J.; HERMALIN, A. I.; and HENSHAW, S. K. 1981. The impact of family planning clinic programs on adolescent pregnancy. *Family Planning Perspectives 13:* 109–116.

FREDERICKSEN, L. W., SOLOMON, L. J., and BREHONY, K. A. (Eds.) 1984. *Marketing health behavior*. New York: Plenum Press.

FREIMAN, J. A.; CHALMERS, T. C.; SMITH, H., JR.; and KNEBLER, R. R. 1978. The importance of Beta, the Type II error and sample size in the design and interpretation of the randomized control trial. *The New England Journal of Medicine 299:* 690–694.

FRIEDMAN, H. 1982. Simplified determinations of statistical power, magnitude of effect and research sample sizes. *Educational and Psychological Measurement 42:* 521–526.

FRIEDMAN, P. J. 1990. We need to find new ways to help scientists avoid ethical problems without overly limiting research. *The Chronicle of Higher Education*, Oct. 31, p. A48.

FRY, L. J., and MILLER, J. 1975. Responding to skid row alcoholism: Self-defeating arrangements in an innovative treatment program. *Social Problems 22:* 673–687.

GELLER, E. S. 1990. Preventing injuries and deaths from vehicle crashes: Encouraging belts and discouraging booze. In *Social influence processes and prevention*, ed. J. D. Edwards, R. S. Tindale, L. Health, and E. J. Posavac. New York: Plenum.

GILBERT, J. P.; LIGHT, R. J.; and MOSTELLER, F. 1975. Assessing social innovations: An empirical base for policy. In *Evaluation and experiment*, ed. A. R. Lumsdaine and C. A. Bennett. New York: Academic Press.

"Good News—crime is up!" 1983. *Chicago Tribune*, May 8, sec. 2, p. 2.

GOOZNER, M. 1990. Pay inequity grew in '80s, study says. *Chicago Tribune*, Sept. 3, sec. 1, pp. 1, 4.

GOSFIELD, A. 1975. PSRO: *The law and the health consumer*. Cambridge, Mass.: Ballinger.

Graph-in-the Box. 1987. Greenwich, Conn.: New England Software, Inc.

GRAY, B. H.; COOKE, R. A.; and TANNENBAUM, A. S. 1978. Research involving human subjects. *Science 201:* 1094–1101.

GREENE, J. C. 1987. Stakeholder participation in evaluation: Is it worth the effort? *Evaluation and Program Planning 10:* 379–394.

GROSS, D. M., and SCOTT, S. 1990. Proceeding with caution. *Time*, July 16, pp. 56–62.

GUBA, E. G., and LINCOLN, Y. S. 1981. *Effective evaluation*. San Francisco: Jossey-Bass.

GUBA, E. G., and LINCOLN, Y. S. 1989. *Fourth generation evaluation*. Newbury Park, Calif.: Sage.

GUTTENTAG, M. 1977. Evaluation and society. *Personality and Social Psychology Bulletin 3:* 31–40.

HAENSLY, P.A., LUPKOWSKI, A. E., and MCNAMARA, J. F. 1987. The Chart Essay: A strategy for communicating research findings to policymakers and practitioners. *Educational Evaluation and Policy Analysis, 9:* 63–75.

HAKEL, M. D. et al. 1980. *Making it happen: Designing research with implementation in mind.* Beverly Hills, Calif.: Sage.

HANKE, S. H., and WALKER, R. A. 1974. Benefit-cost analysis reconsidered: An evaluation of the Mid-State project. *Water Resources Research 10:* 898–908.

HARRIS, M. B., and BRUNER, C. G. 1971. A comparison of a self-control and a contract procedure for weight control. *Behavior Research and Therapy 9:* 347–354.

HASTORF, A. H., and CANTRIL, H. 1954. They saw a game. *Journal of Abnormal and Social Psychology 49:* 129–134.

HAVEMAN, R. H., and WATTS, H. W. 1976. Social experimentation as policy research: A review of negative income tax experiments. In *Evaluation Studies Research Annual,* vol. 1, ed. G. V. Glass, Beverly Hills, Calif.: Sage.

HAYS, W. L. 1988. *Statistics.* 4th ed. New York: Holt, Rinehart and Winston.

HEDGES, L. V., and OLKIN, I. 1985. *Statistical methods for meta-analysis.* New York: Academic Press.

HEGARTY, T. W., and SPORN, D. L. 1988. Effective engagement of decisionmakers in program evaluation. *Evaluation and Program Planning, 11:* 335–340.

HELLER, K. 1990. Social and community intervention. *Annual Review of Psychology, 41:* 141–168.

HENDRICKS, M. 1986. A conversation with Michael Wargo. *Evaluation Practice, 7*(6): 23–36.

HOUGLAND, J. G., JR. 1987. Criteria for client evaluation of public programs: A comparison of objective and perceptual measures. *Social Science Quarterly, 68:* 386–394.

HOUSE, E. R. 1976. Justice in evaluation. In *Evaluation Studies Review Annual,* vol 1. ed. G. V. Glass. Beverly Hills, Calif.: Sage.

HOUSE, E. R. 1988. *Jesse Jackson and the politics of charisma: The rise and fall of the PUSH/Excel program.* Boulder, Colo.: Westview Press.

HOUSE, E. R. 1990. Methodology and justice. In *Evaluation and social justice: Issues in public education,* ed. K. A. Sirotnik. San Francisco: Jossey-Bass.

HOUSE, P. W., and SHULL, R. D. 1988. *Rush to policy: Using analytic techniques in public sector decision making.* New Brunswick, NJ: Transaction Books.

HUNTER, J. E., and SCHMIDT, F. L. 1990. *Methods of meta-analysis.* Newbury Park, Calif.: Sage.

ILLICH, I. 1976. *Medical nemesis.* New York: Pantheon Books.

ISAACSON, W. 1983. The winds of reform. *Time,* March 7, pp. 12–16, 23, 26–30.

JASON, L. A., and LIOTTA, R. F. 1982. Assessing community responsiveness in a metropolitan area. *Evaluation Review 6:* 703–712.

JOGLEKAR, P. N. 1984. Cost-benefit studies of health care programs: Choosing methods for desired results. *Evaluations & the Health Professions, 7:* 285–303.

JOHNSON, P. L. 1990. A conversation with Joseph S. Wholey about the Program for Excellence in Human Services. *Evaluation Practice, 11*(2): 53–61.

JOHNSTON, J. 1983. The status of evaluation as an enterprise. *ERS Newsletter 7*(2): 1, 7.

JOINT COMMITTEE ON STANDARDS FOR EDUCATIONAL EVALUATION. 1981. *Standards for evaluations of educational programs, projects, and materials.* New York: McGraw-Hill.

JUDD, C. M., and KENNEY, D. A. 1981. *Estimating the effects of social interventions.* New York: Cambridge University Press.

JULNES, G., and MOHR, L. B. 1989. Analysis of no-difference findings in evaluation research. *Evaluation Review, 13:* 628–655.

KAHNEMAN, D., and TVERSKY, A., 1974. Judgment under uncertainty: Heuristics and biases. *Science 185:* 1124–1131.

KAHNEMAN, D., SLOVIC, P., and TVERSKY, A., eds. 1982. *Judgment under uncertainty: Heuristics and biases.* New York: Cambridge University Press.

KANE, R. L., and KANE, R. A. 1978. Care of the aged: Old problems in need of new solutions. *Science 200:* 913–919.

KARWATH, R. 1990. Jury's out on pregnant teens plan. *Chicago Tribune*, Aug. 28, sec. 2, p. 4.

KAYNE, N. T., and ALLOY, L. B. 1988. Clinician and patient as aberrant actuaries: Expectation-based distortions in assessment of covariation. In *Social cognition and clinical psychology: A synthesis* (pp. 295–365), ed. L. Y. Abramson. New York: Guilford Press.

KEATING, K. M., and HIRST, E. 1986. Advantages and limits of longitudinal evaluation research in energy conservation. *Evaluation and Program Planning 9:* 113–120.

KELLING, G. L., et al. 1976. The Kansas City preventive patrol experiment: A summary report. In *Evaluative studies review annual*, vol. 1, ed. G. V. Glass. Beverly Hills, Calif.: Sage.

KERSHAW, D. N. 1972. A negative income tax experiment. *Scientific American 227:* 19–25.

KIMMEL, A. J. 1988. *Ethnics and values in applied social research.* Newbury Park, Calif.: Sage.

KIRK, R. E. 1982. *Experimental design: Procedures for the behavorial sciences.* Rev. ed. Belmont, Calif.: Brooks/Cole.

KNAPP, M. 1977. Applying time-series research strategies to program evaluation problems. Paper presented at a meeting of the Evaluation Research Society, October, Washington, D.C.

KOLATA, G. B. 1977. Aftermath of the new math: Its originators defend it. *Science, 195:* 854–857.

KORAN, L. M., et al. 1983. Changing hospital work environments: An example of a burn unit. *General Hospital Psychiatry 5:* 7–13.

KRAUSE, M. S., and JACKSON, J. C. 1983. The validity of some routine evaluative data: A study. *Evaluation Review 7:* 271–276.

KREITNER, R. 1977. People are systems, too: Filling the feedback vacuum. *Business Horizons 20* (November): 54–58.

KRUEGER, R. A. 1988. *Focus groups: A practical guide for applied research.* Newbury Park, Calif.: Sage.

KYTLE, J., and MILLMAN, E. J. 1986. Confessions of two applied researchers in search of principles. *Evaluation and Program Planning 9:* 167–177.

LAWLER, E. E., III, and HACKMAN, J. R. 1969. Impact of employee participation in the development of pay incentive plans: A field experiment. *Journal of Applied Psychology 53:* 467–471.

LAZAR, I. 1981. Early intervention is effective. *Educational Leadership*, January, pp. 303–305.

LEIK, R. K., and CHALKLEY, M. A. 1990. Parent involvement: What is it that works? *Children Today*, May–June, pp. 34–37.

LENIHAN, K. J. 1977. Telephones and raising bail. *Evaluation Quarterly* 1: 569–586.

LESOURNE, J. 1990. OR and the social sciences. *Journal of the Operational Research Society, 41:* 1–7.

LEVIN, H. M. 1982. A world without evaluation. Paper given at the meeting of the Evaluation Research Society, October, Baltimore.

LEVIN, H. M. 1983. *Cost-effectiveness: A primer.* Beverly Hills, Calif.: Sage.

LEVINE, M., et al. 1978. Adapting the jury trial for program evaluation: A report of an experience. *Evaluation and Program Planning 1:* 177–186.

LEVITON, L. C., and BORUCH, R. F. 1983. Contributions of evaluation in education programs and policy. *Evaluation Review 7:* 563–598.

LICHT, M. H. 1979. The Staff-Resident Interaction Chronograph: Observational assessment of staff performance. *Journal of Behavioral Assessment 1:* 185–198.

LIGHT, R. J., and PILLEMER, D. B. 1984. *Summing up: The science of reviewing research.* Cambridge, Mass.: Harvard University Press.

LINCOLN, Y. S. 1990. Program review, accreditation processes, and outcome assessment: Pressures on institutions of higher education. *Evaluation Practice, 11:* 13–23.

LINCOLN, Y. S. and GUBA, E. G. 1985. *Naturalistic inquiry.* Beverly Hills, Calif.: Sage.

LIPSEY, M. W. 1990a. Theory as method: Small theories of treatments. In *Research methodology: Strengthening causal interpretations of nonexperimental data.* ed. L. Sechrest, E. Perrin, and J. Bunker. Rockville, Md.: U.S. Department of Health and Human Services, Agency for Health Care Policy and Research, (PHS) 90–3454.

LIPSEY, M. W. 1990b. *Design sensitivity: Statistical power for experimental research.* Newbury Park, Calif.: Sage.

LIPSEY, M. W., CROSSE, S., DUNKLE, J., POLLARD, J., and STOBART, G. 1985. Evaluation: The state of the art and the sorry state of the science. In *Utilizing prior research in evaluation planning,* ed. D. S. Cordray. San Francisco: Jossey-Bass.

LIPSEY, M. W., and POLLARD, J. A. 1989. Driving toward theory in program evaluation: More models to choose from. *Evaluation and Program Planning, 12:* 317–328.

LotusWorks. 1990. Cambridge, Mass.: Lotus Development Corp.

LOVE, A. J. 1986. Using evaluation to identify service gaps in mental health services to youth. Paper presented at the meeting of the American Evaluation Association, October, Kansas City, Mo.

MADAUS, G. F., SCRIVEN, M. S., and STUFFLEBEAM, D. L. 1983. *Evaluation models.* Boston, Mass.: Kluwer-Nijhoff.

MAGER, R. F. 1972. *Goal analysis.* Belmont, Calif.: Fearon Publishers.

MAJCHRZAK, A. 1986. Keeping the Marines in the field: Results of a field experiment. *Evaluation and Program Planning 9:* 253–265.

MALCOLM, M. T., MADDEN, J. S., and WILLIAMS, A. E. 1974. Disulfiram implantation critically evaluated. *British Journal of Psychiatry, 125:* 485–489.

MALITZ, D. 1984. The costs and benefits of Title XX and Title XIX family planning services in Texas. *Evaluation Review 8:* 519–536.

MANOFF, R. K. 1985. *Social marketing: New imperative for public health.* New York: Praeger.

MARK, M. M., and SHOTLAND, R. L., eds. 1987. *Multiple methods in program evaluation.* San Francisco: Jossey-Bass.

MARSHALL, T. O. 1979. Levels of results. *Journal of Constructive Change 1*(1): 5.

MAXWELL, G. S. 1985. Problems of being responsive: Reflections on an evaluation of a program for training motorcycle riders. *Evaluation and Program Planning 8:* 339–348.

McCALL, R. B. 1990. *Fundamental statistics for the behavioral sciences.* 5th ed. New York: Harcourt Brace Jovanovich.

McCARTHY, M. 1978. Decreasing the incidence of "high bobbins" in a textile spinning department through a group feedback procedure. *Journal of Organizational Behavioral Management 1:* 150–154.

McCLEARY, R., and HAY, R. A., JR. 1980. *Applied time series analysis for the social sciences.* Beverly Hills, Calif.: Sage.

McCLINTOCK, C. C. 1983. Internal evaluation: The new challenge. *Evaluation News 4*(1): 61–62.

McCONKEY, D. D. 1983. *How to manage by results.* 4th ed. New York: AMACON.

McCRACKEN, G. D. 1989. *The long interview.* Newbury Park, Calif.: Sage.

McKAY, H., et al. 1978. Improving cognitive ability in chronically deprived children. *Science 200:* 270–278.

McKILLIP, J. 1987. *Need analysis: Tools for human services and education.* Beverly Hills, Calif.: Sage.

McKILLIP, J. (in press). Effect of Illinois' marriage HIV testing law on frequency of marriage in Illinois and in bordering and comparison states. *American Journal of Public Health.*

McKILLIP, J., and BALDWIN, K. 1990. Evaluation of an STD education media campaign: A control construct design. *Evaluation Review, 14:* 331–346.

McKILLIP, J., et al. 1985. Evaluation of a responsible alcohol use media campaign on a college campus. *Journal of Alcohol and Drug Education. 30:* 88–97.

McLAUGHLIN, M. W. 1974. *Evaluation and reform: The Elementary and Secondary Education Act of 1965. Title I.* Santa Monica, Calif.: The Rand Corporation.

MEADOWS, D. L., and PERELMAN, L. 1973. Limits to growth. In *The future in the making: Current issues in higher education*, ed. D. W. Vermilye. San Francisco: Jossey-Bass.

Medical World News. May 30, 1977. Hypertension compliance. *18:* 20–22; 24–25; 28–29.

MEEHL, P. E. 1978. Theoretical risks and tabular asterisks: Sir Karl, Sir Ronald, and the slow progress of soft psychology. *Journal of Consulting and Clinical Psychology, 46:* 806–834.

MEEHL, P. E. 1990. Appraising and amending theories: The strategy of Lakatosian defense and two principles that warrant it. *Psychological Inquiry, 1:* 108–141.

MILES, M. B., and HUBERMAN, A. M. 1984. *Analyzing qualitative data: A source book for new methods.* Beverly Hills, Calif.: Sage.

MILLENSON, M. L. 1987. System puts doctors, cost cutters at odds. *Chicago Tribune,* June 15, sec. 1, pp. 1, 11.

MILLSAP, R. E., and HARTOG, S. B. 1988. Alpha, beta, and gamma change in evaluation research: A structural equation approach. *Journal of Applied Psychology, 73:* 574–584.

MIRVIS, P. H., and BERG, D. N., eds. 1977. *Failure in organizational development and change: Cases and essays for learning.* New York: Wiley-Interscience.

MOSKOP, J. C. 1987, April. The moral limits to federal funding for kidney disease. *Hastings Center Report,* pp. 11–15.

MOSTELLER, F. 1981. Innovation and evaluation. *Science, 211:* 881–886.

MUELLER, D. J. 1986. *Measuring social attitudes: A handbook for researchers and practitioners.* New York: Teachers College Press.

NAGEL, S. S. 1983a. Nonmonetary variables in benefit-cost evaluation. *Evaluation Review 7:* 37–64.

NAGEL, S. S. 1983b. Factors facilitating the utilization of policy evaluation research. Paper presented at the meeting of the Evaluation Research Society, October, Chicago.

NATIONAL INSTITUTE OF MENTAL HEALTH, 1971. *Planning for creative change in mental health services: A distillation of principles on research utilization.* Washington D. C.: Department of Health, Education, and Welfare. Publication No. (HSM) 73–9148.

National Standards for Community Mental Health Centers. 1977. Rockville, Md.: Department of Health, Education and Welfare.

NEIGHER, W., et al. 1982. Evaluation in the community mental health centers program: A bold new approach? *Evaluation and Program Planning 5:* 283–311.

Newsweek. May 9, 1977. Health-cost crisis. *89:* 84, 89, 90.

NICHOLSON, N. 1977. Absence behavior and attendance motivation: A conceptual synthesis. *The Journal of Management Studies 14:* 231–252.

NIENSTEDT, B. C., and HALEMBA, G. J. 1986. Providing a model for agency program evaluation. *State Evaluation Network 6*(1): 2–4.

NUNNALLY, J. C. 1975. The study of change in evaluation research: Principles concerning measurement, experimental design, and analysis. In *Handbook of Evaluation Research,* vol. 1, ed. E. L. Struening and M. Guttentag. Beverly Hills, Calif.: Sage.

NUNNALLY, J. C., and DURHAM, R. L. 1975. Validity, reliability, and special problems of measurement in evaluation research. In *Handbook of Evaluation Research,* vol. 1, ed. E. L. Struening and M. Guttentag. Beverly Hills, Calif.: Sage.

NUNNALLY, J. C., and WILSON, W. H. 1975. Method and theory for developing measures in evaluation research. In *Handbook of Evaluation Research,* vol. 1, ed. E. L. Struening and M. Guttentag. Beverly Hills, Calif.: Sage.

O'DOHERTY, H. 1989. Mediation evaluation: Status report and challenges for the future. *Evaluation Practice 10*(4): 8–19.

OFFICE OF INSPECTOR GENERAL. 1990. *Technical assistant guides for conducting program evaluations and inspections.* Washington, D.C.: Department of Health and Human Services.

OKRENT, D. 1980. Comment on societal risk. *Science 208:* 372–75.

On a diet? Don't trust your memory. 1989. *Psychology Today,* October, p. 12.

PALCA, J. 1990. Trials and tribulations of AIDS drug testing. *Science, 247:* 1406.

Patton, M. Q. 1980. *Qualitative evaluation methods.* Beverly Hills, Calif.: Sage.

Patton, M. Q. 1986. *Utilization-focused evaluation.* 2nd ed. Beverly Hills, Calif.: Sage.

Patton, M. Q. 1989. A context and boundaries for a theory-driven approach to validity. *Evaluation and Program Planning, 12:* 375–377.

Paul, G. L., ed. 1986. *Assessment in residential settings: Principles and methods to support cost-effective quality operations.* Champaign, Ill.: Research Press.

Pearce, D., and Markandya, A. 1988. Pricing the environment. *The OECD Observer, 151* (April/May): 23–26.

Pendery, M. L.; Maltzman, I. M.; and West, L. J. 1982. Controlled drinking by alcoholics? New findings and a reevaluation of a major affirmative study. *Science 217:* 169–175.

Perloff, R. 1983. The uses of roles for evaluation research in the private sector. Paper presented at the Eastern Evaluation Research Society Conference, June.

Peterson, R. D. 1986. The anatomy of cost-effectiveness analysis. *Evaluation Review 10:* 29–44.

Popham, W. J. 1988. *Educational evaluation,* rev. ed. Englewood Cliffs, N.J.: Prentice Hall.

Posavac, E. J. 1975. *Survey of past residents in the Clinical Pastoral Education Program.* Park Ridge, Ill.: Lutheran General Hospital.

Posavac, E. J. (in press). Communication of applied social psychology: An art and a challenge. In *Methodology in applied social psychology,* ed. F. B. Bryant, J. D. Edwards, R. S. Tindale, E. J. Posavac, L. Heath, Y. Suarez-Balcazar, and E. Henderson. New York: Plenum.

Posavac, E. J., and Hartung, B. M. 1977. An exploration into the reasons people choose a pastoral counselor instead of another type of psychotherapist. *The Journal of Pastoral Care 31:* 23–31.

Posavac, E. J., and Sinacore, J. M. 1984. Reporting effect size in order to improve the understanding of statistical significance. *Knowledge: Creation, Diffusion, Utilization, 5:* 503–508.

Posavac, E. J., et al. 1985. Increasing compliance to medical treatment regimens. *Evaluation & the Health Professions 8:* 7–22.

Potemkin Factory. 1980. *Time,* Feb. 25, p. 36.

Prue, D. M., et al. 1980. Managing the treatment activities of state hospital staff. *Journal of Organizational Behavior Management 2:* 165–181.

Rahe, R. H. 1978. Life stress and illness. Presented at the Stress and Behavioral Medicine Symposium, May 20, Chicago, Ill.

Rawls, J. 1971. *A theory of justice.* Cambridge, Mass.: Harvard University Press.

Ray, M. 1973. Marketing communication and the hierarchy of effects. In *New models for mass communication research,* ed. by P. Clarke. Beverly Hills, Calif.: Sage.

Reichardt, C. S. 1979. The statistical analysis of data from nonequivalent group designs. In *Quasi-experimentation,* ed. T. D. Cook and D. T. Campbell. Boston: Houghton Mifflin.

Rezmovic, E. L.; Cook, T. J.; and Dobson, L. D. 1981. Beyond random assignment: Factors affecting evaluation integrity. *Evaluation Review 5:* 51–67.

Rice, S. A. 1929. Contagious bias in the interview. *American Journal of Sociology 35:* 420–423.

Rich, E. C., Gifford, G., Luxenberg, M., and Dowd, B. 1990. The relationship of house staff experience to the cost and quality of inpatient care. *JAMA, 263:* 953–957.

Richardson, V. 1990. At-risk programs: Evaluation and critical inquiry. In *Evaluation and social justice: Issues in public education,* ed. K. A. Sirotnik. San Francisco: Jossey-Bass.

Richmond, F. 1990. Internal evaluation in the Pennsylvania Department of Public Welfare. In *The demise of internal evaluation in governmental agencies: Cause for concern or auction?* N. L. Ross (Chair), panel presented at the meeting of the American Evaluation Association, October, Washington, D.C.

Riecken, H. W., and Boruch, R. F., eds. 1974. *Social experimentation: A method for planning and evaluating social intervention.* New York: Academic Press.

Rimland, B. 1979. Death knell for psychotherapy? *American Psychologist, 34:* 192.

Rivlin, A. M. 1990. *Evaluation and public policy.* Invited address presented at the meeting of the American Evaluation Association, October, Washington D.C.

Rook, K. S. 1987. Effects of case history versus abstract information on health attitudes and behavior. *Journal of Applied Social Psychology, 17:* 533–553.

Rosenhan, D. L. 1973. On being sane in insane places. *Science 179:* 250–258.

Rosenthal, R. 1984. *Meta-analytic procedures for social research.* Beverly Hills, Calif.: Sage.

Ross, H. L. 1975. The Scandinavian myth: The effectiveness of drinking-and-driving legislation in Sweden and Norway. *Journal of Legal Studies 4:* 285–310.

Ross, N. L. 1990. Internal evaluation in the Florida Department of Health and Rehabilitative Services. In *The demise of internal evaluation in governmental agencies: Cause for concern or action?* N. L. Ross (chair), panel presented at the meeting of the American Evaluation Association, October, Washington, D.C.

Rossi, P. H. 1978. Issues in the evaluation of human services delivery. *Evaluation Quarterly, 2:* 573–599.

Rossi, P. H., ed. 1982. *Standards for evaluation practice.* San Francisco: Jossey-Bass.

Rossi, P. H. 1983. Pussycats, weasels or percherons? Current prospects for social science under the Reagan regime. *Evaluation News 4*(1): 12–27.

Rossman, G. B.; and Wilson, B. L. 1985. Numbers and words: Combining quantitative and qualitative methods in a single large-scale evaluation study. *Evaluation Review 9:* 627–644.

Roth, J. 1990. Needs and the needs assessment process (reprinted from 1978). *Evaluation Practice, 11:* 141–143.

Rothchild, M. L. 1979. Advertising strategies for high and low involvement situations. In *Attitude research plays for high stakes,* ed. J. Maloney and B. Silverman. New York: American Marketing Association.

Schmidt, R. E.; Scanlon, J. W.; and Bell, J. B. 1979. Evaluability assessment: Making public programs work better. *Human Services Monograph Series,* no. 14, November.

Schneider, A. L., and Darcy, R. E. 1984. Policy implications of using significance tests in evaluation research. *Evaluation Review 8:* 573–582.

Schneider, M. J., Chapman, D. D., and Voth, D. E. 1985. Senior center participation: A two-stage approach to impact evaluation. *The Gerontologist, 25:* 194–200.

Schnelle, J. F., et al. 1977. Patrol evaluation research: A multiple-baseline analysis of saturation police patrolling during day and night. *Journal of Applied Behavior Analysis 10:* 33–40.

Schnelle, J. F., et al. 1978. Police evaluation research: An experimental and cost-benefit analysis of a helicopter patrol in a high crime area. *Journal of Applied Behavior Analysis 11:* 11–21.

Schultz, R. F. 1990. *Sisyphus: A software program for outpatient mental health workers.* Salt Lake City, Utah: Author.

Schwandt, T. A., and Halpern, E. S. 1988. *Linking auditing and metaevaluation: Enhancing the quality of applied research.* Newbury Park, Calif.: Sage.

Scriven, M. 1967. The methodology of evaluation. in *Perspectives of curriculum evaluation,* ed. R. W. Tyler, R. M. Gagne, and M. Scriven. Chicago: Rand-McNally.

Scriven, M. 1980. *The logic of evaluation.* Inverness, Calif.: Edgepress.

Scriven, M. 1981. *Evaluation thesaurus.* 3rd ed. Inverness, Calif.: Edgepress.

Scriven, M., and Roth, J. 1990. Special feature: Needs assessment (reprinted from 1976). *Evaluation Practice, 11:* 135–140.

Sechrest, L. 1984. Social science and social policy. Will our numbers ever be good enough? In *Social science and social policy,* ed. R. L. Shotland and M. M. Mark. Beverly Hills, Calif.: Sage.

SECHREST, L., PERRIN, E., and BUNKER, J. 1990. *Research methodology: Strengthening causal interpretations of nonexperimental data.* Rockville, Md.: U. S. Department of Health and Human Services, Agency for Health Care Policy and Research, (PHS) 90–3454.

SELIGMAN, C., and DARLEY, J. M. 1977. Feedback as a means of decreasing residential energy consumption. *Journal of Applied Psychology 62:* 363–368.

SELIGMAN, C., and FINEGAN, J. E. 1990. A two-factor model of energy and water conservation. In *Social influence processes and prevention,* ed. J. Edwards, R. S. Tindale, L. Heath, and E. J. Posavac. New York: Plenum.

SELIGMAN, C., and HUTTON, R. B. 1981. Evaluating energy conservation programs. *Journal of Social Issues 37:* 51–72.

SHADISH, W. R., JR., et al. 1985. The subjective well-being of mental patients in nursing homes. *Evaluation and Program Planning 8:* 239–250.

SHEPARD, L. A. 1990. "Inflating test score gains": Is it old norms or teaching the test? Los Angeles: UCLA Center for Research on Evaluation, Standards, and Student Teaching, CSE Technical Report 307.

SHIPLEY, R. H. 1976. Effects of companion program on college student volunteers and mental patients. *Journal of Consulting and Clinical Psychology 4:* 688–689.

SHOTLAND, R. L., and MARK, M., eds. 1985. *Social science and social policy.* Beverly Hills, Calif.: Sage.

SHRAUGER, J.S., and OSBERG, T. M. 1981. The relative accuracy of self-predictions and judgments by others in psychological assessment. *Psychological Bulletin 90:* 322–351.

SILVERMAN, M., RICCI, E. M., and GUNTER, M. J. 1990. Strategies for increasing the rigor of qualitative methods in evaluation of health care programs. *Evaluation Review, 14:* 57–74.

SIMON, H. A. 1976. *Administrative behavior.* 3rd ed. New York: Macmillan.

SINGH, B.; GREER, P. R.; and HAMMOND, R. 1977. An evaluation of the use of the Law in a Free Society materials on "responsibility." *Evaluation Quarterly 1:* 621–628.

SIROTNIK, K. A., ed. 1990. *Evaluation and social justice.* San Francisco: Jossey-Bass.

SJOBERG, G. 1975. Politics, ethics, and evaluation research. In *Handbook of evaluation research,* vol. 2, ed. M. Guttentag and E. L. Struening. Beverly Hills, Calif.: Sage.

SMITH, M. L., and Glass, G. V. 1977. Meta-analysis of psychotherapy outcome studies. *American Psychologist 32:* 752–760.

SMITH, N. L. 1981. The certainty of judgments in health evaluations. *Evaluation and Program Planning 4:* 273–278

SMITH, N. L., ed. 1982. *Communication strategies in evaluation.* Beverly Hills, Calif.: Sage.

SOBELL, M. B., and SOBELL, L. C. 1978. *Behavioral treatment of alcohol problems.* New York: Plenum.

SOLOMON, A. 1975. Charges of resigned aide on prisons will be probed. *Madison Capitol Times,* Sept. 12.

SPEER, D. C., and TRAPP, J. C. 1976. Evaluation of mental health service effectiveness. *American Journal of Orthopsychiatry 46:* 217–228.

SPIELBERGER, C. D., ed. 1972. *Anxiety: Current trends in theory and research,* vol. 1. New York: Academic Press.

SPIRO, S. E., SHALEV, A., SOLOMON, Z., and KOTLER, M. 1989. Self-reported change versus changed self-report: Contradictory findings of an evaluation of a treatment program for war veterans suffering from post-traumatic stress disorder. *Evaluation Review, 13:* 533–549.

SPORN, D. L. 1989. A conversation with Gerald L. Barkdoll. *Evaluation Practice, 10*(1): 27–32.

SPORN, D. L. 1989. A conversation with Michael Hendricks. *Evaluation Practice, 10*(3): 18–24.

SPORN, D. L. 1990. A conversation with Richard C. Sonnichsen. *Evaluation Practice, 11,* 63–67.

Spotlight: Program evaluation and accountability in Minnesota. 1982. *State Evaluation Network* 2(5), 2.

STEELE, S. 1990. *The content of our character.* New York: St. Martin's Press.

STEIN, S., and RECKTENWALD, W. 1990. City parks are no place to play. *Chicago Tribune,* Nov. 11, sec. 1, pp. 1, 18.

STRAW, M. 1978. Informal presentation delivered at Loyola University, May 22, Chicago, Ill.

STRUPP, H. H., and HANDLEY, S. W. 1977. A tripartite model of mental health and therapeutic outcomes: With special reference to negative effects in psychotherapy. *American Psychologist 32:* 187–196.

Students cheated in college sports. 1990. *Chicago Tribune,* Sept. 10, sec. 1, p. 12.

SUDMAN, S., and BRADBURN, N. M. 1982. *Asking questions.* San Francisco: Jossey-Bass.

SULLIVAN, J. M., and SNOWDEN, L. R. 1981. Monitoring frequency of client problems. *Evaluation Review 5:* 822–833.

SUSSNA, E., and HEINEMANN, H. N. 1972. The education of health manpower in a two-year college: An evaluation model. *Socio-Economic Planning Science 6:* 21–30.

TESCH, R. 1990. *Qualitative research: Analysis types and software tools.* New York: The Falmer Press.

The trouble with dependent variables. 1990. *Dialogue: Society for Personality and Social Psychology,* Spring, p. 9.

THOMPSON, M. S. 1980. *Benefit-cost analysis for program evaluation.* Beverly Hills, Calif.: Sage.

TIERNEY, W. M., MILLER, M. E., and MCDONALD, C. 1990. The effect on test ordering of informing physicians of the charges of outpatient diagnostic tests. *The New England Journal of Medicine, 322:* 1499–1504.

Time, July 24, 1978. Psst! Wanna good job? *112:* 18, 19.

TROCHIM, W. M. K. 1984. *Research design for program evaluation: The regression discontinuity approach.* Beverly Hills, Calif.: Sage.

TROCHIM, W. M. K., ed. 1986. *Advances in quasi-experimental design and analysis.* San Francisco: Jossey-Bass.

TROCHIM, W. M. K. 1990. The regression-discontinuity design. In *Research methodology: Strengthening causal interpretations of nonexperimental data,* ed. L. Sechrest, E. Perrin, and J. Bunker. Rockville, Md.: U.S. Department of Health and Human Services, Agency for Health Care Policy and Research, (PHS) 90–3454.

TUFTE, E. R. 1983. *The visual display of quantitative information.* Cheshire, Conn.: Graphics Press.

TUKEY, J. W. 1977. *Exploratory data analysis.* Reading, Mass.: Addison-Wesley.

TURNER, A. J. 1977. Program goal setting in an evaluation system. Paper presented at the Conference on the Impact of Program Evaluation in Mental Health Care, January, Loyola University of Chicago.

TVERSKY, A., and KAHNEMAN, D. 1973. Availability: A heuristic for judging frequency and probability. *Cognitive Psychology, 5:* 207–232.

TYSON, T. J. 1985. The evaluation and monitoring of a Medicaid second surgical opinion program. *Evaluation and Program Planning 8:* 207–216.

U.S. News & World Report, April 21, 1975. $301 million a day for HEW—and no end in sight. *79:* 45–47.

VAN SANT, J. 1989. Qualitative analysis in developmental evaluations. *Evaluation Review, 13:* 257–272.

WALDO, G. P., and CHIRICOS, T. G. 1977. Work release and recidivism: An empirical evaluation of a social policy. *Evaluation Quarterly 1:* 87–108.

WALLIS, C. 1983. Death of a gallant pioneer. *Time,* April 4, pp. 62, 63.

WALSH, J. 1983. Congress questions NBS [National Bureau of Standards] budget cuts. *Science 220:* 176, 177.

WARHEIT, G. J., BELL, R. A., and SCHWAB, J. J. 1977. *Needs assessment approaches: Concepts and methods.* Rockville, Md.: National Institute of Mental Health.

WASKOW, I. E., and PERLOFF, M. B., eds. 1975. *Psychotherapy change measures*. Rockville, Md.: National Institute of Mental Health.

WEBB, E. J., et al. 1981. *Nonreactive measures in the social sciences*. 2nd ed. Boston: Houghton-Mifflin.

WEST, S. G., HEPWORTH, J. T., and McCALL, M. A. 1989. An evaluation of Arizona's July 1982 drunk driving law: Effects on the city of Phoenix. *Journal of Applied Social Psychology, 19:* 1212–1237.

WHITMORE, E., and RAY, M. L. 1989. Qualitative evaluation audits: Continuation of the discussion. *Evaluation Review, 13:* 78–90.

WHOLEY, J. S. 1979. *Evaluation: Promise and performance*. Washington, D.C.: Urban Institute.

WILLS, F. 1987. A conversation with Joy Frechtling. *Evaluation Practice, 8*(2): 20–30.

Winner of the 1988 President's Problem. 1989. *Evaluation Practice, 10*(1): 53–57.

WOOD, G. 1978. The knew-it-all-along effect. *Journal of Experimental Psychology: Human Perception and Performance, 4:* 345–353.

WYE, C. G. 1989. Increasing client involvement in evaluation: A team approach. In *Evaluation and the federal decision maker*, eds. G. L. Barkdoll and J. B. Bell. New Directions for Program Evaluation, no. 41. San Francisco: Jossey-Bass.

YEATON, W. H., and SECHREST, L. 1986. Use and misuse of no-difference findings in eliminating threats to validity. *Evaluation Review, 10:* 836–852.

YEATON, W. H., and SECHREST, L. 1987. Assessing factors influencing acceptance of no-difference research. *Evaluation Review, 11:* 131–142.

YIN, R. K. 1984. *Case study research: Design and methods*. Beverly Hills, Calif.: Sage.

ZAMMUTO, R. F. 1982. *Assessing organizational effectiveness*. Albany, N. Y.: SUNY Press.

ZIGLER, E., and TRICKETT, P. K. 1978. IQ, social competence, and evaluation of early childhood intervention programs. *American Psychologist 33:* 789–798.

ZIMRING, F. E. 1975. Firearms and federal law: The Gun Control Act of 1968. *Journal of Legal Studies 4:* 133–198.

ZINOBER, J. W., and DINKEL, N. R., eds. 1981. *A trust of evaluation: A guide for involving citizens in community mental health program evaluation*. Tampa, Fla.: The Florida Consortium for Research and Evaluation.

Name Index

Brown, F. G., 73, 305
Bruner, C. G., 188, 309
Bryant, F. B., 313
Bryk, A. S., 28, 305
Bunda, M. A., 98, 305
Bunker, J., 177, 306, 307, 311, 315, 316
Burtle, V., 87, 305
Bussigel, M., 294, 305

Cagle, L. T., 115, 305
Caidin, M., 150, 305
Campbell, D. T., 17, 33, 70, 88, 141,
    142, 147–149, 151, 157, 159,
    160–162, 166, 168, 169, 172, 173,
    177, 179, 181, 183, 188, 189,
    192, 222, 225, 226, 305, 306,
    308, 313
Cantril, H., 183, 309
Caporaso, J. A., 163, 305
Capper, J., 17, 305
Carey, R. G., 17, 31, 92, 179, 249, 305
Carley, M., 104, 305
Carter, D. E., 76, 77, 196, 305
Carver, R. P., 73, 305
Centra, J. A., 148, 305
Chalkey, M. A., 44, 310
Chalmers, T. C., 251, 308
Channell, J. J., 53, 305
Chapman, C., 96, 305
Chapman, D. D., 196, 314
Chapman, R. L., 127, 305
Chelimsky, E., 2, 305
Chen, H., 54, 306
Chiricos, T. G., 251, 316
Ciarlo, J. A., 255, 304
Cicarelli, V. G., 43, 96, 168, 169, 306
Clarke, P., 313
Cleveland, W. S., 240, 306
Cohen, F., 303
Cohen, J., 251, 306
Colburn, D., 196, 306
Cole, D. A., 153, 304
Connor, R. F., 115, 306
Cook, T. D., 2, 6, 13, 15, 19, 22, 30,
    31, 33, 36, 54, 56, 58, 62, 68,
    88, 98, 142, 148, 157, 165, 166,
    172, 177, 179, 189, 192, 211,
    213, 222, 225, 226, 229, 306, 313
Cook, T. J., 313
Cooke, R. A., 88, 308
Cooper, W. H., 306
Cordray, D. S., 173, 258, 306, 311
Cornes, R., 14, 306
Cowan, M., 117, 307
Crano, W. D., 169, 186, 306

Cronbach, L. J., 17, 40, 306
Crosse, S., 258, 311
Culliton, B. J., 196, 306

Darcy, R. E., 96, 314
Darley, J. M., 133, 315
Darlington, R. B., 96, 306
Datta, L., 79, 168, 188, 254, 307
Davidson, W. S., 22, 308
Davis, D. D., 12, 307
Davis, D. F., 26, 307
Day, C. R., Jr., 200, 307
DeFriese, G. B., 54, 239, 307
Demone, H. W., Jr., 193, 307
De Neufville, J. I., 106, 307
Deniston, O. L., 179, 307
Derby, A., 206, 307
Devine, E. C., 56, 306
Dinkel, N. R., 95, 317
Dixon, M. G., 124, 307
Dobson, L. D., 313
Dowd, B., 165, 313
Dryfoos, J. G., 290, 293, 307
Dunkle, J., 258, 311
Durham, R. L., 84, 312

Eckert, P. S., 268
Eddy, D. M., 156, 183, 307
Edwards, J. D., 308, 313, 315
Egan, G., 117, 259, 307
Egdahl, R. H., 15, 307
Egelhof, R. H., 160, 307
Ehrenreich, B., 50, 307
Eisenberg, L., 144, 307
Elliott, E. J., 69, 307
Ellsworth, R. B., 67, 307
Endicott, J., 67, 307
Ericson, D. D., 90, 307
Erlebacher, A., 168, 169, 179, 305, 308
Evans, J. W., 169, 308
Evans, R. G., 204, 308
Evans, R. I., 55, 308

Fairweather, G. W., 22, 308
Fang, W. L., 304
Ferriss, A. L., 104, 308
Filling, C., 294, 305
Finegan, J. E., 56, 315
Fischhoff, B., 242, 308
Flay, B. R., 181, 308
Forrest, J. D., 289, 293, 308
Frechtling, J., 234
Fredericksen, L. W., 115, 308
Freiman, J. A., 240, 251, 308
Friedman, H., 240, 308

Webb, E. J., 70, 317
Webber, S. J., 306
West, L. J., 313
West, S. G., 79, 88, 96, 153, 181, 303, 317
Whitmore, E., 224, 317
Wholey, J. S., 11, 32, 45, 309, 317
Williams, A. E., 51, 311
Williams, R. C., 139, 304
Wills, K., 234, 317
Wilson, W. H., 84, 312
Wilson, B. L., 226, 314

Wolfson, S. M., 69, 304
Wood, G., 242, 317
Wye, C. G., 253, 304

Yeaton, W. H., 251, 317
Yin, R. K., 229, 317

Zammuto, R. F., 12, 317
Zasslow, M., 262
Zigler, E., 69, 317
Zimring, F. E., 256, 317
Zinober, J. W., 95, 317

Subject Index

biases
  evaluator's, 69
  idiosyncratic, 67
  systematic, 67
binomial distribution, 150
black box model of evaluation, 25–27, 49,
  53
blood pressure, high, 115
bloodletting, 144
budget, example, 195, 196

case studies, 110, 112, 260–299
case study, 229
Case Study 1, 262–267
Case Study 2, 172, 268–274
Case Study 3, 181, 275–284
Case Study 4, 199, 285–293
Case Study 5, 215, 294–299
causal effects, 256
causal relationships, 159, 172
causes, analysis of, 178–192
census, 104, 105, 239
change, 143, 147
  alpha, 153
  beta, 153
  gamma, 153
  residualized, 145, 146
  scores, 144–146
citizen evaluation model, 95
Class X crimes, 90
classroom tests, 73
clients of programs, 29
clinical judgment, 183
college entrance examinations, 223
column graph, 239–242
common-sense plausibility, 252
communication, 230, 266
communication plan, 231–233, 244
community forum, 111–113
community indexes, 67, 68
community surveys, 106, 107, 112
comparison groups, 250
  problems in selecting, 167
competence of evaluators, 16
confidence interval, 251
confidentiality, 34, 64, 88, 109, 288
confirmability, 223
conflict of interest, 89
conflicts, 18
construct validity, 153, 222, 223
constructivist philosophy, 27
consultant evaluator, 16–18, 89, 259
consumer movement, 13
consumer satisfaction, 49, 253
Consumer Price Index, 104

Consumer Reports, 26
contact report, 127, 130, 131
context of evaluation, 40
contraception, 285–293
controlled drinking, 88, 96
cost analyses
  assumptions of, 206
  criticisms of, 205–207
  not complete, 206, 207
  units of, 201, 202
cost-benefit, 191, 287
  analysis, 11, 21, 197–199, 207, 261
  using, 204, 205
  ratio, 292, 293
cost-effectiveness, 191, 227
  analysis, 11, 199–200, 207
  using, 204, 205
cost-utility analysis, 200
costs, 30
  and outcomes, 193–208
  direct, 196, 207
  fixed, 194, 207
  future, 202, 203
  hidden, 195, 207
  incremental, 194, 207
  indirect, 196, 207
  nonrecurring, 195, 207
  obvious, 195, 207
  opportunity, 202, 203, 207
  program, 57, 58
  recurring, 195, 207
  sunk, 194, 207
  variable, 194, 207
credibility, 17, 223
criminal justice and evaluation, 4
criteria, 27, 31, 34, 41, 83, 239, 250,
  256, 277
  behavioral, 71
  corrupted, 69
  credible, 61
  importance of selecting, 43–46
  limitations on selecting, 60, 61
  poor choice of, 71
  selecting, 42–62
Crusade of Mercy, 14

data analysis, 226
data
  choice of, 68, 69
  collection, 33, 34, 38
  collectors, 91
  expense of, 257
  sources of, 63–69
database program, 137
deadline for report, 60

findings
no-difference, 250, 251
unexpected, 154
fiscal evaluation, 26
focus groups, 111, 113, 117, 229
Food and Drug Administration, 30, 230
foreign aid, 114, 115
formative evaluation, *see* evaluation, formative
freedom to fail, 247, 248
functional status, 129, 134, 136
functioning, global, 77
funding, 224

generalization, threat to, 189
goal, 27
goal setting, 260
goal-based evaluation, 25
goal-free evaluation, 25
goals, 211, 214, 216, 296–298
goals
abstract, 46
complex, 213
conflicting, 213
developing, 46–49
implementation, 47–49, 53
intermediate, 48, 49
outcome, 48, 49
program, 49, 113, 211
types of, 47
vague, 211, 212
graduate admissions, 209–212
grant applications, 6
Graph-in-the-Box, 240
graphs, 35, 239–242, 278
Gross National Product, 104
gun control, 256

Head Start, 43, 44, 96, 168, 188
health care and evaluation, 3
Health and Human Services, 15, 243
helicopter patrol, 164, 197–199
high bobbins, 165
hindsight bias, 242
history, 162, 181
HIV (AIDS) Testing Law, 161
human resources and evaluation, 21
hypotheses, 226, 252

impact model, 32, 56, 61, 62
implementation, 27, 30, 46, 51, 61, 68, 92, 93, 97, 115, 181, 185, 227, 243, 252, 257, 263, 275–279
improvement, 155, 156, 169
incidence, 102

income maintenance, 187–189
income supplements, 187
independent variable, 56, 141, 146
individual assessment, 7
industry and evaluation, 4
informants, expert, 117. *See also* key informants
information needs, 231
information, ownership of, 90
information systems, 9
informed consent, 88
innovation, 38, 248
instrumentation, 175, 181
instruments
published, 79
specially constructed, 79–83
standardized, 79
intelligence tests, 73
intent of program, 43
interaction, 281
intermediate goals, 52, 53, 117
intermediate outcomes, 68
intermediate results, 54
internal evaluator, 5, 15–17, 28, 32, 37, 89, 95, 143, 247, 258, 259
internal validity, 159, 222, 223, 228, 230
threats to, 141, 146–152, 157, 176, 178, 179, 189–191, 193, 256, 262
compensate the controls, 190, 191
diffusion of the program, 189
history, 147, 148
instrumentation, 151, 152
interactions, 152
maturation, 147
mortality, 149. *See also* attrition, dropout
local history, 190
regression, 149–151
resentful demoralization, 190
rivalry, 190
selection, 148
testing, 151
interpersonal relationships, 227, 242
interpretations, alternative, 141
interrupted time series, 163, 172, 176, 268
interviewers, 92, 153
interviewing, 217
interviews, 34, 75, 78, 91, 255, 270, 277, 296
telephone, 78

job, getting, as an evaluator, 19
Joint Committee on Standards for Educational Evaluation, 86

key informants, 110, 111
kidney dialysis, 196

leadership, 277
legislation and evaluation, 15
Legislative Auditor, 15
level of function, 201
level-of-functioning scale, 76
local history, 148
LotusWorks, 240

management, 14
management audit, 120, 121. *See also* audit
management information system (MIS), 117, 121, 139, 257, 258
problems in, 137–139
management spy, 216
Marine Corps, 275–284
market forces, 3
marketing research, 57
matching, 168, 179, 279
maturation, 162, 169, 175, 181
measurement, 61, 222, 228
principles, 63–84
measures
cost-effective, 75
edumetric, 73
psychometric, 73
reliable, 72, 73
sensitivity to change, 73, 74
valid, 71
MED-LINE, 33
media, 160, 165, 260, 268–274
influence of, 100
Medicaid, 5, 15, 204
medical education, 295
medical regimen, 254
medical research, 226
medical residents, 294–299
Medicare, 5, 15, 204, 249
meta-analysis, 240, 258
methodology, 33–36
Metro Chicago Information Service, 104
military, 19
mixed results, 246, 252–257
monitoring, 19, 21, 117, 190, 275, 277, 278. *See also* program monitoring
threatening use of, 133
morale, 263, 266
multiple measures, 69, 83
multiple sources, 69, 70, 83

narrative, 226
National Institute of Health, 196

National Research Council, 206
naturalistic evaluation, 27, 229
need
assessment of, 50, 239
context of, 114
definition of, 101, 117
denial of, 115
evaluation of, 8, 209, 227
unmet, 103, 117
use in planning, 116, 117
negative evaluation, 38. *See also* outcome, negative
negative findings, 91, 246, 251
negative income tax, 213
negative outcomes, 125
negative side effects, 96, 97–99
New Math, 51
Nigeria, 114
nondirective probes, 219
nonequivalent comparison groups, 172–175. *See also* nonequivalent control groups
nonequivalent control groups, 163, 166–170, 176
weakness in, 168
nonparticipant observation, 214, 215
norms, 53
notes, interview, 217
null hypothesis, 251
nutritional supplements, 187

objectives, 27, 31, 52, 53, 260, 276–278
developing, 46–49
official, 59
objectives-based evaluation, 49, 59
objectivity, 17, 49, 214, 221, 223
observational methods, 215
observations, 44, 67, 151, 261, 294, 296
across time, 160
naturalistic, 294, 296, 298
qualitative, 207
Office of Inspector General, 15, 243
open-ended questions, 80, 81, 111, 112
operational audit, 120
operations research, 14
organizational development, 248
outcome evaluation, 9, 10, 13, 21, 120, 227, 256
outcomes, 10, 32, 227, 286
costs and, 193–208
final, 55
goals, 53, 117, 118, 139
intended, 2
intermediate, 55, 56, 61
level achieved and goals, 52

outcomes (*cont.*)
  measures of, 37
  multiple, 261
  negative, 17, 18
  reprehensible, 90
  variables, 279
overhead, 196

Parents Too Soon, 53
participant observation, 214, 216
participatory action research, 255
pastoral care, 249, 250
patch-up design, 173, 179
performance appraisal, 30, 39
performance-monitoring, 184
personal presentations, 233–236, 245
personal qualities of evaluators, 17. *See
  also* attitudes of evaluator
physical medicine and rehabilitation, 249
pie charts, 239
planner, 19
planning, 120, 226
planning and evaluation, 20, 21
planning and need assessment, 116, 117
planning committee, 103
planning programs, 46
polarization, 256
policy makers, 252
polite persistence, 92
politics, 252
population, target, 117
posttest-only design, 141
Potemkin Factory, 9
power, statistical, 251
press releases, 243–245
pressure, inappropriate, 37. *See also*
  politics
pretest-posttest design, 141–147, 149–151,
  153, 157, 162, 166, 174, 261–267,
  280
pretests, retrospective, 153
prevalence, 102
preventive programs, 285
primary nursing, 179
privacy, 88, 125
probing, 219
  nondirective, 219
process, evaluation of, 8, 209–229
productivity, 200
program, intensity of, 116
program analyst, 19
program audit, 120
program context, 212
program descriptions, 93, 221, 295
program development, 61

program evaluation. *See also* evaluation
  attitudes toward, 36–40
  definition of, 1
  reasons for, 6, 7
program evaluation and organizations,
  1–22
program goals, 97, 139
program management, 255
program monitoring, 119–139
program participants, 32, 34, 64–66, 95,
  97, 123, 142, 151, 155, 178, 238,
  256, 258, 261, 294
  characteristics of, 143–146
  motivating, 64
program personnel, 28–31, 35–39, 248,
  249, 253. *See also* program staff
program planners, 49, 55, 278
program planning, 113, 253
program quality, 38
program records, 64, 75
program resources, 39, 40, 54, 57
program sponsors, 28–31, 253
program success, criteria of, 214
program staff, 66, 71
program theory, 54, 61
program traces, 216, 217
programs, kinds of, 4
proposal, 29, 35, 39, 46
providers of service, 123
pseudo-participant, 216
Psychological Abstracts Search and
  Retrieval (PASAR), 33
public administration and evaluation, 4
purposive sample, 33
PUSH/Excel, 10

qualitative data, 214
qualitative evaluation, 27
qualitative methods, 191
qualitative observations, 27
qualitative understanding, 38
quality of life, 226
quality of service, 1
quantitative data, 224
quantitative evaluations, 221, 225–227
quantitative methods, 226
quasi-experimental design, 191, 222, 261,
  268
questionnaires, 221, 280
questions, open-ended, 218

random assignment, 34, 88, 179, 180,
  188, 189, 191, 279
random sample. *See* sample, random
random selection, 276

random variation, 97
rapport, 218
ratings, 72, 76, 77, 239
reaccreditation, 46
reactivity, 69, 70, 83, 151
recidivism, 251
recommendations, 32, 71, 94, 193, 230,
    237, 243, 244, 247, 248, 253,
    256, 298
records, 34, 49, 124
    usefulness, 125
regression adjustment, 145
regression to the mean, 144, 149, 168,
    169, 281
regression-discontinuity design, 170,
    171
regulation, 3
reliability, 18, 44, 72, 73, 97, 142, 222,
    256
    interrater, 73
    split-half, 73
    test-retest, 73
remedial programs and regression, 151
replication, 154, 182, 271
report, 31, 32, 35
    appendix of, 239, 242, 243
    draft, 38, 234, 296
    evaluation, 221, 226, 228, 230–245
    final, 235, 243, 259
    new client, 127, 129
    oral, 252. *See also* personal presentation
    outline, 237, 244
    progress, 243–245
    summary of, 238
    table of contents of a, 243
    terminated clients, 132
    written, 230, 233, 236, 237, 244, 252,
        259
representativeness, 34
Requests for Proposals, 16
research and evaluation, 20
research design, 18, 33, 34, 43, 223
    unethical, 92
    sensitivity of, 74
research rigor, 214
residency program, 237, 295, 296
residualized change, 145, 146
resources
    alternative uses of, 58
    limitations on, 14
response rates, 75
results, measurement of, 2. *See also*
    findings, outcome
return on investment, 59
role conflicts, 89–91, 99

sample
    random, 33, 148, 273, 280
    representative, 106, 148
    self-selected, 240
sample size, 240, 251
    small, 143
sampling, 34
    error, 52
SAT, 104
scale, 72
secondary analysis, 257
selection, 173–175
self-report, 239
sensitivity, 143
Sesame Street, 30, 58, 98, 236
side effects, 1, 7, 176
    negative, 49, 59, 125
    of programs, 59
significance. *See* statistical significance
significance tests, 224
significant others, 66, 67
single-group designs, 141–158
    usefulness of, 155–157
SISYPHUS, 137
slam-bang effect, 36
social indicators, 104–106, 117
    corrupted, 106
social justice, 58, 90
social marketing, 115
social science model of evaluation, 24, 25
Social Security, 5, 50
speeding, crackdown on, 160, 161, 166,
    172, 173
stakeholders, 28, 31, 32, 34, 35, 37, 45,
    46, 52, 61, 89, 90, 221, 225, 228,
    231, 236, 240, 242–247, 250, 252,
    256, 257, 259, 261, 294, 295, 298
stakeholder needs, 93, 143
standard error of estimate, 72
standard error of the mean, 72
standards, 298
    importance of selecting, 43–46
    selecting, 42–62
state, measures of, 73
statistical analyses, 33, 34, 142, 259
statistical conclusion validity, 142, 222,
    224, 228
statistical significance, 18, 35, 251, 253
stratification, 288
stress, 262–267
    post-trauma, 153
stroke patients, 249
student admissions, 216
subjectivity, 221
summary, 238, 244